A NATION OF VICTIMS?

GERMAN MONITOR No. 67
General Editor: Ian Wallace

A NATION OF VICTIMS?

Representations of German Wartime Suffering from 1945 to the Present

Edited by
Helmut Schmitz

Amsterdam - New York, NY 2007

Cover photo: Gerhard Marcks, *Totenmal für Ohlsdorfer Friedhof*, 1951, courtesy of Gerhard-Marcks-Stiftung, Bremen 2007.

Cover design: Aart Jan Bergshoeff

The paper on which this book is printed meets the requirements of "ISO 9706:1994, Information and documentation - Paper for documents - Requirements for permanence".

Transferred to digital printing 2008

ISBN-13: 978-90-420-2209-6
©Editions Rodopi B.V., Amsterdam - New York, NY 2007
Printed in the Netherlands

Table of Contents

3. Memory and Representation of Air Raids

4. Representations of Suffering in Contemporary Literature and Film

Introduction:
The Return of Wartime Suffering
in Contemporary German Memory Culture,
Literature and Film

The introduction provides an overview over central issues in the recent debates about representations of Germans as victims of war and expulsion as well as the growing academic work on this subject. Addressing a number of crucial aspects of the re-emergence of a German 'victim discourse' such as the tension between public and private forms of memory, the issue of trauma, mourning and taboo, and the issue of Holocaust imagery and memory, it relates these issues to the history of public commemorations of German suffering.

Over the Christmas period of 2005, travellers and visitors to Cologne railway station were greeted with a nativity display that was set in 1945 in a ruined church amongst the rubble in the destroyed city. The second stop on the popular 'Kölner Krippenweg',[1] the display serves as one indicator among many of how deeply the 'return' of memory of German suffering in the Second World War is affecting contemporary German life.

Indeed, the topic of German wartime suffering is omnipresent in contemporary Germany. On its publication in February 2002, Günter Grass's novella *Im Krebsgang* pushed John Grisham and two Harry Potters off the *SPIEGEL* bestseller lists, possibly aided by Guido Knopp's extremely popular five part TV series *Die Große Flucht* on the expulsions of ethnic Germans from the eastern territories. The series was broadcast between 20 Nov and 18 Dec 2001, attracting an audience of over 5 million or 16% of viewing figures. Published in spring 2003, Uwe Timm's memoir *Am Beispiel meines Bruders* about the death of his brother, a member of a *Waffen-SS* regiment, on the Eastern Front, was in its fourth edition by the time of the Frankfurt book-fair in October that same year. Jörg Friedrich's 600 page account of the air war *Der Brand* (2002), detailing the destruction of German cities in the 'Leideform', has sold over 200,000 copies in hardback alone.[2] The two-part 'event movie' *Dresden* – a love story between an English bomber pilot and a German nurse set during the firebombing of the city and broadcast by the *Zweites Deutsches Fernsehen* (ZDF) on 5 and 6 March 2006 – had viewing figures of over 30%. The two state-owned German television channels ARD and

ZDF are practically falling over themselves in the production of a series of high-calibre visualisations of German suffering. While teamworx, the company responsible for *Dresden*, is currently producing another two-part 'event movie' about 'Flucht und Vertreibung' for the first German TV channel ARD, ZDF has quickly created the three part 'Doku-Drama' *Die Kinder der Flucht* under the editorial supervision of Guido Knopp. Similar to the melodramatic plot in *Dresden*, the series, broadcast on 28 November, 5 and 12 December 2006 at prime time, tells the love story between a Polish boy, resettled by the Soviet occupiers to East Prussia in 1945 and a German girl, expelled from there soon after, closing with their wedding sixty years later. Not counting the innumerable autobiographical *Leidensgeschichten* of expellees and bombing victims, since the mid 1990s mainstream German literature has produced a stream of works that address the memory of German wartime experience and its lasting legacy throughout the post-war generations.

As Laurel Cohen-Pfister notes, the theme of wartime suffering has been slowly rising since the 1980s.[3] However, the recent surge in representations of German suffering amounts to the greatest shift in German memory discourse since 1979, when the screening of the US TV series *Holocaust* again brought the theme of Nazi extermination policies to the fore of German public memory.[4] This shift is all the more astonishing as it appears to revert and contest the institutionalisation of the memory of the Holocaust in the memory culture of the Berlin Republic in the 1990s.

As images of suffering Germans move back into the cultural mainstream for the first time in a generation, the issue is subject to a wide and ongoing public and academic debate. The representation of Germans as suffering victims of the Allied bombing campaign and the expulsions from the East or the violence and mass rape of women at the hands of the Red Army seems to be at odds with the general view of them as Nazi perpetrators and bystanders. Lothar Kettenacker sums up the problem in his introduction to the volume *Ein Volk von Opfern?*: 'Dürfen sich auch die Deutschen als Opfer betrachten, angesichts des Leids, das sie in die Welt gebracht haben?'[5] It is beyond the scope of this introduction to provide a comprehensive overview over the entire debate that has taken place both nationally and internationally.[6] Over the following pages I will address a number of issues that arise from the current obsession with German suffering.

Memory Culture in a Unified Germany: Public vs. Private Memory

For the unified Germany, the memory of National Socialism is a matter of national politics and identity building. It is not only that the Third Reich is the last moment of shared history between the two partial German states, in both the old Federal Republic and the GDR memory of the Nazi past was tied up with both national and Cold War commemorative politics. Bill Niven argues that 'the existence of two Germanies worked against, rather than in the interest of, coming to terms with National Socialism'.[7] After 1990, the memory of Nazism returned to the cultural sphere with unprecedented force. Over the decade after unification, the Nazi past, and particularly the Holocaust, appeared to be institutionalised at the centre of cultural memory of the Berlin Republic.[8] A series of controversial debates – around the Berlin Holocaust memorial, Daniel Jonah Goldhagen's book *Hitler's Willing Executioners*, the Walser-Bubis affair, and the travelling exhibition *Vernichtungskrieg: Verbrechen der Wehrmacht 1941-1945* – focused public attention and memory on the Nazi crimes. The Holocaust memorial in Berlin, planned throughout the 1990s and finally opened in 2005, puts the memory of Nazi crimes at the heart of memory culture of unified Germany. With this, *Vergangenheitsbewältigung*, a contentious and troublesome issue for the largest part of the history of the Federal Republic, seemed to have been completed, resulting in a sense of 'ownership' of that history.[9] This process of institutionalisation and appropriation of the legacy of the Holocaust is in itself not unproblematic as it instrumentalises the Holocaust for the creation of a collective identity based on responsibility for Nazi crimes. Furthermore, while individual memories are by nature heterogeneous, institutionalised forms of memory tend to be homogenising. Aleida Assmann speaks of 'Gedächtnisrahmen' in this respect, a framework that produces a common cultural narrative about the past: 'Wo immer kollektiv homogenisierende Impulse festzustellen sind, die ein narratives Raster über die heterogenen individuellen Erinnerungen legen, ist die Wirkungsmacht sozialer oder politischer Gedächtnisrahmen am Werke.'[10] The problem with a normativisation of the memory of the Holocaust is thus that it 'runs the risk of producing a rigid remembrance culture' that is at odds with the memories of individuals and groups.[11]

There is thus a tension between homogenising and public and heterogeneous, private memory, or, between cultural memory operating through forms of institutionalisation and ritual, and communicative memory. The results of the research project 'Tradierung von Geschichtsbewusstsein' indicate that, while public memory is dominated by images of Nazi crimes, private and family memory predominantly communicate experiences of suffering, hardship and heroism.[12] The images of National Socialism in public memory, it appears, are incompatible, even mutually exclusive with those passed on in family memory. What is remarkable is that the shift from a memory centred on the victims of Nazism to a 'perpetrator-centred' memory occurs, almost antithetically, subsequently to the institutionalisation of the memory of the Holocaust at the heart of contemporary German historical identity.[13] The last years have thus seen a pluralisation of divergent memories of National Socialism. One of the pivotal moments in this shift is the Walser-Bubis debate which threw into sharp relief the divergence between public and private memory of the Nazi era in Germany. In the acceptance speech for his reception of the Peace Prize of the German Book Trade in 1998, Walser objected to the public forms of commemoration of National Socialism as alienated and politically correct, insisting on his different perspective and his private conscience as more 'authentic' forms of remembrance. The speech triggered a controversial public debate that exposed the rift between official public memory of the Nazi past and private or family memory.[14] The amount of public support Walser received for his act of dissidence from official memory culture indicated that a lot of Germans did not feel their personal memories of the Nazi period represented in official memory culture. From this perspective, the 'flooding back of memory' of German suffering, as Aleida Assmann calls it,[15] appears to be either a substitution, or, depending on one's perspective, a completion of the image of Nazi perpetrators with those of suffering Germans.

The 'Resurgence of Memory' and the Globalisation of Memory Culture

'Warum erst jetzt' asks someone later identified as the voice of Grass's alter ego in the opening line of *Im Krebsgang* with respect to the apparently forgotten tragedy of the sinking of the *Wilhelm Gustloff* and the death of over 7,000 refugees off the coast of Danzig in January 1945.[16] Indeed, the debate around the resurgence of memories of German suffering is accompanied by the suggestion of belatedness, the idea that German wartime experience has not yet been sufficiently commemorated, communicated or represented. This belatedness is frequently explained with recourse to the politicised history of *Vergangenheitsbewältigung*, the displacement of German wartime suffering by Nazi atrocities in memory culture by a 'taboo' on speaking of Germans as victims and the force of trauma which only comes to light after a prolonged period of latency. I will engage with these issues which are all, in one way or another, tied up with an inner-German memory culture in detail below. The shift towards a communicative and family-centred memory of German suffering occurs at the intersection of two important developments, the passing away of witnesses and the emotionalising of history. A number of critics suggest the 'epoch-threshold' (Jan Assmann) of the foreseeable death of the *Zeitzeugen* as one of the reasons for the resurgence of a 'German-centred' memory of Nazism and the war. Niven remarks on the extraordinary impact of the travelling exhibition *Vernichtungskrieg: Verbrechen der Wehrmacht 1941-1944* on communication between the generations and within families.[17] This phenomenon goes hand in hand with a generational shift from second to third post-war generation. In contrast to the student movement of 1968, which drew a sharp line between themselves and their parents, the third generation is concerned with family genealogy and the exploration of the haunting legacies of the past. This re-appropriation of German wartime experience is facilitated by the inclusion of the memory of National Socialist crimes in the official self-image of the Federal Republic which replaced the issue of guilt by collective responsibility. Together with the replacement of the 'experiential generation' by the 'confessional generation',[18] the end of the discourse of guilt and contrition marks a shift from a judgemental attitude to one of listening: 'Das verschafft den Nachgeborenen Raum für genaueres Hinsehen, erlaubt es in gewisser Weise erst.'[19]

This renewed interest in family legacies coincides with a significant shift both in historiographical and popular discourse from a history of 'hard' facts to 'story', human interest and emotionalisation. Referring to the period 1995-2005 as the 'Decade der Zeitzeugen',

Norbert Frei notes that 'Täter, Opfer, Mitläufer, sowohl in der historiographischen als auch der medialen Vergegenwärtigung vor allem als Kollektivsubjekte präsent, bekamen Gesichter'.[20] Daniel Fulda speaks of a 'Subjektivierung des Geschichtsdiskurses' after 1989 in both academic and public discourse, an increasing focus on oral history and the plight of the individual.[21] This recharging of history with emotions is regarded by historians with some suspicion as it tends to disregard historical contexts and replace structures, processes and complexes with a focus on individual and group experience.[22] Above all, the 'gefühlte Geschichte', as Norbert Frei calls it, facilitates a re-appropriation of the history of German suffering by sentiment, the 'Wiederbelebung dieser Vergangenheit im Modus des emotionalen Nacherlebens'.[23] This is most perceivable in mass media constructions, such as *Die große Flucht*, *Dresden* or *Die Kinder der Flucht* which has been criticised for its sentimentalised creation of a 'fahrlässige Opferperspektive'. History turns into 'Histotainment'.[24]

The increasingly emotionalised and individualised approach to history coincides with both a pluralisation of historical narratives – a renunciation of historical 'master narratives' – and a globalisation of Holocaust memory which inscribes the Holocaust as universal victim narrative into a (western) transnational collective memory. This has important consequences for German memories of wartime suffering as it ironically facilitates their return. Niven argues that the globalisation of Holocaust memory moves Germany from the status of a 'pariah amongst nations' to 'one of many nations with a duty to remember', a shift which opens up a space for the re-discovery of German suffering.[25] With the shift towards German victim memory, Germany appears to follow a trend towards an international 'victim culture'.[26]

Taboo, Trauma and Mourning: The 'Silence' about German Wartime Suffering

One of the most contentious issues in the debate around German suffering is that of a taboo on speaking about or representing Germans as victims. There are two aspects to the allegation of a taboo; one is to do with the politicised history of commemoration in both parts of the divided Germany and the other with the issue of trauma. Both aspects are intertwined to a certain extent. In the thesis of a representational taboo the differences and complexities of post-war German memory discourse are quickly homogenised and glossed over in favour of a uniform narrative of non-representation and repression of German suffering. It is therefore important to not only distinguish between memory discourses in the Federal Republic and the GDR but also between different aspects of suffering, such as the bombings, the suffering of the soldiers and POW's, the expulsions and the mass rapes, all of which were talked about and represented or repressed and silenced in different ways. It is furthermore important to distinguish between the articulation of German suffering in public, private, political and cultural discourses.

The spreading of the taboo-thesis can be observed with respect to the reception of W.G. Sebald's lectures *Luftkrieg und Literatur*, given in Zurich in autumn 1997 and published in 1999.[27] Sebald argued, that post-war German literature had failed to inscribe the experience of the air war into collective memory. Furthermore, Sebald extended his assessment from literature to public discourse as a whole, alleging that the question of the moral justification of the Allied strategic bombings of German cities had never been 'Gegenstand einer öffentlichen Debatte'.[28] Both points were quickly picked up by the German review pages. While critics, in particular Volker Hage,[29] quickly pointed out Sebald's oversight of various novels, such as Gert Ledig's *Die Vergeltung* and Dieter Forte's *Der Junge mit den blutigen Schuhen*, Sebald's thesis of a general collective silence on the devastating nature of the bombing experience was widely adopted and extended to the issue of German suffering as a whole. Frank Schirrmacher in the *Frankfurter Allgemeine Zeitung* asserted: 'Es gibt bis heute keine literarische Verarbeitung der Vertreibung'.[30] Aleida Assmann speaks of Sebald as 'penetrating' the 'Schleier des Tabus [...] der über deutsche Opfererinnerungen gehängt worden war', using the same phrase as Sebald: 'In den ersten Jahrzehnten nach dem Krieg gab es zudem einen verbreiteten Konsens. Weder die Schuld noch die Leidenserfahrung zum Gegenstand einer öffentlichen Debatte zu machen.'[31]

The reception of Grass's *Im Krebsgang* was likewise accompanied by the assertion that the novella was breaking with a representational taboo. Indeed, the novella itself subscribes to this idea. Spanning three generations of German post-war memory, *Im Krebsgang* suggests that the memory of the sinking of the *Wilhelm Gustloff*, which metaphorically stands for the issue of German suffering as a whole, had been a 'gesamtdeutsches' taboo, due to Cold War politics and the politicisation of memory discourse in post-war Germany. While the memory of suffering at the hands of the advancing Red Army had been unwelcome in the GDR for political reasons, Grass's novella asserts, in West Germany the student movement with its exclusive focus on the parents' role as perpetrators had blocked empathy with their parents' wartime suffering. With respect to the GDR, Grass was to a certain extent correct. Official GDR rhetoric referred to the expellees as 'Umsiedler' or resettlers, thus obscuring the forced origin of the expulsions. Furthermore, the considerable hostility the expellees encountered in the GDR could not become a public issue due to the ideology of the Socialist people's community. While the memory of the forced expulsions from the eastern territories was harmonised for political expediency, the mass rapes by the Red Army could not be addressed at all.[32] In the early Federal Republic, the memory of Red Army violence was only articulated (and articulable) within a Cold War rhetoric.[33] The bombing of Dresden, though widely commemorated in the GDR, was quickly instrumentalised for anti-Western bloc Cold War propaganda.

In West Germany, the issue is rather more complicated due to the interference of memories of German suffering with the slowly rising acceptance of the legacy of National Socialism in the official culture of the Federal Republic, something the GDR remained largely untroubled by due to the incorporation of anti-Fascism into its official self-image. In the re-evaluation of German memory culture over the last few years, the issue of silence on the traumatic experiences has been central. The argument is that the traumatic experience of German suffering could not have been properly addressed as it was tied up with and obscured by the culture of guilt for Nazi crimes. There are two facets to this argument. The first takes its cue from the Mitscherlichs' theses on the German 'inability to mourn', suggesting that the silence on German crimes and the silence on German traumatic experience are intertwined. The second suggests that the post-1945 confrontation with Nazi crimes in the Allied re-education campaign had caused a traumatic 'shock', creating a perception of Germans as perpetrators that has obscured and inhibited consideration of their victim experience.[34]

In *Luftkrieg und Literatur* Sebald had suggested a connection between the post-war German silence on their own trauma and the silence about their guilt and responsibility for the crimes committed in their name: 'Der Katalysator war [...] der bis heute nicht zum Versiegen gekommene Strom psychischer Energie, dessen Quelle das von allen gehütete Geheimnis der in die Grundfesten unseres Staates eingemauerten Leichen ist [...].'[35] Sebald argued that the Germans' energy for the reconstruction and the economic miracle originated in a silent collective refusal to engage with the responsibility for the Nazi past, and that this affected the ability to address their own traumatisation. This is basically a restatement of the Mitscherlichs' theses in their seminal 1967 study *Die Unfähigkeit zu trauern*.[36] Propagators of a theory of silence about German suffering due to the belated nature of trauma generally follow Sebald's and the Mitscherlich's assertion of a nexus between guilt, shame, denial and trauma.[37]

The notion of a trauma that could not have been addressed due to its disruptive intensity is central to contemporary representations of German suffering and their reception.[38] As Sebald suggested, the undoubtedly traumatic experiences, together with the 'unbewältigte Vergangenheit', appear to have left lasting legacies within the German family which have only in the recent decade begun to be explored.[39] Particularly the recent wave of 'family novels' testifies to the issue of transgenerational transmission of family secrets, trauma and silence.[40] However, as the research of Robert G. Moeller and Norbert Frei has shown, there is little evidence of an overall silence on German suffering in the immediate post-war period. The early history of the Federal Republic, both politically and culturally, is virtually founded on the sense that the Germans had been victims of the war, Hitler and the Allies. Arguing that the 1950s are a decade of political integration of the general image of suffering into the institutional framework of society and state, Moeller claims that the alleged silence about German suffering in the post-war era is a myth; both East and West Germany 'devoted considerable energy to assessing the losses and incorporating victim status into public memory, [...] in the political arena and forms of commemoration, stories of German loss and suffering were ubiquitous'.[41] The public commemoration of the war victims and expellees, as well as their representation in films, had a predominantly formative function that also held at bay issues of guilt and responsibility: 'the past to be overcome [...] the past to be incorporated systematically as part of the present was not the past of

German crimes but of German suffering.' 1950s victim memory thus created a 'usable past': 'By telling stories of the enormity of their losses, West Germans were able to reject charges of 'collective guilt' […] and claim status as heroic survivors.'[42] Moeller uses precisely the term 'debate' to characterise the issue of German suffering in the public sphere with respect to the expellees and the returning POW's: 'Post-war debates over shared fates circumscribed a community of suffering and empathy among Germans, joined by the common project of distributing the cost of the war.'[43] In fact, the expellees are so visible, in the first two decades of the Federal Republic, both politically and culturally, that Aleida Assmann speaks of their hegemonising the entire discourse of victimhood.[44] Research into the commemoration of bombings shows that this is not completely correct. Daniel Fulda remarks on a virtually uninterrupted commemoration of the firestorm in the city of Hamburg until 1973 when interest began to wane due to a generation shift and the aftermath of the student movement.[45]

Over the course of the 1960s, the focus of attention shifted from Germans as victims to Nazi victims and German crimes. The change from over 20 years of CDU-led governments to an SPD government in 1969 led to a redrawing of Germany's politics towards Eastern Europe, resulting in the *Ostverträge* and the recognition of the loss of the eastern territories. The change towards the liberal left and the subsequent dissolution of the *Bundesministerium für Vertriebene, Flüchtlinge und Kriegsgeschädigte* moved the political wing of the expellees, the *Bund der Vertriebenen* (League of Expellees, *BdV*) which had always refused to recognise the post-war boundaries, onto the political fringe. While the political demands of the expellee organisations became increasingly anathema, the issue of the expulsions did not altogether disappear from the scene. It simply moved from the political centre to the cultural sphere of popular literature, television and memoirs.[46]

Two issues thus emerge: first, in the 1950s the 'silence' about the past only extends to Nazi victims, German responsibility and guilt.[47] Secondly, the issue of German wartime suffering is re-inscribed into a narrative of the economic miracle and the successful overcoming of hardship while being politicised and instrumentalised into a foundational myth of the young Federal Republic. The question is not *whether* German suffering has been addressed but *how* and in what manner. While there is no evidence of any absence of public and cultural commemoration of German losses in the immediate post-war period, there remains the argument that, due to its instrumentalisation, German suffering had always been framed by political interests, economic rebuilding and denial of guilt and thus had no chance to be 'properly' mourned and articulated with empathy.

The re-inscription of the issue of mourning for German losses into the Mitscherlichs' thesis of the 'inability to mourn' is part of the contemporary debate about the legitimacy of representations of German suffering. Of particular importance in this is the argument that the student movement had continued the 'inability to mourn' with respect to their parents' suffering. It is here that the narrative of a 'taboo' acquires its most polemical force. There is now general agreement that the student movement, in their forceful disconnection from their parents, showed little empathy for their suffering. Norbert Frei refers to a 'Selbstimmunisierung' of the student generation against the apologetic tendencies of the German victim discourse.[48] While the discourse of German suffering was in the hands of the right, the student movement is regarded as responsible for instrumentalising a 'politically correct' binary discourse of guilt in which the Germans came to figure exclusively as perpetrators. It is alleged that the cultural hegemony of the liberal left after 1968 resulted in a broad scale de-legitimation of empathy for and articulation of the German experience of suffering, creating a rigid classification of perpetrators and victims that excluded ambivalences.[49] The argument is thus that the one-dimensional focus of the student movement on Nazi atrocities had continued the 'inability to mourn' for German losses. Ian Buruma observed in 1994:

> But the mourning of the German dead – the soldiers, and the civilians killed by allied bombs or by vengeful Polish, Czech or Slovak neighbours, who drove them from their homes – such mourning was an embarrassing affair, left largely to right-wing nationalists and nostalgic survivors, pining for their lost homelands.[50]

Consequently, the re-emergence of images of wartime suffering at the centre of German memory culture has gone hand in hand with a critical re-evaluation of the student movement and its role within the commemorative culture of the federal Republic. The suggestion is that after the end of the guilt discourse, it is now possible for the first time to listen to stories of German suffering with empathy. Aleida Assmann refers to a 'Rückgewinnung deutscher Opfererinnerungen aus ihrer Erstarrung und Verkapselung', arguing that these memories had 'had no chance to be communicated in their humane dimension and shared with empathy in the public sphere', as their inclusion in public memory had been blocked both by the right's political instrumentalisation of these memories and by the left's resistance to acknowledging them.[51] I have described this elsewhere as 'belated' empathy, the children and grandchildren of the wartime generation re-empathising with the suffering of their ancestors.[52] While it is certainly correct that after the 1960s the image of Germans as victims was anathema on the German left, the idea that memories of German wartime experience and suffering had, at any point in the history of the Federal Republic, been repressed or remained unrepresented in culture, is simply untrue. Rather, one could speak of a continuous stand-off between left and right.[53] The idea that the German losses had never been properly mourned and that the recent 'return' of these memories represents some form of belated mourning and healing is, nevertheless, suggested frequently.[54] As with the issue of *Vergangenheitsbewältigung*, this puts the post-war generations in a position of proxy, of mourning on behalf of the 'experiential generation' (Aleida Assmann) that has, allegedly, been unable to mourn. Mourning is precisely the term Moeller uses for the public commemorative rituals of the 1950s, arguing that the Germans 'demonstrated a striking ability to mourn' for their own losses.[55] The argument that the commemorative rituals of the past do not constitute a 'proper' way of mourning as they are predominantly in the interest of nation-building and thus side-step the issue of trauma, is somewhat disingenuous. Public commemorative rituals are by their very nature community-constitutive and involve representation and thus politics. Collectives are not traumatised in the same way as individuals are and they do not mourn in the same ways that individuals do. The lament that, in the past, representations of German suffering were always tied up with political, national and group interests implicitly assumes or desires that this could be dispensed with. An unpoliticised or non-instrumentalisable representation of Germans as victims is, however, hard to come by.

Therefore, the virtues of belated mourning are to a certain extent dubious. For the post-war generations, the ruined German cities are less bound up with loss than with feelings of origin and nostalgia, as Sebald suggested.[56] In explorations of German wartime trauma that take their cue from Sebald, one thing is frequently overlooked, namely

Sebald's laconic conviction that the time for assessing the human damage of the air war is irrevocably past. Sebald suggests that contemporary engagement with the horrors of the bombings are somewhat voyeuristic, arguing, 'dass es unmöglich ist, die Tiefen der Traumatisierung in den Seelen derer auszuloten, die aus den Epizentren der Katastrophe entkamen'.[57] This is not least problematic as representations of German wartime suffering frequently borrow from images and tropes otherwise associated with the Holocaust. However, aesthetic and historiographical representations of the Holocaust usually stress the impossibility of deriving a collective or foundational meaning out of the Nazi genocide.[58] In contrast to this, contemporary representations of German suffering are pervaded by notions of healing and redemption. Representations of Germans as victims are thus exercises in collective meaning creation, and almost inevitably are in the interest of re-forming an 'imaginative community'.[59] That is to say, Germans are configured as suffering ancestors and thus re-collectivised alongside a contemporary concept of German nationhood that, however, remains fundamentally ethnic. Not only does this exclude the ethnic plurality of contemporary Germany, it also runs the risk of re-invoking the homogeneous Nazi *Volksgemeinschaft*.

Politicised Memory: Victims vs. Perpetrators or Competing with Auschwitz

The passing of the discourse of guilt and contrition in the 1990s appears to erode both the split between left and right on the issue of German suffering and the binary discourse of perpetrators and victims that constructs Germans exclusively as perpetrators. Jörg Friedrich, the author of *Der Brand*, is a man with solid liberal-left credentials. In 2003, the late Peter Glotz, a noted SPD politician, published a historical assessment on the expulsions, *Die Vertreibung*, and supported the attempt of the *Bundesverband der Vertriebenen* to build a permanent exhibition on expulsions in the 20th century in Berlin.[60] A number of critics argue that the evolution of a more 'inclusive picture' (Niven) allows for the representation of Germans as both perpetrators and victims, without reverting to reactionary politics, because the historical responsibility of German perpetration has been securely established within public memory:

> because only now that a social framework and discourse has come into existence in which German sufferings dating back to the Second World War can be

separated from reactionary and revisionist arguments and, freed of the danger of political exploitation, do they have a chance to be heard with empathy.[61]

However, Norbert Frei, Harald Welzer and Hannes Heer, the most outspoken critics of the shift in memory discourse argue that the empathetic representation of Germans as victims de-historicises the Nazi past and produces 'erstaunlich unpolitische Töne einer privatistischen Geschichtsbetrachtung, in der sich die Unterschiede zwischen Tätern, Opfern und Mitläufern verwischen'.[62] Where Aleida Assmann sees a widening of perspectives, Frei, Welzer and Heer see a paradigm shift that replaces perpetrators with victims.

The term 'victim' for the classification of German wartime experiences is thus highly contested. The representation of Germans as victims encounters a double binary, the clear distinction between perpetrators, victims and bystanders in Holocaust studies as well as the historical bifurcation of left- and right-wing discourses with their exclusive focus on either German perpetration or victimhood.[63] The issue is complicated further by the fact that in German the term 'Opfer' denotes both victim and sacrifice. Moreover, while within the framework of historiography of National Socialism and the Holocaust, the terms victim and perpetrator have precise meanings, suggesting innocent passivity on the one hand and responsibility and agency on the other, the use of the term victim for referring to Germans abstracts from the political and judicial framework that determines the concept of victim. This is to say that, while in Holocaust historiography the term victim implies the agency of an identifiable act of perpetration, in 'Germans as victims' the term victim is used according to its colloquial usage, one where there need not be a perpetrator. Speaking of 'deutsche Bombenopfer' is thus, at least potentially, semantically akin to 'victim of an accident'.[64]

There are, however, a number of problems with this. The 'neutral' use of the term victim threatens to historically de-contextualise German wartime experience and makes it eminently re-inscribable into a narrative of survival or (Christian) redemptive sacrifice.[65] This has been referred to as a re-moralisation of history that abstracts from historical context in favour of constructing empathy.[66] Furthermore, as the Holocaust becomes the universal signifier of traumatic excess, this facilitates the appropriation of Holocaust imagery for representations of German suffering, something that is repeated with a disturbing frequency in contemporary representations of German suffering.[67] Despite the recurrent attempts to either implicitly or explicitly compare German wartime suffering with Holocaust trauma or intensity, the difference between Nazi victims and suffering Germans is of critical importance as it illustrates the problems and difficulties of adequate commemoration. Holocaust and Nazi victims are victims of National Socialist racial, biological and *völkisch* politics, their status as victims lies outside a context of guilt or individual responsibility. The German population suffers as a result of war, started by Nazi Germany. This means that the suffering Germans are simultaneous members of a murderous Nazi *Volksgemeinschaft*. While Jörg Friedrich is right to point out that the allied bombs fell indiscriminately on Germans, allied POW's, Nazi workslaves, mental hospital inmates and children alike,[68] in empathetic representations of 'German' wartime suffering, the victims are configured on an axis of German-ness that is frequently divested of the taint of Nazism. Consequently, representing German suffering opens up an empathetic minefield. How to adequately portray German wartime experience without either suppressing their status as members of a Nazi community or having constantly to refer to Nazi crimes to ward off potential accusations of levelling German responsibility?

Aleida Assman's answer to the question of how to integrate the 'divergent and even contradictory memories into a generally acceptable framework' is the hierarchisation of memory, claiming that the Holocaust is the normative framework of German memory 'into which all the other memories have to be integrated'.[69] The argument for an integrative approach to the issue of German victimhood that puts the 'German experience' into a subordinate position to Nazi crimes and German perpetration creates a hierarchy in which German perpetration and German victimhood are not equal. However, this apparent unevenness between guilt/responsibility and suffering is exactly the issue around which the entire representational discourse of German victim experience circles. Indeed, representations of and debates about German suffering turn around a perceived inequality and competition with the dimensions of Jewish suffering since 1945. Moeller has demonstrated how the Holocaust became the 'implicit' model for German suffering in the 1950s project of recording the suffering of the expellees, undertaken by the *Bundesministerium für Vertriebene, Flüchtlinge und Kriegsgeschädigte* under the direction of post-war historiography doyen Theodor Schieder: 'The Schieder project recorded precisely such pictures, in the form of detailed memories, in which Germans compared their suffering with the suffering of some Jews persecuted by Nazis.'[70] The parallelising of Jewish and German suffering is thus in the interest of projecting an image of German innocence, abstracting from their role as members of a Nazi community.[71]

There is, however, a subtle difference between post-war and contemporary evocations of the Holocaust in comparison with German suffering, one that is facilitated by the inscription of Holocaust imagery in public memory over the last decades. While in the post-war period the argument that the Germans had also suffered served to ward off a perceived accusation of collective guilt, the recourse to Holocaust tropes, images and metaphors in contemporary representations of German suffering mostly seeks to validate traumatic excess. Aleida Assmann may be correct in arguing that the current interest in German suffering has a therapeutic and not a political agenda.[72] Nevertheless, the de-Nazification of the German wartime community in conjunction with the undoubtedly traumatic horrors of the war opens up the possibility of comparing German and Jewish suffering on an implicitly equal footing. Niven describes this as one of two strategies of turning Germans into 'absolute' victims, the other being the comparison of Allied war strategies with Nazi crimes, thus suggesting the Germans suffered at the hands of the Allies just as much as the Jews suffered at the hands of the Germans.[73] While the first strategy relativises Jewish suffering in comparison to German suffering, the second relativises German crimes in comparison with Allied war aims. There are thus some startling continuities between the self-representation of Germans as victims in the 1950s and today; the attempt to 'establish equivalence of different crimes against humanity was not new; it conformed to established patterns of public memory' in the Federal Republic.[74]

Looking back over 60 years of German memory of National Socialism and the war, two issues are emerging with increasing clarity. One is the continuity of images of German suffering and victimhood, especially in cultural representations throughout the history of the Federal Republic, the other is the pendulum swing in public commemorative discourse from a predominant focus on German suffering to a focus on German crimes. The pluralisation of memory in post-1990 Germany may offer the chance, for the first time, to represent German losses side by side with German responsibilities for the crimes committed under National Socialism. As German memory discourse moves into the 6th decade after the war, the potential lifting of a rigid binary perpetrator/victim discourse in favour of a more inclusive picture is to be welcomed.

Over the course of the 1990s the issue of whether Germany was or could ever be a 'normal' nation was subject to recurrent debates.[75] In these debates the history of Nazi Germany and particularly the Holocaust figured as the prime obstacle to a desired national normality. In the context of the Walser-Bubis debate in 1989, Saul Friedlander noted that the German memory discourse is untypical. Instead of commemorating its own victims, Germany was a nation that commemorated the victims of its policies.[76] It is doubtful whether the recent resurgence of German victim memory is likely to substantially alter this prioritisation of the Holocaust. However, it marks a shift towards forms of commemoration that, at least potentially, move German civilian dead side by side with Nazi victims. In this climate, German suffering can quickly be re-appropriated and exploited for political ends. The *BdV*'s campaign for building a Centre Against Expulsions in Berlin, modelled on the Washington Holocaust Memorial Museum, is just one example of a political pressure group that is attempting to institutionalise a particular memory as collective and national memory. In August 2006 Hermann Schäfer, organiser of the celebrated 1995 exhibition *Flucht Vertreibung Integration* in the Haus der Deutschen Geschichte in Bonn and deputy minister for culture, was invited to give the opening address at the Kunstfest Weimar which since 2003 has been opened with a concert in memory of the victims of nearby Buchenwald concentration camp. Schäfer's speech failed to refer to the concentration camp victims, instead focusing entirely on the plight of the German expellees. The audience's protest led to the speech being aborted. Schäfer's failure to mention the victims of Buchenwald in an event named after the location of their suffering makes for a fitting symbol of the continuity of the temptation, desire and ease with which German victims are sometimes substituted for Nazi victims in public discourse.[77]

The Present Book
The chapters in this book address and elaborate a number of the issues discussed above. The book opens with a section on discourses of

German victimhood in literature and film in the immediate post-war period and the 1950s. The first three chapters illustrate that Moeller's argument that the 'rhetorics of victimisation were central parts of the civic culture of the early Federal Republic' can be applied to various forms of cultural production as well.[78] Gregor Streim's chapter addresses a little researched topic – autobiographical and fictional camp narratives by authors active under National Socialism who were interned by the Allies after the war. Locating these texts in the context of the *Vergangenheitspolitik* of the young Federal Republic, Streim argues that these works represent a discursive attempt to establish a sense of victimhood in the collective memory of the young Federal Republic, salvaging a sense of continuity from the lost war. With the exception of Ernst von Salomon, whose influential satire on Allied de-Nazification, *Der Fragebogen*, is still in print, these authors, who were widely read in the early 1950s, are now by and large forgotten, given that their symbolic continuity with the Third Reich was not compatible with the Federal Republic's western ethos. However, their strategies of re-codifying the Germans as the true victims of the war are also present in cultural products from the younger generation that came to define post-war German culture. This is illustrated by Hans-Joachim Hahn's chapter which looks at the representation of Jewish characters in the first post-war German film, Wolfgang Staudte's *Die Mörder sind unter uns* (1946) and in the early work of Wolfgang Weyrauch, a once influential author of the early Federal Republic. Weyrauch was the originator of the term 'Kahlschlag-Literatur' that came to represent the literary programme of Alfred Andersch's, Hans-Werner Richter's and Walter Kolbenhoff's journal *Der Ruf* and the early *Gruppe 47*.[79] Hahn's thesis is that both Staudte and Weyrauch de-particularise Jewish experience to establish a universal (and Christian) code of suffering that can be applied to Jews and Germans alike. Helen Wolfenden's analysis of two popular films about German soldiers' experience from the mid-late 1950s – *Hunde wollt ihr ewig leben* and *Der Arzt von Stalingrad* – shows that the films not only serve as a form of cultural rehabilitation of the *Wehrmacht* Soldier as innocent victim of Hitler but also that *Der Arzt von Stalingrad* in particular reiterates Nazi racial stereotypes.

The next section of this book deals with political issues arising from the recent re-appearance of the *Bund der Vertriebenen* on the political and cultural stage. The current sensitisation of the public for issues of German suffering provides the *BdV* with an opportunity to re-attach their particularist politics to mainstream culture. Samuel Salzborn discusses the concept of victimhood that is used by the *BdV*, arguing that the *BdV* operates with a universal concept of victim that de-historicises the expulsions. In particular, their attempt to get the expulsions recognised as 'Unrecht' denotes a political move to establish the experience of a particular group as national tragedy in collective memory. Arguing that the *BdV* operates with a strategy of historical decontextualisation, Salzborn's chapter makes clear that an 'unpolitical' focus on the suffering of individuals is easily hijacked for political ends. This is all the more pertinent as the *BdV*'s claim for a cultural recognition of the expellees' victim status is tied up with demands for political consequences of this cultural recognition. The cultural praxis of this kind of hijacking is the focus of Bill Niven's chapter which discusses the effect of the *BdV*'s politics on German relations with Poland and the Czech Republic. Analysing the recent exhibition on expulsions in the 20th century, *Erzwungene Wege,* organised by the *BdV*, Niven claims that the exhibition represents a 'new departure' for *BdV* rhetoric, parallelising the suffering of Armenians (1915/16), the Greek/Turkish resettlements (1922/23), the expulsions of Jews from Germany after 1933 and the expulsions of ethnic Germans from the East. While the *BdV* has hitherto been keen on equating German with Jewish suffering, the exhibition moves the suffering of ethnic Germans into proximity to that of the Armenians. This, argues Niven, suggests a status of 'innocent' victim for the expelled Germans while the exhibition simultaneously seeks to overwrite the Holocaust as its inclusion would have put the claim to innocence into dispute. As the exhibition is run as a kind of model of the Centre Against Expulsions which the *BdV* intends to build in Berlin, this gives an indication of the ongoing rhetoric of equation and de-historisation at the heart of this organisation.

The third section focuses on memories and representations of the air raids, the area of German wartime suffering for which a taboo of traumatised silence has been claimed most vigorously. Gilad Margalit's chapter demonstrates how much memory culture in the GDR was influenced by Cold-War politics, looking at the changing structure of commemorations of air raids in Dresden and Hamburg from 1945 to the 1970s. While immediately after the war public organs in both cities stressed German and Nazi responsibility for the destruction, Margalit argues, from the beginning of the Cold War the GDR adopted a narrative of Western Allied mass murder of innocent civilians as part of its anti-Western propaganda. Margalit demonstrates how this narrative of the military uselessness of the bombing of Dresden was disseminated westwards in the 1950s and was eventually adopted by Hamburg. One of the central issues in the representation of German wartime suffering is the re-recreation of the traumatic intensity of the experience. Heinz-Peter Preußer analyses the literary construction of immediacy in a number of historiographical, photographic and fictional representations of the air war. Discussing Jörg Friedrich's, Gert Ledig's, Hans Erich Nossack's and Alexander Kluge's works, Preußer creates a typology of staging immediacy to mediate traumatic experience to the reader/viewer. Annette Seidel Arpacı discusses the issue of the Holocaust as subtext in Sebald's *Luftkrieg und Literatur* and Jörg Friedrich's *Der Brand*. Arguing that Sebald works with a universalised concept of historical trauma, she reads Sebald's text and its reception by German and international critics as a form of historical forgetting of the processes of coming to terms with the bombings in the 1950s.

The final section of the book deals with representations of German suffering in contemporary literature and film. While the issue of German suffering in the arena of politics and public commemoration remains a contentious issue, there appears to be widespread consensus among critics that literature is a medium that can address all the issues surrounding German wartime experience with greater complexity and ambiguity than other discourses.[80] Odile Jansen opens this section with a discussion of the representation of expulsion in writings by Christa Wolf. Wolf was born in 1929 and, like Günter Grass (born 1927), had been active in a Nazi youth organisation, the *Bund deutscher Mädel* (BdM).[81] Jansen traces the crisis in self-perception and perception of the past triggered by the post-war confrontation with Nazi atrocities in Wolf's autobiographical writings, arguing that the trauma of flight and expulsion and the awareness of historical inculpation causes a personality split in which the authenticity of the traumatic personal experience becomes de-realised. Wolf's autobiographical writings, notes Jansen, represent an attempt to re-integrate the divergent parts of identity by re-empathising with oneself. Empathy is maybe *the* central issue of current representations of German suffering. Starting with a discussion of the role of the student movement as empathy-prohibitors in the recent debate, Helmut Schmitz's chapter provides a theoretical investigation of the issue of empathy in representations of German suffering. Distinguishing between historicist, sentimental and critical empathy, Schmitz analyses Uwe Timm's memoir *Am Beispiel meines Bruders* as a work that manages to empathise with the suffering of his brother and father as soldiers on the Eastern Front without losing sight of the historical context. Stuart Taberner looks at the representation of the expulsion in recent fiction by both West-German and former GDR authors, discussing the loss of *Heimat* and the issue of transgenerational or 'secondary' trauma in Arnold Stadler's *Ein hinreißender Schrotthändler* (1999), Hans-Ulrich Treichel's *Der Verlorene* (1998), Christoph Hein's *Landnahme* (2004) Reinhard Jirgl's *Die Unvollendeten* (2003) and Günter Grass's *Im Krebsgang*. Taberner argues that these literary works are not evidence of a revisionist agenda but represent a sensitive and critical exploration of German suffering and its family legacy, engaging with the serious questions that representation of this historically contentious issue brings up. Subtle and sophisticated, these texts represent a return of 'socially engaged' literature. Taberner sees this serious writing in stark contrast to sensationalist or sentimentalising representations, particularly visual media. Paul Cooke's chapter discusses one such example, the most successful of recent German films, Oliver Hirschbiegel's *Der Untergang*. Discussing the film both within the context of 1950s German war films and contemporary international popular filmmaking, Cooke argues that the film utilises a 1950's image of Germans as Hitler's victims to maximise its commercial appeal.

Seven of the twelve chapters in this book date from the conference 'German Suffering/Deutsches Leid – Representations', organised by Yuliya Komska and Ole Frahm at Cornell University in spring 2004. I am grateful to Dr Komska for allowing me to publish revised versions of the papers here. Four chapters were contributed by participants in the AHRC-funded research project 'From Perpetrators to Victims? Discourses of "German Wartime Suffering" from 1945 to the Present', located at the German Department of the University of Leeds. My sincere thanks to these colleagues and friends for their support. I am furthermore grateful to the Gerhard Marcks Stiftung, Bremen, for granting me the right to reproduce a photograph of Gerhard Marcks' sculpture 'Charonsnachen' free of charge. Finally, thanks are due to Lynn Guyver for checking my translations.

Helmut Schmitz
February 2007

Notes

[1] Since 1996, the 'Kölner Krippenweg' provides citizens and tourists with a guided tour around the city's most beautifully crafted and decorated nativity scenes – or 'Krippen' – linking churches and Christmas markets throughout the city. In 2005 there were 98 stations. The display in the station is traditionally the second stop after the one in the cathedral. In 2006 the display was exhibited again, this time updated to 1946.

[2] Jörg Friedrich, *Der Brand. Deutschland im Bombenkrieg 1940-1945*, Propyläen: Munich, 2002, quoted from the paperback edition, Berlin: List, 2004, p. 542.

[3] Laurel Cohen-Pfister, 'The Suffering of the Perpetrators: Unleashing Collective Memory in German Literature of the Twenty-First Century,' *Forum for Modern Language Studies*, 2 (2005), 123-135 (here: p. 125). One of the first writers to turn the attention from issues of addressing the legacy of Nazism to the legacy of inter-familial trauma was Hanns-Josef Ortheil in his 1983 novel *Hecke*. See the chapter on Ortheil in my *On Their Own Terms. The Legacy of National Socialism on Post-1990 German Fiction*, University of Birmingham Press: Birmingham, 2004, pp. 27-54.

[4] Both Cohen-Pfister and Aleida Assmann refer to 2003 as the year in which the representation of German suffering reached some kind of peak. See Cohen-Pfister, p. 126 and Aleida Assmann, 'On the (In)Compatibility of Guilt and Suffering in German Memory,' in: *German Life and Letters*, 2 (2006), 187-200 (here: p. 188).

[5] Lothar Kettenacker, 'Vorwort des Herausgebers,' in: Kettenacker, ed., *Ein Volk von Opfern? Die neue Debatte um den Bombenkrieg 1940-45*, Berlin: Rowohlt, 2003, pp 9-14 (here: p. 11).

[6] The most complete overview over both the German debate and the international secondary literature is found in Elizabeth Dye's as yet unpublished thesis *Painful Memories. Literary Representations of German Wartime Suffering* (PhD Nottingham, 2006). Bill Niven provides a sober and concise overview over the political as well as the historical field of German suffering in his introduction to his invaluable collection *Germans as Victims. Remembering the Past in Contemporary Germany*, Palgrave MacMillan: Basingstoke, 2006, pp. 1-25. Aleida Assmann's *Der lange Schatten der Vergangenheit. Erinnerungskultur und Geschichtspolitik*, C.H.Beck: Munich, 2006, is a comprehensive attempt to synthesise the whole discourse on (international) memory culture, trauma theory, politics of history and aesthetic representation. See also the essays in the special edition of *German Life and Letters* on German Suffering, 57 (2004), and Graham Jackman's bibliography in that volume, 343-356.

[7] Bill Niven, 'Introduction: German Victimhood at the Turn of the Millenium', in: Niven, *Germans as Victims*, p. 1.

[8] See Bill Niven, *Facing the Nazi Past*, Routledge: London, 2002, 'Introduction: the inclusive picture,' pp. 1-9.

[9] See Niven, *Facing the Nazi Past*, p. 2. See also Niven, 'Introduction: German Victimhood at the Turn of the Millenium,' p. 1.

[10] Aleida Assmann, *Der lange Schatten der Vergangenheit*, p. 157.

[11] Anne Fuchs, 'From *Vergangenheitsbewältigung* to Generational Memory Contests in Günter Grass, Monika Maron and Uwe Timm,', *German Life and Letters*, 2 (2006), 196-186 (here: p. 176).

[12] See Harald Welzer, Sabine Moller, Karoline Tschuggnall, *'Opa war kein Nazi'. Nationalsozialismus und Holocaust im Familiengedächtnis*, Fischer: Frankfurt am Main, 2002, pp. 81ff. See also Olaf Jensen's study *Geschichte machen. Strukturmerkmale des intergenerationellen Sprechens über die NS-Vergangenheit in deutschen Familien*, edition discord: Tübingen, 2004, esp. ch. 5.

[13] Laurel Cohen-Pfister argues that the boom in memories of German suffering 'denotes a break with official cultural memory of the Federal Republic and its generally sensitive reflection on the Holocaust,' p. 125. Niven suggests that the focus on German experience is in part motivated by a 'protest' against the culture of *Vergangenheitsbewältigung, Germans as Victims*, p. 10.

[14] See the chapter on Walser in my *On Their Own Terms*, pp. 181-216.

[15] Aleida Assmann, *Der lange Schatten der Vergangenheit*, p. 189.

[16] Günter Grass, *Im Krebsgang*, Steidl: Göttingen, 2002, p. 7.

[17] Niven, *Facing the Nazi Past*, pp. 144f.

[18] Aleida Assmann, 'On the (In)Compatibility of Guilt and Suffering in German Memory,' p. 191.

[19] Frei, *1945 und Wir*, p. 10.

[20] Norbert Frei, *1945 und Wir. Das 'dritte Reich' im Bewußtsein der Deutschen*, C.H.Beck: Munich, 2005, p. 9.

[21] See Daniel Fulda, 'Abschied von der Zentralperspektive. Der nicht nur literarische Geschichtsdiskurs im Nachwendedeutschland als Dispositiv für Jörg Friedrichs *Der Brand*,' in: Wilfried Wilms and William Rasch, eds., *Bombs Away! Representing the*

Air War over Europe and Japan, Rodopi: Amsterdam, 2006, pp. 45-64 (here: pp. 58-59).

[22] See Norbert Frei, 'Gefühlte Geschichte,' *DIE ZEIT*, 21 October, 2004. See also Fulda, p. 59.

[23] Aleida Assmann, *Der lange Schatten der Vergangenheit*, p. 194.

[24] See Christian Buß, 'Unter Wölfen', *SPIEGEL-online,* 28 November 2006: http://www.spiegel.de/kultur/gesellschaft/0,1518,451125,00.html. Aleida Assmann refers in this context to the 'Knoppisierung der Vergangenheit, *Der lange Schatten der Vergangenheit*, p. 214.

[25] Bill Niven, 'The Globalisation of Memory and the Rediscovery of German Suffering,' in: Stuart Taberner, ed., *German Literature in the Age of Globalisation*, Birmingham: University of Birmingham Press, 2004, pp. 229-246 (here: p. 237). Aleida Assmann speaks of a 'transnationale Erinnerungsgemeinschaft' that establishes the Holocaust in western states as a common point of reference, *Der lange Schatten der Vergangenheit*, p. 272.

[26] Aleida Assmann notes a shift from sacrificial to victimological forms of memory, i.e. collective losses are remembered as victims, rather than national scarifices. Assmann, *Der lange Schatten der Vergangenheit*, p. 76.

[27] W.G. Sebald, *Luftkrieg und Literatur*, Carl Hanser Verlag: Munich, 1999. References to the paperback edition, Fischer: Frankfurt am Main, 2001. Daniel Fulda argues that, while Sebald's book triggered a wide debate in the German review pages, it was only Jörg Friedrich's *Der Brand*, sections of which appeared in the tabloid *BILD*, that moved the topic to the mass media, p. 45.

[28] Sebald, p. 21.

[29] Volker Hage attempted to refute Sebald's thesis of a post-war literary silence in his collection *Zeugen der Zerstörung. Die Literaten und der Luftkrieg*, assembling a wealth of literary evidence on the presence of the air war in post-war literature. However, while asserting that the gap noted by Sebald, was one of reception rather than production, he conceded that there was no single volume that would qualify as a 'popular account'. Volker Hage, *Zeugen der Zerstörung. Die Literaten und der Luftkrieg*, Fischer: Frankfurt am Main, 2003, p. 115.

[30] The reviews are collected in Volker Hage et.al., eds., *Deutsche Literatur 1998. Ein Überblick*, Reclam: Stuttgart, 1998, pp. 249-90. Frank Schirrmacher's review 'Beginnt morgen die deutsche Nachkriegsliteratur?' from the *Frankfurter Allgemeine Zeitung*, 15 January 1998 is on pp. 262-267 (here: p. 265).

[31] Aleida Assmann, *Der lange Schatten der Vergangenheit*, p. 185 and p. 101.

[32] Both Christa Wolf and Erwin Strittmatter were forced by GDR censors to edit sections of their novels that addressed Red Army violence and rape. I am grateful to Bill Niven for pointing this out to me.

[33] Aleida Assmann refers to a 'Trauma, das nicht einmal im Familiengedächtnis seinen Platz fand', *Der lange Schatten der Vergangenheit*, p. 184.

[34] See for example Aleida Assmann and Ute Frevert, *Geschichtsvergessenheit – Geschichtsversessenheit. Vom Umgang mit der deutschen Vergangenheit nach 1945*, DVA, Stuttgart, 1999, esp. pp. 112ff. Dagmar C. Barnouw's ill researched and prejudicial study *The War in the Empty Air. Victims, Perpetrators, and Postwar Germans*, Indiana University Press: Bloomington and Indianapolis, 2005 puts forward the untenable thesis of a continuous silence on German suffering due to a culture of collective guilt that originates in the Allied perception of Germans as Nazis which focused exclusive attention on Nazi victims. Barnouw's study, which ignores virtually all research on German memory culture over the last decade, conflates a probably justified critique of the public image of Germany and Germans in the US with post-war German memory culture, asserting a homogeneous epoch of silence and taboo that culminates in a conspiracy theory of Jewish hegemony over German war memories. It is regrettable that Barnouw's position is picked up in the introduction to the otherwise valuable collection *Bombs Away!*

[35] Sebald, *Luftkrieg und Literatur*, p. 20.

[36] Alexander und Margarete Mitscherlich, *Die Unfähigkeit zu trauern*, Piper: Munich, 1977 [first 1967], pp 15-90.

[37] See for example Aleida Assmann, *Der lange Schatten der Vergangenheit*, pp. 108-112; Stuart Taberner, 'Hans-Ulrich Treichel's *Der Verlorene* and the Problem of German Wartime Suffering,' *Modern Lanuage Review*, 1 (2002), 123-134 (here: p. 126); Wilfried Wilms and William Rasch, 'Introduction,' p. 10; Werner Bohleber, 'Trauma, Trauer und Geschichte,' in: Burkhard Liebsch, Jörn Rüsen, eds., *Trauer und Geschichte*, Böhlau: Cologne, 2001, pp. 111-127.

[38] For a discussion and critique of trauma psychology and its use in cultural and academic debates see Susanne Vees-Gulani, *Trauma and Guilt. Literature of Wartime Bombing in Germany*, Walter deGruyter: Berlin and New York, 2003, pp. 11-30.

[39] See for example Anita Eckstaedt, *Nationalsozialismus in der 'zweiten Generation'*, Suhrkamp: Frankfurt am Main, 1992 and the collection by Jörn Rüsen and Jürgen Straub, eds., *Die dunkle Spur der Vergangenheit. Psychoanalytische Zugänge zum Geschichtsbewußtsein*, Suhrkamp: Frankfurt am Main, 1998. For a Cultural Studies approach to the issue of transgeneral traumatisation see Sigrid Weigel, 'Telescopage im Unbewussten. Zum Verhältnis von Trauma, Geschichtsbegriff und Literatur,' in: Elisabeth Bronfen, Birgit R. Erdle, Sigrid Weigel, eds. *Trauma. Zwischen Psychoanalyse & kulturellem Deutungsmuster*. Böhlau: Cologne, Weimar, Vienna, 1999, pp. 51-76.

[40] Examples of (fictional and non-fictional) narratives over several generations are Marcel Beyer, *Spione* (2000), Tania Dückers, *Himmelskörper* (2003), Günter Grass, *Im Krebsgang*, Stephan Wackwitz, *Ein unsichtbares Land* (2003), Thomas Medicus, *In den Augen meines Großvaters* (2004), Wibke Bruns, *Meines Vaters Land* (2004). Examples of variations of the 'parent novel', exploring wartime family trauma are Hanns-Josef Ortheil, *Hecke* (1983) and *Abschied von den Kriegsteilnehmern* (1992), Hans-Ulrich Treichel, *Der Verlorene* (1998), Ulla Hahn, *Unscharfe Bilder* (2003) and Uwe Timm, *Am Beispiel meines Bruders* (2003).

[41] Robert G. Moeller, 'The Politics of the Past in the 1950s: Rhetorics of Victimisation in East and West Germany,' in: Niven, *Germans as Victims*, pp. 26-42 (here: pp. 27-28). Norbert Frei's *Vergangenheitspolitik* makes a similar point with respect to official Federal Republic politics and its amnesty and social reintegration of the 'army of *Mitläufer*' for the stabilisation of the state. According to Frei, the real extent to which Nazi perpetrators were able to benefit from the Federal Amnesty Law in 1949 and the second law of amnesty in 1954 remains in the dark due to lack of statistics. However, he refers to circumstantial evidence pointing to 'Zehntausende von NS-Tätern', Frei, *Vergangenheitspolitik*, C.H.Beck: Munich, 1996, quoted from the paperback edition, dtv: Munich 2003, p. 18.

[42] Robert G. Moeller, *War Stories. The Search for a Usable Past in the Federal Republic of Germany*, University of California Press: Berkeley and Los Angeles, 2001, p. 85 and p. 3.

[43] Moeller, *War Stories*, p. 49.

[44] Aleida Assmann, *Der lange Schatten der Vergangenheit*, p. 190. The expellees had their own ministry, the *Bundesministerium für Vertriebene, Flüchtlinge and Kriegsgeschädigte*, founded in 1949 and dissolved in 1969. Between 1953 and 1961 the ministry published the five-volume *Dokumentation der Vertreibung der Deutschen aus Ost-Mitteleuropa* under the aegis of the doyen of West German historiography, Theodor Schieder. The edition was republished for dtv paperback in 1984. Moeller refers to the expellees' 'continuous presence in 1950s entertainment film', *War Stories*, pp. 123f.

[45] Fulda, p. 46.

[46] Louis Ferdinand Helbig's study *Der ungeheure Verlust. Flucht und Vertreibung in der deutschsprachigen Belletristik der Nachkriegszeit*, Harrassowitz: Wiesbaden, 1988, contains a comprehensive 25-page bibliography of literature dealing with the expulsion from the eastern territories, 11 of which list literary or autobiographical works, pp. 270-95. Ruth Whittlinger in Niven, *Germans as Victims*, pp. 62-75, refers to 500 academic publications on expellees by 1989, and over 500 publications of so-called *Heimatbücher* 'representing 20% of all regional history accounts published in Germany', p. 73.

[47] 'Aus der massenhaft praktizierten Diskretion, die sich im Persönlich-Privaten keineswegs erschöpfte, erwuchs ein Triumph des 'Beschweigens', dessen Ausmaß, Tiefe und Bedeutung historiographisch nicht einmal in Ansätzen erforscht ist.' Frei, *Vergangenheitspolitik*, p. 15.

[48] Frei, *1945 und Wir*, p. 13. See also Aleida Assmann, *Der lange Schatten der Vergangenheit*, p. 202, Fulda, p. 48, as well as Peter Schneider's article 'Die Deutschen als Ofper? Über ein Tabu der Nachkriegsgeneration,' in: Kettenacker, pp. 158-165.

[49] See Assmann, *Der lange Schatten der Vergangenheit*, p. 201.

[50] Ian Buruma, *The Wages of Guilt. Memories of War in Germany and Japan*, Cape: London, 1994, p. 303.

[51] Assmann, *Der lange Schatten der Vergangenheit*, p. 186 and Assmann, 'On the (In)Compatibility of Guilt and Suffering in German Memory', pp. 191-192.

[52] See the Introduction to my *On their Own Terms*, p. 15. Norbert Frei speaks of 'nachgetragene Empathie', *1945 und Wir*, p. 14.

[53] Aleida Assmann, describes the student movement as the 'other side of the coin' of the League of Expellees, *Der lange Schatten der Vergangenheit*, p. 202. Fulda argues that both left and right play off victims versus perpetrators, 'auf der einen Seite so, auf der anderen Seite andersherum,' Fulda, p. 48.

[54] See Cora Stephan, 'Wie man eine Stadt anzündet,' in: Kettenacker, pp. 95-102 (here: p 102); Assmann, *Der lange Schatten der Vergangenheit*, pp. 108-112.

[55] Moeller, *War Stories*, p. 174.

[56] Sebald, pp. 77-78.

[57] Sebald, p. 95 and p. 104.

[58] Reinhard Kosellek argues that '[e]s gibt keine Sinnstiftung, die rückwirkend die Totalität der Verbrechen der nationalsozialistischen Deutschen einholen oder einlösen könnte,' quoted in Assmann, *Der lange Schatten der Vergangenheit*, p. 14. Dominick LaCapra warns of the temptation to configure historical trauma into 'founding traumas [...] that paradoxically become the valorized or intensely cathected basis of identity for an individual or group.' LaCapra, *Writing History, Writing Trauma*, Johns Hopkins University Press: Baltimore, 2001, p. 23. Adorno remarked with respect to Arnold Schönberg's composition 'Ein Überlebender aus Warschau' that aesthetic representations of the Holocaust are invariably caught up in the paradox of the categorical imperative of remembrance and the aesthetic transformation of suffering into something delectable for the audience: 'Aber indem es [the suffering, HS] trotz aller Härte und Unversöhnlichkeit zum Bild gemacht wird, ist es doch, als ob die

Scham vor den Opfern verletzt wäre. Aus diesen wird etwas bereitet, Kunstwerke, der Welt zum Fraß vorgeworfen, die sie umbrachte.' Adorno, 'Engagement,' in: *Noten zur Literatur*, <u>Gesammelte Werke</u>, 11, Suhrkamp: Frankfurt am Main, 1997 [1974], pp. 409-430 (here: p. 423).

[59] See Frank Schirrmacher's allegation that the trauma of German suffering has remained 'unerzählt, also unerlöst'. Schirrmacher, p. 265. Benedict Anderson, *Imagined Communities*, Verso: London, 1983, pp. 6f.

[60] Peter Glotz, *Die Vertreibung. Böhmen als Lehrstück*, Ullstein: Berlin, 2003.

[61] Assmann, 'On the (In)Compatibility of Guilt and Suffering in German Memory,' p. 198 and *Der lange Schatten der Vergangenheit*, p. 188. See also Wolfgang Sofsky, 'Die halbierte Erinnerung,' in Kettenacker, pp. 124-126 (here: p. 126), Niven, *Germans as Victims*, p. 18 and Fuchs, p. 177. Pfister, p. 132 argues that the 'focus on human frailty in the context of Third Reich policies and the war creates a realm where perpetrator and victim exist as concurrent identities.'

[62] Frei, *1945 und Wir*, p. 14. See also Harald Welzer, 'Schön unscharf. Über die Konjunktur der Familien- und Generationenromane,' *Mittelweg 36*, 1 (2004), 53-64.

[63] See for example Dominick LaCapra who argues that the 'grey zone' (Primo Levi) of victims becoming involved in the act of extermination as, for example, the Jewish Kapos in the death camps or the Jewish police in the Ghettos, does not extend to the perpetrator side. LaCapra, pp. 79-80.

[64] This is visible from Daniel Fulda's use of the term 'Opfer' as denoting someone suffering violence: 'Opfer ist im Sprachgebrauch des vorliegenden Beitrages, wer Gewalt erleidet,' Fulda, p. 49, footnote 12.

[65] On the Christian tradition of victimology see Assmann, *Der lange Schatten der Vergangenheit*, pp. 72ff. Niven notes that recent representations of German suffering are 'at times characterised by a post hoc construction of absolute victimhood which depends for its viability on ignoring issues such as historical context, processes of cause and effect, action and reaction, and questions of the moral responsibility of those upon whom reactions impinge.' *Germans as Victims*, p 16.

[66] Frei, *1945 und Wir*, p. 10, Assmann, *Der lange Schatten der Vergangenheit*, speaks of an 'ethische Wende des Erinnerns', pp. 76ff.

[67] For a list of examples see my 'The Birth of the Collective from the Spirit of Empathy,' in Niven, *Germans as Victims*, pp. 93-108. See also Samuel Salzborn's, Bill Niven's, Heinz-Peter Preußer's and Annette Seidel Arpacı's chapters in this volume.

[68] Friedrich, esp. the section 'Land', pp. 179-363.

[69] Assmann, 'On the (In)Compatibility of Guilt and Suffering in German Memory,' pp. 197-188.

[70] Moeller, *War Stories*, pp. 78-79.

[71] This has remained the discursive praxis of the far right and the League of Expellees until today. In January 2005 the twelve members of the neo-Nazi party NPD in the regional parliament of Saxony left their seats in protest during a minute's silence for the victims of Nazi violence. During a debate on the bombing of Dresden, the NPD section used the term 'Bomben-Holocaust'.

[72] Assmann, 'On the (In)Compatibility of Guilt and Suffering in German Memory,' p. 186.

[73] Niven, *Germans as Victims*, p. 13.

[74] Moeller, *War Stories*, p. 2. Moeller quotes a *SPIEGEL* poll from 8 May 1995 where 36% of all and 40% of over 60s answered yes to the question whether the 'expulsion of the Germans from the East [was] just as great a crime against humanity as the Holocaust'. Moeller also demonstrates that the comparison of the bombing of Dresden with Nazi crimes goes back to the 1950s, 'The Politics of the Past', p. 36.

[75] On the issue of normality see the essays in Stuart Taberner and Paul Cooke, eds., *German Culture, Politics, and Literature into the Twenty-First Century. Beyond Normalization*, Rochester: Camden House, 2006.

[76] Saul Friedlander, 'Die Metapher des Bösen,' *Die Zeit*, 48, 1998.

[77] Wagner's letter of invitation to Schäfer refers to his role as organiser of the exhibition 'Flucht, Vertreibung, Integration' which Schäfer claims to have understood as a request for a commemorative speech on the expulsions. See Julia Spinola, 'Eklat um Buchenwald,' *Frankfurter Allgemeine Zeitung*, 27 August 2006.

[78] See Moeller, 'The Politics of the Past in the 1950s,' p. 33.

[79] In a recent article on Wolfgang Borchert, the iconic writer of the immediate post-war period whose play *Draußen vor der Tür* is one of the foundations of post-war German literature, Friedemann Weidauer demonstrates how Borchert compares the effect on Germans of the Allied de-Nazification questionnaire to being gassed. See Fiedemann Weidauer, 'Sollen wir ihn reinlassen? Wolfgang Borchert's *Draußen vor der Tür* in neuen Kontexten,' *German Life and Letters*, 1 (2006), 122-139 (here: p. 136).

[80] See Assmann, *Der lange Schatten der Vergangenheit*, p. 214, Niven, *Germans as Victims*, p. 17, Pfister, p. 132, Taberner, 'Hans-Ulrich Treichel's *Der Verlorene* and the Problem of German Wartime Suffering', p. 126, Dye, *Painful Memories*.

[81] Grass's revelation in summer 2006 that he had been a member of the *Waffen-SS* for three months cannot be dealt with here. Although the admission by the author whose *Im Krebsgang* had, like no other recent book, contributed to the re-canonisation of the theme of German suffering in serious literature was subject to a ferocious media debate, it had no discernible de-legitimising influence on the discourse of German suffering. What was remarkable, though, was that the focus of the debate was not on any ethical implications of Grass's membership in the *Waffen-SS* but on his late admission. See Anne Fuchs, '"Ehrlich, du lügst wie gedruckt": Günter Grass' Autobiographical Confession and the Changing Territory of Germany's Memory Culture,' *German Life and Letters,* forthcoming.

Gregor Streim

Germans in the *Lager*.
Reports and Narratives about Imprisonment in
Post-War Allied Internment Camps

The chapter focuses on a still largely unexplored, early example of a discourse on German victimisation. It deals with the literary memoirs of authors such as Bruno Brehm, Ernst von Salomon, Franz Tumler, Hans Venatier, and Heinrich Zerkaulen, who were interned in Allied civilian camps in Germany and Austria between 1950 and 1953. These narratives – some fictional, some factual – must be understood as an attempt to establish the perspective of the German victim in the collective memory of the young Federal Republic. In this respect, they competed with reports on National Socialist concentration camps that recounted the memories of the Nazi regime's victims.[1]

I.

In 1988, one year before German unification, Martin Walser gave a public speech in Munich in which he invoked the unifying features of a Germanness that transcended ideological and historical ruptures. Inevitably, he had to consider the question of how to deal with the knowledge about the crimes committed in the name of Germany during the Third Reich. He took recourse to the 'Unschuld [seiner] Erinnerung' on this point: 'Es ist mir nicht möglich, meine Erinnerungen mit Hilfe eines inzwischen erworbenen Wissens zu belehren. [...] Das erworbene Wissen über die mordende Diktatur ist eins, meine Erinnerung ist ein anderes.'[2] Walser's speech is directed against a relationship with the National Socialist past that is dominated by the discourse of guilt, something that, in his view, excludes authentic private memory from the 'official' image of history. With this critique of the 'politically correct' form of remembrance in the former Federal Republic Walser prepared the ground for the public debate about German experience of suffering during the Second World War, which began with great emotional energy in the 1990s and still continues. The thematisation of 'German suffering' – whether the experience of Allied bombing raids or the expulsion from the Eastern territories – was and is always legitimised with recourse to the authenticity of individual memory and memory is presented as a means for breaking with a historical taboo. This created the impression that only now has it become possible to articulate and accept an experience that had been blocked for a long time for psychological and/or political reasons.

This revaluation of remembering was to a certain extent supported by the recent popularisation of memory theory and its distinction between (private) communicative and (political) cultural memory. Aleida Assmann, for example, argued that with his plea for the 'innocence of memory', Walser had defended the communicative memory of his generation.[3] However, the opposition between biographical experience on the one hand and knowledge or judgement on the other cannot be explained solely or primarily with the distinction of temporally and medially different types of memory. The insistence on 'authentic' remembering is obviously less a phenomenon of memory history than of memory politics. This becomes particularly evident when one compares the contemporary thematic presence of memory with narratives of German 'victim experience' from the early years of the Federal Republic. On the one hand these sources confirm that 'German suffering' had indeed a literary presence during that period and was not just articulated in private conversations. On the other hand, the texts show that the remembering of suffering had been tied to similar arguments and conflicts as they determine the contemporary debate. For example, the opposition between memory and knowledge is already central for the historical texts. And, like Walser in 1988, the writers in the post-war period took recourse to the 'Unschuld des Erinnerns'.

II.

In what follows, I would like to present a number of texts, by and large unknown today, that were published between 1950 and 1953. These texts deal with a chapter of early post-war history that was of great concern to the German public at that time, a chapter that has subsequently been largely forgotten and that is unlikely to attract much media attention in the future despite the boom in contemporary memory culture: the Allied civilian internment camps in the western occupied zones after 1945.[4] After some brief remarks on the function and history of these camps, I will discuss central political aspects of the internment narratives in the context of discourse history and politics around 1950. Finally, I will consider the theme of remembering in the texts themselves.

The civilian internment camps that the Western Allies erected in Germany after the surrender were part of an extensive programme of arrests that had been developed by the Americans before the end of the war and that was adopted with limitations by the other Western Allies.[5] This programme had military as well as political aims. First, it was supposed to eliminate persons and groups who could pose a threat to the security of occupational forces. Furthermore, the means of 'automatic arrest' was used to filter out those characters from the group of internees who were politically responsible for the war crimes and crimes against humanity committed by National Socialism, in order to put them on trial.[6] Thus the programme of arrest was closely connected to the de-Nazification programme, something that is a recurrent cause for polemic criticism in the literary representations of internment. Moreover, the programme was not only directed against war criminals, high ranking Nazi officials and members of the SS but, as Lutz Niethammer has shown, also targeted smaller social and administrative functionaries as well as all persons who were suspected of being a potential enemy of the occupational forces. Thus in the first quarter of the occupation 117,500 persons were arrested in the US zone alone, 50% of whom were released within a year.[7]

Although a relatively large part of the population was affected by the programme of arrest either directly or indirectly, the internment has hardly played any role at all both in historiography and in the public discourse of the later Federal Republic – in stark contrast to the theme of war captivity. The memory of internment became a domain of military and National Socialist memoirs and their reception by right wing radicals. This has remained unchanged until today. From the present perspective, this situation is rather obvious, as the experience of internment is rather less 'innocent' than that of the POW's or the bombing victims, especially as it was shared by Nazi functionaries and officials. Nevertheless, the internment was an object of wide public debate in the early years of the Federal Republic and it is the object of a number of fictional and non-fictional narratives that frequently attracted high sales figures.

The most prominent of these – and the only one that is still known today – is Ernst von Salomon's 'autobiographical report' *Der Fragebogen*. The book was published in April 1951 and sold over 200,000 copies in two years, triggering the first political-literary controversy of the Federal Republic.[8] From the outset, Salomon

conceived the book as a provocation, as a demonstrative violation of
the discourse of guilt and as ironic commentary on the theory and
praxis of de-Nazification. The book narrates Salomon's own life story
as fictive answer to the 131 questions of the notorious 'large'
American de-Nazification questionnaire. By answering even the
simplest questions about religious affiliation or party memberships
with pages of anecdotal memories, he attempted to demonstrate the
absurdity of the schematism of de-Nazification. His purpose was to
reveal it as a control of convictions ultimately motivated by ideology.
The most violent public reaction was triggered by the final part of his
autobiographical report, some 200 pages long. Here, Salomon reports
under the section title 'Remarks/Bemerkungen' on his fifteen months
of internment in various civil internment camps.[9] While the previous
passages dealing with the Weimar Republic and the Third Reich are
narrated as burlesque, the final section is dominated by a tone of
accusation and nationalist confession. Especially the sympathetic
description of the interned Nazi leaders and the demonstrative
equation of American CIC (Counter Intelligence Corps) officers who
were in charge of the camp, with the Gestapo was considered
provocative (or liberating for others).[10] The narrative closes with the
memory of the fellow internee, SA-leader Hanns Ludin (who was later
executed as a war criminal), quoting his (supposedly) final words: 'Es
lebe Deutschland!'[11]

Despite the heated debate that followed the publication of *Der
Fragebogen*, it was by no means the only and not even the first
literary treatment of Allied internment. It was only the most well
known representative of a whole series of representations that treated
internment in a similar fashion and that, as provisional research seems
to suggest, were published predominantly in the period between 1950
and 1953. Their authors can without exception be attributed to the
National Socialist, or like Salomon, to the national revolutionary
camp. An important common feature of the texts is that although they
frequently approach the genre of factual report, they mostly choose
the form of a story for the depiction of internment, either a factual,
autobiographical or fictional narrative.

Franz Tumler's novel *Heimfahrt* which appeared in 1950, a year
before Salomon's *Fragebogen*, focuses on a fictional protagonist.[12]
Tumler, a former member of the SA-group 'Alpenland' and a war
participant, tells the story of the soldier Leberecht, who is holding his

post at an anti-aircraft gun on the North Sea coast until the last days of the war and who is arrested and interned during his attempt to fight his way through to his Austrian home after the dissolution of his unit. At the heart of the novel is the experience of internment, embedded in a story of a soldier returning home from war. After an odyssee through several camps where he experiences humiliation and hunger but also the comradeship of his fellow internees, Leberecht manages to get home with cunning and luck, where he learns, however, that the Heimat outside the lager is occupied and under foreign administration, too.[13]

A similar pattern is used by Richard Euringer in his autobiographical novella *Die Sargbreite Leben* which bears the subtitle 'Wir sind Internierte', written in 1950 and published in 1952.[14] Euringer's novella begins with the arrest of the protagonist and similarly ends with an incomplete 'Heimkehr' after some 350 pages.[15] Here, the first person narrator has to get to grips with the fact that his house has been occupied by the family of a British officer that employs his wife as a house maid. Like Salomon, Euringer, a Nazi of the first hour, attempts to communicate the authenticity of the experience by employing the style of a report, making no secret of his *völkisch* convictions and his contempt for the American occupiers.

In Heinrich Zerkaulen's autobiographical novella *Zwischen Tag und Nacht. Erlebnisse aus dem Camp 94* (1951) the first person narrator is arrested at home due to a denunciation. After internment in various US camps and interrogations by the CIC he is finally released, his health affected but his spirit unbroken.[16] When he returns home, he learns that his house has been looted and expropriated. Zerkaulen's narrative adds the task of the chronicler to the viewpoint of the autobiographically legitimised witness. At the beginning of his narrative, the narrator remarks that he had to promise his comrades in the camp, 'die Geschichte unserer Gefangenschaft aufzuzeichnen.'[17]

In Bruno Brehm's novel *Aus der Reitschul'!* (1951) the internment camp is the (preliminary) final station of a long German passion that extends backwards to the time before the First World War.[18] Brehm tells the life story of Herbert Hörmann, son of an officer in the army of the Austro-Hungarian empire. Hörmann is an idealist believer in the German mission and to his chagrin experiences the step-by-step defeat of Germanness in middle and Eastern Europe. In his missionary enthusiasm he joins the First World War, suffers inflation, democracy and ultimately the Second World War, finally being interned in a US camp, accused of being a 'Hauptkriegsverbrecher'.[19] At the end of this *deutschnational* story of German suffering Brehm's protagonist, too, returns home, maltreated but unshaken in his political creed.

In Hans Venatier's novel *Der Major und die Stiere* (1953), which is formally different from the texts mentioned so far, the internment camps play a rather marginal role.[20] In this ironic parable of de-Nazification, the camps and the time of occupation are presented as a historically overcome period. It is the only text that uses comic effects. Modelled on Giovanni Guareschi's popular comic novel *Don Camillo und Peppone* (1950),[21] Venatier recapitulates the history of de-Nazification as a personal confrontation between an officer of the US occupation forces and a Bavarian farmer, the 'Kolterner' who has been forcefully enlisted by the CIC as interpreter. The ironic punchline of the novel is that ultimately it is not the 'Amy' who has re-educated the Germans but the Germans who have re-educated the American. The American major who cannot tear himself away from 'diesem damned beloved country' sends for his wife and his 'Sonnyboy' to join him in Germany: [22]

> 'Daddy, Daddy,' hat der Sonnyboy [...] gestrampelt, 'wo sind die Nehsis?' Der Major hat seinen Arm über den Marktplatz gereckt. 'Dies alles sind Nazis.' Vor Schreck hat sich der Sonnyboy die Hand an den Mund gehalten. 'O Daddy, die sehen ja aus wie richtige Menschen!' Da hat der Major aber lachen müssen, hat den Sonnyboy hochgehoben geküßt und gelobt: 'Wie schnell du dahinter gekommen bist, Sonnyboy!' Und die liebe Mutter hat ganz stolz hinzugefügt: 'Dafür ist ja unser lieber Daddy zu den Germans gegangen, daß er Menschen aus ihnen macht!'[23]

What is most surprising from a contemporary perspective in these texts, which I have only been able to outline here, is particularly the way in which the US internment camps are nonchalantly described as 'KZs' and the de-Nazification is equated with Nazi methods. Cynical remarks like the following narrator's commentary from Venatier's novel are a fixed part of the repertoire of this genre: 'Recht haben s' daran getan, die Amerikaner, daß s' die Lager, die s' eben leer gemacht haben, gleich wieder aufgefüllt haben, sonst wären s' ja unrentabel geworden.'[24]

The unbroken continuity of *völkisch* and anti-western ideology in these texts is less surprising, however, than the fact that they had such a large distribution around 1950 and apparently could count on large-scale acceptance. How then can it be explained that these 'Lager-Erzählungen' became popular in the period between 1950-1953 only to quickly lose importance as a literary genre? This question can only be answered in the context of discursive and political history of the time.

III.

What is important for the understanding of these texts is the difference between narrated time – internment and de-Nazification 1945-1948 – and the time of publication. The end of the de-Nazification programme in 1948 as a result of increasing tensions beween the Western Allies and the Soviet Union and the opening of the Bundestag in 1949 effected a fundamental change in the public approaches to the Nazi past. Whereas in the immediate post-war period the acknowledgement of the Nazi crimes and Nazi victims had been at the centre of public statements, now domestic politics was predominantly concerned with the acknowledgement and rehabilitation of the victims of de-Nazification – the interned, the POW's, the party members who had been forced out of office, even the sentenced war criminals and Nazi perpetrators. Norbert Frei has analysed the political process of the years 1949 to 1953 as a foundational time of the 'Vergangenheitspolitik' of the Federal Republic, the constituent elements of which were 'Amnestie, Integration und Abgrenzung'.[25] The texts which we are concerned with here encountered a political and discursive constellation where the focus on the 'victims' of de-Nazification increasingly displaced the confrontation with German responsibility for the crimes of the Third Reich. The prominence of these texts between 1950 and 1953 can thus not only be explained by the abolition of censorship. Rather, one has to read them as an attempt to fix the German perspective of victimhood securely in collective memory, supported by the 'Vergangenheitspolitik' of the young Federal Republic. The political structures that characterise collective memory are clearly evident in these narratives.[26]

The first important aspect is the competition with Nazi victims. The memory of Allied internment in these narratives is in veiled but clearly recognisable competition with the memory of Nazi victims and the remembrance of Nazi victims. The internment narratives read in parts like a copy of reports about Nazi concentration camps which had attracted immense public attention in the early post-war period.[27] This is recognisable in the stylised representation of the Allied camps as copies of the Nazi camps, in the description of registration, marches, roll-calls and accommodation. Reports from Nazi camps are also thematised directly, specifically the function these reports fulfilled within the re-education programme. The way in which such parallels are drawn is ambiguous. On the one hand, the suffering represented in the photographs and films from liberated Nazi camps is de-legitimised due to its propagandistic use and its mediated nature. On the other hand, the Germans' own suffering is ennobled in an ironic way by comparison with these images. This becomes clear from the following passage from Salomon's *Fragebogen*:

> Der alte Herr hatte überhaupt kein Fleisch mehr auf den Knochen und unter der Haut. Er war wirklich nur noch ein Skelett. Ich rief ihn an, er sollte sich neben die Bilder von Mauthausen stellen, die der Kommandant hatte an einer Barackenwand annageln lassen. Herr Alinn hatte längst mit Stolz festgestellt, daß er sich in bezug auf die Kunst der Abmagerung vor den Opfern des Mauthausener KZs nicht zu verstecken brauche.[28]

Simultaneously, the German camp community is distinguished in their own consciousness from Nazi camp victims by their undefeated 'Glauben' and 'Kameradschaft'. See Zerkaulen:

> In jeder Stube waren bis unter die Decke Verschläge gebaut worden, Käfige, Menschenkäfige. Nun konnten wir sogar übereinander liegen, immer zwei Mann in einem 'Bett'. Äußerlich [...] war jetzt wenig Unterschied zwischen den Abbildungen der an uns zur Verteilung gekommenen kleinen Bildhefte über die Zustände in Buchenwald und unserer Situation in Kornwestheim! Wenn wir diesen Unterschied nicht selber in uns aufrichteten, würden wir genauso verkommen, wie jene dort.[29]

Zerkaulen takes the victim competition to the point that he not only turns the interned Germans into fellow sufferers but also into advocates of those murdered and abused in National Socialist camps. Thus the victim-perpetrator-relation is subtly reversed. In a conciliatory tone, Zerkaulen hopes the example of the Germans suffering in American 'KZs' could 'die Menschheit endlich davon abbringen, solche grausamen Lager einzurichten':

> Vielleicht wird man auch euch erzählen von den Verbrechen in Dachau und Buchenwald, daran ihr keinen Anteil hattet, die ihr verabscheut haben würdet, wie wir es tun. Und wenn nur dies die Menschheit lernt, endgültig Schluß zu machen mit ihren Konzentrationslagern des Hungers und aller seelischen und körperlichen Qual – dann war auch unsere Inhaftierungszeit der Besinnung nicht umsonst.[30]

A second, political, aspect of these narratives is their clearly recognisable purpose to found a group identity, that is, a common German identity. This is, above all, the function of the metonymic figuration of the camp. In all narratives, the internment camp represents the occupied Germany as *pars pro toto*. The internment camp is a means of making the occupation, regulation and control that the whole country is subject to, particularly visible. Thus Euringer's interned first person narrator maintains:

> Die guten Landsleutchen, die da draußen jetzt nur an ihre Eier denken, an ihre Milch und ihren Markt, merken das vielleicht noch nicht. [...] Offenbar sehen sie den Stacheldraht nicht, der auch uns hier umdrahtet, und doch sind sie mitinterniert.[31]

To support this logic of the proxy, all narrators strive to portray the camp community as a representative section of the population.[32] They not only point out that next to former SS-men and convinced Nazis representatives from all other social groups are present in the camp,[33] but attempt to level the difference between the different groups. The question of responsibility and guilt is demonstratively ignored, at most it is identified as a means of Allied propaganda, aiming at the disintegration of the camp community. The authors are particularly intent to blur the distinction between civilian internees and POW's by presenting both groups as victims of an arbitrary procedure that is, as is recurrently stated, in contravention of international law.[34]

The recourse to the foundational figure of the victim in all of the narratives under consideration can be regarded as a third aspect of the politics of memory and remembrance at stake in these texts. By representing internees and POW's as victims without distinction, these texts mobilise a pattern of experience that possesses a particular power of integration.[35] However, the figure of the victim does not just have an integrating function, it is aimed at de-legitimising the Allied victorious powers and the occupation. If the internees are victims, law and morality are not on the side of the victor; none of the narratives leaves its readers in any doubt that the internment has no legal and moral basis and is thus totally arbitrary. The authors spend a lot of narrative energy on discrediting the reasons and motives of the occupation and the internment. Numerous scenes of interrogation portray in drastic and sometimes comic fashion how CIC officers grill the German prisoners only because they adhere to the wrong 'creed', one that is not western. From this perspective, de-Nazification, even occupation and the war itself appear as a problem of cultural difference, as becomes evident from Brehm's *Aus der Reitschul'!*:

> Am nächsten Morgen wurde Hauptmann Hörmann zum Verhör gerufen; als er nach fünf Minuten zurückkam, fragten die Kameraden, was man von ihm habe wissen wollen. 'Eigentlich gar nichts. Der Ami hat gefragt, wen ich für bedeutender halte: Spengler oder Toynbee.' 'Und was hast Du gesagt?' wollte der

Arzt wissen. 'Spengler.' 'Deshalb kutschiert man uns im Land herum', murrte der
Arzt.[36]

The humiliation and deprivation of one's rights by the occupational
forces, the endless interrogations and meaningless prescriptions, are
experienced by the internee as a form of heroism that turns him into a
proxy for the disgraced nation. Thus a fourth aspect becomes clear:
The situation of internment does not only metonymically point to the
occupation, but also presents a model of orientation for national self-
assertion and new beginning. All the authors explain thoroughly how
the subordinate mass of internees is changing slowly into a camp
community. The camp creates structures of communication and
develops a characteristic ethos amongst the internees that proves the
American re-education measures to be futile. The camp community
actually renews the set of virtues of the ideology of the
Volksgemeinschaft, the force of which is beginning to wane outside
the camp – comradeship, honesty and sense of duty.[37] Naturally,
German women who enter into relationships with American –
sometimes even black! – soldiers function in this context as a negative
topos. In this constellation, the internee does not only suffer for the
whole of Germany by proxy, his suffering also appears as a personal
sacrifice (Opfer) that he makes to the fatherland. Zerkaulen speaks of
a 'Zeit der Prüfung', imposed by God.[38] Euringer, author of the
Deutsche Passion (1933) rhymes: 'Verfemt, geschlagen und beraubt./
Warum?/ Ich habe geopfert und geglaubt'.[39] This idea of martyrdom
with religious overtones also plays a significant role in Carl Schmitt's
autobiographical writings where he reflects on his various arrests by
the Americans, for example in his *Gesang eines Sechzigjährigen*:

Ich habe die Escavessaden des Schicksals erfahren,
Siege und Niederlagen, Revolutionen und Restaurationen,
Inflationen und Deflationen, Ausbombungen,
Diffamierungen, Regimewechsel und Rohrbrüche,
Hunger und Kälte, Lager und Einzelhaft.
Durch alles das bin ich hindurchgegangen,
Und alles ist durch mich hindurchgegangen.
[...]
Sohn dieser Weihe, du sollst nicht erbeben –
Horche und leide![40]

The figure of self-sacrifice (Selbstopfer) likewise has a political
function, albeit in different fashion from the victim of war or de-
Nazification. It has a restorative tendency: the self-sacrifice of the
internee salvages the values of Germannness and *völkisch* identity

from the military defeat and transfers them to future history. Zerkaulen formulates the meaning of the 'Prüfung' imposed on him and his fellow internees: 'Unsere Aufgabe heißt, ein ganzes Leben über Pfeiler der Brücke zu sein zwischen den Kriegen zu einem neuen Deutschland hin.'[41]

In contrast to the critique of de-Nazification, this restorative, nationalist aspect of the camp narratives was not compatible with the 'Vergangenheitspolitik' of the early Federal Republic. While its purpose was the correction of the de-Nazification programme, it simultaneously wanted to ensure a strict differentiation from remaining groups of National Socialism and potential neo-Nazis. This discrepancy might be among the reasons that the victim-centered memory of the internment camps was not able to enter the collective memory of the Federal Republic for long and instead sedimented into the group memory of right wing radicalism as a form of 'counter memory'.

IV.

The internment narratives of the early 1950s can be read as a perfect example of the political function of historical memory in literature. Because of their symbolic reductionism and their allegorical or parabolic narratives these texts pursue an obvious strategy of rendering meaningful and foundational structures out of defeat and occupation. These texts are of particular interest because they also topicalise memory, or rather, the function of narrative within memory politics. The texts discussed above do not only legitimise the authenticity of the presented experience by recourse to the autobiographical pact. Of no less importance is the narrative gestus of oral communication of this experience. Thus the narratives present themselves in a form that Aleida Assmann has described as genuine communicative memory. The narrator's voice on the one hand imitates characteristics of oral communication, as can be seen, for example, in the narrator's use of dialect in Venatier's novel. On the other hand the novels and reports about the interment camps contain numerous examples of storytelling amongst the characters themselves. One could say that the community of internees is only created in the act of mutual exchange of experience. Zerkaulen writes 'Es waren jene Stunden, in denen der geborene Erzähler sich erweisen konnte, auch wenn er nie im Leben eine Zeile geschrieben hatte', and specifies this act of narration further: it was 'dieses echte Erzählenkönnen aus dem Stegreif des eigenen, kleinen, oft so unscheinbaren und dennoch so trächtigen Beispiels heraus'.[42] The foundational power of storytelling is accentuated particularly in its juxtaposition to the interrogations by the CIC. This is evident from Salomon's *Fragebogen* the whole purpose of which is to counteract the schematic principle of the questionnaire by 'authentic' memory and autobiographical storytelling. The other texts likewise report again and again with gratification how the CIC interrogators fail to grasp the German 'Wesen'. Like Salomon, Zekaulen presents his autobiographical narrative as a counter model to the interrogations:

> Meinen Kameraden im Camp habe ich versprechen müssen, die Geschichte unserer Gefangenschaft aufzuzeichnen. Ich habe es auch bei jener langen und denkwürdigen Unterredung mit C.I.C. (Counter Intelligence Corps) versprechen müssen, mit jenen also, die so viel von uns wußten und noch mehr wissen wollten, um endlich hinter das Geheimnis zu kommen, das für uns Deutschland heißt. Aber wenn einer auch nach bestem Gewissen noch so zahlreiche Fragebögen ausfüllte, wie es uns im Camp zu tun befohlen war, – er hätte sein ganzes Leben Stunde für Stunde vor ihnen ausbreiten müssen, um am Ende doch nicht verstanden zu werden![43]

The interrogations and endless questionnaires, presented as 'Instrument einer Inquisition des zwanzigsten Jahrhunderts',[44] tend to dissolve community with their incomprehensible codes, and are, in the views of the narrators and their characters used by the Americans for this purpose. In contrast to this, the internees feel reassured whenever they take possession of their individual experience in the medium of oral communication and storytelling. Moreover, they increasingly acknowledge as their most important task the keeping of their own memories 'unverstellt im Gedächtnis', a task that transcends their individuality.[45] This is evident from the following passage from Tumler's novel:

> So redeten Leberecht und Gehlen zusammen, und die Zeit, die vordem leer überhandgenommen hatte, verwandelte sich ihnen zu einem Aufenthalt für Gespräch und Erinnerung. Etwas stand still, oder: etwas anderes bewegte sich auf einmal. [...] Auch auf die Leute in der Stube wirkte diese Verwandlung. Sie kam nicht eigentlich von Gehlens Erzählung, sondern von dem, was er selber vorstellte: er hatte sich nicht übermächtigen lassen, vielmehr statt dessen ein Beispiel gegeben, daß einer, der elend ist, noch aufstehen und sagen kann: ich muß mir selber helfen, ich will mich erinnern![46]

In the internment narratives, orally transmitted memory enters into a partially veiled, partially open competition with the propaganda of re-education and the overwhelming media presence of reports of

National Socialist crimes. These reports are viewed with increasing scepticism, not only because of their propaganda function but especially because of their nature as media. This can be seen from Euringer's description of a screening of a concentration camp film in the internment camp:

> Unter Harmoniumsuntermalung eröffnet eine Grabesstimme als Ansage die Scheußlichkeiten. Bald freilich fällt die Technik auf, die erschwert, Text und Bild als Dokument in Einklang zu bringen. Vor einem Haufen verstümmelter Leichen – darunter eine schamlos aufgenommene Frauenleiche – wird z.B. nicht gesagt: 'Dies ist ein Berg im Konzentrationslager soundso Hingemordeter', sondern: 'Dies war einmal eine Frau'. Alsbald macht sich unter denen, die Dokumente erwartet hatten, denn auch Unruhe bemerkbar. Je entsetzlicher sich die einzelnen Szenen folgen, desto häufiger melden sich Zwischenrufe, die [...] laut protestieren. [...] Diese Zusammenstellung, nicht würdig der Tragödie, selbst der Verbrechen, die sie behauptet, bewies sie nicht so unzweideutig, daß sie überzeugen konnte. [...] Sie wendet sich an die niedrigsten Instinkte, peitscht – unter Mißbrauch sakraler Musik – mit unlauteren Mitteln zum Haß auf, dient aber letztlich nicht der Erkenntnis. Etliche abgefeimte Züge charakterisieren das Ganze als Machwerk.[47]

In her study of the use of photographs in the re-education campaign Claudia Brink has noted that the pictures from the concentration camps were seen by many Germans as an instrument to establish the thesis of collective guilt and were subsequently rejected[48] This is confirmed by the texts discussed here. In addition, it becomes clear that the distrust awakened by the propagandist use is immediately connected with the criticism of the media in use. This can be shown in an exemplary section from Euringer, who comments on the newspapers distributed in the internment camp:

> Es liegen nun so viele Zeitungen auf, auch amerikanische, daß man danach nicht mehr anstehen muß. [...] Aufschlußreich sind Zeichnungsfolgen im Stil von Bilderbogenstreifen. Da werden Kindern die Greueltaten, z.B. der SS so pädagogisch eingeträufelt. Einer dieser Streifen schließt so: 'Und nun zu Bett! Und brav geschlafen! Sonst erzähle ich dir morgen nicht wieder von deutschen Naziverbrechern.' Zwischen solchen Streifen, Kriminalgeschichten, Hochzeitsberichten und Modeschauen finde ich als Füllsel Bibelworte eingestreut.[49]

Newspaper reports, comics, photographs and films are seen as inauthentic media due to their technical and propagandist manipulation of pictures and words; the knowledge about National Socialist crimes transmitted by these media thus becomes implausible and untrustworthy. In contrast, 'living' individual memory certifies the authenticity and in an emphatic sense the truth of that which is remembered. Storytelling thus attains the function of guaranteeing the biographical continuity and of defending the legitimacy of one's own experience against the implied attributions of guilt from interrogations and concentration camp film screenings. This is evident from the following passage from Zerkaulen:

> An Regentagen oder in jenen Stunden, die es bisweilen zwischen den Appellen gab, die in ihrer qualvollen Langsamkeit alles Denken zu lähmen und Herz und Glieder gleichermaßen zu ertöten schienen, da hatte dieser und jener in einem Anfall von Schwermut plötzlich begonnen, laut aus sich heraus zu reden. Zwei oder drei hörten eine Weile zu, schließlich ein ganzer Haufen. Rede und Gegenrede entstand. Es wurde von alten Berufsdingen gesprochen, von dem, was einst gut und schön war, bis der böse und sinnlose Krieg sich dazwischen gedrängt hatte [...].[50]

What is at stake is the protection of one's continuity of memory, and thus simultaneously one's national identity, from fragmentation and disintegration as a result of roll-calls, interrogations and confrontation with an 'alien' knowledge about unimaginable crimes. Thus it becomes clear that the conflict between knowledge and memory is a fundamental presupposition of these literary representations of memory. In Jan Assmann's terminology one could say that these texts develop a communicative memory in the context of the memory politics of the early Federal Republic and the struggle for collective memory. In this context, the topos of the 'Unschuld des Erinnerns' is anything but innocent.

Translation by Helmut Schmitz

Notes

[1] A shorter version of this article appeared in *Mittelweg 36*, Oktober/November 2005, pp. 77-91 under the title 'Die "andere" Lagerliteratur'.

[2] Martin Walser, 'Über Deutschland reden (Ein Bericht),' in: Walser, *Über Deutschland reden*, Suhrkamp: Frankfurt am Main, 1988, pp. 76-100 (here: pp. 76-77). The speech was given in the Munich Kammerspiele on 30 October 1988 and appeared first in the weekly *DIE ZEIT* on 3 November 1988.

[3] See Aleida Assmann, Ute Frevert, *Geschichtsvergessenheit – Geschichtsversessenheit. Vom Umgang mit deutschen Vergangenheiten nach 1945*, Deutsche Verlags-Anstalt: Stuttgart, 1999, pp. 38-39.

[4] An overview over the historiographical research that began relatively late can be found in Lutz Niethammer, 'Alliierte Internierungslager in Deutschland nach 1945. Vergleich und offene Fragen,' in: Christian Jansen, Lutz Niethammer und Bernd Weisbrod, eds., *Von der Aufgabe der Freiheit. Politische Verantwortung und*

bürgerliche Gesellschaft im 19. und 20. Jahrhundert. Festschrift für Hans Mommsen zum 5. November 1995, Akademie Verlag: Berlin, 1995, pp. 469-492.

[5] The special camps of the NKWD in the Soviet zone of occupation which are not comparable to the camps of the Western Allies both with respect to their historic form and their public reception are not considered here. On the differences see Niethammer, 'Alliierte Internierungslager', pp. 481-482.

[6] See Niethammer, 'Alliierte Internierungslager', p. 480.

[7] Ibid., p. 474.

[8] On this issue see Gregor Streim, 'Unter der "Diktatur" des Fragebogens. Ernst von Salomons Bestseller *Der Fragebogen* (1951) und der Diskurs der "Okkupation"', in: Gunther Nickel, ed., *Literarische und politische Deutschlandkonzepte 1938-1949 (Zuckmayer-Jahrbuch 7)*, Wallstein: Göttingen, 2004, pp. 87-115.

[9] Ernst von Salomon (1902-1972) joined the Free Corps after the First World War and was involved in the 1920 *Kapp-Putsch* as well as in the assassination of the Weimar Republic's foreign minister Walter Rathenau in 1922. He described his experiences as a cadet and free corps fighter in the novels *Die Geächteten* (1930) and *Die Kadetten* (1933). During the Third Reich Salomon, who held national-revolutionary convictions, kept his distance to Nazi politics and worked as a writer of film scripts, among other things. After the war he was taken under 'automatic arrest' by the Allies on 11 June 1945 due to his right-wing terrorist past and his participation in the assassination. He was interned for 15 months in the camps Natternberg, Plattling, Langwasser and Landsberg.

[10] See Ernst von Salomon, *Der Fragebogen*, Rowohlt: Hamburg, 1951, p. 663.

[11] Ibid., p. 806. Hanns Ludin, former German envoy in occupied Slovakia was interned with Salomon in the camp Nuremberg-Langwasser for a while. He was executed as a war criminal in Preßburg (Bratislava) on 9 December 1947. Malte Ludin's recent documentary film *2 oder 3 Dinge, die ich von ihm weiß* (2005) explores the image of Ludin as an upright Nazi and innocent victim of victor's justice, to which Salomon contributed.

[12] Franz Tumler, *Heimfahrt. Roman*, Pilgram: Salzburg, Cologne, Zurich, 1950. Tumler (1912-1998) came from Southern Tyrol and was among the first followers of National Socialism in Austria. His novels (e.g. *Das Tal von Lausa und Duron*, 1935; *Der Ausführende*, 1937) received several prizes during the Third Reich. He voluntarily joined the army in 1941 and was briefly interned as a marine soldier at the end of the war.

[13] Tumler's protagonist is interned in the camps Mühlhausen (Thuringia) und Naumburg.

[14] Richard Euringer, *Die Sargbreite Leben. Wir sind Internierte*, Grote: Hamm, 1952. Richard Euringer (1891-1953) was a pilot and head of a pilot school during the First World War. He joined National Socialism in the early 1920s. Many of his works (e.g. the novel *Fliegerschule 4*, 1929) combine the heroic image of the soldier with the Nazi ideology of the *Volksgemeinschaft*. In 1933 he was awarded the first national book prize by Goebbels for his radio play *Deutsche Passion 1933*. Many works by Euringer, for example the biography *Dietrich Eckart. Leben eines deutschen Dichters* (1936), can be categorised as National Socialist propaganda literature. During the Second World War he was an officer in the general staff with the section of the *Wehrmacht* that was concerned with the historiography of war.

[15] The places of internment in this case are the camps Garmisch-Partenkirchen, Augsburg, Berchtesgaden, Reichenhall, Bischofswiesen, Marburg, Schreufa and Darmstadt. In between, Euringer's protagonist is interned for interrogation in Camp Latimer (England) und Camp Zedelghem (Belgien).

[16] Heinrich Zerkaulen, *Zwischen Nacht und Tag. Erlebnisse aus dem Camp 94*, Hieronymus Mühlberger: Munich, 1951. Heinrich Zerkaulen (1892-1954) was a soldier in the First World War and first published war poems in the 1920s before turning to romanticised historic and *Heimat*-novels. His drama *Die Jugend von Langemarck* (1933), which glorifies the 'Heldentod' of the young volunteers of the First World War, was one of the most frequently staged plays in the Third Reich. Zerkaulen's texts from this period, for example the novel *Hörnerklang der Frühe* (1934), are characterised by a nationalism with religious overtones. After the Second World War, Zerkaulen was interned briefly in the camps Herfa und Kornwestheim.

[17] Ibid., p. 12.

[18] Bruno Brehm, *Aus der Reitschul'!* Roman, Leopold Stocker: Graz, 1951. Bruno Brehm (1892-1974) was born in what is now Slovenia as the son of an officer in the army of the Austro-Hungarian Empire and participated in the First World War as a volunteer. The experience of war and his belief in a future *Reich* that would comprise Germany and Austria is the topic of most of his literary works, particularly the trilogy *Apis und Este* (1931), *Das war das Ende* (1932) and *Weder Kaiser noch König* (1933), for which he received the national book prize from Goebbels in 1939. After the annexation of Austria Brehm became a member of the NSDAP and a member of the council of the city of Vienna. In 1941 he became president of the *Wiener Kulturvereinigung*. During the Second World War he was a major and an aide-de-camp.

[19] Ibid., p. 379. Brehm's protagonist is interned in the camps Salzburg and Gmunden. Brehm himself was interned at first in Ried (northern Austria) and then in Glasenbach near Salzburg.

[20] Hans Venatier, *Der Major und die Stiere*. Roman, F. M. Bourg: Düsseldorf, 1953. Hans Venatier (1903-1959) was born in Silesia. His historical novels *Vogt Bartold. Der große Zug nach Osten* (1943) and *Narren Gottes. Historischer Roman über die*

schlesischen Glaubenskämpfe (no date) deal with the theme of the 'German East'. During the Third Reich he worked in teacher training. He edited the series 'Lesebogen für die höhere Schule im Dritten Reich' and was made a National Socialist lecturer at the *Lehrerhochschule* Breslau in 1941.

[21] The first Italian edition of *Il mondo piccolo de 'Don Camillo'* was published in 1948.

[22] Venatier, *Der Major und die Stiere*, p. 345.

[23] Ibid., p. 337.

[24] Ibid., p. 65.

[25] Norbert Frei, *Vergangenheitspolitik. Die Anfänge der Bundesrepublik und die NS-Vergangenheit*, dtv: Munich, 1999 [first 1996], p. 14.

[26] On the political character of cultural memory see Aleida Assmann, Jan Assmann, 'Das Gestern im Heute. Medien und soziales Gedächtnis', in: Klaus Merten, Siegfried J. Schmidt, Siegfried Weischenberg, eds., *Die Wirklichkeit der Medien. Eine Einführung in die Kommunikationswissenschaft*, Verlag für Sozialwissenschaft: Opladen, 1994, pp. 114-140; Assmann, Frevert, *Geschichtsvergessenheit – Geschichtsversessenheit*, pp. 36-41.

[27] Erhard Schütz has observed a similar appropriation of 'victim iconography' in the literature about POW-experiences. See Erhard Schütz, 'Von Lageropfern und Helden der Flucht. Kriegsgefangenschaft Deutscher – Popularisierungsmuster in der Bundesrepublik,' in: Wolfgang Hardtwig, Erhard Schütz, eds., *Geschichte für Leser. Populäre Geschichtsschreibung in Deutschland im 20. Jahrhundert*, Franz Steiner: Stuttgart, 2005, pp.181-203.

[28] Salomon, *Der Fragebogen*, p. 736.

[29] Zerkaulen, *Zwischen Nacht und Tag*, pp. 166f.

[30] Ibid., p. 74.

[31] Euringer, *Die Sargbreite Leben*, p. 53.

[32] See e.g. Salomon, *Der Fragebogen*, p. 698.

[33] Especially the US zone had wide ranging criteria for the arrests. Lutz Niethammer has shown with respect to the camp at Garmisch that 80% of internees were local and regional functionaries. See Lutz Niethammer, *Entnazifizierung in Bayern. Säuberung und Rehabilitierung unter amerikanischer Besatzung*, Fischer: Frankfurt am Main, 1972, p. 258.

[34] Since members of the military high command and of the general staff were interned in the course of 'automatic arrest' as well, a mix between civilian and military internees was common. Moreover, there were general similarities between war captivity and internment with respect to accommodation, food, and process. See Niethammer, 'Alliierte Internierungslager', pp. 488-490. The problem of POW's and internees is historically 'nicht eindeutig abgrenzbar' (Ibid., p. 488). Likewise, the genre of internment narratives can only with difficulty be differentiated from the much larger genre of reports and narratives about war captivity, as becomes clear with respect to Tumler's novel. An overview of the latter can be found in Schütz, 'Von Lageropfern und Helden der Flucht',

[35] On the difference between 'victim memory' (Opfergedächtnis) and 'memory of the defeated' (Verlierergedächtnis) see Assmann, Frevert, *Geschichtsvergessenheit – Geschichtsversessenheit*, p. 44.

[36] Brehm, *Aus der Reitschul'*, p. 386.

[37] Historical reality is likely to have been different. For example, Hanns Johst reports in his unpublished notes from the camps Fürstenfeldbruck, Darmstadt und Moosbach near Munich that interned high SS-officials had been treated with hostility by former members of the army. See Rolf Düsterberg. *Hanns Johst: 'Der Barde der SS'. Karrieren eines deutschen Dichters*, Ferdinand Schöningh: Paderborn, 2004, pp. 326-328.

[38] Zerkaulen, *Zwischen Nacht und Tag*, p. 49.

[39] Euringer, *Die Sargbreite Leben*, p. 105.

[40] Carl Schmitt, *Ex Captivitate Salus. Erfahrungen der Zeit 1945/47*, Greven: Cologne, 1950 pp. 92-93.

[41] Zerkaulen, *Zwischen Nacht und Tag*, p. 155.

[42] Ibid., p. 122.

[43] Ibid., pp. 12f.

[44] Euringer, *Die Sargbreite Leben*, p. 319.

[45] Tumler, *Heimfahrt*, p. 455.

[46] Ibid., p. 540.

[47] Euringer, *Die Sargbreite Leben*, p. 175.

[48] See Claudia Brink, *Ikonen der Vernichtung. Öffentlicher Gebrauch von Fotografien aus nationalsozialistischen Konzentrationslagern nach 1945*, Akademie Verlag: Berlin, 1998, pp. 97-99.

[49] Euringer, *Die Sargbreite Leben*, pp. 167-168.

[50] Zerkaulen, *Zwischen Nacht und Tag*, pp. 65-66.

Hans-Joachim Hahn

'Die, von denen man erzählt hat, dass sie die kleinen Kinder schlachten'. Deutsche Leiderfahrung und Bilder von Juden in der deutschen Kultur nach 1945. Zu einigen Texten Wolfgang Weyrauchs

The chapter analyses the representation of Jewish characters in Wolfgang Staudte's 1946 film *Die Mörder sind unter uns* and in a number of Wolfgang Weyrauch's works, reading Weyrauch's literary construction of Jews in the context of representations of victims and perpetrators in the immediate post-war period. It argues that Staudte and Weyrauch either de-particularise the Jewish experience of victimisation in favour of a universalised concept of suffering that can be applied to Nazi victims and Germans alike or that Jews and Germans exchange places. Texts from the early post-war period thus constitute an important source for the establishment of a post-war German victim mentality.

In seinem Resümee zur Debatte um eine Veröffentlichung von Hans Jürgen Syberberg aus dem Jahr 1990 zitiert Lothar Baier zwei Aussagen des Filmregisseurs und Autors. Die erste entstammt Syberbergs Notizbuch-Veröffentlichung *Die freudlose Gesellschaft. Notizen aus dem letzten Jahr* von 1981:

> Die Juden gibt es bei uns nicht mehr, seit fünfunddreißig Jahren [...] und im Bereich des Films, wo sie am radikalsten verschwunden sind, sieht man, was sich verändert hat – alles wurde unsagbar böse, ungeschmeidig im Witz oder Denken und Diskutieren, Wunden werden geschlagen, an denen weder Opfer noch Täter bittere Freude finden können, die geistige Freude der Produktivität.[1]

Diese Proposition setzt Baier in Beziehung zu dem Wort von der 'unseligen Allianz einer jüdisch-linken Ästhetik gegen die Schuldigen' und der Behauptung: 'Wer mit den Juden ging wie mit den Linken, machte Karriere.'[2] Letztere entstammen dem Essay *Vom Unglück und Glück der Kunst in Deutschland nach dem letzten Krieg* (1990), mit dem Syberberg ein Jahr nach der deutschen Vereinigung die einhellige Ablehnung des liberalen Feuilletons von *ZEIT* bis *FAZ* auf sich zog. Baier fragt, ob etwa Syberberg, der in dem Zitat von 1981 das Verschwinden der Juden aus dem deutschen Kulturleben bedauerte, inzwischen einen radikalen Wandel durchlebt hätte, oder aber, ob er mit beiden Aussagen nicht vielmehr einer 'Spur' folge, die in Deutschland Tradition besitze und die dazu zwinge, in dem

scheinbaren Widerspruch eine Ergänzung zu sehen. Im Sinne der von
ihm als Alternative formulierten zweiten Hypothese gelangt Baier
dann zu einer eigenen Definition des modernen Antisemitismus in
Deutschland. Dieser zeichne sich durch eine Gleichzeitigkeit des
antisemitischen Vertreibungs- und Vernichtungswunsches mit einer
betonten Hochschätzung der den Juden zugeschriebenen positiven
Eigenschaften aus. So seien 'die Juden' für die Nationalsozialisten
zwar das ganz Fremde gewesen, ebenso aber auch 'den Deutschen'
zum Verwechseln ähnlich. Gerade die paradoxe Verbindung beider
Vorstellungen hätte von den Anhängern der nationalsozialistischen
Reinheitslogik verlangt, sich der Juden zu entledigen. Die
Rachephantasien nationalsozialistischer Täter hätten sich nicht aus der
Verachtung Minderwertiger gespeist, sondern aus der Furcht vor
Überlegenen. Baier beschließt diesen Gedankengang mit der
Zuspitzung, erst die 'Koexistenz von Haß und Bewunderung' habe
den Antisemitismus in Deutschland mörderisch gemacht.

In seiner Argumentation nutzt Baier diese Deutung des
nationalsozialistischen Antisemitismus, um das auf den ersten Blick
widersprüchlich Erscheinende an Syberbergs Aussagen über Juden
und die Kultur in Deutschland nach 1945 miteinander in Beziehung zu
setzen. Die scheinbaren Gegensätze werden so erkennbar als
zusammengehörige Teile eines projizierten Bildes von 'Juden', worin
diese gleichzeitig als fremd und als ähnlich wahrgenommen werden.
Tatsächlich konstruiert der eliminatorische Antisemitismus der
Nationalsozialisten Juden als fremdartige Täter, die den 'gesunden
Volkskörper' bedrohen. In dem berüchtigten Kapitel 'Volk und Rasse'
aus Hitlers *Mein Kampf* werden sie zur tödlichen Bedrohung stilisiert.[3]
Um sie derart darstellen zu können, müssen 'Juden' eine Macht
besitzen, also Eigenschaften, die sie dem 'arischen' Kollektiv als
mindestens potentiell überlegen zeigen. Die nationalsozialistische
Bewegung freilich evoziert diese 'jüdische Gefahr', um sich selbst als
Retter anzuempfehlen.

Es muss jedoch nicht erst auf Hitler verwiesen werden, um das
scheinbare Paradox des Zusammenhangs von Fremdheit und
Ähnlichkeit in der Struktur des Antisemitismus zu entdecken. Die
zentralen semantischen Regeln des modernen, weltanschaulichen
Antisemitismus begegnen uns, wie vor allem Klaus Holz gezeigt hat,
bereits ebenso in Treitschkes nationalliberalem Antisemitismus Ende
der 1870er Jahre in Deutschland wie auch in Edouard Drumonts

berüchtigtem Pamphlet im Frankreich der dritten Republik.[4] Dazu gehört neben der Täter-Opfer-Umkehr – die eigene Aggression der Antisemiten ist legitim, weil sie immer als reaktiv verstanden wird – auch das Eröffnen einer Lösungsperspektive auf die von der antisemitischen Logik erst erzeugte 'Judenfrage'. Freilich sind der liberale und der nationalsozialistische Antisemitismus nicht gleichzusetzen; diskursiv-semantisch unterscheiden sie sich vor allem in der Radikalität ihrer 'Lösungsperspektiven'. Gemein ist ihnen jedoch – und hier tritt jetzt das zweite Moment hinzu –, dass für sie 'die Juden' gerade deshalb so bedrohlich erscheinen, weil sie sich äußerlich seit Beginn ihrer bürgerlichen Gleichstellung und der Überwindung der Ghettos immer weniger von der Mehrheitsbevölkerung unterscheiden. Es ist also weniger die Verbindung aus unterstellter Fremdheit und scheinbar positiven Eigenschaften – wie z.B. der 'jüdischen Schlauheit' oder ähnlichen Stereotypen –,[5] die Juden zugeschrieben werden, aus denen sich der Antisemitismus speist, als vielmehr die *Ununterscheidbarkeit* von 'den Juden' und der eigenen, nationalen Wir-Gruppe, die von den Antisemiten als unheimlich und bedrohlich imaginiert wird. Baier zielt also im Grunde genommen über den Antisemitismus hinaus auf eine weitere Ambivalenz im Blick der Mehrheitsbevölkerung auf Juden. Auch die Zuschreibung positiver Eigenschaften, was häufig mit dem Stichwort des Philosemitismus bezeichnet wird, bedeutet noch nicht das Verlassen der Projektionsspirale. Darin knüpft die Zeit nach 1945 an die Zeit davor an: Weiterhin unterliegt die Darstellung jüdischer Charaktere der projektiven Fantasie von Nichtjuden (wo nicht die wenigen Überlebenden selbst kulturelle Bilder von Juden kreierten). Zwar wurde der eliminatorische Antisemitismus durch den alliierten Sieg über das nationalsozialistische Deutschland beendet und Antisemitismus insgesamt nach dem 8. Mai 1945 delegitimiert. Der Anti-Nationalsozialismus bildete den Grundkonsens im Selbstverständnis der beiden Nachfolgestaaten des Deutschen Reichs, in der Bundesrepublik in seiner Variante als Antitotalitarismus und in der DDR als Antifaschismus. Abgesehen davon, dass dieser Grundkonsens jedoch keineswegs unumstritten war, unterlag auch die Bewertung von Ursachen und Gegenstand des Nationalsozialismus Wandlungen. Dessen zentrales Verbrechen, der 'totale' Genozid an den europäischen Juden, stand in den ersten Jahrzehnten weder im Zentrum der offiziellen noch der nichtöffentlichen Erinnerung.[6] Vor

diesem Hintergrund liegt es nahe, vor allem Werke zu analysieren, in
denen sich die Darstellung jüdischer Figuren mit einer
Auseinandersetzung mit dem Nationalsozialismus verbindet. Denn
hier, wo eine 'Aufarbeitung' des Nationalsozialismus mit den Mitteln
der Kultur versucht wurde, ist das Verhältnis der
Mehrheitsbevölkerung zu den Juden wegen des Holocaust immer
Gegenstand, auch da, wo es nicht explizit erwähnt wird.[7]

Der erste deutsche Nachkriegsfilm, Wolfgang Staudtes *Die Mörder
sind unter uns* (1946), scheint zunächst einmal nichts weiter mit dem
deutsch-jüdischen Verhältnis nach dem Holocaust zu tun zu haben.
Erzählt wird die Geschichte des Kriegsheimkehrers und Arztes Hans
Mertens, der als Wehrmachtssoldat an der Ostfront erfolglos bei
seinem Kommandanten, einem Herrn Brückner, gegen die
willkürliche Erschießung von Männern, Frauen und Kindern
protestiert hatte. Zynisch und larmoyant bringt Mertens nach dem
Krieg in der Berliner Trümmerlandschaft seine Tage mit Alkohol und
Cabaret-Besuchen durch, bis er in seiner heruntergekommenen
Wohnung auf deren frühere Mieterin, Susanne Wallner trifft, die als
nichtjüdische Überlebende aus einem Konzentrationslager
zurückgekehrt ist. Die Zuschauer erfahren nichts über ihre Zeit im KZ,
die an der Gestalt der Susanne Wallner merkwürdig spurlos
vorbeigegangen zu sein scheint. Über die Gründe, warum sie verhaftet
wurde, verrät der Film lediglich, dass es 'wegen ihres Vaters' war. Im
Mittelpunkt der Geschichte steht dagegen die Konfrontation zwischen
Mertens und Brückner, der ebenfalls den Krieg überlebt hat und
inzwischen als Vater dreier Söhne ein beschauliches Familienleben
führt, sowie als Produzent von Kochtöpfen, die er aus vormaligen
Stahlhelmen herstellt, sein Auskommen hat. Susanne Wallner kann
schließlich im letzten Augenblick verhindern, dass Mertens an
Brückner Selbstjustiz übt. Unter den Nebenfiguren des Films gibt es
einen alten Optiker, der Mondschein heißt und im Souterrain des
Hauses lebt, in dem auch Susanne Wallner und Hans Mertens wohnen.
Jahrelang wurde von Kritikern übersehen, dass eine Reihe subtiler
Hinweise Herrn Mondschein als jüdischen Überlebenden
kennzeichnen, der auf die Rückkehr seines Sohnes wartet.[8] Dafür
nennt Ulrike Weckel drei einleuchtende Gründe: zum einen erinnere
der Name Mondschein an jüdische Namen. Zum anderen betonen
Susanne Wallner und Hans Mertens wiederholt, es sei ein Wunder,
dass Mondschein überlebt hätte. Da aber das Mietshaus, in dem er

lebt, ebenso wie alle seine Bewohner von den Bomben, die die Umgebung verwüsteten, verschont blieb, wäre es an sich wenig erstaunlich, dass ein Bewohner eben dieses Hauses überlebt hat. Dagegen sei es aus der Sicht des Filmpersonals durchaus 'verwunderlich', dass ein Jude den Holocaust in Deutschland überlebt habe – unabhängig davon, in welchem Haus er lebte. Schließlich, fügt sie noch an, erhält Mondschein – allerdings erst nach seinem Tode – einen Brief von seinem Sohn, der nun in den USA lebt.[9] Wird Mondschein als jüdischer Überlebender gedeutet – und die genannten Hinweise lassen kaum einen anderen Schluss zu, – so fällt das erstaunliche Missverhältnis auf, dass der Film zwischen den Geschichten der tatsächlichen Opfer des Nationalsozialismus, Herrn Mondschein und Susanne Wallner, und der zentralen Erzählhandlung enthält, die um die Larmoyanz und Gerechtigkeitsfantasien des Mitläufers Hans Mertens kreisen. Die Tatsache, dass Mondschein nicht explizit als jüdischer Überlebender ausgewiesen wird, kann vor dem Hintergrund einer Tendenz zur Universalisierung der Opferpositionen gedeutet werden, die in dem Film auch an anderer Stelle zum Ausdruck kommt. So ist einmal kurz eine Zeitungsschlagzeile zu sehen, die auf die nationalsozialistischen Verbrechen und das Vernichtungslager Auschwitz verweist, die lautet: '2 Millionen Menschen vergast!'. Dass es sich dabei um Juden handelt wird nicht genannt. Deshalb können auch die Protagonisten im Film potentiell als Opfer dieser Verbrechen erscheinen und sich die deutschen Besucher des Films als ein Kollektiv überwiegend von Opfern empfinden. Insgesamt konstruiert der Film eine deutsche Nachkriegsgesellschaft in nuce, in der Mitläufer, KZ-Überlebende und Ausgebombte den Denunzianten, Mördern und skrupellosen Kriegsgewinnlern – ineins gesetzt in der Gestalt des Fabrikbesitzers Brückner – gegenübergestellt werden. Es ist daher sicherlich richtig, hinsichtlich des Films *Die Mörder sind unter uns* ein 'Verschwinden der Opfer' zu konstatieren.[10] In Bezug auf die Darstellung des Juden Mondschein ist ein Dialog zwischen ihm und Hans Mertens zusätzlich bemerkenswert. Mertens sagt: 'Ich bewundere Ihren Kinderglauben.' Mondschein erwidert: 'Wenn er kommt, wird das Haus bereitet sein.' Wenn Mertens von Mondscheins 'Kinderglauben' spricht, wird dieser damit in die Nähe von den Kindern gerückt, die am Anfang des Films die Szenerie beherrschen und denen die 'Zukunft' gilt.[11] Konkret jedoch bezieht sich die Aussage auf Mondscheins Hoffnung, sein

Sohn würde jetzt, nach dem Ende des Kriegs und der Nazizeit, wieder zu ihm zurückkehren. Diese denunziert Mertens als 'Kinderglauben'; die Filmhandlung allerdings gibt letztlich dennoch Mondschein recht, denn der Brief mit der Nachricht seines Sohnes trifft ja schließlich ein, auch wenn er ihn nicht mehr lebend erreicht. Warum aber bedient sich der nur durch indirekte Verweise als ein jüdischer Überlebender gekennzeichnete Mondschein einer Anspielung auf das christliche Gleichnis vom verlorenen Sohn ('das Haus werde bereitet sein'), um seiner Hoffnung Ausdruck zu verleihen? Die dem Filmnarrativ eigene Tendenz zur Universalisierung, scheint sich auch hier Bahn zu brechen. Die vom Film propagierte und gegen die Selbstjustiz an den Mördern gerichtete Botschaft zur Errichtung einer besseren, gerechteren Welt, erinnert unterschiedslos an die Leiden von Ausgebombten, Kriegsheimkehrern sowie Überlebenden aus Konzentrationslagern. Genau in dieser Universalisierung steckt jedoch der dialektische Umschlag, denn angesprochen werden soll die partikularistische deutsche Nachkriegsgesellschaft – und die interessierte sich nicht für den Genozid an den Juden und die Traumatisierung der Überlebenden. Auch die Figur Mondscheins ist also nicht frei von Ambivalenzen. Einerseits erfüllt sie eine affirmative Funktion zur Bekräftigung der Neubegründung einer gesellschaftlich-familiären Solidarität im Gegensatz zur im Film ironisierten 'Volksgemeinschaft', die durch die anderen Hausbewohner dargestellt wird. Andererseits aber erinnert sie an die eigentlichen Opfer des Nationalsozialismus, deren Geschichten der Film jedoch nicht erzählt. In diesem Sinne markiert sie eine Leerstelle im Diskurs über den Nationalsozialismus. Damit erscheint mir diese Gestalt ein Beleg für die These eines Projektionsfeldes des 'Jüdischen', das sich weder als Anti- noch als Philosemitismus beschreiben lässt, sich allerdings aus beiden Tendenzen speist. Im Zusammenhang mit einer Darstellung des Nationalsozialismus dienen diese Projektionsgestalten auch der Rechtfertigung einer Darstellung deutscher Opfererfahrung. Z.B. wird dabei Leiden generell universalisiert, so dass aus deutschen Wehrmachtssoldaten Opfer ihrer Vorgesetzten werden können und generell nichtjüdische deutsche mit jüdischen Opfern gleichgesetzt werden.

Diese These werde ich anhand einiger Texte Wolfgang Weyrauchs (1904–1980) zu belegen versuchen. Weyrauch wurde insbesondere wegen seiner beiden Nachkriegsanthologien *Die Pflugschar* (1947) und *1000 Gramm* (1949) als einer der Neubegründer der deutschen Literatur nach 1945 wahrgenommen. Im Nachwort zu *1000 Gramm* prägte er den erfolgreichen Terminus von der 'Kahlschlag-Literatur'.[12] Allerdings war er, 1945 schon über vierzig Jahre alt, bereits seit 1929 als freier Autor tätig und zählte zu denjenigen Autoren, die wie etwa Günter Eich, Peter Huchel oder Wolfgang Koeppen auch während des Nationalsozialismus schon veröffentlichten. Von 1929-1933 arbeitete er als freier Mitarbeiter für die *Frankfurter Zeitung*, von 1932-1938 für das *Berliner Tageblatt* und 1933-1934 auch für die *Vossische Zeitung*. Außerdem war er in den dreißiger Jahren als Verlagslektor tätig. Am Zweiten Weltkrieg nahm er als Obergefreiter in einer Luftnachrichteneinheit teil. 1945 kam er in russische Gefangenschaft, aus der er im August entlassen wurde. Nach dem Krieg war er zunächst drei Jahre lang als Redakteur der in Berlin erscheinenden Zeitschriften *Ulenspiegel* und *Ost und West* tätig. Von 1950-1958 arbeitete er als Lektor für den Rowohlt-Verlag, ab 1959 dann wieder als freier Schriftsteller.[13] Mit einigem Recht kann heute im Hinblick auf das Werk Weyrauchs ein 'Forschungsdefizit der Literaturwissenschaft' festgestellt werden.[14] Bereits vor einem Vierteljahrhundert wurde bemerkt, dass es sich bei ihm um einen Autoren handelt, 'dessen Namen jeder, der sich mit der Nachkriegsliteratur beschäftigt, schon einmal gehört hat, dessen umfangreiches Gedicht-, Prosa- und Hörspielwerk dennoch merkwürdig unbekannt geblieben ist.'[15] Auch der seit 1979 jährlich an deutschsprachige Autor(inn)en vergebene Wolfgang-Weyrauch-Förderpreis hat daran wenig zu ändern vermocht. Bislang liegen, wie Ulrike Landzettel vermerkt, weder eine Werkausgabe seiner Schriften noch eine Biographie Weyrauchs vor.[16] Sie fasst den Forschungsstand mit der Formel zusammen: 'Es gab eine Rezeption und vereinzelte Ansätze von Sekundärliteratur, aber keine Forschung.'[17] In ihrer Dissertation unternimmt sie den Versuch, Weyrauchs Entwicklung als Schriftsteller vor dem Hintergrund ihrer historischen, gesellschaftspolitischen und kulturgeschichtlichen Entstehungsbedingungen zu rekonstruieren. Dabei misst sie dem Verhältnis von Kontinuität und Diskontinuität der vor und nach 1945 verfassten Texte Weyrauchs einen besonderen Stellenwert zu.[18] In dieser Hinsicht hält sie ihn für einen 'exemplarischen Fall': ihn als Vertreter einer 'nichtnationalsozialistischen Literatur' während des Nationalsozialismus beschreibend, geht sie von Kontinuitätslinien seines Schreibens aus, die von vor 1945 bis in die Nachkriegszeit reichen.[19] Das Interesse am 'Gegenstand' der Texte Wolfgang Weyrauchs speist sich daher nicht in erster Linie aus deren ästhetischer Qualität, sondern aus der Bedeutung Weyrauchs für die Transformation der deutschen Literatur aus der Zeit des Nationalsozialismus in die Literatur der Nachkriegszeit. In dieser Perspektive situiert sich auch der hier vorgestellte Blick auf drei Texte des Autors, in denen es um das Verhältnis der nichtjüdischen deutschen Umgebung zu Juden geht. Es handelt sich um die beiden Erzählungen 'Die Liebenden' (1947) und 'Mit dem Kopf durch die Wand' (1958) sowie das Hörspiel 'Woher kennen wir uns bloß' (1952). Die jeweilige Thematisierung des deutsch-jüdischen Verhältnisses nimmt dabei unterschiedlichen Raum ein.

Eine seiner ersten Prosaarbeiten nach dem Kriegsende ist *Die Liebenden*, 1947 mit Erlaubnis der US-amerikanischen Militäradministration bei Kurt Desch in München erschienen.[20] Die Johannes R. Becher gewidmete, durchaus umfangreiche Erzählung (115 Seiten) besteht aus Rollenprosa, die den beiden 'Liebenden' Thomas Scherer, einem Studenten, und der Stenotypistin Maria Dobert, als Sprachrohren des Erzählers in den Mund gelegt ist.[21] Formal untergliedert sich der Text in einzelne kurze Kapitel, die nach Berliner U-Bahn-Stationen benannt sind. Die Kapitel wiederum sind unterteilt in Abschnitte, die dem Studenten Thomas Scherer, der Stenotypistin, sowie 'dem Verfasser' zugewiesen sind. Darüber hinaus enthält jedes Kapitel auch eine Rubrik 'Geister', in der neben unterschiedlichen Gruppen von Toten auch personifizierte Gegenstände zu Wort kommen. Zusätzlich wird diese Struktur noch um einige Gespräche zwischen den beiden Protagonisten ergänzt. Das abschließende Kapitel 'Friedrichstrasse' weicht von dieser Form ab; hier berichtet ein Erzähler – es ist nahe liegend, ihn mit der vorher eingeführten Instanz des Verfassers zu identifizieren – unter dem Eintrag '20.10.1945, 9 Uhr früh' aus einer Überblicksperspektive über Personen in Berlin.[22] Der hier gesetzten Zeitangabe korrespondiert eine vorausgegangene, die das erste Treffen und Kennenlernen der 'Liebenden' auf den '19.10.1945, 4.55 Uhr nachmittags' festlegt.[23] Der kurze Erzählzeitraum unterstreicht die eigentliche Bedeutungslosigkeit der Liebesgeschichte für diesen Text. Vom Erzähler wird daran in seinem resümierenden Schlusswort kein Zweifel gelassen: 'Und der Student Thomas Scherer kam aus der

Französischen Straße und dachte an die Stenotypistin Maria Dobert, aber er dachte nicht viel an sie, nur gerade in diesem Augenblick, und über ein Kurzes würde er sie vergessen haben'. Analoges erfahren wir eine Seite weiter auch über Maria Dobert.[24] Damit wird die Begegnung der beiden zur kurzen, göttlich inspirierten Epiphanie und die namentlich eingeführten Handlungsträger zur reinen Staffage: 'Gott ist imstande, alles mit allem zu verknüpfen, wie, wo, wann immer es ihm beliebt.'[25] Die handlungsarme Erzählung, die nur durch die Fragmentarisierung des Erzählten modern erscheint, wird durch die Erzählperspektive eines monologischen Erzählers zentriert, der im Text das göttliche Prinzip darstellt. Dessen Gedanken verteilen sich auf die Personen, die beiden Liebenden und die Verfassergestalt. Auf der inhaltlichen Ebene auch als 'Reflexion' des Nationalsozialismus lesbar, der allerdings an keiner Stelle direkt benannt wird, hat der christliche Glaube an Gott eine zentrale ordnende Funktion.[26] So sollen die 'Geister' gebannt werden, die in der U-Bahn mitfahren. Und hier, verschoben in das Reich der untoten Toten, tauchen u.a. verschiedene Opfergruppen auf, die allerdings wiederum nicht unmittelbar als Opfer *des Nationalsozialismus* erscheinen. So sind die ersten Geister die erschlagener junger Mädchen (wo, wann und von wem diese erschlagen wurden, wird nicht erzählt); deren Aussage besteht in der Affirmation und Verwandlung ihres Todes in eine Sinnstiftung: 'Wir erschlagenen jungen Mädchen sind glücklich darüber, daß wir erschlagen sind.' Denn: 'Wir lieben die Möglichkeit, daß das Entsetzen nichts mehr ist, daß aber die Freundschaft unter den Menschen alles ist.'[27] Unbenannt bleibt das zurückliegende Verbrechen, dessen Opfer jedoch als Opfer legitimiert und daher als Versöhnungsinstanz autorisiert erscheinen. Den Toten wird zugemutet, die Welt der Lebenden zu versöhnen. Eine solche Aufladung und Funktionalisierung erfahren auch anthropomorphisierte Tiere und Pflanzen als Geister. So setzen 'die Rosen' der Frage 'der Bienen', ob sie von den Menschen verschlungen worden seien, entgegen: 'Wir blühen, wir wachsen, wir welken, wir spenden.'[28] Die Welt als Schöpfung Gottes erfährt eine umfassende Sinngebung; die ungenannten Verbrechen und Zerstörungen des Nationalsozialismus erscheinen darin aufgehoben. Wie sehr der ganze Text als ein auf abstrakte, religiös motivierte Versöhnung ausgerichtetes Konstrukt angelegt ist, zeigt auch eine kleine, weitere 'Geistergeschichte', in der es um das deutsch-jüdische

Verhältnis geht. Es ist wiederum ein Dialog zwischen zwei Kollektiven, von denen das eine als 'Juden' identifiziert wird, das andere im Gesamtkontext der Erzählung als eine Gruppe nichtjüdischer Deutscher erscheint. Die ganze Stelle sei hier im Wortlaut wiedergegeben:

Was seid ihr für welche?
Wir sind Juden.
Ach, dann seid ihr die, von denen man erzählt hat, daß sie die kleinen Kinder schlachten, um ihnen das Blut abzuzapfen und es zu trinken?
Ja, die sind wir.
Wieso kommt es aber, daß wir uns nicht fürchten?
Weil ihr euch nicht zu fürchten braucht.
Wieso nicht?
Wir schlachten keine kleinen Kinder, sondern wir lieben sie.
Ihr seht ja auch ganz freundlich aus.
Wir schlachten nur Rinder und Ochsen, damit ihr etwas zu essen habt.
Das ist aber nett von euch.
Ihr braucht euch nicht zu bedanken.
Und was wollt ihr dafür haben?
Nichts. Höchstens, daß ihr hingeht und den erwachsenen deutschen Leuten von uns erzählt.
Was sollen wir ihnen erzählen?
Was ihr mit uns erlebt habt, sonst nichts.[29]

Die fiktiven nichtjüdischen Fragesteller des Jahres 1947 haben von Juden nur gehört, sind aber offenbar bislang noch keinen begegnet. Damit ist das Gespräch den tatsächlichen Zeitumständen Nachkriegsdeutschlands mit dem vorausgegangenen Nationalsozialismus und dessen Erlösungsantisemitismus enthoben. Gerade in der letzten Phase des 'Tausendjährigen Reichs' waren Juden als Zwangsarbeiter und auf den Todesmärschen nach der Evakuierung der Konzentrations- und Vernichtungslager für weite Teile der deutschen Bevölkerung, sofern sie nicht ohnehin direkt an den Verbrechen beteiligt waren, durchaus sichtbar und als Opfer nationalsozialistischer Politik präsent. Aufschlussreich ist an dieser 'Stunde Null' des Antisemitismus jedoch, dass den nichtjüdischen Geistern[30] antijüdische Vorstellungen vertraut erscheinen, die älter sind als die Entstehung des modernen, national und/oder rassentheoretisch begründeten Antisemitismus des 19. Jahrhunderts. So wissen die Gesprächspartner, mit wem sie es zu tun haben, weil sie das mittelalterliche christlich-antijüdische Stereotyp vom Ritualmord kennen. Damit ist aber die moderne Verfolgungsgeschichte, die im

Holocaust kulminiert, ausgeblendet. Angeknüpft wird vielmehr an Vorstellungen, die christliche Mehrheitsbevölkerungen in Europa den Juden seit dem Mittelalter bis zur Aufklärung zuordneten. Die in ihrem Verhältnis zu den Juden ambivalente europäische Aufklärung wiederum wollte Juden zwar als Menschen emanzipieren und ihnen bürgerliche Rechte zugestehen, nicht aber *als Juden*. An diese Ambivalenz knüpft auch Weyrauchs Dialog noch an. Erkennbar ist, noch in seiner Entstellung, der Ansatz, über Vorurteile aufklären zu wollen. Dass jedoch nach dem Holocaust jüdische Geister in der Konstruktion des nichtjüdischen deutschen Autors die Rolle zugewiesen bekommen, den erwachsenen nichtjüdischen Deutschen zu erklären, dass sie vor Juden keine Angst zu haben bräuchten, kann nach dem Genozid kaum als Gesprächsgrundlage dienen. In diesem Sinne ist der Dialog gespenstisch, ein Geistergespräch. Immerhin hält die letzte Zeile des Dialogs als Erkenntnis fest, die gegen den manifesten, erneut Projektionen festschreibenden Textinhalt gelesen werden kann, dass reale Erlebnisse zum Ausgangspunkt der Darstellung gemacht werden sollen, nicht die literarischen Fantasmagorien, aus denen sich Anti- und Philosemitismus speisen.

1952 produziert der Nordwestdeutsche Rundfunk (NWDR) unter der Regie von Gustav Burmester Wolfgang Weyrauchs Hörspiel 'Woher kennen wir uns bloß', das am 4. November des Jahres erstmals gesendet wird.[31] Das deutsch-jüdische Geistergespräch wird hier fortgesetzt. Schon der Titel erinnert an die Amnesie der nichtjüdischen Geister aus dem Dialog in den *Liebenden*: wer waren das eigentlich, die Juden? Jetzt stehen sich zwei abstrakte Charaktere gegenüber, die einen Dialog führen, an dessen Ende sie ihre Positionen tauschen und damit einen unheimlichen Rollenwechsel vornehmen. Diese Sprecher des Hörspiels heißen 'Jude' und 'Polizist'. Die Abstrahierung geht also von asymmetrischen Bezeichnungen aus: während 'Polizist' eine, eher verschleiernde, Berufsbezeichnung darstellt – wo eigentlich die SS gemeint ist, wie sich zeigen wird –, bezieht sich 'Jude', wie sich ebenfalls im Verlauf des Stücks herausstellt, auf die Angehörigen einer Gruppe von zehn in einem Ghetto verschanzten Personen, die von der 'Geheimpolizei' tödlich verfolgt werden. Das Konstrukt 'Jude' bestimmt sich aus dem Gegensatz zum 'Polizist' und wird daher primär auf die Eigenschaft des Verfolgten festgelegt. Gleichzeitig tauchen in den Redebeiträgen des Polizisten weitere, negative Zuschreibungen auf, denen dann im

Dialog widersprochen wird.[32] Eindeutige rassenantisemitische
Äußerungen macht dieser 'Polizist' jedoch nicht. Aus einem SS-Mann
ist ein 'Polizist' geworden.

Die Dialogsituation wird zu Beginn des Stücks im ersten
Redebeitrag der Figur 'Jude' als ein Gedankenspiel vorgestellt. Dieses
richtet sich an eine/n Leser/in bzw. Hörer/in, der/die sich vorstellen
soll, es sei der 9. Oktober 1952, 'kurz nach Büroschluß' und der
Sprecher stehe an einer Hamburger Straßenkreuzung am dortigen
Stephansplatz.[33] Ähnlich wie in *Die Liebenden* wird so das abstrakte
Lehrstück zeitlich wie räumlich genau fixiert und somit beansprucht,
gegenwärtig stattzufinden. Gegenwart jedoch nicht als Abbildung von
Wirklichkeit, sondern als Imagination einer fiktiven Gestalt, die in
relativer zeitlicher Nähe zu den Hörenden/Lesenden spricht. In diesem
ersten Monolog der Figur 'Jude' erfahren wir, dass er eine Freundin
hat, mit der er später in den US-amerikanischen Film 'Ehekrieg' mit
Spencer Tracy und Katherine Hepburn gehen will. Vorausdeutend auf
den dann im Hörspiel entwickelten Konflikt, lässt sich im Filmtitel ein
Hinweis auf die Allgegenwart kriegerischer Auseinandersetzung
vermuten, die im Zentrum des Dialogs steht und die so auch in den
privaten Raum der Ehe hineingetragen erscheint. Schließlich ist in
diesem ersten Monolog noch die Anähnlichung von Bedeutung, die
die Figur 'Jude' gegenüber der Figur 'Polizist' vornimmt: 'Ein Mann,
wie ich es bin. Er könnte ich sein, und ich könnte er sein.'[34] Der
Verlauf des Gesprächs führt dann eine Veränderung vor, die sich in
den Einstellungen von 'Jude' und 'Polizist' ergibt und in einen
angedeuteten Rollentausch mündet. Tatsächlich wird diese
Veränderung – als didaktisch gemeinter Prozess zur Belehrung des
Publikums – jedoch weniger in Handlung übersetzt, als behauptet.
Anders formuliert: die deiktischen Hinweise überwiegen die
Handlungselemente – wiederum sehr ähnlich wie in *Die Liebenden*.

Zu den vom Text thematisierten Vorurteilen gehört die Vorstellung
des 'Polizist', der 'Jude' und 'seinesgleichen' könne ihm und
'seinesgleichen' etwas antun. Diese für den modernen Antisemitismus
zentrale Idee einer Täter-Opfer-Umkehr, die die eigene Aggression als
'Notwehr' gegen 'die Juden' begründet und legitimiert, erscheint hier
zwar als falsches Bewusstsein, was auch umständlich dialogisch
entwickelt und widerlegt wird, nicht aber als Teil antisemitischer
Ideologie. Denn nicht der Antisemitismus wird in diesem Text

analysiert und entlarvt, sondern eine abstrakte Theorie gesellschaftlicher Machtverhältnisse skizziert:

> POLIZIST Du fragst und fragst. Du hast mir noch nichts getan, aber du könntest mir jeden Augenblick etwas tun, und nicht bloß du allein, sondern du und deinesgleichen mir und allen meinesgleichen.
>
> JUDE Die Juden haben nichts gegen die Polizisten, wenn die Polizisten nichts gegen die Juden haben.
>
> POLIZIST Aber die Polizei hat sehr viel gegen die Juden, gegen die Juden und alle anderen, die so sind wie sie.
>
> JUDE Mein Gott, wie sind wir denn?
>
> POLIZIST Ihr seid wie fast alle anderen, die von einer Straßenseite zur anderen gehen.
>
> JUDE Also arm und schwach und unglücklich und verwirrt und gefoltert und brüderlich zu denen, die arm und schwach und unglücklich und verwirrt und gefoltert sind.

Am Ende dieser für das gesamte Hörspiel symptomatischen Passage nimmt die Figur 'Jude' eine Verallgemeinerung vor, die ihn mit *allen* schwachen, unglücklichen, verwirrten und gefolterten Menschen identifiziert. So dreht sich der Hörspieltext um eine einfache These, mit deren Hilfe gesellschaftliche Konflikte beschrieben und erklärt werden sollen. Es ist dies die wohlbekannte Vorstellung vom 'kleinen Mann', der machtlos ist – und also für das Geschehene, die angedeutete Vernichtung von Juden in einem Ghetto, keine Verantwortung tragen kann. Über diese Vorstellung werden 'Jude' und 'Polizist' – in absurder Travestie der historischen Konstellation von SS und den verfolgten und ermordeten Juden Europas – einander angenähert. Es ist die Figur 'Jude', die dies ausspricht: 'Ich bin ein kleiner Mann, du bist auch ein kleiner Mann. Die kleinen Leute sind ohnmächtig, und die großen Leute sind mächtig.'[35] Die Bedeutung dieses Erklärungsmusters für den Text kann wohl kaum überschätzt werden. So vermutet der 'Polizist', der 'Jude' wolle aus 'Ohnmächtigen Mächtige' und aus 'Mächtigen Ohnmächtige' machen und erhält als Antwort: 'Kann sein.'[36] Text und Autor wollen 'Veränderung' erreichen; die beiden Figuren sind dabei Zeichen in einer Versuchsanordnung des Autors. Oder, wie Weyrauch sich ausgedrückt haben soll: 'Wenn da der Jude und der SS-Mann sich unterhalten, eine halbe Stunde lang, und dann kommt ein Resümee, dann sind (...) diese Figuren ja doch, lassen Sie mich's pathetisch sagen, Emanationen des Autors. Der Autor ist ja der Jude, der Autor ist ja der SS-Mann.'[37] Was aber passiert, wenn ein nichtjüdischer deutscher Autor 1952 glaubt, er sei gleichermaßen SS-Mann und 'Jude'? Sein fantasmagorischer Dialog zwischen 'Jude' und 'Polizist' endet mit der Drohung des Polizisten, es werde sich alles umkehren. Und diese Umkehrung der Verhältnisse spricht der 'Jude' dann aus:

> Wir wollen das Gute und vergessen darüber, wie wir es anstellen, daß wir das Gute erreichen. Wir wittern, daß etwas nicht stimmt, aber wir wissen nicht, was los ist. Wir kriegen ein schlechtes Gewissen. Da beschließen wir, daß das, was wir tun, gut sei, aber wir untersuchen nicht, ob es nicht vielleicht böse statt gut ist. Dabei bleiben wir. Keiner darf uns widersprechen. Wer trotzdem widerspricht, ist böse. Wer böse ist, ist schädlich. Wer schadet, muß unschädlich gemacht werden.[38]

An dieser Stelle folgt der Ruf nach 'dem Geheimpolizisten'. Aus dem Wunsch nach 'dem Guten' ist unversehens das 'Böse' geworden. Dass auch ihm dies passieren könne, davor fürchtet sich der 'Jude'. Und damit ist unter der Hand 'das Böse', die Ermordung der europäischen Juden, zu einer Sache geworden, die aus dem Wunsch entstand, 'das Gute' zu erreichen. Die Positionen von 'Jude' und 'Polizist' sind austauschbar geworden; mehr noch, es ist der 'Polizist' der aus dem Gespräch etwas 'mitgenommen' hat.[39] So kulminiert in diesem Text die dialogisch ausgebreitete Idee eines Lernprozesses *der deutschen Nachkriegsgesellschaft* im Hinblick auf den Holocaust, der in Form der Darstellung eines Ghettoaufstands und Polizei (als SS) angedeutet wird,[40] ausgerechnet in der Vorstellung, auch ein 'Jude' könne – wenn wir nicht alle wachsam bleiben – eines Tages das Gute wollend das Böse erreichen.

Die Erzählung 'Mit dem Kopf durch die Wand' (1958) ist ein innerer Monolog einer Überlebenden, deren Eltern vergast worden sind und die selbst vor dreizehn Jahren am Ende des Zweiten Weltkriegs ihrer Ermordung durch Erschlagen zufällig entgehen konnte.[41] Der Monolog setzt mit der Rückkehr in ihre Wohnung ein, nachdem sie einen stundenlangen Spaziergang unternommen hatte, 'zum erstenmal, seitdem ich zurückgekommen bin'.[42] In dieser Wohnung in einer Mietskaserne, die sie in mimetischer Annäherung an die Ermordung ihrer Eltern als Zelle erlebt, verbarrikadiert sie sich. Tür- und Fensterritzen wurden von ihr abgedichtet, damit kein Gas eingeleitet werden kann. In ihrer Vorstellung dauert die nationalsozialistische Vergangenheit an. Die Außenwelt stellt sich ihr als feindlich dar: dort laufen Menschen herum, die sie mit Hilfe der Erzählung von Kain und Abel in 'gut' und 'böse' unterteilt. Die dichotome Zuordnung macht die Ich-Erzählerin dabei an den Augen fest: 'Den guten Augen sah ich das Gute an, wie man es überall beobachten kann. Aber das Böse in den Augen der Fußgänger war ein anderes Böses, als man es anderswo sieht. Es war das Böse, wie ich es aus den Lagern kenne.'[43] Im Unterschied zu den *Liebenden* ebenso wie dem Hörspiel 'Woher kennen wir uns bloß' wird hier ein spezifisches Böses der 'Lager' benannt. Das Spezifische verliert sich jedoch in der nachfolgenden Aufzählung von Eigenschaften: 'Es war das Mörderische, verborgen unter Gleichgültig, gespielter Gleichgültigkeit, Höflichkeit, alltäglicher Bosheit, Hoffärtigkeit, Geschäftigkeit, Gedankenlosigkeit, Abwesenheit, verborgen, fast verborgen, kaum verborgen, aber es war das Mörderische.'[44] Bei ihrem Spaziergang hatte sie den Menschen, denen sie begegnet war, Fragen gestellt, die sich auf Stationen der nationalsozialistischen Verfolgung der Juden beziehen, wie z.B. die Einführung des 'gelben Stern' 1941, um herauszufinden, was sie damals gedacht und getan hätten. So stellte sie diese Menschen auf die 'Probe', die unterschiedlich reagierten. Von einigen erinnert sie, sie seien weitergegangen, ohne zu reagieren. Diese kann sie nicht verurteilen, weil sie Zweifel hat, ob sie sich damals tatsächlich schuldig gemacht hatten. Das entscheidende Erlebnis, ein novellenartiger Umschlagspunkt, ist die erneute Konfrontation mit 'Birkenmännern', Soldaten, die nach dem Wegwerfen ihrer Gewehre am Ende des Kriegs noch mit jungen Birken ihre Opfer tot zu schlagen versucht hätten:

> Sie antworteten folgendes: ich will so tun, als hätte ich Ihre Frage überhört, Sie können froh sein, daß ich so gut gelaunt bin, sonst hätten Sie etwas anderes von mir gehört, Sie können Gott danken, daß Sie kein Mann sind, ich wünschte, ich könnte so, wie ich wollte, machen Sie, daß Sie dahin kommen, wo man Sie damals vergessen hat.[45]

Durch diese Begegnung gewinnt die wahnhafte Vorstellung der Ich-Erzählerin von einer mörderischen Weiter-Verfolgung ihren Realitätsgehalt. Am Ende ihres Monologs erwartet sie von einem Pfeil getroffen zu werden.[46] Die Figur einer jüdischen Überlebenden, die unter Verfolgungswahn leidet, ist Weyrauch in dieser Erzählung das Medium, um vom Weiterwirken des Nationalsozialismus zu erzählen. Anders als in den beiden hier behandelten früheren Texten des Autors gibt es in 'Mit dem Kopf durch die Wand' weder eine Universalisierung von Kriegsleiden noch einen Rollentausch. Allerdings bleibt die Wahl einer jüdischen Ich-Erzählerin dennoch irritierend: unter ihrem Blick auf ihre Umgebung, die deutsche Gesellschaft der späten fünfziger Jahre, entdeckt sie verallgemeinernd und in einer, von Weyrauch bekannten christlich-anthropologischen

Perspektive, 'gute' und 'böse' Menschen, wie das anderswo auch der Fall sei. Zwar gibt es mörderische 'Birkenmänner' in dieser Gesellschaft, aber eben auch andere, über die sie sich nicht anmaßen will zu urteilen. Obendrein relativiert ihre wahnhaft verschobene Realitätswahrnehmung die Textaussage. Schließlich geht es tatsächlich auch gar nicht um das Fortwirken des Nationalsozialismus in der Gegenwart sondern um das Vorhandensein von Mördern in einer Gesellschaft; das Morden wird essentialisiert und Menschen zugeordnet, die 'böse' sind, nicht aber aus einer mörderischen Politik, einer solchen Ideologie, aus konkreten historisch-gesellschaftlichen Bedingungen heraus analysiert.

Schlussbetrachtung

Jüdische Figuren in der deutschen Nachkriegskultur erfüllen diskursive Funktionen. Im Hinblick auf die Auseinandersetzung mit dem Nationalsozialismus folgen sie festgelegten Rollen. Die hier analysierten Texte Wolfgang Weyrauchs und der Exkurs zu Wolfgang Staudtes *Die Mörder sind unter uns* weisen dabei ein Spektrum auf, das teilweise auch antisemitisch ist, insgesamt aber aus sehr heterogenen Vorstellungen von 'Juden' zusammengesetzt erscheint. So sind die jüdischen Geister aus Weyrauchs Erzählung *Die Liebenden* gespenstische Versöhnungsfiguren, während der Optiker Mondschein in Staudtes Film vielschichtiger angelegt ist; als jüdischer Überlebender, dessen Geschichte unerzählt bleibt, kann er einerseits im Film ein abstraktes 'Prinzip Hoffnung' verkörpern. Andererseits erinnert Mondschein auch daran, dass die *eigentliche* Opfergeschichte, der Genozid an den Juden Europas, im ersten deutschen Nachkriegsfilm offenbar (noch) nicht erzählt werden konnte. Insgesamt bestätigen die Textanalysen eine Tendenz in der Nachkriegszeit in Deutschland, 'deutsche Opfer' jüdischen Opfern gleichzusetzen und das Kollektiv der Nachkriegsdeutschen mit Hilfe antinationalsozialistischer Opfererzählungen mit sich selbst zu versöhnen.[47] Bei dieser Selbstversöhnung kommen jüdischen Gestalten festgelegte Funktionen zu, die sie als projektive Fantasien und Entlastungsfiguren benötigen; innerhalb dieses Funktionsfeldes können sie dabei gleichzeitig durchaus unterschiedlich gestaltet sein.

Anmerkungen

[1] Hans Jürgen Syberberg, *Die freudlose Gesellschaft. Notizen aus dem letzten Jahr*, Carl Hanser Verlag: München und Wien, 1981, S. 8. Eine ähnliche Stelle findet sich auf S. 55. Gleichzeitig finden sich bereits in *Die freudlose Gesellschaft* eine Reihe von Relativierungen des Holocaust (u.a. 'Atomarer Holocaust', S. 24) oder antisemitischen Äußerungen (angesichts der fiktiven 'neuesten Meldung', die US-amerikanische Fernsehserie 'Holocaust' solle als obligatorisches Unterrichtsfach eingeführt werden, befindet Syberberg z.b.: 'Die jüdischen und zionistischen Organisationen reagierten weltweit mit Genugtuung auf das Wiedererwachen des deutschen Geistes, das so fast die Qualität einer jüdischen Anekdote erreicht.' (S. 77).

[2] Lothar Baier, 'Eine ungeheuerliche Neuigkeit? Nachfragen zur Debatte um den Pamphlettisten Syberberg,' *Neue Rundschau*, 1 (1990), S. 117-138 (hier: S. 125). Vgl. außerdem Hans Jürgen Syberberg, *Vom Unglück und Glück der Kunst in Deutschland nach dem letzten Kriege*, Matthes & Seitz: München, 1990, S. 14.

[3] Adolf Hitler, 'Volk und Rasse,' in: Ders. *Mein Kampf*. Zwei Bände in einem Band. Ungekürzte Ausgabe, Franz Eher Nachf.: München, 1934, S. 311-362.

[4] Dazu insbesondere Klaus Holz, *Nationaler Antisemitismus. Wissenssoziologie einer Weltanschauung*, Hamburger Edition: Hamburg, 2000.

[5] Vgl. Sander Gilman, *Die schlauen Juden. Über ein dummes Vorurteil*, Claassen: Hildesheim, 1998.

[6] Das heißt nicht, dass es keine Berichte jüdischer Überlebender oder jüdischer Historiker gegeben hätte; auch stößt die Bühnenfassung des *Tagebuchs der Anne Frank* ab 1957 z.b. auf eine breite Rezeption. Allerdings steht hier die Vernichtung nicht im Zentrum und das Stück erlaubt sehr unterschiedliche Aneignungen, die nicht notwendig mit einer Auseinandersetzung mit der 'Endlösung der Judenfrage' in Zusammenhang stehen müssen.

[7] Saul Friedländer bezeichnet die Vernichtung der Juden als 'das eigentliche Kernstück der Auseinandersetzung mit der NS-Zeit'. Dies bleibe es auch dann, wenn die Vernichtung in Diskursen nicht direkt erwähnt werde (vgl. Saul Friedländer: *Kitsch und Tod. Der Widerschein des Nazismus*, Carl Hanser Verlag: München³, 1999, S. 143). Der Holocaust bestimmt fundamental das Verhältnis von Juden und Nichtjuden in der deutschen Gesellschaft nach 1945. Daher sind alle Darstellungen von Juden durch Nichtjuden in der deutschen Kultur auf die eine oder andere Weise von dieser 'Vorgeschichte' geprägt. Vgl. auch Hans-Joachim Hahn, *Repräsentationen des Holocaust. Zur westdeutschen Erinnerungskultur seit 1979*, Winter: Heidelberg, 2005, S. 13-17.

[8] Ulrike Weckel, 'The *Mitläufer* in Two German Postwar Films. Representation and Critical Reception,' *History & Memory*, Vol. 15, 2 (Fall/Winter 2003), S. 64-93 (hier: S. 85).

[9] Ulrike Weckel, ebd., S. 93, Endnote 51.

[10] So die gleichlautende Formel, die Ulrike Weckel in einem früheren Aufsatz über den Film bereits im Titel nennt. Vgl. Ulrike Weckel: *'Die Mörder sind unter uns* oder: Vom Verschwinden der Opfer,' *WerkstattGeschichte 9*, 25 (2000), S. 105-115.

[11] Kinder sind ein durchgängiges Motiv, auf das im Film immer wieder Bezug genommen wird. Ein Teil der von Brückner verantworteten erschossenen Personen sind Kinder. Auch ist es ein kleines Mädchen, das bezeichnenderweise auch noch einen jüdischen Namen - Edith - trägt, das von Mertens durch eine Notoperation gerettet wird. An anderer Stelle schließlich bekommen die Zuschauer ein von Susanne Wallner entworfenes Plakat zu sehen, auf dem der Aufruf 'Rettet die Kinder!' zu lesen ist.

[12] Vgl. Wolfgang Weyrauch, *Tausend Gramm. Ein deutsches Bekenntnis in dreißig Geschichten aus dem Jahr 1949.* Mit einer Einleitung von Charles Schüddekopf. Rowohlt: Reinbek bei Hamburg, 1989, S. 175-183 (hier: S. 178).

[13] Angaben zur Biographie Wolfgang Weyrauchs finden sich online in der Wikipedia-Enzyklopädie unter http://de.wikipedia.org/wiki/Wolfgang_Weyrauch.

[14] Vgl. Ulrike Landzettel, *Identifikation eines Eckenstehers. Der Schriftsteller Wolfgang Weyrauch (1904 - 1980)*, Inauguraldissertation, Marburg 2003, S. 9; URL: deposit.ddb.de/cgi-bin/dokserv?idn=973877707&dok_var=d1&dok_ext=pdf& filename=973877707.pdf.

[15] Reinhard Döhl, 'Zu den Hörspielen Wolfgang Weyrauchs,' in: Ders. und Bernhard Willms, *Zu den Hörspielen Wolfgang Weyrauchs*, Massenmedien und Kommunikation Bd. 14, hrsg. von Irmela Schneider und Karl Riha, Forschungsschwerpunkt Massenmedien und Kommunikation an der Universität Siegen: Siegen, 1981, S. 10-34 (hier: S. 11).

[16] Landzettel, *Identifikation eines Eckenstehers*, S. 9.

[17] Ebd., S. 14.

[18] Ebd., S. 10.

[19] Ebd., S. 27.

[20] In der Studie von Landzettel wird die Erzählung 'Die Liebenden' lediglich an einer einzigen Stelle erwähnt, ohne jedoch analysiert zu werden: 'Es folgten die Erzählungen *Die Liebenden* (1947) und *Die Davidsbündler* (1948), in denen Weyrauch, wie schon am Ende des Textes *Auf der bewegten Erde* für den Glauben an Gott plädiert.' Vgl. Landzettel, *Identifikation eines Eckenstehers*, S. 266.

[21] Inwiefern dieser Text eine 'autobiographische Orientierung' aufweist, wie Landzettel auch für die nicht explizit als solche ausgezeichneten Texte Weyrauchs vermutet, soll hier nicht untersucht werden. Für diese Annahme spräche u.a., dass der Student Thomas Scherer als früherer 'Obergefreiter' bezeichnet wird, was mit Weyrauchs eigenem Dienstgrad übereinstimmt. Vgl. Landzettel, *Identifikation eines Eckenstehers*, S. 28; Wolfgang Weyrauch, *Die Liebenden*, Kurt Desch: München, 1947, S. 12.

[22] Wolfgang Weyrauch, *Die Liebenden*, S. 110.

[23] Ebd., S. 21.

[24] Ebd., S. 112 und S. 113.

[25] Ebd., S. 21.

[26] Der Nationalsozialismus wird schlicht als das 'Andere' bezeichnet. Am Ende des Textes heißt es in dem Bericht des Erzählers: 'Die Leute unterhielten sich ja auch über Deutschland, über den Krieg und über den Frieden, der noch keiner war, aber eines Tages würde er einer sein. [...] Und über das Glück, daß jenes Andere vorbei wäre'. Ebd., S. 114.

[27] Ebd., S. 11.

[28] Ebd., S. 15.

[29] Ebd., S. 44. Vgl. auch Hahn, *Repräsentationen des Holocaust*, Fußnoten auf S. 51-52.

[30] Ebenfalls plausibel wäre es, in der anderen, am Gespräch beteiligten Gruppe U-Bahn-Fahrer(inne)n zu vermuten. Durch die Wahl der U-Bahn als Ort dieser Geistergespräche ist deren Status als untergründig, als jenseits der Welt des Tageslichts oder als unbewusst angedeutet.

[31] Vgl. die Angaben dazu bei Reinhard Döhl, 'Zu den Hörspielen Wolfgang Weyrauchs,' S. 41. Hier ist auch zu erfahren, dass die Angaben in der Anthologie *Wolfgang Weyrauch, Dialog mit dem Unsichtbaren. Sieben Hörspiele. Mit einem Nachwort von Martin Walser*. Walter: Olten und Freiburg i. Breisgau, 1962, über eine Stuttgarter Produktion unter der Regie von Martin Walser falsch seien. Die Analyse des Stücks bezieht sich ausschließlich auf die gedruckte Fassung von 1962.

[32] Ein Beispiel: Der 'Polizist' sagt, 'ihr Juden' seid 'rechthaberisch und eingebildet und voreingenommen'. Der 'Jude' entgegnet ihm dann: 'Ihr Juden, ihr Juden, wir sind Menschen wie alle anderen auch, mit Fehlern und Hoffnungen und Einbußen.' Vgl. Weyrauch, 'Woher kennen wir uns bloß', in: *Dialog mit dem Unsichtbaren*, S. 7-27 (hier: S. 16).

[33] Weyrauch, 'Woher kennen wir uns bloß', in: *Dialog mit dem Unsichtbaren*, S. 7-27 (hier: S. 10).

[34] Ebd., S. 10.

[35] Ebd., S. 13.

[36] Ebd.

[37] Zit. nach Döhl, 'Zu den Hörspielen Wolfgang Weyrauchs', S. 20.

[38] Weyrauch, 'Woher kennen wir uns bloß', S. 27.

[39] 'Ich nehme das mit, was du gesagt hast. Ich durchsuche dich nicht. Ich verhafte dich nicht. Solch einen Geheimpolizisten hat man sicher noch nie gesehen.' Ebd.

[40] Auch die Asche der Ermordeten und in den Krematorien Verbrannten wird, wenn auch völlig verschoben, erwähnt. Der geschilderte Ghettoaufstand hat nur zwei 'Überlebende', den Sprecher und einen zweiten, der übrigbleibt und von dem er sagt: 'Der Mann war einfach weg. Wie Asche, die vom Feuer übrigbleibt.' Ebd.

[41] Wolfgang Weyrauch: 'Mit dem Kopf durch die Wand,' in: Ders. *Das war überall. Erzählungen*. Hrsg. und mit einem Vorwort von Fritz Deppert, Kranichsteiner: Darmstadt, 1998, S. 127-135. Zu den Eltern ebd. S. 127, auf S. 132 der Hinweis auf die Ich-Erzählerin als Frau. Landzettel gibt an, die Erzählung sei am 27. September 1958 erstmals in der *FAZ* abgedruckt worden. Vgl. Landzettel, *Identifikation eines Eckenstehers*, S. 398.

[42] Ebd., S. 129.

[43] Ebd., S. 130.

[44] Ebd.

[45] Ebd., S. 134.

[46] Ebd., S. 135.

[47] Siehe dazu Robert G. Moeller, 'The Politics of the Past in the 1950s,' in: Bill Niven, ed., *Germans as Victims. Remembering the Past in Contemporary Germany*, Palgrave MacMillan: Basingstoke, 2006, pp. 26-42, und ausführlicher Robert G. Moeller, *War Stories. The Search for a Usable Past in the Federal Republic of Germany*, University of California Press: Berkeley and Los Angeles, 2001.

Helen Wolfenden

The Representation of *Wehrmacht* Soldiers as Victims in Post-war West German Film: *Hunde, wollt ihr ewig leben?* and *Der Arzt von Stalingrad*

In the late-1950s two films focusing on the experiences of the *Wehrmacht* on the Eastern Front during World War Two were released in West Germany: Frank Wisbar's *Hunde, wollt ihr ewig leben?* (1959) and Geza von Radvanyi's *Der Arzt von Stalingrad* (1958). Although members of the *Wehrmacht* were responsible for many war crimes, particularly in the East, the narratives depict German soldiers as victims of National Socialism and communism, rather than perpetrators of Nazi atrocities. It may therefore be argued that these films attempt to rehabilitate the *Wehrmacht* at the expense of historical accuracy.

Between 1952 and approximately 1957 the West German government actively encouraged film directors to produce war films in an attempt to gain public support for its rearmament programme. Since the West German film industry was indirectly controlled by the state, it can be argued that these early war films needed to promote a positive image of the military in order to receive financial backing. Consequently, until very recently, critics of post-war West German film focused mainly on the correlation between remilitarisation and the re-emergence of the war film genre in West Germany.[1] Yet even after West Germany had established a military force, and it was no longer necessary to promote rearmament, films that depicted the *Wehrmacht* in a favourable light continued to be produced. It cannot therefore be claimed that war films which were released towards the end of the 1950s fostered a positive image of the military solely to facilitate the government's policy of remilitarisation. Rather, the most striking features of these very popular films appear to be the rhetoric of avoidance with regard to atrocities committed by the *Wehrmacht* during World War Two, and the depiction of *Wehrmacht* soldiers as victims not just of National Socialism, but also of communism. Thus it can be maintained that war films from the era propagate the myth of a *saubere Wehrmacht* that was, and to a certain extent is still, prevalent in West Germany.

The myth of the innocent *Wehrmacht* soldier was a prominent narrative in post-war historiography, which has only been relativised very recently. In the aftermath of World War Two, war crimes trials proved that atrocities had been committed by individual members of the *Wehrmacht*, yet the *Wehrmacht* as an institution was found to be not guilty of war crimes.[2] This acquittal arguably contributed to the public and private propagation of the notion of the *saubere Wehrmacht*. Moreover, this idea was fostered in post-war literature, from the *Trümmerliteratur* of *Gruppe 47*, such as Heinrich Böll's 1951 novel *Wo warst du, Adam?*, to memoirs published by former *Wehrmacht* officers, and the positive portrayals of *Wehrmacht* soldiers in *Landser-Hefte*. In the 1950s, the myth was also encouraged by the Western Allies in an attempt to promote West German remilitarisation, and by the West German government, who publicly proclaimed repatriated *Wehrmacht* soldiers to be innocent of war crimes.[3] A similar rhetoric of innocence can be found in war films of the 1950s, and is particularly apparent in two films dealing with the war on the Eastern Front: Frank Wisbar's 1959 film, *Hunde, wollt ihr ewig leben?*, which centres on the Sixth Army's experiences during the Battle of Stalingrad, and Geza von Radvanyi's 1958 film *Der Arzt von Stalingrad*, which is set in a Soviet prisoner of war camp.

Hitler's sacrifice of the Sixth Army: *Hunde, wollt ihr ewig leben?*

Hunde, wollt ihr ewig leben? is set in winter 1942/43 and focuses on a young officer's experience of the war on the Eastern Front. *Oberstleutnant* Wisse is an idealistic officer, who initially supports the National Socialist regime, but, whilst fighting with the Sixth Army in Stalingrad, gradually becomes disillusioned with Hitler and the war. Wisbar based his film version of the Battle of Stalingrad on three books published in the 1950s: Heinz Schröter's historical account, *Stalingrad – bis zur letzten Patrone*; a collection of soldiers' letters, *Letzte Briefe aus Stalingrad*; and Fritz Wöss's semi-autographical novel, *Hunde, wollt ihr ewig leben*.[4] However, whereas these books give a somewhat unfavourable representation of the German army by relating episodes where Russian prisoners of war are maltreated and Russian villages are looted, such images are not included in Wisbar's film. Rather, Wisse and all the on-screen German officers, excepting Major Linkmann who appears to be a cowardly individual, are portrayed as honourable and brave soldiers, who are victims of National Socialism.

Wisbar's favourable portrayal of Wisse and the Sixth Army is problematic in that it is well documented that members of this division were involved in war crimes on the Eastern Front. For example, in 1941, Walther von Reichenau, Commander-in-Chief of the Sixth Army, ordered his troops to eliminate the Bolshevist threat, leading to the murders of thousands of communists and Jews in the east.[5] *Generalfeldmarschall* Erich von Manstein was one of the officers responsible for ensuring that Reichenau's order was adhered to by *Wehrmacht* soldiers, and it is therefore clear that the *Vernichtungskrieg* was not only carried out by the SS, but also by members of the army with the full knowledge of superior officers. Considering the fact that von Manstein had a public trial in 1949, where he was sentenced to eighteen years imprisonment for war crimes, it can be assumed that many cinemagoers would have known that atrocities had been perpetrated by the *Wehrmacht* on the Eastern Front.[6] In view of the covert censorship that existed in the West German film industry in the 1950s, Wisbar's depiction of the *Wehrmacht* is perhaps not surprising, yet the film arguably goes beyond merely appeasing the censors, and appears to be an attempt at propagating the myth of a *saubere Wehrmacht* at the expense of historical fact. This argument is given added weight by the fact that Wisbar employs a documentary style for the film, which gives an impression of authenticity to his fictional account of the Battle of Stalingrad.

The documentary style that dominates the film gives a measure of verisimilitude to the narrative. This is accentuated by the fact that the film has neither opening nor closing credits, intimating that it is a true documentary and that the on-screen characters are not played by actors.[7] Instead of credits, an opening sequence combines shots of documentary footage of an army parade with the off-screen commentary of a voice-over narrator. Since this narrator is a disembodied voice, that is, one outside the screen and the fictional events, he is given an air of authority, and together with on-screen titles, keeps the viewer informed of the date and time at key points in the narrative, thereby implying that the events depicted are historically accurate. An examination of the opening scenes demonstrates the extent to which, as a result of this style, the viewer is manipulated into believing the fiction. Since the positive portrayal of the Sixth Army contradicts evidence proving that *Wehrmacht* officers did commit war crimes, this manipulation may be perceived as being necessary in order to give Wisbar's fictional account of the Battle of Stalingrad credibility.

The film begins with two introductory scenes that combine documentary footage with the commentary of the voice-over narrator, and act as a prologue to the main narrative. The first scene opens with a drum roll and close-up shots of soldiers marching past Hitler in documentary footage of a military parade. We hear the military band playing, and see shots of Hitler inter-cut with goose-stepping soldiers proudly carrying flags bearing the Swastika. The camera then pans out to a long shot that gives an overview of the parade, and the narrator begins to speak over the music:

> Paraden sind prächtig anzusehen. Zu aufreizender Musik schlagen die blankgeputzten Stiefel den Asphalt. Die Augen blitzen. In gleichem Schritt und Tritt geht es voran, und endet erst, wenn Schnee und Wind die Leichentücher wiegen, um zuzudecken, was so strahlend und siegesgewiss begann. Einem toten Soldaten ist es egal, wer den Krieg gewann oder verlor.

The fact that the narrator only begins to comment on the visuals when the screen shows an overview of the procession gives him added authority, in that it is implied that he too has an overview of events. After the narrator says, 'und endet erst', the music stops and the film cuts to shots of dead soldiers lying in the snow, with the sound of distant gunfire. Since the glamorous parade is replaced by images of death, and the jubilant, proud music is substituted by the noise of battle, the contrast between the glamour of the parade and the reality that soldiers do die is emphasised, and an emotional anti-war message is conveyed to the viewer. The first scene ends with a full screen shot of a banner proclaiming: 'Mit dem Führer zum Sieg!' Thus the cynical tone of the narrator is reflected by the irony of the visuals, and the viewer is guided to believe that soldiers in the Sixth Army were victims of National Socialism.

In the second introductory scene carefully arranged images combined with the voice-over narration indicate how the viewer is supposed to receive the film. At a military briefing, an officer points out the Sixth Army's position on a map, indicating that it is so weak that if the Russians were to launch an attack, a defeat would be inevitable. Thus, from the outset, the viewer is aware that the outcome of the war in the East is not a forgone conclusion, and that the Sixth Army is in a precarious position. As the officer speaks, the camera pans out to show a silhouette of Hitler looking towards the map. It is now apparent that Hitler has access to the same information as the viewer, and has full knowledge of the danger that the Sixth Army faces. However, the lighting of this scene contradicts the narrative: whilst the map and the adviser are well lit, Hitler is standing in shadow. Hence, even while the adviser is attempting to inform him as to the true situation on the Eastern Front, it is visually apparent that Hitler is not enlightened. This suggestion is then confirmed by the voice-over of the narrator, who comments:

> Aber Hitler nannte solche Warnungen idiotische Schwarzseherei, und befahl der Sechsten Armee unter General Paulus, Stalingrad für ihn zu erobern. Dieser Befehl wurde zum Hinrichtungsbefehl für die Sechste Armee.

It is therefore emphasised that Hitler's determination to win at Stalingrad overrides all military sense. Following the military strategist telling Hitler he cannot win at Stalingrad, as if from a slide show, we see assorted shots of Stalingrad burning, and the narrator tells us that German soldiers are buried under the rubble. This technique ensures that the viewer connects the loss of the Sixth Army to Hitler, and by showing us where many soldiers are entombed, conveys the horror of their deaths. Moreover, the term 'Hinrichtungsbefehl' implies that the army was sacrificed because of Hitler's poor decisions, thus manipulating the viewer into blaming Hitler for the soldiers' deaths.

As a result of techniques used in the introductory scenes, the viewer is guided towards the narrator's point of view and is predisposed to trust his commentary on subsequent events. This means that we are more likely to accept the narrator's stance that Hitler and the Nazi party misled the German public over events at Stalingrad. For example, prior to the scene in the hospital, the screen fills with shots of Stalingrad burning, and the narrator reports: 'In dieser Nacht brennt Stalingrad von einem Ende bis zum anderen. In dieser Nacht feiert Herr von Göring den zehnten Jahrestag der Machtübernahme.' At this point the scene cuts to documentary footage of the tenth anniversary celebration in Germany, leading the viewer to compare the two images. In this instance the narrator influences the viewer so that when we see Göring on screen we are inclined to believe that he is deceiving the German public. Thus the narrative demonstrates not only that the celebrations are inappropriate when brave German soldiers are risking their lives as a result of Nazi policy, but also that the Nazis are responsible for the horror at Stalingrad.

Various forms of actual media coverage of the war on the Eastern Front are incorporated into the fictional scenes. For example, we see newspaper reports, radio programmes and documentary film footage, which not only appear to add to the veracity of the fiction, but also illustrate just how effective Nazi propaganda was on the German public. The opening footage of the military parade shows how Hitler wanted the *Wehrmacht* to be perceived, consisting of soldiers who proudly march in front of their *Führer* with great pomp. The sharp cut to shots of dead soldiers, however, immediately negates the glamour of the parade, and reveals the reality of war that Hitler tried to keep hidden from the public eye. Thus, from the outset, the film demonstrates an awareness of the propaganda that was disseminated during the Nazi era, and appears to highlight how Hitler misled both the German public and *Wehrmacht* soldiers.

Wisse's experiences on the Eastern Front confirm the notion that Hitler duped the Germans. During a train journey, for instance, *Oberstleutnant* Kesselbach draws Wisse's attention to a newspaper report that prematurely declares a win at Stalingrad. The report is clearly part of Hitler's propaganda and shows how the Nazis deceived the German public. This idea is continued during the hospital scene when Göring's radio broadcast claims Hitler has held the Eastern Front. A travelling shot of the hospital reveals the sheer number of horrifically wounded men, including Wisse's friend Fuhrmann, a pianist, who has had his hands blown off. Wisse's brief conversation with a doctor shows the hopelessness of the situation. There are simply too many wounded and not enough medical supplies to help. Although all the injured soldiers know that Göring's radio broadcast is untrue, the public at home in Germany would not. Hence the narrative demonstrates that only those fighting on the Eastern Front could have known the truth, and offers the contemporary German viewer a defence for believing Nazi propaganda during the war. As a result, the film exonerates not only the *Wehrmacht*, but also the German nation from involvement in Nazism.

The rhetoric of innocence is further assisted by the clear separation of *Wehrmacht* soldiers from the Nazi regime, which suggests that the true Nazis are the Nazi elite in Germany, rather than soldiers on the Frontline or the German public. Thus Hitler and Göring are portrayed as having deceived the German public, whilst soldiers in the Sixth Army are shown to have been sacrificed by Nazi leaders. This narrative is highlighted by the fact that only two characters are shown to believe in Nazism: Major Linkmann and Wisse. Whilst Linkmann is negatively portrayed as a cowardly individual, who deserts his troops when they come under bombardment, the narrative indicates that Wisse's belief in Nazism is a psychological rather than political one. That is, he has been indoctrinated by Nazism as a result of his education at an *Ordensburg*, a school for the Nazi elite.

At the beginning of the film Wisse unquestioningly believes Hitler's propaganda, but gradually realises he has been duped. In an early scene at a Russian farmhouse, Wisse tells Kesselbach of his education: 'Ich bin auch auf der Ordensburg erzogen worden. Wir haben gelernt, uns auf uns selbst zu verlassen, und sind damit recht gut gefahren.' Kesselbach, who has evidently become disillusioned by the war, responds: 'Bis euch mal der Reifen platzt'. In the final scene of the film, as the soldiers march out of Stalingrad to a prisoner of war camp, Wisse refers to this conversation, telling Kesselbach: 'Damals haben Sie mir prophezeit, dass der Reifen mal platzen würde. [...] Ich muss Ihnen wohl sehr dämlich vorgekommen sein.' This is evidence that Wisse has been changed by his experiences in Stalingrad. Moreover he has survived the war with his reputation intact: he has committed no atrocities; no longer believes in Hitler; and has fought bravely and honourably on behalf of Germany. He could therefore be perceived by the post-war West German audience to be an ideal role model for a *Bundeswehr* officer.

In making a distinction between the Nazis and *Wehrmacht* soldiers, and depicting the Sixth Army as having been sacrificed at Stalingrad by Hitler, *Hunde, wollt ihr ewig leben?* conforms to the notion that *Wehrmacht* soldiers were victims of Nazism rather than perpetrators of Nazi atrocities. This representation would arguably have been welcomed by the post-war West German audience, since it allowed them to be proud of their former soldiers who had endured hardships on their behalf. Moreover, it allows the audience to separate themselves from Nazism, and hence be removed from Nazi atrocities. A similar rhetoric can be found in Geza von Radvanyi's film *Der Arzt von Stalingrad*, which was released in 1958. However, whereas *Hunde, wollt ihr ewig leben?* focuses on soldiers as victims of Nazism, Radvanyi's film additionally portrays them as victims of communism, thereby conforming to the Cold War narrative that was prevalent in West Germany in the 1950s.

Wehrmacht soldiers as victims of communism: *Der Arzt von Stalingrad*

Der Arzt von Stalingrad is set in 1949 and focuses on the experiences of Dr Fritz Böhler in a prisoner of war camp in the Soviet Union, where conditions are poor and the German prisoners are forced to do hard labour even when ill. In a similar approach to the narrative in *Hunde, wollt ihr ewig leben?*, there is a noticeable lack of Nazis amongst the German characters, and German soldiers are portrayed as being victims of the war, rather than as soldiers who engaged in war of aggression. This idea is reinforced by the fact that the soldiers are imprisoned on Soviet soil four years after the end of World War Two, and are treated inhumanely by their captors. Thus Radvanyi's film confirms the predominant rhetoric of the late 1950s regarding the representation of the *Wehrmacht*.

The opening sequence of the film manipulates the viewer into an anti-war sentiment and immediately establishes the notion that Hitler is responsible for the loss of millions of German soldiers in the Soviet Union. Prior to the credits, the film opens with an off-screen voice that sounds like Hitler giving a political speech. Astute viewers with knowledge of German history will recognise the speech as being adapted from one given on 8 November 1942 at the Munich *Löwenbräukeller* on the anniversary of the 1923 Putsch.[8] Over a blank screen, Hitler's voice claims: 'Damals war es der Kaiser...' The screen is then illuminated by a light and the camera focuses on a loud speaker while the speech continues:

> Jetzt bin ich es. Nur ein Unterschied ist: Der Kaiser von damals war ein Mann, dem jede Stärke im Widerstand gegen diese Feinde abging; in mir haben sie nun einen Gegner gegenüber, der an das Wort Kapitulieren überhaupt gar nicht denkt. Das Deutschland von einst hat um dreiviertel zwölf die Waffen niedergelegt - ich habe grundsätzlich immer erst fünf Minuten nach zwölf aufgehört.

As the speech continues, the shot changes to show an inn where men are drinking and listening to the radio. Subsequent images of warfare contrast with this peaceful scene. Over off-screen cries of 'Sieg Heil', we see documentary footage of gunfire, planes, burning houses and fire, which are then replaced by the dramatic shot of the words 'Stalingrad 1943' written in fire. Whilst Hitler disseminates his propaganda to the German nation, Stalingrad is literally and symbolically burning.

The opening sequence suggests not only that Hitler was directly responsible for the defeat at Stalingrad, but also that he lied to the German public by claiming that the battle was almost won despite the fact that the German army was being overwhelmingly defeated at Stalingrad. This notion is accentuated by contrasting visual images of warfare with a second off-screen broadcast of Hitler addressing the German public:

> Die Inbesitznahme von Stalingrad, die auch abgeschlossen werden wird, wird diesen Riegel nur vertiefen und wieder verstärken. Und Sie können der Überzeugung sein, dass uns kein Mensch mehr von dieser Stelle wegbringen wird. Was nun die weiteren Ziele betrifft, so werden Sie wieder verstehen, dass ich darüber nicht rede, weil es sich um Ziele handelt, die zur Zeit verfolgt werden. Darüber spricht Mister Churchill.

The contents of the speech, with the emphasis on taking Stalingrad at all costs, are undermined by the noise of bombs and gunfire, and images of a row of injured soldiers in a military hospital. As a result of this technique, the film indicates that the German public were misled, and the *Wehrmacht* let down by Hitler. The words are taken from a speech given by Hitler in Berlin on 30 September 1942, where he optimistically declared that the worst of the fighting was over and that Germany would win at Stalingrad.[9] By combining the two speeches, which are taken out of chronological order, the film implies that they are part of the same speech even though the second was given one and a half months earlier than the first. This gives the impression that they have been carefully selected by Radvanyi to ensure that the viewer is receptive to the idea of Germans as victims of Nazism, and that Hitler is blamed for the defeat at Stalingrad.

The scene where the main characters are captured by the Soviets clearly intimates that the Germans are also victims of Soviet brutality. A panned shot of injured soldiers reveals that the action is set in a cellar being used as a military hospital, whilst the sound of gunfire reveals that the battle is nearby. Dr Böhler is in the middle of an operation on a German soldier when Soviet soldiers burst in, remove the patient, and force him at gunpoint to operate on one of their comrades. The Soviets are therefore instantly portrayed in a negative manner, in that they apparently make no allowances for the fact that they are in a military hospital. Furthermore, the fact that they are armed and are invading the defenceless hospital suggests that the Soviets, rather than the Germans, are the aggressors.

The opening credits that immediately follow this scene are accompanied by still shots of the ruins of Stalingrad combined with documentary footage of a seemingly endless column of German soldiers marching out of the city. The actual footage fades and is replaced by a close up shot of Böhler marching through the snow with his fellow soldiers. Thus the viewer is reminded that thousands of German soldiers were captured following the Battle of Stalingrad and Böhler is merely one of them. By integrating actual footage with fictional scenes an air of authenticity is given to the film, implying that the fiction that follows is based on fact. Yet, although the opening sequence does show shots of the destruction that has been caused during the Battle of Stalingrad, the camera mainly focuses on the hardships of the German soldiers as they march into captivity; hence the viewer is manipulated into sympathising with the prisoners of war, rather than with the Soviets who have had their city destroyed. In other words the viewer is led into identifying with the aggressors rather than with the defenders of Stalingrad, and the Soviet victims of German aggression are not represented on screen. This omission is at odds with the apparent desire to give the film a measure of authenticity.

The opening sequence clearly evokes the idea that German soldiers were victims of Hitler's desire to take Stalingrad, and leads the viewer to empathize with their plight as they are captured. This sentiment is continued throughout the film. Following the credits, over a background shot of the camp, the years 1945 to 1949 flash on screen. This device not only establishes a clear time frame for the subsequent action, but also highlights the passing of time, and visually demonstrates that German soldiers are still imprisoned four years after the end of World War Two. Since the opening scenes showed that Böhler and his comrades were captured during the Battle of Stalingrad in 1943, yet only the post-war years are highlighted, it is suggested that the film is not disputing the imprisonment of German soldiers between 1943 and 1945, but that they should have been repatriated at the end of the war. As it is visually emphasised that they were not, it is implied that the Soviet regime is acting inhumanely.

The inhumane behaviour of the Soviets is further highlighted by the narrative which demonstrates that life in the camp is unpleasant: the prisoners do not receive enough food, are physically and mentally abused, and are forced to do hard labour even when they are ill. This representation is consistent with reports that life for captured German soldiers was extremely harsh in Soviet camps: typhus was rife, food was scarce, and it was extremely cold in winter; hence many were too weak to endure the enforced manual labour. However, although it can be argued that the film depicts the severity of camp life, the portrayal is not as terrible as the reported reality. Out of approximately one hundred and twenty thousand soldiers who were captured by the Soviets between November 1942 and February 1943, it has been estimated that between sixty and seventy thousand did not survive the first four months of imprisonment.[10] Radvanyi's film does not show German deaths due to poor conditions and maltreatment in the camp, rather the only on-screen German deaths are the killing of Grosse, the informant, by his fellow prisoners, and the shooting of Dr Sellnow by the Soviet officer Markow in a jealous rage. Thus, even though life in the camp is undoubtedly unpleasant, and the guards do abuse the prisoners, the true horror of Soviet prisoner of war camps is not shown. Moreover since it is not the Soviet regime that is responsible for the on-screen deaths, Radvanyi's decision not to screen large numbers of German deaths may indicate a shift towards a more tolerant representation of the Soviets than was prevalent in West Germany in the mid-1950s. Alternatively, the lessening of the horror can perhaps be explained by the fact that the film only focuses on a small group of prisoners, who can be seen to be representative of the prisoners of war as a whole. Consequently two deaths in this group are a comparatively large proportion, and the anti-communist rhetoric is upheld.

Although the narrative informs us that the prisoners of war are on meagre rations and are treated badly by their captors, this is undermined by the appearance of the main characters. Böhler, Sellnow, Grosse and Pelz do not look as if they are starving, nor do any of the prisoners have their heads shaved which was customary in Soviet camps. They are therefore neither consistent with the traditional portrayal of prisoners of war as seen in posters and on stamps in the post-war era, nor with the reality that many soldiers repatriated from Soviet camps were undernourished and suffering from psychological problems.[11] In 1946, West German doctors had inadvertently assisted the development of the rhetoric of Germans as victims by diagnosing many former prisoners of war as suffering from dystrophy, with symptoms such as liver damage, depression and loss of sexual desire.[12] The appearance of the prisoners in the film, however, suggests they have managed to endure captivity without being dehumanised. Hence it can be argued that the prisoners of war are not only shown to be victims, but also survivors of an inhumane communist regime. It also means that they can still be perceived as being ideal representatives of the German *Volksgemeinschaft*, which separates the German survivors of Soviet captivity from survivors of Nazi concentration camps. The film therefore shows German victims to be stronger than the victims of the Germans.

In post-war West German medical theory, one of the main symptoms of prisoner of war dystrophy was loss of sexual desire, and the returning prisoners of war were often portrayed in medical journals as being emasculated by their captivity.[13] Radvanyi's film does not however conform to this theory. Even though the prisoners are in a largely masculine environment, the film strongly emphasises that they have heterosexual desires, which the camera voyeuristically follows. An early scene, for example, shows a prisoner working in Kasalinsskaja's bedroom. The camera first focuses on him looking towards a screen, before cross-cutting to show the silhouette of Kasalinsskaja undressing behind the screen, then to Markow sat stroking a cat and watching the prisoner. The implication is that the German has sexual desires, whilst Markow is more interested in his cat than looking at Kasalinsskaja. Similarly when Pelz is in a hurry to steal a scarf for an emergency operation, he makes time to look at the naked female kitchen workers in the sauna. Thus the film contradicts the traditional portrayal of the asexual dystrophic prisoner of war. This contradiction is enhanced by the fact that the German prisoners are also shown to be sexually attractive to the female Soviet captors: Tamara is attracted to Schultheiß, and Kasalinsskaja finds Sellnow physically attractive. Furthermore Kasalinsskaja's preference for Sellnow at Markow's expense shows that a German is preferable to a Russian, even when imprisoned. This rhetoric is strengthened by comparing the appearance of the two men. Markow only has one hand, which suggests he is physically lacking, whilst Sellnow, although imprisoned, is a complete man. This indicates that German men are physically strong enough to survive inhumane treatment in Soviet camps, and, even when imprisoned, are preferable to Soviet men.

Der Arzt von Stalingrad evidently gives a positive representation of prisoners of war in the Soviet Union. By showing the Germans to be maltreated by the Soviets after the end of the war, the rhetoric of Germans as victims of a communist regime is upheld, and Hitler's responsibility for their plight is lessened. However, by showing that the Germans are not dehumanised by their captivity, but are sexually attractive to Soviet women, the prisoners are portrayed as survivors of a communist regime. A predominant post-war narrative frequently equated the suffering of prisoners of war to that of Jews in concentration camps, yet Radvanyi's representation of German soldiers as being not only strong enough to survive mental and physical maltreatment, but also physically attractive even in captivity, is the complete opposite of the representation of Jewish victims in post-war West Germany. Thus the film gives the impression that the German prisoners of war were stronger than Jewish concentration camp victims, hence were able to survive poor conditions. It is this emphasis on survival that dominates the film and it is therefore possible to argue that *Der Arzt von Stalingrad* not only perpetuates anti-Soviet ideology, but also, perhaps subconsciously, National Socialist thought that declared Germans to be the superior race.

Both *Hunde, wollt ihr ewig leben?* and *Der Arzt von Stalingrad* clearly demonstrate the tendency of post-war West German filmmakers to show *Wehrmacht* soldiers suffering on behalf of Germany. The films are therefore consistent with the West German government's official stance with regard to the *Wehrmacht* during the 1950s, which was arguably a result of the campaign to repatriate German soldiers incarcerated in Soviet prisoner of war camps. That is, that the soldiers had behaved honourably during the war, and had been victims of Nazism and communism, rather than war criminals. Focusing on the predicament of the prisoners of war rather than German involvement in crimes against humanity not only added to the anti-communist sentiment that was prevalent in the 1950s, but also enabled West Germans to view themselves as victims of a brutal regime rather than perpetrators of war crimes. Thus the films helped to propagate the myth of the *saubere Wehrmacht* that was not publicly confronted in West Germany until the opening of the now celebrated exhibition documenting the *Wehrmacht's* involvement in atrocities committed on the Eastern Front, *Vernichtungskrieg: Verbrechen der Wehrmacht*, in Hamburg in March 1995. The exhibition caused extreme public reactions, resulting in demonstrations and counter-demonstrations, political debates, and historians querying the legitimacy of some photographs.[14] The controversy surrounding the exhibition indicates just how prevalent the myth of the *saubere Wehrmacht*, with its roots in the immediate post-war era, was, in that even in the 1990s many Germans were still unwilling to confront the notion that the *Wehrmacht* had been involved in Nazi atrocities.

Notes

[1] See for example: Klaus Kreimeier, *Kino und Filmindustrie in der BRD*, Scriptor: Kronberg, 1973; Wilfried von Bredow, 'Filmpropaganda für Wehrbereitschaft: Kriegsfilme in der Bundesrepublik,' in: Wilfried von Bredow and Rolf Zurek, eds., *Film und Gesellschaft in Deutschland: Dokumente und Materialien*, Hoffmann & Campe: Hamburg, 1975, pp. 316-326; Heinz Ungureit, 'Filmpolitik in der Bundesrepublik,' *Filmkritik*, 1 (1964), 9-16.

[2] Regarding the *Wehrmacht*, one tribunal stated: 'The Tribunal believes that no declaration of criminality should be made with respect to the General Staff and High Command. [...] The Tribunal has heard much evidence as to the participation of these officers in planning and waging aggressive war, and in committing war crimes and crimes against humanity.' See Tim Coates, ed., *The Judgment of Nuremberg, 1946: The International Military Tribunal for the Trial of German Major War Criminals*, The Stationery Office: London, 2001, pp. 273-276.

[3] See Klaus Naumann, 'The "Unblemished" Wehrmacht: The Social History of a Myth', in Hannes Heer and Klaus Naumann, eds., *War of Extermination: The German Military in World War II, 1941-1944*, Berghahn: New York, 2000, pp. 417-429; Robert G. Moeller, 'In a Thousand Years, Every German will Speak of this Battle: Celluloid Memories of Stalingrad,' in Omer Bartov, Atina Grossmann and Mary Nolan, eds., *Crimes of War: Guilt and Denial in the Twentieth Century*, The New Press: New York, 2002, pp. 170-171; 'Kriegsgefangene aus Ungarn eingetroffen', *Frankfurter Rundschau*, 26 October 1953, p. 2. See also Robert G. Moeller, 'Victims in Uniform. West German Combat Movies from the 1950s,' in: Bill Niven, ed., *Germans as Victims: Remembering the Past in Contemporary Germany*, MacMillan: Basingstoke, 2006, pp. 43-61 (here: p. 43).

[4] Heinz Schröter, *Stalingrad – bis zur letzten Patrone*, Kaiser: Klagenfurt, 1958; *Letzte Briefe aus Stalingrad*, Bertelsmann: Gütersloh, 1954; Fritz Wöss, *Hunde, wollt ihr ewig leben*, Ullstein: Frankfurt am Main, 1958; It may be significant that Theodor Plievier's account of Stalingrad is not mentioned by the film, even though Wöss's novel appears to be a counter-text to Plievier's *Stalingrad* (1946).

[5] Quoted in Christian Streit, *Keine Kameraden: Die Wehrmacht und die sowjetischen Kriegsgefangenen 1941-1945*, Dietz: Bonn, 1991, p.115.

[6] Peter Reichel, *Vergangenheitsbewältigung in Deutschland: Die Auseinandersetzung mit der NS-Diktatur von 1945 bis heute*, C.H.Beck: Munich, 2001, p.116; Jay Lockenour, *Soldiers as Citizens: Former Wehrmacht Officers in the Federal Republic of Germany, 1945-1955*, University of Nebraska Press: Lincoln, 2001; Christian Hartmann, Johannes Hürter, Ulrike Jureit, eds., *Verbrechen der Wehrmacht: Bilanz einer Debatte*, C.H.Beck: Munich, 2005.

[7] Contemporary audiences were handed a leaflet containing the film credits as they left the cinemas. See 'Frei nach Schiller,' *Der Spiegel*, 15 April 1959, p. 68.

[8] The full speech is printed in Max Domarus, *Hitler: Reden und Proklamationen 1932-1945*, 2 vols in 4 parts, Süddeutscher Verlag: Munich, 1965, II, p. 1935.

[9] The full speech is printed in *Kölnische Zeitung*, 1 October 1942, pp. 1-2.

[10] Guido Knopp, *Die Gefangenen*, Goldmann: Munich, 2005, p. 24.

[11] Knopp, p. 384.

[12] See Frank Biess, 'Survivors of Totalitarianism: Returning POWs and the Reconstruction of Masculine Citizenship in West Germany, 1945-1955,' in: Hanna Schissler, ed., *The Miracle Years: A Cultural History of West Germany, 1949-1968*, Princeton University Press: Princeton, 2001, pp. 57-82 (here: pp. 59-63); Robert G. Moeller, 'Remembering the War in a Nation of Victims: West German Pasts in the 1950s,' in Schissler, pp. 83-109.

[13] See Biess, pp. 59-62.

[14] Omer Bartov, 'The Wehrmacht Exhibition Controversy: Politics of Evidence', in *Crimes of War*, pp. 41-60.

Samuel Salzborn

The German Myth of a Victim Nation: (Re-)presenting Germans as Victims in the New Debate on their Flight and Expulsion from Eastern Europe

Various German expellee organisations have lobbied for a Centre Against Expulsions to be built in Berlin, in 'historical and spatial proximity' to the Holocaust memorial. Their designs for the Centre place their own, 'German suffering', at the core of German collective memory both geographically and politically. The article argues that the implicit aim of the project is to ascribe to the collective body of the nation the role of a victim while relativising the German past, specifically National Socialism and World War II. The article analyzes how the topos 'Germans as victims' is represented in the current debate on the Centre Against Expulsions in Germany and examines historical implications of enabling this topos, as well as addressing the conflict between the myth of German innocence and historical reality.

From a sociological perspective it may be surprising that interest groups that were founded in reaction to an event 60 years ago continue to be of social and political relevance. The *Vertriebenenverbände* (expellee organisations)[1] which are the subject of this article might easily have lost their immediate significance and given up their existence after the admission and integration of the refugees into the social and economic fabric of the Federal Republic. Although this integration was not without its problems, it was generally accomplished by the late 1950s/early 1960s. Had it been the case that the expellee organisations had been founded with the sole purpose to represent the social and economic interests of those who had been displaced by flight and re-settlement as a result of National Socialism and the Second World War, this loss of significance would have most likely been the case. In this case only a few elderly people would still be telling stories about the former Eastern German territories, for example when they talked to their grandchildren about their own childhood. In the near future these territories would have the same social and political status that they have had in historiography and international law for quite some time: that of a closed chapter of German history.[2] However, the expellee organisations, which were founded illegally immediately after the unconditional surrender of

Nazi Germany,[3] were by no means conceived as a lobby with exclusively domestic political ambitions.[4] The concept of 'landsmannschaftlicher Gedanke'[5] was developed at an early stage, running counter to concepts of integration of the refugees into the Federal Republic. 'Landsmannschaftlicher Gedanke' implies that all refugees and re-settlers should not only live in their new 'Heimat' in the Federal Republic but should maintain a parallel mental existence in their 'alte Heimat' in order to safeguard a real German future for it. The identity of the new Federal citizens was supposed to be rooted in a *Landsmannschaft*, something that was articulated with a clearly recognisable territorial aspect. Since it was not just supposed to be concerned with the memory of times past but with the earliest possible restitution of the lost territories, the expellee organisations' concept of *Heimat* resulted in political demands that could only be perceived by the East European neighbour states as a provocation and a threat. Of particular importance here is the insistence on 'das Recht auf die Heimat' in the statutes of the expellee organisations. The definite article 'die' is still being stressed today. What is at stake is not that every human being should have a right to live wherever s/he happens to dwell but a concept of *Heimat* that is tied to a particular region or territory. In the case of the expellee organisations, their 'Heimat' has (again) become the home of Poles, Russians, Czechs and others. The claim to 'die Heimat' in the expellee organisations thus implicitly questions the right of East European neighbours to their home. This generally *völkisch* conception of 'die Heimat' in the expellee organisations' foreign policy ambitions was underlined by the fact that the re-settlers had already found a new home, either in the Federal Republic or in parts of the GDR. However, the political activities of the expellee organisations continue to this day, since they were not satisfied with this situation.

The political influence of the expellee organisations is certainly weaker today than it was 30 or 40 years ago – a time when they constituted a decisive factor in domestic policy and elections in West Germany. Nevertheless, the expellee organisations still make claims with respect to (foreign) policy and frequently manage to arouse public interest. The political claims that the expellee organisations stand for are linked to the moral function they have for a 'self-confident' German foreign policy. This can be illustrated by the fact that the expellee organisations have received generous financial support from past and present Federal governments, irrespective of which party was in power. That the ideas and demands of the expellee organisations still find an audience today is related to the new claim to sovereignty and normality in the politics of the Federal Republic which results from the transformations in Eastern Europe after 1989/90. Part of this new 'normality' is the 'levelling of the Nazi past'[6] in everyday consciousness; people's concrete historical knowledge about National Socialism is in decline and loses the meaning it had for the old Federal Republic. This goes hand in hand with a tendency to detach historical realities, events and developments from their concrete socio-political context in favour of a moralising view. One of the most prominent examples of this is the representation of flight and expulsion of Germans from the eastern territories, a development which is not seen in the context of National Socialism's politics of expansion and extermination. Thus flight and expulsion can be morally condemned (e.g. as condemnation of violence) without taking into account the historical and social responsibilities for those consequences of National Socialism.

This moralising approach to the German past is becoming increasingly significant in a time where an alleged 'taboo' on empathy with German experience is evoked continuously, while simultaneously the Nazi past is addressed everywhere, especially by politicians. The Federal Republic is at pains to correct the image of Germany abroad, for example by stressing the lessons Germany has learnt from history, by making statements against the far right or by introducing political measures against neo-Nazis. Simultaneously, the world is expected to recognise that the Germans, too, had been victims. The historical-political arguments of the expellee organisations are part of a larger discourse about the image of German history which has been the subject of controversial debates over the last twenty years, particularly from the conservative end of the political spectrum.[7] The aim of these conservative attempts to redefine Germany's relation to its Nazi past was the 'normalisation' of German history; the removal of the limitations on German politics (e.g. military interventions) due to the Nazi past was supposed to facilitate a renewed German geo-politics.[8] Conservative historians and politicians negated the historically exceptional status of National Socialism and the Holocaust in particular, attempting to exonerate the German past by applying concepts from 1950s totalitarianism theory that essentially equated

Nazism with Stalinism.[9] This line of argument essentially aims to relativise the political, historical and social relevance of National Socialism. The expellee organisations supplement this with an attempt to redefine the perpetrator-victim relationship. This is of extreme importance for their image of history and the narratives of political legitimacy that are derived from it. The ultimate aim of a rewriting of the perpetrator-victim relationship is the moral and historical legitimation of their hegemonic interests, that is, the claim to financial compensation by the Polish or Czech state. Simultaneously, this allows them to play a passive or innocent role through the 'construction of a victim community',[10] since the German responsibility for flight and expulsion is negated. The aim of this redefinition of the victim-perpetrator paradigm is to legitimise the image of the 'self-confident nation' as it was, for example, developed by the so-called 'New Right' in the 1990s.[11] The motivation of the expellee organisation is thus of a political nature rather than being concerned with a historically adequate interpretation of the past.

* * *

In the old Federal Republic, the expellee organisations frequently aroused negative public opinion, especially when they presented their claims rather aggressively. The recent shift in public discourse with respect to German wartime suffering, however, has furnished them with a more positive image and has allocated them a privileged role within that discourse. The expellee organisations' central argument is that flight, expulsion and resettlement at the end of the Second World War constituted an injustice in terms of international law. The ultimate goal is the inscription of this perspective within German historical memory in order to support their struggle for the 'Recht auf die Heimat' in the arena of international politics.

In the past, this argument has been presented with some restraint by the expellee organisations in the knowledge that these ideas and claims would lead to considerable political and diplomatic irritation on behalf of East European countries. However, since the expansion of the EU eastwards and the admission of Poland and the Czech Republic, their tone has become much harsher. Additionally, the legitimate basis of their argument was supposed to be made visible for everyone in the capital of the 'Berlin Republic' in the shape of a

Zentrum gegen Vertreibungen (Centre Against Expulsions). Erika Steinbach, president of the *Bund der Vertriebenen* (League of Expellees, *BdV*) and member of parliament for the CDU, is quite open about the benefits of this Centre for the expellee organisations. The Centre is supposed to be placed in 'historical and spatial proximity' to the Berlin Holocaust memorial.[12] The conceptual model for the project is the Holocaust Memorial Museum in Washington.

Considering the large number of memorial sites and their considerable divergence with respect to content – from German war memorials to the memorials for Nazi victims – the creation of the Centre against Expulsions does not immediately appear to be very significant. The commitment that is expressed in the plural of 'expulsions' in the Centre's title even seems to be a sign against inhumanity and crime, and thus seems to abstract from the usual historical revisionism of the expellee organisations.[13] And if there wasn't the issue of the German past and the Nazi *völkische* politics of extermination, and if history was merely a succession of dates rather than a nexus of causalities, this would probably be the case.

However, the desired spatial closeness to the Holocaust memorial takes the flight and expulsion of the Germans out of its historical context. The purpose of this is to lend legitimacy to the claim that the Germans, too, had been victims, since they had suffered under Hitler. While this certainly applies to Hitler's racial and political victims as well as to those who were designated 'inferior' by Nazi ideology, it is certainly incorrect with respect to the majority of Germans.[14] Above all, the Germans are supposed to have suffered 'after Hitler' or 'from the consequences of Hitler'. Opinion polls on behalf of the German daily *Frankfurter Allgemeine Zeitung* (23 October 2003) and the Polish newspaper *Gazeta Wyborcza* (21 October 2003) found that over 90% of Germans are of the opinion that the Germans are victims of the Second World War.

The expellee organisations' desire for 'historical' proximity of their Centre to the Holocaust memorial is thus directly connected to their desire for a discursive proximity of the expulsion to the German mass murder of European Jews, or more precisely, to their status as victims. The intended location of the Centre Against Expulsions in the nation's capital turns the expellee organisations into representatives of a national tragedy. This ascribes victim status to the Germans as a whole and implicitly puts them historically on the same footing with the murdered Jews. In Erika Steinbach's words: 'Im Grunde genommen ergänzen sich die Themen Juden und Vertriebene miteinander. Dieser entmenschte Rassenwahn hier wie dort, der soll auch Thema in unserem Zentrum sein.'[15]

This comparison turns history upside down. The expulsion of the Germans was a reaction to National Socialism, to the racial policies of the Nazi state and the Holocaust. In contrast to Nazi policy, it was established in the Potsdam Agreement (article XIII) in accordance with the principles of international law. Furthermore, the term 'Rassenwahn' is inappropriate with respect to the resettlement of Germans from the eastern territories. The resettlement was not racially motivated but a reaction to the conflict potential of National Socialism's racial policies. The German minorities in Eastern Europe (a large part of the later expellees) had stirred up social and political conflicts and had played an active part in the Nazi policies of Germanisation. The most well known example of this is the 'Volkstumskampf' by large sections of the *Sudeten* German minority against Czechoslovakian democracy.[16] The Allies' objective was thus to prevent future conflict.

This politics of destabilising neighbouring countries with *völkisch* organisations was the basis of Nazi foreign policy at least until Nazi Germany pursued its interest by military means. This *Volkstumspolitik*, which was to lead ultimately to the resettlement of the German population in the East, was a central aspect of the preparation and execution of Nazi imperial and genocidal policies. Recent research in social history has exposed a structural connection between German *völkisch* and minority policies in Eastern Europe and the mass extermination of European Jewry.[17]

The expellee organisations' desire to represent themselves as victims with their Centre Against Expulsions implies thus a forgetting of the anti-Semitic and genocidal policies pursued by National Socialism and German minorities. Furthermore, it implies a denial of the fact that the Allied decision to resettle the Germans from the eastern territories was not ethnically but politically motivated. While the cruelties that occurred during the expulsion are doubtlessly morally reprehensible, this does not change the historically legitimate and legal character of the resettlement.

Erika Steinbach's statement that the 'topics of Jews and expellees' were complementary is not just a distortion of history; the Centre

Against Expulsions would cost an estimated 82 million Euros in contrast to the Holocaust memorial which cost around 25.5 million Euros.[18] Instead of putting the expulsions into a historical context, the Centre Against Expulsions would obscure the causal connections between Nazi *völkisch* and genocidal politics in the East and flight and expulsion of the Germans from the eastern territories.

In order to devalue any critique of the planned Centre Against Expulsions its supporters take recourse to morality, which appears without doubt to be on their side. Who is not moved by the terrible photographs that depict people fleeing from the East? Who is not morally outraged at the sight of these images? However, the code of politics is different from the code of morality, as Hans-Magnus Enzensberger has poignantly noted.[19] It is important to make this distinction; historical arguments in the debate about a Centre Against Expulsions cannot and should not be devalued politically by emotive attitudes. The purpose of a moralist reduction of flight and expulsion to the aspect of violence is to abstract from German historical and political responsibility and to project that responsibility onto the Allies. Simultaneously, it abstracts from the concrete historical situation as well as from the political interests that are the basis of this situation. The main problem here is that a Centre Against Expulsions in Germany would further detach the past from its historical and political context. The Centre would remove not only the chronological but above all the causal connection between Nazi settlement and extermination policies and flight and expulsion from collective memory. The goal is thus not a realistic and historically appropriate view of the past but a sanctioning of flight and expulsion as collective injustice for which there is no individual responsibility or guilt on the German side. The social philosopher Theodor W. Adorno noted in his *Minima Moralia* that the concept of universal wrong obscures any individual responsibility: 'In der abstrakten Vorstellung des universalen Unrechts geht jede konkrete Verantwortung unter.'[20]

The problem here is not the topic of flight and expulsion as such and the search for an adequate interpretation and historisation. Rather, the way in which this engagement with the past takes shape in the Centre Against Expulsions is to be criticised. The former vice president of the *Bundestag*, Antje Vollmer, criticised the approach of the expellee organisations when she noted that their political approach to the topic of flight and expulsion has to be understood as a wish to keep the memory of the experience alive, however, 'nicht im Sinne des Mitleids, sondern im Sinne einer offenen Rechnung'.[21] The new German victim discourse is thus less an encounter with the suffering of individuals than it is an attempt to conceive and represent flight and expulsion as collectively experienced injustice. The central aim is not the enlightenment about the past but the creation of a collective victim identity to support the political demands of the expellee organisations. The historian Peter Steinbach notes:

> Die Deutung der Vergangenheit wird dabei nicht nur zum Streitfall, sondern sie kann auch, national wie international, zum Ziel politischer Einflussnahme werden – sei es, um bestimmte Inhalte kollektiver Identität zu beeinflussen, sei es, um politische Gegner mit historischen Argumenten zu bekämpfen, sei es, um in den internationalen Interessenkonflikten Ansprüche historisch zu rechtfertigen.[22]

The collectivising of individual histories aims at a revision of the historical context. On the one hand it negates the historical origins of flight and expulsion, on the other hand it calls the legitimacy of their consequences into question. The fragmentation of history into apparently unconnected events facilitates the contemporary delegitimation of the post-war anti-fascist European order, following the Allied defeat of National Socialism. Only when flight and expulsion are no longer perceived in the context of National Socialism is it possible to morally exonerate and present them collectively as injustice. This is simultaneously a de-politicisation of history as history is no longer presented and interpreted in its causal connections and contexts.

Moralising is an integral part of this process. This can be best observed in the German right's inability to speak of flight and expulsion without resorting to nationalist and delusional terminology.[23] However, the moralising line of argument is also part of a conscious political strategy. The expellee organisations' de-politicised argumentation aims at creating assent precisely by appealing to people's emotions and moral sense.

This process has been described by Sabine Moller as 'Entkonkretisierung'[24] – a moralising perspective that makes everything comparable with everything else because the facts have become completely distorted. The complex nature of historical reality is reduced to apparently omnipresent fragments by emotional regression. Thus every analogy appears to make sense because its addressees are no longer conscious of any epistemological and judgemental context; they merely evaluate historical events according to the criteria of 'good' and 'evil' without taking into account their contexts and political motivations.

This process is best illustrated by recent research into the memory of National Socialism within German families which has shown that the children and grandchildren of Nazi-perpetrators frequently turn their parents and grandparents into victims. The reason for this is that they on the one hand have little knowledge about the Nazi past and the Holocaust and on the other hand perceive their parents and grandparents as victims of Nazi persecution, terror, bombings and war captivity.[25] As the generation of children and grandchildren judges the latter to be 'bad' and 'evil', their own parents and grandparents are re-codified as resistance fighters and victims of National Socialism.

The origin of this kind of reflex is not least the lack of substantial, precise and detailed engagement with National Socialism which is largely dealt with as a moral problem without conscious engagement with its historical and political reality. Any conscious engagement with this period would need to contain the acknowledgement that the Nazi regime enjoyed wide support in the German population – especially in the annexed and invaded Eastern European territories. It would have to acknowledge that the majority of Germans actively and passively participated in the extermination of the Jews (whether by participating in expropriations, lootings, denunciations, killings, deportations etc., or through silence and lack of resistance, by spreading anti-Semitic or racist sentiment or by profiting from forced labour and 'Aryanisation'). Finally, it would have to acknowledge that it was possible to execute the Nazi policies of resettlement and extermination in such a barbaric manner because there was a wide consensus between Nazi leaders and the German population.

The aim of the recent debate about flight and expulsion of Germans as result of National Socialism does thus not constitute an engagement with the individual fates and people's traumatic experiences, experiences that are independent of the victim-perpetrator-paradigm, as Alfred Krozova has convincingly argued.[26] The concept of traumatic experience refers both to violence experienced as well as executed violence. As the result of an experience of violence, traumatic experience does not immediately contain any political or moral judgement or attribution of guilt. Thus it was possible for the Germans as a 'derart in ihren Wahnzielen bloßgestellte, der grausamsten Verbrechen überführte Population' to be first and foremost concerned with themselves, as Alexander and Margarete Mitscherlich put it in their seminal study *Die Unfähigkeit zu trauern*.[27]

Under National Socialism, the German collective followed a doctrine that allocated to the Germans a privileged position in the world. This allowed them to project their own aggression onto designated 'others' who, by that projection, were turned into sub-human creatures. For the overwhelming majority of Germans after the war, this fact did not result in a feeling of shame, instead they resorted to the infantile excuse that they had 'only' obeyed their *Führer*. This explains, as the Mitscherlichs underline, the

> Neigung vieler Deutscher, nach dem Kriegsende die Rolle des unschuldigen Opfers einzunehmen. Jeder einzelne erlebt die Enttäuschung *seiner* Wünsche nach Schutz und Führung; er ist mißleitet, verführt, im Stich gelassen und schließlich vertrieben und verachtet worden, und dabei war er doch nur folgsam, wie die erste Bürgerpflicht es befahl.[28]

This infantile position does not only 'forget' the historical facts, but it turns the victim-perpetrator paradigm upside down. It turns the paradigm to the advantage of the Germans insofar as the remorse expressed in this attitude relates only to the destruction and extermination of the Germans' own character and desires.

The defence mechanisms against guilt and the denial of the past that are manifest in the immediate post-war period went hand in hand with an almost ritual cultivation of one's own innocence and one's own status as a victim. The frequently uttered claim that there had been a social taboo to speak about this topic can be explained by the lack of critical reflection on the repressed causes of flight and expulsion, despite the large amount of historiographical, sociological, political and literary publications on this theme. It is not necessary to refer to the prominent critic Marcel Reich-Ranicki who pointed out the non-existence of such a taboo in an interview with the *Frankfurter Allgemeine Zeitung*;[29] any unprejudiced look at the German past will confirm the impression that flight and expulsion of Germans is a topic that at no time during the history of the Federal Republic had been subject to a taboo. Rather than subject to a taboo, the topic was 'omnipresent' as early as the 1950s and an important medium for the Germans to represent themselves as a 'nation of victims', as Robert G. Moeller points out.[30] Simultaneously, however, the issue of perpetration with respect to the Holocaust was played down in public discourse:[31]

In the diction of the *Vertriebenenverbände*, the expulsions constituted not only a 'crime against humanity and a violation of the basic ethical principles of our civilization'. Because of their indiscriminate brutality and sweeping scope, they amounted to something much worse: 'the greatest collective crime in history' which endowed the expellees with a victim status comparable to that of Jewish survivors of the Holocaust.[32]

The purpose of the Centre Against Expulsions is to situate the Germans' own suffering in the centre of the memory of the Nazi war. What is new about this is not the German feeling of being a nation of victims, this myth had been widespread in Germany already in the 1950s and 1960s. What is new in this claim to victim status is the vehemence and aggression with which it is articulated, especially by the league of expellees. New is also the strategy of international focus, as the moral and political claims against Poland and the Czech Republic are validated under the guise of an allegedly global memory of a 'Century of Expulsions'. The imagined claim of German collective guilt, a concept that was never part of an Allied political strategy,[33] is countered by an interpretation of history that is likely to generate the myth of a German collective innocence.

One central aspect of this inverted representation of historical reality is the collectivisation of individual experiences of German refugees. This results in an undue generalisation of individual memories of German refugees which ignores the political context in favour of a moralised view of the past. However, in this representation of the German past as history of German victims there is no room for disharmonious elements of memory. This means that the generalising term 'expulsion' obscures the ambiguous and contradictory nature of the historically diverse phenomenon which took place in several phases. The 'expulsion', as conservative historian Theodor Schieder argued shortly after the war, is an aggregate of four phases of evacuation, flight, expulsion and deportation/resettlement with permanently changing variables (participants, legal situation, local and temporal micro-context etc). According to Schieder these four phases were distinctly different in character while partially historically overlapping.[34]

This is important for the debate on representations of flight and expulsions insofar as the choice of a *generalising* term, namely a term that is supposed to describe a longer historical process, is made in order to highlight the general, or rather, what can be generalised. However, the term 'expulsion' represents something linguistically that cannot be generalised historically in this way. The events that can be described as 'expulsion' only represent a small part of a larger process. The first phase according to Schieder is the evacuation by German units as 'Ausdruck einer zusammenbrechenden Staatsgewalt ohne tiefere Autorität'. The ensuing flight was followed by a brief phase of 'wild', i.e. inofficial and unorganised, expulsions before the Potsdam Conference. These were in some regions supposed to create 'vollendete Tatsachen vor den Entscheidungen der großen Politik' with respect to borders and transfer of population. The last phase was that of 'organisierten Ausweisungen nach den Potsdamer Beschlüssen'.[35] Evacuation – flight – expulsion – deportation (resettlement): expulsion itself was thus only one of a series of phases.

This insistence on terminological differentiation and on the particularity of detail might seem petty at first sight. However, the reason for this demand for precision is that the term 'Vertreibung' (expulsion) has acquired general acceptance in public discourse until today. It was purposefully introduced after the Second World War despite the fact that historiography had established the above mentioned four phases very early on. The term 'Vertreibung' was intentionally launched as part of victim terminology and as part of a political strategy. The language of 'expulsion' was supposed to underline the status and the representation of the resettled Germans as victims.[36]

The term 'Vertreibung' was thus introduced some years after the end of WWII as official victim term with the purpose of morally legitimising the claims of the expellee organisations. It replaced hitherto commonly used terms like 'Umsiedlung' (re-settlement), 'Ausweisung' (deportation) or 'Flucht' (flight). As the representative 1959 work *Die Vertriebenen in Westdeutschland* explains, 'Wort und Begriff des "Vertriebenen"' implicitly expresses the 'Unrecht der Vertreibung'. The term 'expellee' denotes 'eine andere Würde als der Name Flüchtling'.[37] In this sense one has to understand the 'deutsche Rechtsterminus "Vertriebener"', as 'fortlaufender Protest gegen das Unrecht der Vertreibung'.[38] This is the reason why 'Flüchtling' (refugee) or 'Umsiedler' (re-settler) were rejected as collective terms: the re-settlement was supposed to be understood as passively endured injustice and everything that denoted responsibility or active participation was supposed to be removed from memory. With a view to the planned Centre Against Expulsions, the introduction of the term 'expulsion' anticipates terminologically contemporary attempts to realise the claims by the *League of Expellees* on a political and historically binding level. The demand for a scholarly debate about the generalising tendency of the term 'expulsion' does not call into question historical facts but is in the interest of terminological precision with regard to the interpretation of these facts. The term 'Ausweisung', initially introduced by Theodor Schieder to describe one phase, might be considered as a suitable scholarly overall term. On the one hand, it includes the component of coercion while leaving it open whether this is due to anticipatory action (as in 'Flucht') or whether it happened in conjunction to physical violence (as in 'wilde Vertreibungen'). On the other hand, however, it lacks the moralising overtones of 'Vertreibung', or – on the other side of the political spectrum – 'Umsiedlung' while including semantic indicators that there were historical and political reasons for these events. Moreover, the term 'Ausweisung' points to the legal basis of these events in the framework of international law. Another which might be regarded as too sterile due to its legalese character is that of 'Bevölkerungstransfer' (transfer of population). In contrast to 'Ausweisung', however, it would underline the aspects of the politics of migration and thus implicitly point to the potential for conflict as a result of the transfer process.

A serious scholarly debate about the term 'expulsion' in Germany has yet to take place. The term can only be considered as having been consciously implemented for political reasons; it was ultimately institutionalised in legally binding form though article 16 of the *Basic Law* (1949) and later through Section 1 of the *Bundesvertriebenengesetz* (Federal Law on Expellees, 1953). Those who supported the institutionalisation of this terminology, however, were not primarily concerned with the people affected and their problems. This is evident from the fact that Theodor Schieder, who oversaw the *Dokumentation der Vertreibung der Deutschen aus Ost-Mitteleuropa* comprising several thousand pages,[39] produced a report on behalf of the Federal Ministry for Expellees on the 'gesamten Komplex der Dokumentensammlung' without having seen 'auch nur einen der vorliegenden Zeitzeugenberichte über die Vertreibung am Ende des Zweiten Weltkrieges'.[40] Although Schieder was doubtlessly familiar with the topic and methodologically competent, his approach reveals the political intention of the enterprise, one that abstracts from the individual fate without knowing it. According to Mathias Beer, through this approach historiography was supposed to underpin and legitimise in a scholarly way the 'außenpolitischen Ziele des Staates' and thus could 'nach wie vor national sinnstiftend wirken'. The ultimate purpose of this kind of historiography is to make history manageable for a collective project.[41] This is not about the 'immediate perception of the individual case' as Arnold Sywottek put it.[42] On the contrary, the individual case is de-individualised in order to represent a historical problem. Thus historical events become generalised before a scholarly debate about the possibility to generalise and typify has even taken place. The aim of the representation of Germans as victims is not enlightenment about historical realities but the creation of a certain collective identity.

The Centre Against Expulsions in the way intended by the *League of Expellees* is thus anything but a form of productive engagement with the past – something that is nevertheless necessary. Such an engagement with the past should certainly address the crimes that occurred during flight and expulsion, even if (or because) this topic is one of the most thoroughly researched within recent German history. However, the new German victim discourse is not concerned with a critical reflection of the past, by which, according to Adorno, 'man das Vergangene im Ernst verarbeite, seinen Bann breche durch helles Bewußtsein'.[43] It is instead concerned with the restitution of the 'aufrechte Gang', as the categorical farewell to the past is euphemistically known in Germany.

Translation by Helmut Schmitz

Notes

[1] The expellee organisations possess a wide network of political and cultural organisations, though not all refugees and expellees were members of these organisations. The umbrella organisation *Bund der Vertriebenen* (*BdV*) currently gives a number of two million members. This number is probably inflated, though, and is supposed to give the impression that the expellee organisations still have mass support today.

[2] The historical and legal status of the former Eastern German territories was initially determined at the Potsdam Conference. The bilateral contracts between Germany and

its East European neighbours in the early 1990s confirmed the status of these territories as no longer belonging to Germany. The Two-Plus-Four contract finally established the East German border as definite and fixed with respect to international law.

[3] These types of organisations were initially prohibited by the Allies who feared a renaissance of militarism and nationalism.

[4] Cf. Samuel Salzborn, *Grenzenlose Heimat. Geschichte, Gegenwart und Zukunft der Vertriebenenverbände*, Elefanten Press: Berlin, 2000, pp. 52ff.

[5] A *Landsmannschaft* is a welfare and cultural association for Germans from areas of the former *Reich*.

[6] Gerd Wiegel, *Die Zukunft der Vergangenheit. Konservativer Geschichtsdiskurs und kulturelle Hegemonie*, PapyRossa: Köln, 2001, p. 399.

[7] See the documentation on the 'Historians' Controversy', James Knowlton and Truett Cates, trans., *Forever in the Shadow of Hitler? Original Documents on the Historikerstreit concerning the Singularity of the Holocaust*, Humanities Press: New Jersey, 1993. See also Peter Baldwin, ed., *Reworking the Past: Hitler, the Holocaust and the Historians' Debate*, Beacon Press: Boston/Mass. 1990.

[8] Cf. Wiegel.

[9] See esp. Johannes Klotz, Ulrich Schneider, eds., *Die selbstbewusste Nation und ihr Geschichtsbild. Geschichtslegenden der Neuen Rechten*, PapyRossa: Cologne, 1997.

[10] Hans-Dieter König, 'Ein Neonazi in Auschwitz. Tiefenhermeneutische Rekonstruktion einer Filmsequenz aus Bonengels *Beruf Neonazi* und ihre Wirkung im kulturellen Klima der Postmoderne,' in: Hans-Dieter König, ed., *Sozialpsychologie des Rechtsextremismus*, Suhrkamp: Frankfurt am Main, 1998, pp. 372-415 (here: p. 411).

[11] Cf. Heimo Schwilk, Ulrich Schacht, eds., *Die selbstbewusste Nation. 'Anschwellender Bocksgesang' und weitere Beiträge zu einer deutschen Debatte*, Ullstein: Berlin, 1994.

[12] Cf. Dieter Wonka, 'Vertriebene für Gedenkstätte neben Holocaust-Mahnmal,' *Leipziger Volkszeitung*, 29 May 2000, p. 3.

[13] Cf. Samuel Salzborn, *Grenzenlose Heimat*, pp. 131ff.

[14] Cf. Robert Gellately, *Backing Hitler. Consent and Coercion in Nazi Germany*, Oxford UP: Oxford, 2001; Daniel Jonah Goldhagen, *Hitler's willing executioners. Ordinary Germans and the Holocaust*, Knopf: New York, 1996.

[15] quoted after Wonka, p. 3.

[16] Cf. Volker Zimmermann, *Die Sudetendeutschen im NS-Staat. Politik und Stimmung der Bevölkerung im Reichsgau Sudetenland (1938–1945)*, Klartext: Essen, 1999. In comparison to the *völkische* struggle of the Sudeten-German minority in Czechoslovakia, the activities of German minorities in other regions had been waged with less aggression and destructive force. Nevertheless, these German minorities frequently had a profoundly de-stabilising and disintegrating role during the 1920s and 1930s, which disturbed social cohesion. See the survey of research in Samuel Salzborn, *Ethnisierung der Politik. Theorie und Geschichte des Volksgruppenrechts in Europa*, Campus: Frankfurt am Main and New York, 2005, pp. 73ff.

[17] Cf. Ingo Haar, 'Deutsche "Ostforschung" und Antisemitismus,' in: *Zeitschrift für Geschichtswissenschaft*, 6 (2000), 485-508; Isabel Heinemann, *"Rasse, Siedlung, deutsches Blut". Das Rasse- und Siedlungshauptamt der SS und die rassenpolitische Neuordnung Europas*, Wallstein: Göttingen, 2003.

[18] Cf. Samuel Salzborn, 'Ein neuer deutscher Opferdiskurs. Zur Bedeutung der Vertriebenenverbände und ihrer Anliegen für politische Debatten der Gegenwart,' in: Christoph Butterwegge et al., *Themen der Rechten – Themen der Mitte. Zuwanderung, demografischer Wandel und Nationalbewusstsein*, Leske + Budrich: Opladen, 2002, pp. 147-166 (here: p. 151). The equation of the Holocaust with the resettlement of Germans after the war is part of Erika Steinbach's rhetorics. The newspaper *Frankfurter Rundschau* had already in their edition of 12 December 1998 issued a symbolic red card as 'intellektuellen Platzverweis'.

[19] Hans Magnus Enzensberger, 'Blinder Frieden,' *Frankfurter Allgemeine Zeitung*, 15 April 2003.

[20] Theodor W. Adorno, *Minima Moralia. Reflexionen aus dem beschädigten Leben*, in: Theodor W. Adorno, <u>Gesammelte Schriften</u>, vol. 4, Suhrkamp: Frankfurt am Main, 1997, p. 25.

[21] Antje Vollmer, 'Tiefe Resignation,' Interview, *Süddeutsche Zeitung*, 9 February 2002.

[22] Peter Steinbach, 'Geschichte und Politik – nicht nur ein wissenschaftliches Verhältnis,' *Aus Politik und Zeitgeschichte*, 28 (2001), 3-7 (here: p. 7).

[23] One of the best examples of this in the recent past is Klaus Rainer Röhl's *Verbotene Trauer. Ende der deutschen Tabus*, Universitas Verlag: Munich, 2002.

[24] Sabine Moller, *Die Entkonkretisierung der NS-Herrschaft in der Ära Kohl*, Offizin: Hanover, 1998.

[25] Cf. Harald Welzer/Sabine Moller/Karoline Tschuggnall, *„Opa war kein Nazi". Nationalsozialismus und Holocaust im Familiengedächtnis*, Fischer: Frankfurt am Main, 2002.

[26] Alfred Krovoza, 'Die (west-)deutsche Gesellschaft nach dem Gewaltexzeß von Zweitem Weltkrieg und Judenvernichtung,' in: Loccumer Initiative kritischer Wissenschaftlerinnen und Wissenschaftler, ed., *Gewalt und Zivilisation in der bürgerlichen Gesellschaft*, Offizin: Hanover, 2001, pp. 110-123.

[27] Alexander und Margarete Mitscherlich, *Die Unfähigkeit zu trauern. Grundlagen kollektiven Verhaltens*, Piper: Munich, [13]1980, p. 35.

[28] Ibid., pp. 53f.

[29] Marcel Reich-Ranicki, 'Die Berliner sollten lieber Kleist aufführen!,' Interview, *Frankfurter Allgemeine Zeitung*, 19 February 2002.

[30] Robert G. Moeller, 'Als der Krieg nach Deutschland kam,' *Frankfurter Allgemeine Zeitung*, 8 June 2002; Robert G. Moeller, 'Die Vertreibung aus dem Osten und westdeutsche Trauerarbeit,' in: Brigitta Huhnke/Björn Krondorfer, eds., *Das Vermächtnis annehmen. Kulturelle und biographische Zugänge zum Holocaust – Beiträge aus den USA und Deutschland*, Psychosozial Verlag: Giessen, 2002, pp. 113-148.

[31] Cf. Samuel Salzborn, 'Los perpetradores de la Shoá. Sobre el desarrollo de la investigación acerca de los culpables en Alemania,' *Nuestra Memoria*, 20 (2002), pp. 8-10.

[32] Pertti Ahonen, *After the Expulsion. West Germany and Eastern Europe 1945–1990*, Oxford UP: Oxford, 2003 p. 46.

[33] Cf. Wolfgang Benz, 'Kollektivschuld,' in: Wolfgang Benz, ed., *Legenden, Lügen, Vorurteile. Ein Wörterbuch zur Zeitgeschichte*, dtv: Munich, [5]1994, pp. 117-119.

[34] Theodor Schieder, 'Die Vertreibung der Deutschen aus dem Osten als wissenschaftliches Problem,' *Vierteljahrshefte für Zeitgeschichte*, 1 (1960), 1-16 (here: pp. 10f).

[35] Ibid.

[36] Cf. Karin Böke, '*Flüchtlinge* und *Vertriebene* zwischen dem *Recht auf die alte Heimat* und der *Eingliederung in die neue Heimat*. Leitvokabeln der Flüchtlingspolitik,' in: Karin Böke/Frank Liedtke/Martin Wengeler, *Politische Leitvokabeln in der Adenauer-Ära*, deGruyter: Berlin/New York, 1996, pp. 131-210.

[37] Heinrich Rogge, 'Vertreibung und Eingliederung im Spiegel des Rechts,' in: Eugen Lemberg/Friedrich Edding, eds., *Die Vertriebenen in Westdeutschland. Ihre Eingliederung und ihr Einfluß auf Gesellschaft, Wirtschaft, Politik und Geistesleben* (3 volumes), vol. 1, Hirt Verlag: Kiel, 1959, pp. 174-245 (here: p. 190).

[38] Ibid.

[39] Cf. Mathias Beer, 'Im Spannungsfeld von Politik und Zeitgeschichte. Das Großforschungsprojekt "Dokumentation der Vertreibung der Deutschen aus Ost-Mitteleuropa",' in: *Vierteljahrshefte für Zeitgeschichte*, 3 (1998), 345-389; Mathias Beer, 'Die Dokumentation der Vertreibung der Deutschen aus Ost-Mitteleuropa. Hintergründe – Entstehung – Ergebnis – Wirkung,' in: *Geschichte in Wissenschaft und Unterricht*, 2 (1999), 99-117.

[40] Mathias Beer, 'Der "Neuanfang" der Zeitgeschichte nach 1945. Zum Verhältnis von nationalsozialistischer Umsiedlungs- und Vernichtungspolitik und der Vertreibung der Deutschen aus Ostmitteleuropa,' in: Winfried Schulze/Otto Gerhard Oexle, eds., *Deutsche Historiker im Nationalsozialismus*, Fischer: Frankfurt am Main, 1999, pp. 274-301 (here: p. 281).

[41] Ibid., p. 282.

[42] Arnold Sywottek, '"Umsiedlung" und "Räumung", "Flucht" und "Ausweisung" – Bemerkungen zur deutschen Flüchtlingsgeschichte,' in: Rainer Schulze/Doris von der Brelie-Lewien/Helga Grebing, eds., *Flüchtlinge und Vertriebene in der westdeutschen Nachkriegsgeschichte. Bilanzierung der Forschung und Perspektiven für die künftige Forschungsarbeit*, Lax: Hildesheim, 1987, pp. 69-80 (here: p. 72).

[43] Theodor W. Adorno, 'Was bedeutet: Aufarbeitung der Vergangenheit,' in: Theodor W. Adorno, *Kulturkritik und Gesellschaft II*, Gesammelte Schriften, vol. 10.2, Suhrkamp: Frankfurt am Main, 1997, pp. 555-72 (here: p. 555).

Bill Niven

Implicit Equations in Constructions of German Suffering

The *Bund der Vertriebenen* has both benefited from and played a key role in the recent debates about German suffering. The chapter discusses the revisionist politics of the *Bund der Vertriebenen* with respect to Poland and the Czech Republic since the end of the Soviet Union, before analysing the representation of expulsions in the Berlin exhibition *Erzwungene Wege*, organised by the *Bund der Vertriebenen* as a model for the planned Centre Against Expulsions. It argues that the exhibition attempts to implicitly equate the German expulsions to the suffering of the Armenians, thus writing the Holocaust out of the history of 20th century expulsions.

Preamble

The use of comparisons with National Socialism in the political realm is hardly new. Over recent years, however, such deployment seems, if possible, to have increased. A particularly offensive year was 2002. First of all, former Christian Democratic Chancellor Helmut Kohl compared Social Democrat Wolfgang Thierse, at the time President of the *Bundestag*, to Hermann Göring.[1] In the same month, the then Federal Minister of Justice, Herta Däubler-Gmelin, compared George Bush's alleged attempt to detract from domestic problems by going to war in Irak with the policies of Adolf Hitler.[2] Also in September 2002, Christoph Stölzl, head of Berlin's Christian Democrats at the time, compared the victory of the SPD and Greens in Berlin's regional election to Nazi election victories in 1931/32.[3] In 2003, the Italians demonstrated their flair for such comparisons when Silvio Berlusconi, prime minister at the time, suggested that German EU parliamentarian Martin Schulz would make a good concentration camp guard,[4] while Italy's then Minister of Tourism Stefano Stefani described German tourists as 'supernationalistic blonds' given to invading Italian beaches in a drunken stupor – a comment which provoked such protest that Stefani resigned.[5] The political fall-out from such comparisons can be considerable; as a result of the indignation caused by Däubler-Gmelin's comments, she decided not to stand for reappointment as Minister after the general elections of September 2002. Not all politicians, however, simply resign when the protests start. In that year of offence, 2002, Christian Democrat Minister

President of Hesse, Roland Koch, was so angry at the naming of wealthy citizens by union leader Frank Bsirske in the course of a debate on wealth tax that he accused the latter of introducing 'eine neue Form von Stern an der Brust'.[6] Although Koch apologised in response to the indignation caused by his remarks, he did not step down as Minister President of Hesse.

Not all of these comparisons – witness Kohl's and Däubler-Gmelin's – were made in public. The 'leaking' of a comparison is not the same thing as explicitly making one in the public realm. But the politicians involved are still responsible for their utterances, and surely know the risks attached to being 'overheard'. That such comparisons continue to be made despite the associated protest at their unfairness can surely be put down to the fact that, in the heat of the moment, the temptation to defame a political opponent by calling him a Nazi is simply too hard to resist; equally hard to resist, seemingly, is the wish to align oneself, or the constituents and groups one represents, with the victims of Nazism, particularly the Jews. In the same moment as branding Bsirske a latter-day Nazi, Koch's comparison would have us believe that the wealthy classes are today's Jews. Borrowing from the victim status of the Jews is not a practice restricted to politicians, but the agenda behind it is always political. Cologne Cardinal Meisner's comparison of the murder of millions by Stalin and Hitler with the 'millionfold murder' of unborn children is a good example;[7] the unquestionable victim status of those murdered under totalitarianism is mobilised in an attempt to reinforce the legitimacy of the Church's position on abortion. Another example would be the 'Holocaust on Your Plate' campaign and exhibition launched in 2003 by the American animal rights' organisation, Peta, in protest at the mass farming of chickens, an exhibition which set side by side photographs of the death camps with photographs from animal factory farms and slaughterhouses.[8] The campaign was also launched in Germany a year later.[9]

In the end, such explicit deployments of Nazi and Holocaust comparisons in the public realm come and go in rapid succession without appearing to undermine the general consensus that they are utterly improper; after all, they depend for their effectiveness as publicity stunts, arguably, on their very inappropriateness. But there are forms of comparison which, while less explicit, are more systematic and therefore more insidious and potentially destabilising than any of the above examples, all of which were as ephemeral as they were scandalous. I am thinking here particularly of what I would call a process of *implicit equation* in Germany today between the severity of the crimes of the Germans under Hitler in occupied territories such as Czechoslovakia and Poland, and the sometimes murderous expulsion of the ethnic Germans from Czechoslovakia and Poland at the end of the Second World War. One rarely reads in a German newspaper, or hears a German politician say in a public statement that the treatment of the Sudeten Germans or East Prussian Germans in 1945 bears direct comparison to the treatment of Jews, Poles and Czechs under Nazism. Instead, one can observe developments in the political and public realm in Germany which point implicitly to the belief that such comparison is legitimate, and that there is a need to address a range of political, juridical and ethical issues which stem from this comparability. In short, the view underlying these developments is this: the Czechs and Poles in 1945-1946 treated the ethnic Germans in many ways as badly as the Germans, before that, treated the inhabitants of the territories they had occupied. While the Germans have faced up to their past of murder and misdemeanour, so the (usually) unstated argument runs, the Czechs and Poles have not, and it is about time they did. Equally, there is an implication that the Germans not only have a duty to focus in commemoration on those upon whom they inflicted injustice and suffering, but also a *right* to focus on those Germans upon whom injustice and suffering was inflicted by others.

One might, of course, want to observe that a view of Czech and Polish conduct at the end of the war as comparable with German conduct during it is a much more justified position, say, than a view of Bush as being like Hitler. This can hardly be denied. The comparisons cited at the beginning of the chapter are self-evidently absurd. One might also argue that it is historiographically *necessary* to see the expulsion of ethnic Germans in relation to the discrimination against Jews, Poles and Slavs under Hitler. Was not ethnic hatred and intolerance towards the however defined 'other' a generic twentieth-century phenomenon? And surely it is also necessary as a matter of ethical principle. If one accepts that it was wrong of Hitler to seek to drive out the Jews from Germany, then for the sake of moral consistency one must surely also accept that it was wrong of the Poles and Czechs to drive out the Germans. Equally, can the murder of a

Jew, say, by an SS man really be considered any more horrendous
than the killing of a Sudeten German by Czech militia simply because
he, or she, is a German?

These arguments are, in themselves, very forceful. But it needs to
be stressed that in the climate of cumulative equation I discuss below
there is little contextual discussion of arguments, indeed little
discussion. This is certainly a failing. After all, any serious
comparative engagement would have to acknowledge differences and
sequences as well as similarities: thus the expulsion of the ethnic
Germans was *significantly* motivated by hatred towards Germans
which accumulated during the years of occupation; it was a *result* of
the German war; it did *not* end in genocide, unlike the persecution of
the Jews, whatever the acts of individual murder; while the Jews were
absolute victims, the victimhood of the expellees is *qualified*, certainly
in the case of the Sudeten Germans, by their support of Nazism in the
late 1930s (although the expulsion itself affected mostly women and
children, the latter certainly innocent *without* qualification).
Arguments and counter-arguments are the stuff of true discourse, and
while this discourse may be taking place in historiography, in
Germany's public realm it is rarely engaged in at the level of
complexity that would be necessary.

In the course of this chapter, I should like to examine what I have
identified as a process of implicit equation more closely, concluding
with a discussion of a recent exhibition on ethnic expulsions in Berlin
– *Erzwungene Wege*. This exhibition, I will argue, while including
examples of equation of the fate of the ethnic Germans with that of
other expelled minorities, actually also represented a new departure, in
that it endeavoured to align the fate of ethnic Germans more with that
of the Armenians. At the same time, the makers of the exhibition
appeared more committed to circumnavigating the Holocaust than to
equating aspects of it with the German experience of expulsion. There
are, I believe, several reasons for this, some more worrying than
others.

German-Czech, German-Polish Relations

Part of the process of German unification in 1990 was the removal
from the Basic Law of the clause referring to Germany's rightful
borders as those of 1937, and the conclusion of a border treaty
between Poland and the future Germany. In relations with both Poland

and the Czech Republic, both Chancellor Kohl (CDU) and his successor Gerhard Schröder (SPD) sought, by and large, to develop positive, forward-looking relations based on the wish, for want of a better phrase, to let bygones be bygones. Conciliation and collaboration were the key terms in bilateral relations, the highpoints of which were the conclusion of a Neighbourhood Agreement between Germany and Poland in June 1991, and the German-Czech Reconciliation declaration in January 1997, when Germany acknowledged responsibility for injustices done to Czechs under Hitler, and the Czech Republic acknowledged and regretted the fact of the expulsion of the Sudeten Germans. In December 1997, the German and Czech governments agreed to set up a 'Fund for the Future' to finance joint German-Czech cultural projects, and to compensate Czech victims of Nazism. Yet this appearance of diplomatic rapprochement – itself undermined by moments of political tension at the highest level, and by the contrary position of the Christian Social Union (CSU) – belied the true state of affairs in German-Polish and German-Czech relations, which became particularly fraught in the 1998-2005 period. In fact, the top-level insistence on the need for moving forward, precisely by attempting to abnegate the relevance of the past for current German-Czech and German-Polish relations, merely enabled revisionist groupings in Germany to dominate discourse on the issue of which moral imperatives in the present derive from actions and events in the past. Of course their views were challenged by conciliatory rhetoric from above – but there was no serious discursive engagement with the historical presumptions on which these views were based.

The general background to these revisionist activities was the release of Poland as well as the new Czech and Slovak Republics from the grip of the Soviet Union, and their understandable wish to improve relations with western Europe, and to become integrated into NATO, and the European Union. A key player here is the *Bund der Vertriebenen (BdV)*. The League of Expellees had voted against the 1990 border treaty, *and* against the 1991 Neighbourhood Agreement with Poland because the latter did not commit the Poles to guaranteeing the rights of minorities.[10] Thus began a process of highlighting the inadequate political morality of Poland and the Czech Republic in the present, a process intimately connected to the persistent claim that these countries had failed to take *post hoc* ethical and legal responsibility for the expulsion of the Germans in 1945. These criticisms, in turn, became a pistol which some representatives of the *BdV*, and some in the CSU (particularly in the European Parliament), held at the heads of the Poles and Czechs. Thus in the case of the Czechs, it was argued in 2001 and 2002 by the *BdV* and CSU politicians such as Edmund Stoiber that they could not be allowed into the European Union until they had formally repealed the Beneš Decrees, which had formed the legal basis for the expulsion of the Sudeten Germans. But the Czechs – supported by EU expansion commissary Günter Verheugen (SPD) – argued that these decrees had no judicial force in the present, and thus did not need to be annulled according to EU law. Of course, they could theoretically have been repealed *ex nunc* rather than *ex tunc*, thus circumnavigating Czech fears that their annulment would lead to a flood of restitution and compensation claims from Sudeten Germans.[11] But the judicial status of *ex nunc* annulments is complex, and in any case, Czech politicians were reluctant to be seen to give in to right-wing German politicians. In the face of pressure, they chose the opposite path, lining up behind Beneš. Thus in April 2002, the Czech government and then parliament unanimously voted against repealing the decrees, declaring them inviolable; and in March 2004 a decision was even taken in Prague to promulgate a law declaring that Beneš had acted in the service of the Czech state.

The implicit thrust of German criticism of the decrees was that the Czechs, just as the Germans had done before them, needed to come to terms with their past before they could be considered the moral equal of their western European neighbours. In short, the message being sent to Prague, and indeed to Poland, was: now it's your turn. High on the agenda of some right-wing politicians in Germany, and on that of the *BdV* was the issue of restitution and compensation. In May 2000, the Sudeten German *Landsmannschaft* applied to the Czech-German 'Fund for the Future' for financial support for Sudeten Germans who had suffered severe persecution in the course of expulsion; Milos Zeman, the Czech Republic's Minister President, suggested in 2002 that a humanitarian gesture towards those expellees who had fought against the Nazis might be appropriate, but his idea was immediately rejected by the *Landsmannschaft* because it appeared to aim to split the Sudeten Germans into the deserving and undeserving. Of course, for Zeman most of them were undeserving; he created some indignation in Germany when he described the Sudeten Germans as 'Hitler's Fifth Column' in January 2002, and the then Chancellor Gerhard Schröder promptly cancelled his planned trip to Prague – truly the low-point of German-Czech relations during the years of the Red-Green coalition (1998-2005), although the Red-Green Foreign Minister Joschka Fischer also caused alarm in Prague when he appeared in May and again in July 2003 to call for compensation to be taken from the Czech-German Fund for those Sudeten Germans who had suffered forced labour after the war.

Relations with Poland were also put under considerable strain by the establishment of the so-called *Preußische Treuhand*, a private enterprise offering support to those German expellees wishing to file restitution and compensation claims against Poland. Erika Steinbach, the president of the *BdV*, has distanced herself from this organisation on more than one occasion, and when former Chancellor Schröder attended the commemoration of the 1944 Warsaw Uprising in August 2004, he stated that there was no room today for 'Restitutionsansprüche aus Deutschland, die die Geschichte auf den Kopf stellen', and even asseverated that Germany would resist any such claims if necessary by legal means.[12] However, Schröder was not prepared to commit Germany to paying compensation to the expellees, an idea that had been mooted both by Polish politicians and Erika Steinbach (albeit for different reasons). The unresolved legal and political tensions attendant on the restitution and compensation wishes of former expellees continue to disturb German-Czech and German-Polish relations.[13] As long as they do, they will be grist to the mill of those revisionists in Germany committed to reframing the history of the Second World War as one of general criminality, with Poles, Czechs and Russians appearing no less guilty of perpetration than the Germans. At the same time there is an attempted framing of post-war history as one in which the Germans appear morally superior to the Czechs and Poles because they paid compensation (of sorts), whereas the Czechs and Poles did not.

The implicit positing of historical equivalences and, perhaps worse, the sometimes quite explicit critique of what is perceived to be inferior Czech and Polish *Vergangenheitsbewältigung* are connected to the current preoccupation in Germany with German victimhood during the war. They help to reinforce a widespread feeling that Germans have the *right* to focus public memory on their own victims,

while the Czech Republic and Poland have the *duty* to acknowledge
their history of perpetration. It is this agenda of self-pitying
inculpation which is currently at the root of plans to set up a Centre
Against Expulsions in Berlin. The idea of such a Centre was first
floated by Erika Steinbach in 1999. One year later, the *Stiftung der
deutschen Heimatvertriebenen im BdV* was formed, and from this, on
6 September 2000, the foundation *Zentrum gegen Vertreibungen*, with
Peter Glotz (SPD) and Steinbach (CDU) as presiding chairpersons.
According to the foundation's website, the idea of such a centre was
born of the awareness

> dass es nötig ist, nicht im eigenen Leide, in persönlichen traumatischen
> Erinnerungen zu verharren, sondern ein Instrument zu schaffen, das dazu beiträgt,
> Vertreibung und Genozid grundsätzlich als Mittel von Politik zu ächten.[14]

While this all sounds very noble, the Foundation *Zentrum gegen
Vertreibungen* is regarded with the greatest scepticism in Poland and
the Czech Republic, but also in Germany itself – even more so since
the death of Peter Glotz in 2005, whose role within the Foundation
lent it some credibility. So far, the Foundation has resisted calls for the
planned Centre to be erected in Breslau, insisting instead on Berlin.
This has merely served to intensify suspicion that the Centre is to act
as a kind of counter-memorial to the Holocaust Memorial near the
Brandenburg Gate, and that it will place the central focus on the
German experience of expulsion, as well as contextualising that
experience, problematically, within the history of 20th century
genocide.

Poland and the Czech Republic, faced on the one hand with a
German government committed officially to conciliation and support
for eastward EU expansion, and on the other with the vociferous
criticisms and demands emanating from the CSU and the *BdV*, have
oscillated between expressing a degree of historical self-criticism one
moment, and self-defensive insistence on the legitimacy of the
expulsions and on German culpability the next. In the case of both
Poland and the Czech Republic, self-critical remarks have tended to
come more from left or left-liberal circles. In June 2003, for instance,
Vladimir Spidla, Prime Minister of the Social Democratic coalition
government in power in the Czech Republic at the time, declared the
expulsion of the Sudeten Germans to be 'unacceptable from today's
perspective'. The more self-defensive, morally assertive stance is
typical of conservative and nationalist politicians in both countries.
Undoubtedly, this stance has often been informed by a politics of 'tit-

for-tat', particularly in the case of Poland. In September 2004, following wide publicisation of the activities of the *Preußische Treuhand*, and after it became clear that the German government was not prepared to meet the compensation demands of the expellees, Polish conservatives in the Sejm (Polish parliament) pushed through a resolution calling for Germany to pay reparations for damage done to Poland during the war. While the Polish cabinet refused to bow to parliamentary pressure and distanced itself from the resolution, the message sent out by the Sejm created waves in Germany. It was a clear message: if German organisations were going to demand restitution and compensation, then Poland too could enter the ring with even bigger financial demands for the disastrous effects of German occupation – arguing that the 1953 renunciation of reparations by the Polish government was extracted under Soviet pressure, that the gain of western territories in 1945/1946 did not compensate Poland for the loss of its eastern territories, and that Poland never received the reparations from Germany which it was promised at the Potsdam Conference.

Erzwungene Wege: **An Exhibition in Berlin**
However, on balance, it has not so much been the *Preußische Treuhand*, as the *BdV*'s planned Centre Against Expulsions that has been at the epicentre of tensions between Germany, Poland and the Czech Republic – despite the *BdV*'s repeated protestations that it wished to document the history of 20th century expulsions as a whole, not focus exclusively or even centrally on the German expellees. Germans and non-Germans alike had a chance to judge the true intentions of the *BdV* when it opened a temporary exhibition entitled *Erzwungene Wege* in Berlin's Kronprinzenpalais in August 2006. While there were attempts to defend the exhibition, it has, overall, prompted criticism – largely from Poland, to a lesser degree from the Czech Republic, and also from the left-liberal press in Germany itself. Polish and Czech indignation is understandable. The exhibition avoided sentimentality and strong emotional appeals for the most part, an eschewal which lent it an air of objectivity and critical distance. But its manner was deceptive. For in essence, its presentation and interpretation of history were selective, tendentious and ideological. It came with a smooth urbane veneer, preaching the indivisibility of *humanitas*, pointing to the importance of conciliation, expressing

concern at expulsions in the present – while actually pursuing a historiographical agenda more likely to cause rifts than stimulate consensus.

The problem with *Erzwungene Wege* was implied – unintentionally – by its title. It sought to force history down a path it could not and should not be made to go. In its three rooms, the exhibition brought together different historical examples of expulsion. These included: the suffering of the Armenians (1916/1917); the expulsion and resettlement of Greeks and Turks (1922/1923); the expulsion of Jews from Germany after 1933; the massive population transfers following the Hitler-Stalin Pact and the invasion of Poland; the forced resettlement of Finnish Karelians (1939-1944); the expulsion of the ethnic Germans at the end of World War Two (and of Italians); and the recent expulsions in the former Yugoslavia. Such juxtaposition would have been perfectly in order had the exhibition's organisers used it as a platform for analytical and critical comparison, a process which would surely have resulted in contrast or at least differentiation. But rather the juxtaposition proceeded in a selective and inadequately commentated manner, serving as a means of eliding significant differences.

In the largest room, a chronologically ordered account of expulsions was mapped out over all four walls; the temporal and physical sequentiality of the way the material was presented implied continuity. The exhibition's organisers made it quite clear that they see parallels in the motives behind the featured expulsions: 'die Umsetzung der Idee eines ethnisch homogenen Nationalstaates ist eine der Hauptursachen für Vertreibungen ethnischer Gruppen und Minderheiten im zwanzigsten Jahrhundert. Rassismus und Antisemitismus waren neben dem Nationalismus weitere Antriebskräfte für Vertreibung und Vernichtung.'[15] In order to ensure that the visitor to the exhibition came away with a sense of this correspondence of motives – nationalism, bound up with racism, in all cases – the makers had to obscure fundamental differences. Thus while the exhibition highlighted the fact that Polish, Czech and Soviet national interests played an important part in the expulsion of ethnic Germans at the end of World War Two, it made little reference to the issue of German culpability or the issue of revenge.

Certainly, in the section on Czechoslovakia there was a clear reference to the horrors of the Nazi regime. But this was followed by the sentence, 'die von Konrad Henlein geführte nationalsozialistische Sudetendeutsche Partei hatte zudem die in der Tschechoslowakei lebenden Deutschen als antisemitisch und Hitler-freundlich diskreditiert'.[16] The Germans in the Sudetenland, we infer, were not *really* pro-Hitler; it was rather that Henlein's Party had earned them a bad reputation. The exhibition's makers clearly felt there was no need to underline the enormous support the Sudeten Germans gave to Henlein in 1938. We also read that the Germans in Yugoslavia were 'sich keinerlei Verbrechen bewußt'. Without doubt, the post-war internment of the Danube Swabians in Gakovo in Yugoslavia on the grounds of Nazi collaboration proceeded in an utterly inhumane fashion; but they *had* in considerable numbers collaborated with the Nazis. The issue is not whether the former German ethnic minorities of Yugoslavia had committed crimes, or at least not just; it is also about whether they had supported a criminal regime.

The exhibition's general section on the expulsion of the ethnic Germans claimed that the main motive for it was the westward shift of Poland's borders at Stalin's behest – a shift accepted by the western Allies and the Polish government. Plans for getting rid of the Germans, we read, existed at the beginning of the war already. The Germans were then made 'collectively responsible for the crimes of the Nazi regime'; and the expulsion affected mainly women, children and old people (who, we were meant to infer, were surely innocent). All of these statements were and are true. It would be quite unhistorical to create an exhibition on the expulsion of the Germans which did NOT mention the crucial role of Stalin, or the Polish and Czech governments and national interests. But to round off the picture, the exhibition should have made it clear that the expulsion of the Germans also constituted a (very inhumane) reaction to Nazi inhumanity, that it was a *reactive* policy (to a degree) as well as a *proactive* policy, and that there was a cruel logic to removing the Germans: with few of them left in Poland and Czechoslovakia, future German governments would hardly be able to claim that parts of these countries were really 'German' as a pretext for a renewed invasion. Czech Prime Minister Vladimir Spidla irritated the Germans by claiming in May 2002 that the expulsion of ethnic Germans was 'a source of future peace'.[17] But from the perspective of the mid-1940s, at least, this is exactly what it appeared to be - and not just to the Czechs.

By failing to mention *all* the links in the specific chain of cause and effect, the exhibition implied that the circumstances of the expulsion of the ethnic Germans can be equated with the circumstances surrounding the treatment meted out to the Armenians, the Greek Cypriots, or the Jews. A section on trains, for instance, set side by side descriptions of the fates of deported Jews, Balts and German 'resettlers' – without placing these very different deportations in their respective context. Yet as any observant visitor to the exhibition would have spotted, the Jewish experience of discrimination and deportation was often *not* referenced in the sets of juxtapositions. Thus a section on concentration (and annihilation) camps – apart from one brief use of the word 'Holocaust' – failed to make it clear that Jews perished in their millions at such camps. Another section on 'Camp Life', focusing *inter alia* on Estonians deported by Stalin to Siberia in 1941, and Greek Cypriots put in camps on southern Cyprus in 1974, failed to mention Jews. I also failed to detect a reference to Jews in the section on transit camps. The best that can be said of this approach is that the exhibition was attempting to enhance public awareness of the broader applicability of terms such as 'concentration camps' or 'transit camps'. A more critical interpretation would be that the exhibition wished to distract attention from Jewish suffering and German culpability and focus instead on German victimhood, and on the culpability of the Russians, Czechs, Poles – an indication perhaps of the exhibition's debt to the resurgence of totalitarianism theory. The exhibition was also at pains to condemn the Turks, an expression perhaps of western, Christian right-wing distaste for the prospect of Turkey becoming a member of the European Union.

In addition to one very large room, in which material was chronologically ordered, the exhibition consisted of two smaller rooms which structured their displays thematically. Subsections were grouped around subjects such as 'Gepäck und Memorabilia', 'Lager' and 'Heimat'. In the room focusing on 'Heimat', subsections were wistfully entitled 'Verlorenes Haus', 'Verlorene Natur', and indeed 'Verlorene Heimat'. This grouping helped to reinforce the exhibition's equationist agenda. Thus the subsection on lost homelands provided examples taken from the experiences of Finnish Karelians and Greek Cypriots; the subsection on lost nature focused on the Soviets' disregard after 1945 for the beauties of the East Prussian landscape (reference is made to the near-total annihilation of the native elk population, and to the stationing of Soviet rockets); and the subsection 'Religion und Sprache als Symbol der Heimat' displays books by (among others) Jeffrey Eugenides, Günter Grass, Arno Surminski and Yaşar Kemal. This thematic organisation obviated the need for differentiation by historical context. The room on 'Heimat' was made even more problematic by its neglect of the theme of Jewish loss of homeland. In failing to accord to the Jews any sense of loss, the exhibition unwittingly reproduced the Nazi world-view, which was that Jews knew no bonds of homeland. But the omission of the Jews served another purpose. Had they been included, it would have been necessary to point out that most of them not only lost their homeland, but also their lives – in contrast to the ethnic Germans, most of whom survived expulsion to set up a new home elsewhere.

Against criticism of such omission, it could be said that the exhibition *does*, in its chronological display in the largest room, include a section entitled 'Die Vertreibung der Juden aus Deutschland ab 1933'. However, this section does not extend to a discussion of the Holocaust – an omission which the exhibitors felt they needed to justify by means of the following statement: 'die Darstellung der Ermordung der europäischen Juden ist nicht Thema dieser Ausstellung. Die Ausstellung zeigt vielmehr den schrittweisen Prozess der Vertreibung bis zum Holocaust'.[18] The very fact that such a statement was made smacks of bad conscience. And it provides no rationale for this dubious omission. Was the mass murder of the Jews not the final stage in the destructive process of discrimination, forced emigration, expulsion and deportation? Were the trains that took Berlin's or Hungary's Jews direct to Auschwitz not expelling them in the most radical way imaginable? The exhibition never even fulfilled its intention of at least showing the 'step-by-step process of expulsion up to the Holocaust'. If it had done, it would have featured a close examination of the process of the deportation and ghettoisation of Jews between 1941 and 1945. Nor did the section on forced resettlements as a result of the invasion of Poland give any more than cursory consideration to the 'resettlement' of Jews.

The omission of the Holocaust seemed all the more curious when one considers that the exhibition did make frequent reference to the brutalities endured by the ethnic Germans. The visitor was informed about the loss of Sudeten German life through 'Krankheit, Hunger, willkürliche Morde und Selbstmord'; elsewhere mention was made of the 'willkürliche[r] Tötungen, Hunger und Krankheiten' suffered by the Jugoslavian Germans.[19] Even more curious, surely, is the fact that the exhibition did include a section on 'Der Völkermord an den Armeniern 1915/1916'. There is a consensus among historians that the massacre of the Armenians was a genocide; nevertheless, the consensus is not total, and even historian Norman Naimark has argued that the term genocide 'does not fit the Armenian case perfectly'.[20] Why include a section on a genocide that is still disputed (not least by Turkey), and at the same time omit one that is *undisputed* (except by cranks)? To anger the Turks? To make a political point? Perhaps. But there seem to me to be other reasons for the keenness of the exhibitors to include one genocide while studiously overlooking the other.

The aim of the exhibition was to allow the expulsion of the ethnic Germans to appear as one key scene in a history of repetition – a history in which surely innocent minorities, such as Greek Cypriots, Armenians and, it is implied, ethnic Germans – suffered at the hands of others. While the Jews were also included in this history, the exhibitors had to omit the Holocaust because a focus upon it would have made it clear that a *German* atrocity preceded the expulsion of ethnic Germans; that *German* perpetration in Poland and Czechoslovakia, generally, partly triggered the expulsions of ethnic Germans; and that the suffering and murder inflicted on Jews by *Germans* was of an infinitely more drastic order than that inflicted upon ethnic Germans by Soviets, Poles and Czechs. A focus on the Holocaust would have made it harder for the exhibition to sustain its tone of uncritical empathy for the ethnic Germans, and forced it to portray German perpetration much more comprehensively than it did. But while this explains the omission of the Holocaust, it does not explain the inclusion of the Armenian genocide.

The inclusion of the latter must be understood in relation to the exclusion of the former. For decades, the expellees have felt that memory of the Holocaust has blocked German empathy for the fate of the ethnic Germans. The exhibition attempted a reframing: visitors were to be invited to relate the ethnic German expulsion *not* to the preceding Holocaust, which overshadows subsequent German suffering, but to the much earlier Armenian genocide, which is not linked in any historical chain of causation to the expulsion of the Germans. Without making it explicit, the exhibition hoped to convince the visitor that the Armenian experience is more 'relevant' to German memory of expulsion than the Holocaust because it was a 'genocide by deportation'. Most of the Armenians were killed *during* deportation. Many ethnic Germans, so the exhibition informed us, were also killed *during* deportation. Not that the exhibition referred to the expulsion of the ethnic Germans as a 'genocide'. But it left the visitor to draw his or her own conclusions from references to atrocities committed against Germans. In other words: the inclusion of the Armenian genocide was designed to position the expulsion of the ethnic Germans within a murderous, indeed genocidal history of deportational killing – while decoupling it historiographically from part of its roots in German atrocities against Poles, Czechs and Jews. This decoupling was only possible by simultaneously failing to acknowledge that the Holocaust also included elements of killing during deportation – the most extreme and obvious example being the deaths of countless numbers of Jews in the course of death marches towards the end of the war.

It would not be judicious to claim, however, that the exhibition was seeking to obscure entirely the Jewish experience of discrimination at the hand of the Germans. After all, as already pointed out, a section on the anti-Jewish measures in Germany between 1933 and 1939 made this discrimination clear. However, the exhibition also referred to the discrimination experienced by ethnic Germans prior to their expulsion. It observed with some cynicism that there was no mention of Germans in the name of the new post-World War One state of Czechoslovakia. 'In der Zwischenkriegszeit', the visitor read, 'wurde die deutsche Bevölkerung in den Bereichen Wirtschaft, Kultur und Administration methodisch benachteiligt'.[21] In other words, Czech discrimination against ethnic Germans was, we were meant to infer, just as considerable as Nazi discrimination against Jews in peacetime Germany. Here, then, there *was* an implicit equation with the Jewish experience. It was an extremely dubious one, given that ethnic Germans under Polish and Czechoslovak rule had infinitely more rights than Jews under Nazi rule. Nevertheless, the exhibitors clearly felt that such an equation was sustainable, whereas of course any detailed and explicit attempt to equate the Holocaust with the expulsion of ethnic Germans would have laid them open to charges of unacceptable revisionism. An inclusion of the Holocaust which, in historiographically judicious fashion, drew attention to differences in scale and motive (thus the ethnic Germans were expelled to another country, the Jews to their collective *deaths*), was clearly also unacceptable – in this case to the exhibitors themselves.

Conclusion

The exhibition's most problematic aspects, then, were its attempt to write the Holocaust out of the European history of expulsions, to abnegate the relevance of historical cause and effect, and to align the history of the expulsion of the ethnic Germans with that of the Armenian genocide and indeed with that of the other expulsions which the exhibit included. That it is possible to present the history of the expulsion of ethnic Germans differently was made clear by another exhibition on the subject, which was shown more or less at the same time as *Erzwungene Wege* – and shown exactly opposite the Kronprinzenpalais in Berlin's Deutsches Historisches Museum. This other exhibition, titled *Flucht Vertreibung Integration*, was created by the Haus der Deutschen Geschichte, hardly an organisation known for its self-critical portrayals of German history. Yet to its credit, *Flucht Vertreibung Integration* was far less problematic than *Erzwungene Wege*. This had to do in part with its main focus, which was not on expulsion itself, but on the post-war integration of fugitives and expellees into West and East Germany. It also had to do with the fact that this exhibition honestly admitted to being an exhibition principally about German expellees, whereas the *Erzwungene Wege* exhibition claimed to be an exhibition about the 20th century phenomenon of expulsion generally, while in fact using other examples of expulsion to promote by implication a view of German expellees as in no way responsible for the fate which befell them.

But there is another reason why *Flucht Vertreibung Integration* was less problematic: it acknowledged the measure of German responsibility for the process which led to the expulsion of the ethnic Germans. Thus we read right at the beginning of the exhibition that flight and expulsion had reached 'eine erschreckende Dimension […] infolge des vom nationalsozialistischen Deutschland entfesselten Weltkrieges'. And the exhibition, while highlighting the importance of nationalism as a motor for expulsions in twentieth century Europe, recognised the motive of reaction to German atrocities as a factor in the expulsion of the ethnic Germans. *Flucht Vertreibung Integration*, moreover, used an aesthetic device to stress the need to be aware of immediate historical context as a cause. Thus the visitor entered the section focusing on the expulsion of the Germans through a tilted black box displaying examples of German atrocities against Poles, Czechs and Jews that had gone before. The exhibition's lack of any exculpatory agenda made its portrayal of the suffering of the German fugitives and expellees – which is graphically conveyed – all the more moving.

Erzwungene Wege and *Flucht Vertreibung Integration* were very different in character. *Erzwungene Wege* explored the phenomenology of expulsion as a symptom of ethnic nationalism; it showed the sores and open wounds of the process; it was a lament, a complaint, and a protest. *Flucht Vertreibung Integration* – with the word *Heimat* running vertically through these three terms on the poster and catalogue, each on a separate line – certainly did not ignore the pain of expulsion itself, but its emphasis was more on the *post facto* political, social and psychological process of living with its effects. It therefore historicized the expulsion in a quite different way. It appeared to argue that the loss of *Heimat* triggered a process in which integration into the new environment, and preoccupation with the old one existed in a precarious balance. This preoccupation, according to *Flucht Vertreibung Integration*, could take the form of open revanchism and irredentism on the one hand, and of a more forward-looking and constructive continuation of cultural, social and professional traditions on the other. One of the most exemplary cases of such a cultural transference, as the exhibition showed, was the emergence of Neugablonz, in which the old *Heimat* – understood as a professional pride and tradition – was reborn in the new. Hence the title's interlacing of *Heimat* with *Flucht Vertreibung Integration*; *Heimat* is both lost and preserved, lost and exchanged, lost and in part relocated.

The simultaneous showing of these two exhibitions did something to create precisely that kind of dialogue about the ethnic expulsions of the Germans which has so far been missing in the public realm. However, it was *Erzwungene Wege* which kicked up the most fuss and was focused on the most in the press – not least because it became caught up in the political tensions between Poland and Germany. It is, then, still the League of Expellees which appears to be calling the shots when it comes to representations of German victimhood, and if the Centre Against Expulsions is constructed in Berlin under the supervision of the *BdV*, the tensions between Poland, the Czech

Republic and Germany are likely to be exacerbated. It is not that the Poles and Czechs do *not* have a past to face. The problem is that the *BdV* is insisting that they face a version of the past concocted by the *BdV*, not least by its indefatigable president Erika Steinbach – a version in which ethnic Germans are absolute victims, Czechs and Poles are historical villains every bit as heinous as the Nazi perpetrators, and the Holocaust is seen as less relevant to an understanding of German history than it has been hitherto. All in all, a concoction that the Poles and Czechs, rightly, are reluctant to accept.

Notes

[1] See Christoph Schult, '"Private Gespräche,"' *DER SPIEGEL*, 17/2002, 9 September 2002, pp. 34-35.

[2] Nico Fried, '"Irgendwie irgendwo vorgekommen,"' *Süddeutsche Zeitung*, 21/22 September 2002, p. 5.

[3] Christiane Wirtz, 'Stölzl entschuldigt sich für NS-Parallele,' *Süddeutsche Zeitung*, 25 September 2002, p. 7.

[4] See 'Europäer empören sich über Berlusconi,' *Süddeutsche Zeitung*, 4 July 2003, p. 1.

[5] 'Erleichterung über Stefanis Rücktritt,' *Süddeutsche Zeitung*, 14 July 2003, p. 2.

[6] Detlef Esslinger and Susanne Höll, 'Koch erschreckt die eigene Partei,' *Süddeutsche Zeitung*, 13 December 2002, p. 1.

[7] See Matthias Drobinski, 'Empörung über Kardinal Meisner,' *Süddeutsche Zeitung*, 8/9 January 2005, p. 5.

[8] See http://edition.cnn.com/2003/US/Northeast/02/28/peta.holocaust.

[9] See Hauke Goos, 'Ein Krieg für Tiere,' *DER SPIEGEL*, 12/2004, 15 March 2004, pp. 226-229.

[10] See Thomas Urban, *Der Verlust: Die Vertreibung der Deutschen und Polen im 20. Jahrhundert*, C.H.Beck: Munich, 2004, p. 175.

[11] *Ex tunc* is Latin for 'from the beginning'; *ex nunc* is Latin for 'from now on'. If a ruling is annulled *ex tunc*, then it is considered invalid from the moment it was passed. If it is annulled *ex nunc*, then it is only invalid from a given moment in the present onwards. If the Beneš Decrees were annulled *ex tunc*, this would mean that all expulsions which followed as a result of them were illegal; all those affected by the Decrees could claim compensation. But if they were annulled *ex nunc*, say as of 2006,

then only those measures based on the decrees undertaken *after* 2006 would be illegal – all those expelled on the basis of the decrees before 2006 would have no legal right of redress.

[12] See Nico Fried, "'Versöhnung mit Polen wirkt wie ein Wunder,'" *Süddeutsche Zeitung*, 2 August 2004, p. 1.

[13] For an interesting account of the restitution issues, see Irina Repke, 'Angst vor den Deutschen,' *DER SPIEGEL*, June 2004, pp. 36-42.

[14] http://www.z-g-v.de/aktuelles/?id=34

[15] This statement is included in a display in the exhibition's foyer.

[16] This quotation is taken from a textboard in the exhibition's largest room.

[17] See Daniel Brössler, 'Berlin skeptisch über Ende des Zwists mit Prag,' *Süddeutsche Zeitung*, 29/30 May 2002, p. 8.

[18] This quotation is taken from a textboard in the exhibition's largest room.

[19] This quotation is taken from a textboard in the exhibition's largest room.

[20] Norman M. Naimark, *Fires of Hatred: Ethnic Cleansing in Twentieth-Century Europe*, Harvard University Press: Cambridge, Mass., and London, 2001, p. 36.

[21] This quotation is taken from a textboard in the exhibition's largest room.

Gilad Margalit

Dresden and Hamburg - Official Memory and Commemoration of the Victims of Allied Air Raids in the two Germanies

This chapter compares the official and public commemoration of the air raids in the two cities of Hamburg and Dresden from the immediate post-war period to the present. Putting the changing forms of commemoration in context with the politics in the two German states, it argues that the Cold-War GDR interpretation of the air raid on Dresden as a militarily useless act of aggression and a crime gradually shifted to the West.

Of all the German cities and towns attacked during the Second World War by the Allies' strategic bombing, Hamburg (about 55,000 victims) and Dresden (25,000-35,000 victims[1]) suffered the highest number of civilian casualties. The development of the official memory and commemoration of the victims of the Allied air raids in both cities reflects essential elements of post-war German memory and commemoration cultures that had crystallised in the two Germanys mostly during the Cold War and in response to it.

The Preoccupation with the Bombardment of the German Cities 1945-1949

A. Dresden

Until the outbreak of the Cold War, the official line in the Soviet zone of occupation (SBZ) as well as the dominant narrative of the German press in the Western sectors held the Nazi regime responsible for the Allied bombardment of German cities. The suffering of the German civilian population was thus causally related to the German responsibility for the war. This narrative was embedded within the German guilt discourse that started among the German public after the collapse of the Nazi regime.

On the first commemorative day for the Allied bombardment of Dresden on 13 February 1946, the city's mayor (*Bürgermeister*), Walter Weidauer, published an article in the local *Sächsische Volkszeitung* that read:

> Besonders schlimm sind Katastrophen, die vermeidbar gewesen wären. Aber nichts in der Geschichte unserer Stadt ist vergleichbar mit der Nacht vom 13. bis

14. Februar 1945. Zum Vermeidbaren kommt noch die Tatsache der bewußt von
den faschistischen Verbrechern provozierten Zerstörung Dresdens.

Weidauer closed his article by reproaching the German people with
guilt:

> Mit Schmerz und Trauer gedenken wir heute der Opfer. Mit doppeltem Schmerz,
> weil ihr Opfer sinnlos war, und – sprechen wir es offen aus – weil die politische
> Schwäche des deutschen Volks mit Schuld trägt an diesem Krieg, den wir hätten
> verhindern können, wenn wir dem Beispiel der Hunderttausenden gefolgt wären,
> die Not und Tod auf sich nahmen, die in die Zuchthäuser und Konzentrationslager
> wanderten, weil sie gegen Hitler und den Krieg aktiv kämpften.[2]

The first commemorations for the destruction of Dresden by the Allies
on the night of 13 February 1945 were held on a local basis only and
had no national resonance. The speeches of party activists in Dresden
on those occasions simply ignored the British and American identity
of the bombers and highlighted the responsibility of the Nazi regime
for the destruction of the city. In certain publications and films on the
air raid on Dresden from the period of Democratic anti-Fascism, the
issue was integrated into the discourse on collective German guilt.
Occasionally, the destruction of Dresden was presented quite
explicitly as a punishment for the political guilt of voting for Hitler. In
a scene in *Dresden*, a DEFA film from 1946 about the destruction of
the city, an inmate in the city's prison refers to the National Socialists
ascending to power in a manner typical of the period of Democratic
anti-Fascism: 'In diesem Lande ist alles zu Lügen geworden. Die
Formen sind leer, Deutschland hat kein Gewissen mehr! […] Die
Menschen schweigen, eher würden die Steine sprechen.'[3]

Another DEFA Film on the destruction of Dresden, *Dresden warnt
und mahnt* from 1952, still retains this reproachful tone but, in the
light of Stalinisation of the early Cold War years, the essence of the
German guilt has changed. In contrast to the 1946 DEFA film, the
problem of the German people during the end of the Weimar Republic
and the Third Reich is no longer the loss of conscience and humanity
– it is not listening to and following the Communists: the citizens of
the city and the masses of the German people are blamed for not
following the Communist leader, Ernst Thälman, who had warned
against Hitler. The film thus blames the Germans for preferring to
vote for Hitler, insinuating that they had thus burdened themselves
with a tremendous guilt for the outbreak of the Second World War and
the crimes of the Nazi regime.[4]

B. Hamburg

In an article in the Social-Democratic newspaper *Hamburger Echo* that appeared in July 1946 on the third anniversary of the air attack on Hamburg of July 1943, the anonymous author recalled the bombardment of his hometown and the reactions of his fellow citizens. They had fled from Hamburg after the air raids:

> Sie alle sind mit mir der Meinung, das müsse das Ende des Krieges sein, dieser fürchterliche Luftangriff werde uns auch die Befreiung von der Naziherrschaft bringen. Wir ahnen alle nicht, dass wir von diesem erhofften Ereignis leider noch ein erhebliches Stück entfernt sind.[5]

This kind of depiction of the bombardment of Hamburg as part of the Allied campaign to free the Germans of the Nazi yoke characterised the reactions of anti-Nazis and Jews; but it was certainly not the typical German attitude to the air raids. These reactions recall the happiness of Wolf Biermann's Communist mother in the face of the British bombardment of her hometown, Hamburg. She regarded the bombs as a sign of the coming liberation, although '[e]s war nur so unpraktisch, daß sie uns auf den Kopf flogen'.[6]

Similar responses were also common among the few remaining Jews who still lived in Dresden in February 1945. Henny Brenner was a young Jewish woman who was due to be deported with her family and the rest of the Jews to a concentration camp two days after the notorious Allied bombardment on 13 February 1945. She reported that after her family had received the news about their coming deportation, her father told them 'halb im ernst, halb im Spaß: Das einzige, was uns retten kann, ist ein großer Angriff auf Dresden. [...] Für uns dagegen war der Angriff, so makaber es klingt, die Rettung, und genauso empfanden wir ihn.'[7]

Ordinary Germans usually did not react in this manner with respect to the Allied air raids on German cities. This kind of response of Germans towards the Allied bombardments is most likely a post-war construct and an apologetic attempt to make a distinction between the Nazis and the German people who, it is alleged, opposed Hitler's belligerent policy. No such expressions had been registered in the wartime reports of the Nazi security service (*Sicherheitsdienst*, SD) on dissenting public expressions regarding the Nazi leadership, evoked by the heavy Allied bombardments. The German public was enraged over the helplessness of its anti-aircraft defence and its commander, Air-Marshal Hermann Göring, and hoped for military acts of retaliation against Britain that would put an end to the attacks on the

German hinterland.[8] One of the verses of a parody of the religious hymn 'Komm Herr Jesu' sung in Koblenz in 1943, clearly reflects the common feeling among the German public:

Auf Vergeltung warten wir
Dass es England geht wie hier,
Hilf der Meyer doch, O Gott
Jetzt in dieser großen Not
Gib ihm doch den richt'gen Geist
Dass er wieder Göring heisst.[9]

Such reactions had not changed in essence since the air attack on Hamburg in the summer of 1943. In his biography/memoir, *Am Beispiel meines Bruders*, Uwe Timm quotes from a letter his brother Karl-Heinz, a soldier with the *Waffen-SS* who had fought on the Russian front in early August 1943, had sent home after he had heard about the British bombardments on his home town, Hamburg: '[...] ...täglich werden hier Fliegerangriffe der Engländer gemeldet. [...] das ist doch kein Krieg, das ist ja Mord an Frauen und Kinder – und das ist nicht human.'[10] Karl-Heinz Timm's position regarding the Allied bombing, probably like that of most Germans at the time, was similar to the official Nazi propaganda.[11]

However, the dissenting and critical tones became sharper. There were for example demands to dismiss Göring; this elicited certain fears among the SD and the Nazi leadership. Nevertheless, the SD authors maintained that 'The majority of the population still believe that Germany will win the War'.[12] It is important to note, however, that the Social-Democratic organ, *Hamburger Echo*, in 1947 presented the Nazis and not Britain and its bombers as responsible for the destruction of Hamburg, similar to the above-cited Communist press before the outbreak of the Cold War.[13]

Dresden and the Communist Narrative of the Cold War

The beginning of the Cold War dramatically changed the Communist narrative of the Second World War and, in direct consequence, the attitude toward the bombing of the German cities by Western Allies. The German population was very embittered because of the Allied attacks on civilians. The SED leadership decided to exploit the nationalist feelings and German bitterness toward the Western Allies. The Allied bombings were increasingly manipulated as part of the propaganda struggle of the GDR and its political allies in the Federal Republic against the Western super-powers and the pro-Western politics of the Adenauer administration. The near non-involvement of the Soviet Union in bombardments of German cities facilitated the stigmatisation only of the Western Allies as mass murderers.

After 1949, the SED radically changed its interpretation of the Western Allies' air raids on German cities, especially on Dresden. The narrative of collective German guilt disappeared almost completely and the responsibility of the Western Allies was emphasised. The residents of German cities were depicted as innocent victims and likened to the victims of Nazi persecution. In the framework of a national anti-Western campaign that the SED waged in order to mobilise the Germans and especially the citizens of the Federal Republic towards pro-Soviet feeling, the party did not hesitate to revive Nazi terms, slogans and opinions regarding the Allies and their air raids on German cities, such as the term Anglo-American terror assaults *(Anglo-amerikanische Terrorangriffe)* coined by the propaganda Minister, Dr. Goebbels.[14]

In 1955 the committee of the anti-fascist fighters of the GDR instructed participants to use the following slogan on banners in a ceremony which was planned to be held at the memorial site of the former concentration camp Sachsenhausen: 'Die SS-Mörder von Sachsenhausen und die amerikanischen Luftgangster, die Mörder von Dresden und Berlin, Hand in Hand.'[15] Such expressions equated the American and British air raids with Nazi atrocities.

On the fourth memorial day of the attack on Dresden in February 1949, the SED paper, *Neues Deutschland*, for the first time dedicated one half of its Sunday supplement to this topic. Accompanying the reports of eyewitnesses were photographs of the dead bodies piled up in the city centre, as well as other contributions about the destruction of the city. Included in this supplement was also an article by the mayor (now *Oberbürgermeister*) Walter Weidauer. In this article Weidauer presented his views on the air raid on Dresden, but they were completely different from those which had appeared in the same newspaper on the first remembrance day three years before, in 1946.

In 1949 Weidauer explicitly accused the Americans and the British of bombarding Dresden despite no military need to do so. The air raid was defined as a crime committed by the Western Allies; they and not the Nazis should bear the responsibility for it. Although Weidauer asserts: 'ganz gewiß ist es wahr, daß die Hitlerfaschisten das böse Beispiel dieser barbarischen Kriegsführung gegeben und bis zur raffinierten Vollendung entwickelt hatten', this argument is used to contrast Western Allied strategy with that of the Soviet army. In contrast to the Anglo-American air raids, which followed the Nazi example in their bombarding of Dresden, the Soviet Red Army harboured no barbaric feelings of vengeance and retaliation against the German civilian population, 'trotz Millionen unschuldiger Tote ihrer Zivilbevölkerung'.[16]

These changes mark a dramatic break with the earlier Communist narrative that had depicted the Second World War as a *bellum justum* of the righteous and moral victorious Allies, including Great Britain and the USA, against Nazi barbarism. From now on, the story of the war was mobilised to the needs of the Cold War struggle and the Second World War was depicted as a series of barbaric attacks by Nazis against the German people and the Soviet Union while the Western Allies observed with satisfaction the bloodshed and the exhaustion on both sides.

This propaganda campaign reached its peak in 1955. The remembrance of the destruction of Dresden and other German cities together with emphasis on the suffering of the civilian population was supposed to alert the Germans to the menace of an escalation toward a nuclear war. The SED claimed that the rearmament of the Federal Republic and the latter's entrance into NATO was accelerating the atomic threat. An SED document of 1955 includes the statement:

> Die Pariser Verträge, die Adenauer im Bonner Bundestag durchpeitschen will, bedeuten die Wiederbewaffnung der Mörder von Warschau und Coventry, von Stalingrad und Rotterdam, von Lidice und Oradour und ihr Bündnis mit den Mördern von Dresden und Hamburg, Berlin und Mannheim, Hiroshima und Pjongjang.[17]

In this constellation the American conduct during the Second World War and after is equated with Nazi war-crimes, and the conventional bombing of the German cities is likened to the use of the atomic bomb on Hiroshima and Nagasaki. After 1955 this campaign lost much of its blatant and belligerent force; its contents, however, remained intact and did not change until the end of the GDR.

This new conceptualisation of the Second World War and of the former Western Allies also received its visual expression in the GDR. The design of the *Heidefriedhof*, the cemetery in Dresden where the victims of the notorious air raid on the city were buried, implicitly compared the fate of civilian victims of the Allied air raid with the fate of the anti-Fascist fighters. In 1951 an *Ehrenhain* (a memorial grove) to the memory of anti-Fascist victims of Nazism was planted in the graveyard, situated symmetrically opposite the area where in 1945 civilian victims of the Anglo-American air raid and their remains were interred. It was there that the anti-Fascist fighters were buried. Placing these two groups of victims at opposite poles of the same axis suggests a moral equation of their destiny. In 1964 this admittedly rather obscure suggestion received a much more concrete symbolic form. In the middle of the axis connecting the two graveyards a circular monument was erected which consisted of fourteen stelae that commemorated the victims of the Nazi concentration camps and the cities destroyed during the Second World War. The names of seven Nazi concentration camps were inscribed on seven of these stelae: Auschwitz, Bergen-Belsen, Buchenwald, Dachau, Ravensbrück, Sachsenhausen and Theresienstadt. The names of seven cities destroyed during the war appeared on the other seven pillars: Coventry, Dresden, Leningrad, Lidice, Oradour, Rotterdam and Warsaw. The monument thus equates Dresden with Auschwitz, a symbol of the annihilation of the Jews.

The Gradual Westward Dissemination of the Communist Narrative

During the early days of the Federal Republic the issue of Allied Air raids on German cities during the War became even more delicate. The SED turned this nationalist topic into a central political tool in the Communist campaign against the Federal Republic and the Western bloc. The propaganda about 'Anglo-American war crimes against Germans' was focused first on Dresden, but soon the West German Communist party (KPD) and other pro-Soviet organisations in the Federal Republic imported these issues and slogans into West German cities such as Hamburg and aired them freely during the commemorative ceremonies that were conducted in memory of victims of the Allied air raids. The young Federal Republic, which integrated itself within the Western bloc and entered NATO in the early 1950s, could not tolerate the airing of such propaganda against the former national enemies and the current allies and protectors.

During the early 1950s the local authorities in Hamburg, the most severely damaged West German city, seemed – as elsewhere in the FRG – to consciously limit public preoccupation with the British air raids, on the occasion of the anniversary of the bombardments of July

1943. In contrast to the mass demonstrations held in Dresden almost every year on 13 February, the ceremonies in Hamburg held late in July were of a very modest nature and usually had a very limited public attendance. There were only a couple of thousand participants in Hamburg in comparison with the hundred thousands who participated in the ceremonies in Dresden, reported in the Communist press. In sharp contrast to the aggressive tone against the Allies in the Communist ceremonies, the official commemoration in Hamburg had a conciliatory nature. In the ceremony organised by the Catholic committee in July 1951, a priest from Munich, J.S. Waldmann, gave a speech in which he said: 'Wir sind nicht hergekommen, um Anklage gegen das eigene Volk oder die Völker draußen zu erheben.'[18]

Similar to the speeches expressed on remembrance days during the early 1950s, the treatment that the West German press in general and the local press in Hamburg in particular gave the Royal Air Force attack on Hamburg in the Summer of 1943 was characterised by a moderate and conciliatory tone toward the former enemies. Usually, the national identity of the bombers was not mentioned; however, the opinion in the press probably did not represent public opinion on these issues.

Since 1949, the local and national press of the GDR, and the local Communist organ *Hamburger Volkszeitung*, allocated more space to articles on the Allied air raids on German cities during the Second World War than the non-Communist press of the Federal Republic. Until 1952, the Hamburg press still tried as much as possible to limit articles about the British bombardments of summer 1943. It appears that the press complied with the official policy of the city-state's Senate, and the federal government in general, a policy that was aimed at limiting the stimulation of negative feelings toward the former enemy and still-present British Allied forces in the German public.

In August 1952 the *Hamburger Abendblatt* for the first time published an article under large headlines on the front page concerning the commemoration of the air raid victims. From 1953, the tenth anniversary of the bombardment, the local press started to publish a series of longer articles on every decennial. Whole page articles containing testimonies and photos of the air raids appeared almost every day during July. The West German press separated the discussion of Allied bombardments from the context of the struggle against Nazism during the Second World War and emphasised the enormous suffering of the German civilian population. Gradually, there were more and more allegations that the bombing was an act of mass murder and a war crime.

The Social-Democratic establishment in Hamburg also tried to stick to the pre-Cold War narrative which referred to the bombardments in the context of German collective guilt. The speech of the city's mayor, Max Brauer, in August 1952, on the occasion of the consecration of the memorial for the victims of the air raid on Hamburg in Ohlsdorf cemetery, is typical of this. Brauer asked the audience: 'Warum mußten sie alle sterben? [...] Weil unser Volk die Freiheit verloren hatte, ließ es sich von einer unmenschlichen Diktatur an die Schlachtbank führen. Es regnete Bomben und Feuer über fremde Städte. Dann gingen unsere eigenen Städte in Flammen auf'.[19]

Brauer's straightforward language, comparable to the speeches held in Dresden until the outbreak of the Cold War, might explain the decision of the local SPD leadership in Hamburg to choose a sculpture with a non-Christian character and comfortless subject (although the memorial contained at least one figure that might symbolise consolation). The Hamburg Senate invested a large sum of money in the memorial for the victims of the bombardment. As in Dresden and in Chemnitz, the memorial was erected in the city cemetery and not in the centre of the city as some citizens and politicians had wished. The motif that the memorial's designer, Gerhard Marcks, had chosen was taken from Greek mythology; a sculpture of Charon navigating his boat of the dead over the river Styx of the underworld. Marcks explained his decision to choose a pre-Christian motif for this memorial by claiming that

> [...] hier eine christliche Todesauffassung nicht am Platz war. Weder ist in dieser Art Tod irgend etwas Versöhnliches zu sehen, noch sterben die Bombenopfer als Märtyrer für eine Idee, sondern alle, Männer, Frauen und Kinder wurden in den Wahnsinn der Vernichtung hineingerissen, ohne Antwort auf die Frage: Warum? die auf so vielen Grabkreuzen sich wiederholt.[20]

The figure of Charon shows indifference towards the tragic suffering of the passengers he is carrying on his boat: a sitting man, bent, his hands grasping his head, in a pose that expresses despair and sorrow; a young couple, the woman with her hand on the shoulder of the man, the eyes of both are lowered, a mother putting a protective hand on the head of her little boy who hides his face in her skirt. On the prow of the boat is placed the last figure: a naked man standing and staring at the horizon.

Charon is the largest figure in this monument and the only one who looks directly at the observers of the monument. This figure offers no Christian consolation for the bereaved relatives of the air raid victims. In the text that Marcks wrote on the monument he maintained that 'Charon [ist ein] überlebensgroßer Dämon mit grausamen Zügen: Gleichgültigkeit, organisierter Massenmord.'[21]

These words of Marcks indicate that like many Germans, he also adopted the Nazi propaganda that presented the Allied air raids on German cities as horrendous crimes. Marcks's choice of words insinuates an equation between the bombardment of Hamburg and the language used to describe the mass murder of European Jewry. Max Brauer, the mayor of Hamburg, did not regard the bombardment of his city in the same way as Marcks did. He also did not know that Marcks first sketched the motif of Charon's boat in 1933, under the impression of his emigrating Jewish friends, i.e. those leaving Germany.[22] Brauer was neither a member of the committee that decided to choose Marcks's masterpiece for the memorial, nor was he interested in Marcks's ideas. In the document the committee submitted to the Senate, the choice of Marcks's sculpture is explained with these words:

> [...] der eingereichte Entwurf [erweckt] die Hoffnung auf ein menschlich und künstlerisch bedeutendes, ernstes und allgemein verständliches Mal, das auch an der Aufgabe mitwirken wird, das Gedächtnis an die Opfer des Bombenkrieges aus der Sphäre der Verbitterung zu befreien, ohne ihm Schmerz, Schwere und Tiefe zu nehmen. Indem es die Frage nach dem Sinn des Geschehenen stellt und künstlerisch meistert, wird es auch an den Lebenden bilden.[23]

The alienated character of Marcks's sculpture was probably perceived by the committee as a 'bitterness neutraliser'. It offers only very little consolation for the bereaved relatives of the victims of the British air raids of July 1943. This position chimed with Brauer's claim to regard the bombardments in the political context of the German guilt discourse. Brauer abstained from representing self pity and the idea of being a victim of evil aggression, notions that had been promoted and nurtured in the ceremonies to commemorate the victims of the allied bombardments on the German cities, initiated by the Communist and pro-Soviet organisations in Dresden as in Hamburg at the beginning of the 1950s.

During the 1950s certain West German newspapers published headlines and articles containing Communist propaganda arguments, equating the Western Allies' conventional air attacks on the German cities in the Second World War with the atomic bombs dropped on Japanese cities. They did this, of course, without accepting the ideological contexts of these arguments. Instead, they emphasised that the bombardment of Hamburg and even more so that of Dresden were worse than the effect the atom bombs had on Hiroshima and Nagasaki.[24] As late as the mid 1960s even the liberal supra-regional press over-inflated the figures of the number of people killed during the air raid on Dresden, maintaining that the Allies were responsible for 130,000 German victims, while the atomic bombs killed 'only' 71,000 people in Hiroshima and only 36,000 in Nagasaki.[25]

1963 saw the publication of David Irving's book *The Destruction of Dresden* in Britain with its explicit criticism of the conduct of Sir Arthur Harris, who was 'concerned less with possible interpretations of international law than with winning the war'.[26] The translation of this book into German the following year gave the political culture of the Federal Republic a certain amount of legitimacy to raise charges against the Allied war conduct, charges that up to that time were uttered either by Communists or by the extreme right. During the 1950s such voices had appeared only in the provincial press. In clear affinity to the Communist Cold War interpretation of the attack on Dresden, Irving claimed that the horrible damage caused to the city by Allied aircraft was not intended to accelerate the defeat of Nazi Germany, as the Allies had declared. Instead, Irving maintained, it was designed to demonstrate to the Soviets the superiority of Western air bombers as part of the super- powers' struggle for hegemony in post-war Europe. A review of Irving's book in the weekly *DIE ZEIT* defined the attack on Dresden as '[d]er wahrscheinlich größte Massenmord der gesamten Menschengeschichte, der in der Spanne eines einzigen Tages stattfand'.[27] This change in the published and official judgment of the British air raid had started in the local press of Hamburg in 1963. By 1973, the thirtieth anniversary of the air raid, it had become highly critical.

In 1967 Rolf Hochhuth published his play *Soldaten*. The play accused Churchill's policy of strategic bombing of the German cities, especially of Hamburg, of violating the Geneva Convention. The Allied air raids should therefore be considered a war crime.[28] The final article of a series on the occasion of the thirtieth anniversary of the British air attack on Hamburg, published in that city in 1973, contained an implicit personal accusation against Sir Arthur Harris, Commander-in-Chief of the RAF Bomber Command:

> Das 'Unternehmen Gomorrha' sollte 1943 Hamburg von der Landkarte radieren [...]. Chef dieser Bomber-Armada, die in den großen Nachtangriffen 1943 Hamburg vernichten sollte wie einst Karthago, war Sir Arthur Travers Harris, 'Bomber Harris' genannt. Heute lebt der 81-jährige in Goring-on-Thames in England. War er der Schuldige am Tod von mehr als 40,000 Hamburgern?[29]

The article elicited readers' letters to the *Hamburger Abendblatt*. One of them explicitly accused the Allies of committing war crimes and the mass murder of hundreds of thousands of women and children.[30] Since the 1970s, claims have frequently appeared in the local press of Hamburg that the British bombardment had been aimed not only at destroying the city, but at its complete annihilation (*Vernichtung*). The local press in Hamburg falsely attributed annihilation plans regarding the German cities to Harris and the British leadership, plans of the kind Hitler designed during the Battle of Britain with regard to London and other British cities.

Such allegations are reminiscent of similar claims in the SED organs in the early 1950s, regarding the air raid on Dresden. The choice of terms such as 'annihilation' for the Allied bombardment of Hamburg might also imply another hidden equation of the Allied conduct with that of the Nazi annihilation of the Jews, an equation implicitly used by the SED propaganda in the early 1950s.

The iconisation of 'Bomber Harris' as the sole person responsible for the destruction of the city and the death of its population became even more vivid during the fortieth anniversary of the British air attack on Hamburg in 1983. Harris and not the British cabinet appeared in Germany as the *bête noire* not only in the local press, where a series of articles on the air raid in the *Hamburger Abendblatt* started with one entitled 'Sir Arthur Harris' tödliche Rechnung',[31] but also in a speech given by the city's mayor, Klaus von Dohnanyi, at the central ceremony:

> In der Nacht vom 24. auf den 25. Juli 1943 flogen 800 britische Maschinen aus den Bombergeschwadern des Luftmarschalls Sir Arthur Harris Hamburg an und legten einen Bombenteppich über die dichtbesiedelten Gebiete der Innenstadt und der Stadtteile Altona, Einsbüttel und Hoheluft.[32]

As in Dresden, the ceremonial language emphasised that '[D]en Hamburgerinnen und Hamburgern [...] sind die Massengräber und das Mahnmal in Ohlsdorf [the cemetery where the victims of the British air raid were buried, G.M.] Klage und Mahnung: Nie wieder Krieg'.[33]

Like the earlier Communist propaganda, Dohnanyi also emphasised that the Germans (implicitly in contrast to their former enemies who had bombed the German cities) had learnt the lesson from the air raids of the past and were implementing this lesson regarding the present menace of a nuclear war which might annihilate humanity: This is an implicit claim for German moral superiority; the sinner who had repented of his sins and had learnt a lesson from them, now had a new pacifist mission to preach and to educate humanity for world peace.

However, the implicit accusations regarding the British conduct could hardly be compared with the anti-Western venom of the Communist ceremonies at Dresden during the GDR era. Large scale ceremonies now take place only on the decennial anniversaries. Since the fortieth anniversary in 1983, not only the local media, but the entire German media have commemorated the bombardment of the city. On July 23, 1983, the first German TV channel (ARD) broadcast Hans Brecht's film, *Operation Gomorrha* during prime time. The commemoration of the bombardment of Hamburg on a national level in the FRG in the last three decennial anniversaries resembles the national dimension of the commemoration that was granted to the bombardment of Dresden in the GDR.

During the commemoration of the sixtieth anniversary of the air raid on Hamburg in July 2003, certain voices in the political culture of the Federal Republic echoed Jörg Friedrich's rage at the Allied conduct of strategic bombing in his books *Der Brand* and *Brandstätten*. The post-Cold War atmosphere enabled Friedrich and his adherents to shift the charge of committing war crimes from 'Bomber' Harris directly on to Winston Churchill. Friedrich's insinuated reference to the Allied bombing as a sort of a 'German Holocaust'[34] and his implied moral equation of Churchill with Hitler[35] revives the nationalist narrative of the SED propaganda that likened Dresden with Auschwitz.

The geo-political location of Dresden in the Soviet occupation zone and the later GDR and Hamburg in Western Germany in the formative years of the Cold War determined their status in the German historical consciousness. While Dresden turned into an icon of German suffering, Hamburg occupied only a subordinate role, in spite of the higher number of casualties. Dresden retained this status even after the end of the Cold War. However, gradually and even before the end of the Cold War, the commemoration of the air raid on Hamburg adopted many of the characteristics of the commemorations in Dresden. This process combined with the end of the GDR and the anti-fascist commemorations aligned the ceremonies in Dresden more with those in Hamburg and laid the foundation for a united German commemorative culture.

Notes

[1] Friedrich Reichert, *Verbrannt bis zur Unkenntlichkeit*, DZA Verlag für Kultur und Wissenschaft: Dresden, 1994, pp. 59-62.

[2] Walter Weidauer, 'Zum 13. Februar,' *Sächsische Volkszeitung*, 13 February 1946, p. 2.

[3] Bundesarchiv – Filmarchiv: *Dresden*. A DEFA Film by Richard Groschopp, 1946.

[4] Bundesarchiv – Filmarchiv: *Dresden warnt und mahnt*. A DEFA Film by Heino Brandes 1951.

[5] 'Die Bombardierung von Hamburg. Erinnerung an den July 1943,' *Hamburger Echo*, 20 July 1946.

[6] Wolf Biermann, 'Die Rettung,' in: Volker Hage, ed., *Hamburg 1943. Literarische Zeugnisse zum Feuersturm*. Fischer: Frankfurt am Main, 2003, p. 246.

[7] Henny Brenner, *'Das Lied ist aus'. Ein jüdisches Schicksal in Dresden*, Pendo: Zurich and Munich 2001, p. 86 and p. 88. For a similar experience of Jews in Dresden see: Victor Klemperer, *Ich will Zeugnis ablegen bis zum letzten. Tagebücher 1933-1945*, Aufbau Verlag: Berlin, 1995, Vol. 2, pp. 661ff.

[8] Heinz Boberach, *Meldungen aus dem Reich 1938-1945*, Pawlak Verlag: Hersching, 1984, vol. 14, pp. 5545-5546.

[9] Deutsches Volksliedarchiv, Freiburg: Gr. II 2. Weltkrieg M 300. In 1940 Göring boasted that if enemy aircraft could penetrate the German anti-aircraft defense then, he would no longer be called Göring but 'Meyer'. Thus during the 'Luftkrieg', the people referred to him as 'Meyer'.

[10] Uwe Timm, *Am Beispiel meines Bruders*, Kiepenheuer & Witsch: Cologne, 2003, p. 24. The grammatical error is in the original letter.

[11] E.g. Deutsches Rundfunkarchiv, Wiesbaden: 2945653 - PK-Bericht: Dresden nach den alliierten Bombenangriffen, 20 February 1945: 'Weit entfernt, ist diese barbarische teuflische Kriegsführung, die Mord, Terror und Verbrechen auf Ihre

Fahne geschrieben hat, von unserer Auffassung eines Krieges auch eines totalen Krieges im wahrsten Sinne des Wortes'.

[12] Boberach, pp. 5562f.

[13] 'Als Hamburgs Pulsschlag stockte,' *Hamburger Echo*, No. 58, 22 July, 1947, p. 3.

[14] A typical Nazi reaction to the air raid on Dresden. DRA 2945653, PK-Bericht: Dresden nach den alliierten Bombenangriffen, 20 February 1945; See as well Golo Mann's (at the time an American soldier) answer to the Nazi Propaganda transmitted on radio Luxemburg by the Allies: 'Deutschland in Flammen,' *Frankfurter Allgemeine Zeitung*, 18 February 2005; Tilmann Lahme, 'Rede an eine Nation vor dem Untergang,' *Frankfurter Allgemeine Zeitung*, 18 February 2005.

[15] Archiv der Gedenkstätte Sachsenhausen, AS, KAW, K5/M2, Bl. 133-134. Arbeitskopie aus Unterlagen des Komitees der Antifaschistischen Widerstandkämpfer der DDR. I am very grateful to Dr. Carmen Lange who drew my attention to this document.

[16] Walter Weidauer, 'Vor vier Jahren sank Dresden in Asche,' Sonntagsbeilage *Neues Deutschland*, 13 February 1949.

[17] Bundesarchiv Berlin (BA): 'Politische Richtlinien zum 10. Jahrestag des amerikanischen Terrorangriffes auf Dresden'' 29 January 1955. SAPMO NY 4090/517, Bl. 200-204.

[18] 'Verzeihen aber nicht vergessen. Hamburg gedachte den Opfern des Bombenkrieges,' *Hamburger Abendblatt*, No. 175, 30 July 1951, p. 3.

[19] Speech of mayor Max Brauer on the unveiling of the memorial for the commemoration of the victims of the Hamburg air raid on 16. August 1952. In: *Das Mahnmal für die Opfer des Bombenkrieges. Ein Gang der Erinnerung zu den Gräbern der Bombenopfer auf dem Ohlsdorfer Friedhof*, Förderkreis Ohlsdorfer Friedhof: Hamburg, 1992, pp. 28f.

[20] Beate Manske, 'Auftrag und Botschaft. Mahnmale von Gerhard Marcks,' in: Martina Rudolf, ed., *Gerhard Marcks 1889-1981. Retrospektive*, Hirmer: Munich, 1989, p. 286.

[21] *Gerhard Marcks 1889-1981. Briefe und Werke*, Ausgewählt, bearbeitet und eingeleitet von Ursula Frenzel, Prestel: Munich, 1988, p. 144.

[22] Manske, p. 286.

[23] Denkmalschutzamt Hamburg: 39-430.302 Ehrenmal für die Bombenopfer in Ohlsdorf – Drucksache für die Senatssitzung: Berichtstatter Senator Landahl s.d. (probably written between May and August 1948), p. 2.

[24] 'Dresden war schlimmer als Hiroshima,' *Kasseler Post*, 11 February 1955, 'Schlimmer als die Atombombe,' *Hamburger Abendblatt*, No. 174, 29 July 1953, p. 3: 'Die Katastrophe des Jahres 1943 übertraf noch die Wirkung der Atombombenangriffe auf Hiroshima und Nagasaki'.

[25] Margaret Hofmann, 'Als Dresden in Trümmer sank,' *DIE ZEIT*, 25 September 1964; Wolf Schneider, 'Warum musste Dresden sterben?,' *Süddeutsche Zeitung*, 12 February 1965.

[26] David Irving, *The Destruction of Dresden*, Macmillan: London, 1963, p. 76.

[27] Margaret Hofmann, p. 15.

[28] See for example the dialogue between Bishop Bell and Churchill, Rolf Hochhuth, *Soldiers. An Obituary for Geneva*. Translated by Robert David MacDonald, Grove Press: New York, 1968, pp.190ff.

[29] 'Hamburg die unverzagte Stadt,' *Hamburger Abendblatt*, Nr. 172, 26 July 1973, p. 10.

[30] Alfred Schmidt, 'Waren das Keine Kriegsverbrechen?,' *Hamburger Abendblatt*, No. 174, 28/29 July 1973, p. 28.

[31] 'Sir Arthur Harris' tödliche Rechnung,' in: 'Als das Feuer vom Himmel fiel. Eine Serie von Egbert A. Hoffmann,' *Hamburger Abendblatt*, No. 162, 15 July 1983, p. 7.

[32] 'Dohnanyi gedenkt der Opfer des Bombenangriffs,' *Hamburger Abendblatt*, Nr. 169, 23/24 July 1983, p. 7.

[33] Ibid.

[34] E.g. by calling a British squadron an *Einsatzgruppe* and the Germans *Ausgerottete*. Jörg Friedrich, *Der Brand. Deutschland im Bombenkrieg 1940-1945*, Propyläen: Munich, 2002, pp. 93, 388, 311, 359.

[35] 'Ein Kriegsverbrechen? Das muss jeder für sich selbst entscheiden,' *Die Welt*, 21 November 2002.

Heinz-Peter Preußer

Regarding and Imagining. Contrived Immediacy of the Allied Bombing Campaign in Photography, Novel and Historiography

This chapter is a critical reflection on the debate about Allied bombing of Germany. Its purpose is to show how immediacy is suggestively produced within different media and what problems arise from this. Beginning with an outline of the debate around W.G. Sebald's *Luftkrieg und Literatur* and a theoretical discussion of the shock-effect of images of atrocities the chapter discusses the representation of the horrors of the bombing experience in four different types of texts, Jörg Friedrich's history of the bombing campaign *Der Brand* and his picture book *Brandstätten*, Gert Ledig's novel *Die Vergeltung*, Hans Erich Nossack's *Der Untergang* and Alexander Kluge's fictional-documentary narrative *Der Luftangriff auf Halberstadt am 8. April 1945*.

I. Introductory Remarks

In autumn 1997 W.G. Sebald presented his Zurich 'Poetik-Vorlesungen' on *Luftkrieg und Literatur*, which were met with wide reactions by the press. Sebald's central thesis is that post-war German literature had failed with regard to the horrors of the bombing war that virtually eradicated the German cities during World War Two. Furthermore, Sebald read this failure as part of a problem of collective psychology – as a form of collective repression and taboo formation. He writes:

> Die in der Geschichte bis dahin einzigartige Vernichtungsaktion [!] ist in den Annalen der neu sich konstituierenden Nation nur in Form vager Verallgemeinerungen eingegangen, scheint kaum eine Schmerzensspur [!] hinterlassen zu haben im kollektiven Bewußtsein.[1]

Historically speaking, this sentence is an affront since it specifically omits the victims on the other side (e.g. in the Soviet Union) by its implicit comparison. However, even the diagnosis of a taboo regarding the air war in Germany is incorrect. Sebald himself names several literary examples in the published version of *Luftkrieg und Literatur*, some of which I am going to discuss in this article: Hans-Erich Nossack, Gert Ledig and Alexander Kluge. He also engages with numerous reservations against his theses. The fact remains that about half a million civilians died in the allied bombings; in several cities – Hamburg, Pforzheim, etc. – the number of dead amounted to several tens of thousands. Sebald is also at pains not to be misunderstood as a revisionist. Giving examples of German bombardments – Guernica, Warsaw, Belgrade, Rotterdam, and London – he writes: 'Die Mehrzahl der Deutschen weiß heute, so hofft man zumindest, daß wir die Vernichtung der Städte, in denen wir einst lebten, geradezu provozierten.'[2]

Sebald's lectures produced an astonishing reaction in the press. Volker Hage's edited volume *Zeugen der Zerstörung* collected interviews with Wolf Biermann, Walter Kempowski, Rolf Hochhuth, Dieter Forte or Kurt Vonnegut to refute Sebald's thesis of collective forgetting.[3] The ensuing debate, to which Hage contributed considerably,[4] resulted in the re-publication of Gert Ledig's forgotten novels, making them accessible to a wider public for the first time since the late 1950s.[5]

Into this heady climate Jörg Friedrich published *Der Brand* in 2002.[6] This narrative historiography of the bombing war could almost be imagined to deliver what Sebald claimed to be lacking;[7] Friedrich's account attempts to re-inscribe the bombing war into collective memory. He emphatically describes the Germans as victims of a cynical annihilation, without the gestures of exoneration and exculpation that Sebald was still using. For Friedrich, the air war is not primarily the result of a war of annihilation started by Hitler's Germany, not even a reply to the systematic policy of extermination of Nazi racial ideology but an effect of Allied, specifically British power politics that predominantly affects the innocent, i.e. the civilian population.

Friedrich relativised German responsibility by implicit, not by direct comparisons; this, however, followed suit immediately after the publication of the book. Particularly in the UK the reactions were indignant, as some reviewers saw Churchill described as a war criminal by Friedrich and thus compared to Hitler.[8] Friedrich's revisionism, however, is more indirect. Particularly his choice of language suggests a parallel to the mass extermination of the Holocaust or Germany's attack on the Soviet Union, without explicitly referring to them. Furthermore, he speaks of German suffering within a historical constellation that is articulating the German experience of extreme suffering, for example Günter Grass's novella *Im Krebsgang* on the sinking of the refugee ship *Wilhelm Gustloff* or the series of articles in *SPIEGEL* on the expulsion and flight of Germans from

Eastern Europe. The air war itself became the subject of a prime time TV documentary with the collaboration of Friedrich.[9] All this indicates that the perpetrator-victim dichotomy had begun to de-stabilise.[10]

Hans-Ulrich Wehler hits the nail on the head about why the trauma of German suffering had been so obviously neglected over the past decades: the fear of the accusation of *Aufrechnung* or setting off German crimes against German suffering: 'angesichts der Millionenzahlen des Holocaust und des antislawischen Vernichtungskrieges gab es eine tief sitzende Scheu, diese deutsche Leidensgeschichte zu schreiben.'[11]

Friedrich gives up this inhibition; he provocatively takes up the gesture of 'Gegenredner' to the existing social consensus.[12] He stages the experience of suffering as physically as the medium of the book, and later that of the picture book, allow. Andreas Kilb comments approvingly: 'Fast sechzig Jahre nach Kriegsende geht es nicht mehr darum, Schuld festzustellen. Es geht um die Feststellung des Schmerzes.'[13] The problems of this shift in perception are the subject of the following pages.

II. Shock, Death and Disgust: The Medium of Photography

As Susan Sontag has recently re-established in her essay *Regarding the Pain of Others*, photographs of war work by the almost inevitable shock effect they cause in the beholder.[14] The moving images that determine our media environment affect us less directly and leave a less distinct trace in memory due to their fleeting nature: 'Memory freeze-frames, its basic unit is the single image'. In the discourse about memory, 'the photograph has the deeper bite'. It 'provides a quick way of apprehending something and a compact form for memorising it'.[15] The photograph's medial condition more or less prepares the thematic shock of the horrors of war. Every photograph bursts parts out of the unstructured flow of time. The continuum disintegrates into the instantaneous moment that needs an active observer because temporality is given only in the condition of regarding. As life is existentially dependent on chronological context, since chronology is the essence of being, its destruction reminds us of death, something Roland Barthes touches upon in his essay *La Chambre Claire*.[16] The photographs are still, like the dead whom they keep alive in the memorialising image: but only as divested of life.

Barthes says death is the *eidos* of photography.[17] In peoples with magic beliefs, photography is frequently equalled with the stealing of the soul.[18] The spatial compactness and the temporally isolated nature of photography guide the observer's interest and modify the expectations. Ultimately, war photography reduplicates in representation what is its essence as medium: its affinity to death. It shows transitoriness not in the contemplative gaze of the melancholic subject but in the immediacy of affectedness. The volume *War against War!* by Ernst Friedrich was conceived as shock therapy which sought to morally disqualify military operations by exposing their consequences with a ruthlessness that produced only disgust and abhorrence.[19] Published in 1924, the volume of photographs shows the disfigurations that the First World War left behind: grotesque mutilations, especially of the face, of victims whose survival of their injuries appears to make a mockery of the human form; men who lived without lower jaws, without noses and who were kept from public view.

Disgust cannot, as Kant already knew, be integrated into a contemplation of the beautiful or the sublime. Paintings of battles have to be kept free from it, so not to undermine the distance of the spectator. Otherwise, artistic imagination and nature of the object cannot be told apart.[20] The blurring of object and emotion, which characterises disgust, undermines as well the certainty of individuation. The cause of disgust is close inspection. In the images of decomposition we recognise an anticipation of the dissolution that awaits us as subjects. Georges Bataille has theorised the 'Rückkehr zum gärenden Leben': disgust is an anticipatory feeling of the 'kommende[n] Vernichtung [...] die sich vollständig auf das Wesen, das ich bin, herabsenken wird'.[21] We see the decomposition of the other and feel the amorphous working in ourselves.

III. Reflections of the Real: Icon and Digitalisation
The photograph addresses us more directly, the more abhorrence it causes. We know that the photograph is a reflection of something real, reflex of light from a suffering body. According to Charles Sanders Peirce, its 'existential one-to-one correspondence' connects the photograph with the real event. And via this 'authentication' that, according to Barthes, photographs always desire to be, the images of horror affect us immediately. In the moment the regarding subject is

confronted with his/her own mortality, with that dissolution that produces disgust. The defence may switch over into pleasure, the observer may change into a voyeur. Or he/she feels, from his/her position of safety, pity, if not outrage or even thirst for vengeance. However, the cleansing of emotions that can spring from feelings of disgust, always focuses on one's own self. The close inspection of the object causes the immediacy of affectedness; and it is intensified because the object of the gaze is taken for real.

In his Semiotics, Peirce distinguishes between three classes of signs: index, icon and symbol. An icon gives a transformation of the real based on similarities. Painting or sculpture are approximations of the real; nevertheless, they do not render a point-for-point translation. The symbol, in contrast, is based on convention and thus creates arbitrary relations. We can recognise Saussure's idea of the arbitrariness in language here.[22] Signifier and signified are related to each other by an act of collective training;[23] apart from that nothing connects them. The index is different: Here a causal relation exists between object and sign; and this relation is legitimised physically. Rising smoke signifies a (hidden) fire. Photographs correspond point for point to the original that they represent, only compressed into two-dimensional space. The procedure of photography coerces it into precision.[24]

It is noteworthy that this directness does not disappear, despite the fact that the paradigm of photography is being dissolved at the point of mere physical authentication; digital technology seems to spell the end of the age of photography. This has been described as the entropy of photography, as an irreversible epistemological break.[25] However, we still credit photographs, at first, with authenticity. The meaningful content of the 'what-had-been', which sticks to the photograph since the discovery of the light-sensitivity of silver crystals,[26] has not been fully undermined by the 'dubiative' (i.e. dubious, suspicious) digital image. Whatever may become doubtful by the possibilities of digital editing, the truth content is undermined by the wilful falsifications, not by the procedure itself. The purposeful deception is necessary to shake the trust in the indexical representability. Deception, however, predates digitalisation by which the real can be retouched completely. Victims 'swap sides', depending on who interprets them, who creates the captions.

IV. Contrived Regarding: Jörg Friedrich's *Brandstätten*

The photographs recently collected by Jörg Friedrich in his volume *Brandstätten. Der Anblick des Krieges*, appropriate the idea of re-coding without admitting it. The chapter 'Bergung' (rescue) shows the suffering of the creature: human, but also animal bodies in unspeakable disfiguration. As the reactions from the press alone show, all of these images of 'German suffering' seem to have an *Urbild*, an original image: the Holocaust.[27] One empathises with the victims, because all suffering of the creature has claims on our undivided empathy. However, it is exactly this comparison with the Holocaust which imposes itself upon us and which is pre-structured by the shock of the camp images of 1945 that is problematic about Friedrich's photographs. Friedrich is interested in representing German history as victim history. The image contexts retrospectively found national identity that relativises the victim/perpetrator discourse.

It is certainly in the eye of the beholder to see the association with the Holocaust at all. Piles of corpses are primarily piles of corpses. They show the destruction of life. This evokes, seen out of context, pity and horror. And Friedrich shows photographs of Germans who were subjects of this suffering.[28] However, in Germany, these photographs cannot be regarded without denoting the emblem of industrial mass killing, the destruction of European Jewry. Society is pre-structured in its reception of images to the guilt of the Nazi regime, not least due to the re-education after 1945 and the continuing evocation of this legacy in culture, media and schools. As a German, when looking at the piles of bodies to be burnt in Dresden, one simultaneously recognises Auschwitz. The traumatic experience of the air raids predated the confrontation with the images from the concentration camps. However, throughout the decades, the images from the death camps are more present and more lasting. What is at stake is thus the expectation, especially in Germany, when regarding those images. A point of critique with Friedrich is, in my opinion, that he instrumentalises the cultural pre-structuring of a specifically German perception since he is aware that the piles of Dresden bodies will be perceived as a reply to the Holocaust. This is not just the effect of the single photograph but of his composition of the book and the *Inszenierung* of perception.

The volume which comprises 240 pages with about 400 photographs is divided into 10 chapters with 'Bergung' occupying the centre, being the largest chapter: 68 photographs on 48 pages. The chapter is structured by a recognisable frame which begins with the image of German cities before the bombings [Früher] and ends with images of destruction and rebuilding [Heute]. The loss is supposed to be anticipated and is confirmed at the end: whether in Hamburg or in Halberstadt, Würzburg or Ulm, Leipzig or Magdeburg, Cologne or Bremen. The first photographs waver between idyll and poverty, representation and urban bustle. Consciously, the introduction is concluded with images of the swastika flag being flown in Hannover and of an SS parade in Nuremberg (!). Whenever the observer expects something to be cut out, it appears nevertheless. We see the planning and machinery of aerial warfare, such as the B-17 bombers, the *Flying Fortress*, and B-24, *Liberator*, the dropping of bombs and detonations, cascades of light from parachute flares and anti-aircraft-fire, finally burning buildings and crashed pilots. *Attack* is followed by *defence*. Friedrich presents fighter planes and anti-aircraft-guns, floodlight positions, operations of the Reich's air defence organisation, the securing of unexploded shells and the work of the fire fighting units. The chapter 'Zuflucht' shows cellars, mining shafts and bunkers and life in and in between them.

This is followed by 'Bergung', the chapter which has received the biggest response and the harshest critique.[29] Soldiers are in action but also prisoners of war and forced labourers, locating and rescuing the trapped and recovering the dead, with equipment or with bare hands.[30] On 39 photographs we see swollen, burnt, disfigured corpses, bones and ash, limbs and body parts, disinfection of the human remains, asphyxiated dead in the cellars, victims shrunk to the size of a doll, who have evaporated on stairs and streets and who later were collected in zinc containers. The dead are lying in seemingly endless rows on the streets for identification; to prevent an epidemic the charred bodies are then stacked into large piles and burnt. As if to prevent another objection, the last photographs show the deformed corpses of crashed British bomber crews, then impressions of the German air raids on London, finally, – as a parallel construction, we see a Polish girl mourning her sister who was killed during the German air raid on Warsaw in 1939. The other side is represented by the last image in 'Bergung'; two German sisters watering the garden. Only the caption subverts the idyll and informs us that one of them died shortly before the end of the war during the air raid on Paderborn.

Friedrich has been accused of avoiding the construction of contexts for his photographs.[31] This is not quite correct. What is missing is the grand arch that unambiguously allocated guilt and responsibility to the Germans. In the perceptive horizon of the affected, however, the contextualisation is logical, even too harmonious. The book is excellently composed. The photographs of 'Bergung', which, as Ulrich Raulff noted, are likely to cause 'Magenkrämpfe', are immediately followed by the bustle of 'Versorgung' (supply).[32] The protection from fire, the relief of damage to people's eyes are of immediate concern here, followed by the daily struggle for the essentials: bread and water, hot food, ultimately for compensation. When the SA delivers beer by the crate to those who have been bombed out, the all too self-assertive faces of the 'aides' tell a story. They revive the myth of the German *Volksgemeinschaft* by their gazes alone. The chapter 'Trümmer' (rubble) only shows the devastation to infrastructure, to stone, steel constructions, traffic routes, private living space: bizarre 'last worlds'. 'Trümmerleben' (life among the rubble) puts people into this environment, people who were able to save themselves and possibly others, their possessions reduced to a sack or a suitcase, as well as salvaged goods beside the road. In the last and rather short chapter 'Partei' (party), state representatives seek to dispel anger by words of comfort and ritualised honours. The sum total is given by the chapter 'Heute' (today): a synopsis of once and now that profiles the losses by accentuating the devastation caused by the rebuilding.

Jörg Friedrich's arrangement of the photographs makes clear how the immediate affectedness by the abhorrence of the horrors in 'Bergung' is supposed to be understood: not as index – i.e. not as reference to reality – but as rhetorical transgression. The deformations of the individual bodies are, like the synecdoche, a *pars pro toto*, it is the *Volkskörper* that is disfigured. And this loss is supposed to be felt immediately as the loss of the individual, concrete person. This rhetorical imposition ultimately does make the book, which is in many respects remarkable, untruthful.

V. From the Suffering Self to the German Soul: Jörg Friedrich's *Der Brand*

Seen in the cold light of day, this was already the conception of Friedrich's *Der Brand. Deutschland im Bombenkrieg 1940–1945*. The issue of intensities is also at stake there. In the chapter 'Ich', the text develops that which normally remains exterior to historiography: suffering and particularly the sense of individual suffering. In contrast to the recipient's affectedness by photographs, in *Der Brand* it is the impression itself which is the topic: through the universal prototype of a bombing victim. Against all conventions of historiography Friedrich establishes a first-person narrator, identifies with the suffering of others and turns into this 'Ich' himself (DB, 502). The reader experiences in his/her imagination, how the sensory apparatus changes under the pressure of the bombing, how the experience of time and real time are torn apart, how the emotions are dulled and how this 'I' armours itself under the pressure of the experience.[33]

> Mit dem Rauschen des Abwurfs beginnt das Entsetzen. Der Angriff wirkt auf alle Sinne ein. Die Nase erfaßt Brand- und Geruchsgase, und die Haut spürt die Temperatur und den Luftstrom, den Anstieg der Glut, den Wind, der sie herträgt. Die Gefäße schließlich nehmen die Druckwellen auf oder sie zerspringen, der Sog zerrt die Kleidung vom Leib. (DB, 495)

The first rush of fear needs to be softened. Thus the bombing war is not being 'experienced' in the strict sense: 'Die Reduktion der Anteilnahme, verknüpft mit tüchtigem Zupacken, half ihn überstehen.' (DB, 504) As during anaesthesia the pain, rather than eliminated, is simply not perceived (DB, 505): 'Das Erforderliche vollbringe ich wie außerhalb meiner selbst. Die Empfindungshaut ist dagegen taub.' (DB, 502)

The city of Hamburg, where 40,000 people die during the July attacks of 1943, is described as analogous to this ideal subject of suffering: 'Chiffren des Äußersten, was Waffengewalt der Kreatur zufügte. Nicht wegen der Ströme vergossenen Blutes, sondern der Art wegen, in der Lebewesen von der Welt getilgt wurden mit einem tödlichen Hauch.' (DB, 193) Immediately afterwards the author quotes an anatomical description:

> Leiche eines Jünglings von schätzungsweise sechzehn Jahren. Fechterstellung des rechten Armes, völlig unbekleidet auf der Straße auf dem Rücken liegend. Die Kopfhaare versengt, die Haut der Füße verkohlt, ferner Kinn und Nasenspitze eingetrocknet und verbrannt. Oberflächliche Verkohlung auf der Streckseite der Hände. Hautfarbe rötlich bräunlich. Muskulatur des Rumpfes wie gekocht erscheinend. Zungenoberfläche trocken und bräunlich. Die Lungen gebläht, voluminös, schwer. Im rechten Herzen reichlich eingedicktes Blut. Das linke Herz leer, Leber hart, Milz zerflossen. Zwischen harter Hirnhaut und Schädeldach große Mengen eingedickter, schmierig breiiger rötlicher Massen. Schnitte durch Groß- und Kleinhirn ohne Nachweis von freien Blutungen und pathologischen

Veränderungen. [...] Beurteilung: Der Jüngling ist lebend auf der Straße
verbrannt. (DB, 193f)

Friedrich argues that the world of existence is withdrawn in the
firestorm. The planet is no longer identical with itself, its atmosphere
is exchanged and hostile to life. The interruption of the experienced
horror stops the clock, not just for those affected; Hamburg is a torch,
an 'Unterbrechung der Welt' (DB, 7, 194). Friedrich's narration does
not fall back on the terminology of apocalypse by accident. Like the
individual fate which is extended to the city as a whole, the individual
bombardment is thus extended to the whole nation, indeed, the
Kulturvolk of the Germans. For Friedrich, the soul of German-ness
disappears with the buildings, memorials, paintings and libraries, even
if he does not say so explicitly. The destruction reached back into
history from the atemporal nature of the experience of the event itself.
The fire, suggests Friedrich, shatters the fundament.[34]

VI. On the limits of Imagination: Hans Erich Nossack's *Der Untergang*

'Sprechen ist eine Übersetzung', writes Friedrich, 'die Gewalt dieser
Sinneseindrücke ist aber unübersetzbar' (DB, 497). The photographs
of the volume *Brandstätten* are thus supposed to exceed what
Friedrich was able to narrate historiographically in *Der Brand*.[35] The
first literary reaction to experiences of the bombing campaign was
different, as we know. Instead of relying on immediacy, Hans Erich
Nossack kept the events at a distance. His autobiographical report *Der
Untergang. Hamburg 1943* employs the means of coincidence to
produce this distance. When Hamburg goes up in flames, the first
person narrator is located 15 kilometres south of the city, in a village
on the heath. Thus he experiences as observer what exceeds 'alle
menschliche Vorstellungskraft'.[36] He renders the catastrophe 'von den
Rändern her':[37] 'Der Nordhimmel war rot wie nach
Sonnenuntergang'. (U, 20) Nossack's language fails again and again
at the task of putting into words what he sees: 'vor Entsetzen konnte
man einzelnes nicht mehr wahrnehmen.' (U, 22) It is only
'unvorstellbar grauenhaft', 'unbegreiflich', and appears as a bad
dream.[38] 'Der Abgrund war ganz nah neben uns, ja, vielleicht unter
uns, und wir schwebten nur durch irgendeine Gnade darüberhin.' (U,
58) Everything has become alien in the city: 'Was uns umgab,
erinnerte in keiner Weise an das Verlorene. Es hatte nichts damit zu
tun. Es war etwas anderes, es war das Fremde, es war das eigentlich

Nicht-Mögliche.'³⁹ The observer has dropped out of time like the dead themselves.⁴⁰ 'Wir sind gegenwärtig geworden, wir haben uns aus der Zeit gelöst.' (U, 138) However, Nossack's first person narrator is eventually gripped by the immediacy of affectedness by disgust. In sealed-off parts of the city 'Zuchthäusler in gestreiften Anzügen' are working to recover the dead. But the 'Wirklichkeit' is worse than the stories of the burnings that people tell:

> Sie konnten vor Fliegen nicht in die Keller [zu den Toten] gelangen, sie glitschten auf dem Boden aus vor fingerlangen Maden, und die Flammen mußten ihnen einen Weg bahnen zu denen, die durch Flammen umgekommen waren. Ratten und Fliegen beherrschten die Stadt. Frech und fett tummelten sich die Ratten auf den Straßen. Aber noch ekelhafter waren die Fliegen. Große, grünschillernde, wie man sie nie gesehen hatte. Klumpenweise wälzten sie sich auf dem Pflaster, saßen an den Mauerresten sich begattend übereinander und wärmten sich müde und satt an den Splittern der Fensterscheiben. (U, 99f)

VII. Simultaneity of Sensations: Gert Ledig's *Die Vergeltung*

Gert Ledig's novel *Die Vergeltung* seeks to produce the immediacy of sensation through narrative simultaneity. Whereas Nossack had written his 'report' as early as November 1943, only four months after the Hamburg firestorm, Ledig writes with the temporal distance of more than ten years after the end of the war and constructs a fictional city with a broad cross-section of society.⁴¹ Narrative time and narrated time are poles apart. 200 pages of text render events taking place between 13:01 and 14:10 on July 1944. However, the narrative does not stretch and slow down the action rather it is split into the simultaneity of parallel events and jumps backwards and forwards between the isolated fragments of the story. Like a mosaic, the patterns of the story and its characters only become clear in the course of the narrative. Biographies of characters are inserted into the narrative flow like memorial plaques or court statements. The parallel montage breaks up the chronology of events: the biographical statements mark the vanishing point of the retrospective narrative and provide the distance that allows for reflection. In contrast to this, the quick successive sequences of action within the time of bombardment develop a disorienting narrative current in which the novel's characters appear as displaced, desperate, and lost.

The crew of a bomber, which initially separated above and below, attacker and attacked, crashes into the inferno caused by themselves and becomes a part of the destruction and its victim (V, 48). Ledig creates the fiction of authenticity through a mixture of laconic description and intensifying the sensations that affect the defenceless bodies. One example is the sergeant Jonathan Strenehen, the only member of the bomber crew to survive the plane crash. In the moment of free fall there are 'keine Bilder der Vergangenheit, keine Gedanken an die Zukunft. Es gab nur einen Körper, der durch die Luft flog' (V, 50). The senses work like a machine, a mechanical interplay of nerves, cerebrum, consciousness and fear. The US soldier survives only to become mad and to be humiliated by his targets.[42] Victims turn into sadistic perpetrators, executing lynch justice, and in 'lustful' humiliation of the attacking pilot they take revenge for the destruction.[43]

A scene change: a private has his nose blown off (V, 68f), a steel girder crushes the legs of a priest: both feel nothing; the pain remains 'gefühllos' (V, 85). A man and a woman are buried alive and coincidentally come to lie on top of one another without any possibilities of movement. However, the man exploits the situation and rapes the defenceless woman: 'Wärme drang auf sie ein. Ekel stieg in ihr auf bis zum Mund.' The woman vomits; this however does not stop the man: 'Alles vermischte sich: Schmerz, Ekel, Abscheu. Sie dachte nichts mehr. [...] Die Luft roch nach Exkreten. [...] Über ihr gurgelte er wie ein Tier.' (V, 122) Another scene: a squad leader falls into 'liquid asphalt':

> Es zischte. Der Teer warf Blasen. Von Schmerzen gepeinigt, wälzte er sich als schwarzer Klumpen in zäher Masse. Er schrie nicht, kämpfte nicht. Seine Bewegungen dirigierte die Hitze. Sie krümmte ihn zusammen, warf seinen Kopf hoch. [...] Er glich keinem Menschen mehr, er glich einem Krebs. Er starb nicht nach einer Todesart, die bereits erfunden war. Er wurde gegrillt. (V, 127f)

Murder and improvised drumhead court martial, suicide and torture follow each other in a mad *ronde*. The heat engulfs and swallows up everything: 'Feuer war rings um ihn. In seinem Gehirn, vor seinen Augen, unter der Haut.' Inside and outside world melt down, 'Vernichtung raste überall'. (V, 156f). Phosphorus crackles, flesh cracks (V, 150). 'Eine Stunde genügte, und das Grauen triumphierte', is the résumé of the novel. 'Nach der siebzigsten Minute wurde weiter gebombt. Die Vergeltung verrichtete ihre Arbeit. Sie war unaufhaltsam. Nur das Jüngste Gericht. Das war sie nicht.' (V, 199) In his narrative composition which remains transparent throughout, Ledig constructs and creates distance to the affectedness that he produces over and over again. Nevertheless, the focus of the narrative chronology is on the horrors rendered by Ledig. The sensory apparatus triumphs over the documentation of total destruction.

VIII. The Logic of Emotions: Alexander Kluge's *Der Luftangriff auf Halberstadt*

Alexander Kluge's fictional-documentary narrative *Der Luftangriff auf Halberstadt am 8. April 1945* operates differently, focusing on knowledge instead of experience. Generally, writing produces the distance of judging appraisal. However, in the stance of the reader which is per se distanced, the act of reading on the other hand causes a change in the recipient which, as Wolfgang Iser has noted, restructures the subject itself. The horror as literature is given only in the 'Präsenz des Vorgestellten'.[44] Thus it becomes reality of experience and 'real'. The act of imagination substitutes the immediacy of affectedness, works like its mental *simulacrum*.[45] However, imagination is imprecise, especially where the comparative data to one's own experience are missing. This is the reason why in every account of the bombings we read that the horrors exceeded any imaginative ability. The repeated stressing of these limits is frequently even part of the contrivance of immediacy.

In contrast to this, Kluge skilfully balances imagination and reflection. Logic and emotion belong together. In Kluge's representation the bombing becomes an intelligible act. It is not the distance of the existentially 'thrown', as in Nossack, that is supposed to move us away from false immediacy, but the distance of enlightened reason. This is all the more remarkable since Kluge shares Horkheimer's and Adorno's critique of instrumental reason in *Dialectic of Enlightenment*. Like Ledig, Kluge develops a totality of events, limited to one and a half hours. As in Nossack, Ledig and Friedrich, for Kluge's protagonists clock time 'und die sinnliche Verarbeitung der Zeit [...]' fall apart.[46] But Kluge's aim is never to overpower, on the contrary. When in the cinema 'Capitol' a piece of sky becomes visible because a bomb has 'das Haus geöffnet', the immediacy is undercut by the factuality and coolness of Kluge's language. The 'Erschütterungen' caused by the movie *Heimkehr* are outdone by the reality. However, since the metaphor becomes reality, the scene appears in ironic refraction. Frau Schrader, the owner of the cinema, sees the burning houses all around her; 'wie Fackeln' is the image that comes to her mind. 'Sie suchte nach einem besseren

Ausdruck für das, was sie so genau sah.' Corpses lie in the cellar, 'mit einem Strahl Heizwasser übergossen. Frau Schrader wollte wenigstens hier Ordnung schaffen, legte die gekochten und – entweder durch diesen Vorgang oder schon durch die Sprengwirkung – unzusammenhängenden Körperteile in die Waschkessel der Waschküche.' Then she wants 'an irgendeiner verantwortlichen Stelle Meldung erstatten' (LH, 27f).

Frau Schrader rationalises and begins to work. She experiences what the other narratives and the volume of photographs equally stage as immediacy. However, Kluge's text lets her work it through in a different manner. The same goes for the subsequent retrieval of corpses: 'Was dieser Arbeitsgang nach Ausgraben und Sortieren weiter nützen sollte, war schleierhaft.' (LH, 29) The characters are focused on activity, act according to expediency, adapt their emotions to the demands of the situation. In several parts the text imitates the tone of official documents and reports, interrupted only by the contemporary idioms of its protagonists. Thus Frau Zacke and Frau Arnold, the observers from the tower, are given a concise outline as characters (LH, 35-37). The distancing of address and portrayal of the figures create a unique tension. Gerda Baethe, a woman with three children, summons within seconds 'Leitsätze einer "Strategie von unten"', to produce the correct stance towards the exploding bombs: 'Es war wenigstens so, daß Gerdas Truppe nicht in alle Winde auseinanderfetzte, sondern Hautberührung suchte.' (LH, 43f)

The strategic bombing command and the bomber formation, some 200 machines, operate their 'Strategie von oben' (LH, 48). Charts and diagrams make this clear (LH, 52f, 57f). The structures of rationality are, however, the same. The bomb is a 'Ware' which needs to be delivered: 'Es sind ja teure Sachen. Man kann das praktisch auch nicht auf die Berge oder das freie Feld hinschmeißen, nachdem es mit viel Arbeitskraft zu Hause hergestellt ist.' Everything must go according to plan, a 'vernünftige Angriffslinie' has to be found, the bombs must not be 'verkleckert', as brigadier Anderson says retrospectively in an interview (LH, 61, 59). The bombing, even the *moral bombing*, follows a logic of optimisation. In Halberstadt it was successful; even if the fire-fighters had 'fachlich gewachsen' after the extensive blazes in Hamburg, Darmstadt and Cologne (LH, 77). To the question of the *Neue Zürcher Zeitung* 'Bombardieren Sie aus Moral oder bombardieren Sie die Moral?' staff officer Williams replies: 'Wir bombardieren die Moral. Der Widerstandsgeist muß aus der gegebenen Bevölkerung durch Zerstörung der Stadt entfernt werden.' (LH, 65). Only two months later, the success of this strategy can be recorded. A questionnaire distributed amongst the bombarded produces an astonishing result: 82% would like to emigrate to the USA: 'Hatten wir uns Freunde unserer Nation herangebombt?' was the baffled question. Nobody wants to remember what happened, however, especially if the questioned person had been immediately affected. One woman questioned writes: 'An einem gewissen Punkt der Grausamkeit angekommen, ist es schon gleich, wer sie begangen hat: sie soll nur aufhören.' (LH, 80-82)

Translation by Helmut Schmitz

Notes

[1] W. G. Sebald, *Luftkrieg und Literatur. Mit einem Essay zu Alfred Andersch* [1999], Fischer: Frankfurt am Main, 2003, p. 11f.

[2] Ibid., p. 109 f.

[3] Volker Hage, *Zeugen der Zerstörung. Die Literaten und der Luftkrieg. Essays und Gespräche*, Fischer: Frankfurt am Main, 2003, esp. pp. 113-131. Cf. the collection of sources in Volker Hage, ed., *Hamburg 1943. Literarische Zeugnisse zum Feuersturm*, Fischer: Frankfurt am Main, 2003. See esp. the texts by Nossack, Borchert, Biermann, Hubert Fichte, Ralph Giordano and Uwe Timm, as well as Sebald himself.

[4] Hage's essays are collected in his volume *Zeugen der Zerstörung* (footnote 3).

[5] See Gregor Streim, 'Der Bombenkrieg als Sensation und als Dokumentation. Gert Ledigs Roman *Vergeltung* und die Debatte um W. G. Sebalds *Luftkrieg und Literatur*,' in: Heinz-Peter Preußer, ed., *Krieg in den Medien*, Rodopi: Amsterdam, New York, 2004, pp. 293-312.

[6] Jörg Friedrich, *Der Brand. Deutschland im Bombenkrieg 1940-1945*, Propyläen: Munich, 2002. Further references as (DB, page number). Cf. Martin Walser, 'Bombenkrieg als Epos,' *Focus*, 9 December 2002, reprinted in: Lothar Kettenacker, ed., *Ein Volk von Opfern? Die neue Debatte um den Bombenkrieg 1940-45*, Rowohlt: Berlin, 2003, pp. 127-30.

[7] Cf. Volker Ulrich, 'Weltuntergang kann nicht schlimmer sein,' *DIE ZEIT*, 28 November 2002.

[8] Cf. Oliver Reinhard and Jochen Wittmann, 'Wer Wind sät, erntet Feuersturm,' *Sächsische Zeitung*, 26 November 2002. See also the interview with Jörg Friedrich

'Ein Kriegsverbrechen? Das muss jeder für sich selbst entscheiden,' *Die Welt*, 21 November 2002. See also Lothar Kettenacker, 'Wollen sich die Deutschen etwa als Opfer sehen?,' *DIE ZEIT*, 5 December 2002.

[9] Jörg Müllner and Anja Greulich, *Der Bombenkrieg*, TV documentary, *Zweites Deutsches Fernsehen*, 2002, broadcast on 4 February 2003, 20:15 (90 mins). See the review by Lorenz Jäger, 'Bleib übrig, sagte man damals,' *Frankfurter Allgemeine Zeitung*, 6 February 2003. The success of Friedrich's book was supported by a serialisation of parts of the book in the tabloid newspaper *BILD*, 18/19/20/21 November 2002. This was preceded by the Helmut Böger's detailed article 'Warum Deutschlands Städte starben,' *BILD am Sonntag*, 17 November 2002.

[10] See Hans-Ulrich Wehler's review, '*Der Brand*,' *DeutschlandRadio*, 'Politisches Buch,' broadcast on 6 December 2002, 17:50.

[11] Ibid.

[12] See Michael Jeismann, 'Gegenredner,' *Frankfurter Allgemeine Zeitung*, 22 November 2002.

[13] Andreas Kilb, 'Das Zeugnis,' *Frankfurter Allgemeine Zeitung*, 22 November 2002.

[14] Susan Sontag, *Regarding the Pain of Others*, Hamish Hamilton: London, 2003, p. 20.

[15] Ibid., p. 19.

[16] Roland Barthes, *Camera Lucida* [1980, *La Chambre claire*], translated by Richard Howard, Vintage: London, 1993, esp. pp. 99-104.

[17] Ibid. p. 24. Siegfried Kracauer notes something similar in his early essay on photography (*Frankfurter Zeitung*, 28 October 1927). Reprinted in: *Das Ornament der Masse. Essays*. Afterword by Karsten Witte, Suhrkamp: Frankfurt am Main, 1977, pp. 21-39, esp. pp. 30 and 35. See also Bernd Busch, *Belichtete Welt. Eine Wahrnehmungsgeschichte der Fotografie*, Carl Hanser Verlag: Munich, 1995, pp. 364-366.

[18] After-effects of the fear of black magic can still be felt in modern photography. See Henri Cartier-Bresson, 'Der entscheidende Augenblick' [1952], in: Wilfried Wiegand, ed., *Die Wahrheit der Photographie. Klassische Bekenntnisse zu einer neuen Kunst*, Fischer: Frankfurt am Main, 1981, pp. 267-282 (here: p. 274). See also Roland Barthes, pp. 21-23 and Friedrich Kittler, *Grammophon Film Typewriter*, Brinkmann u. Bose: Berlin, 1986, p. 21.

[19] Ernst Friedrich, *Krieg dem Kriege, War against War, Guerre à la Guerre, Vojna Vojně*, Berlin: Freie Jugend, 1926, two volumes.

[20] Immanuel Kant, *Kritik der Urteilskraft* [1790], Karl Vorländer ed., Meiner: Hamburg 1974, p. 166, § 48.

[21] Georges Bataille, *Die Erotik*. Translated with an introductory essay by Gert Bergfleth. Matthes & Seitz: Munich, 1994, p. 57.

[22] Ferdinand de Saussure, *Grundfragen der Allgemeinen Sprachwissenschaft* [Cours de linguistique générale, 1906-1911; [1]1916, [2]1922]. Ed. by Charles Bally and Albert Sechehaye, translated by Herman Lommel. 2. editon, deGruyter: Berlin 1967 [[1]1931], pp. 79-82.

[23] Cf. Roland Barthes, *Elemente der Semiologie* [1965], translated by Eva Moldenhauer, Suhrkamp: Frankfurt am Main, 1983, p. 13. *Langue* 'ist im Wesen ein kollektiver Vertrag, dem man sich [...] rückhaltlos unterwerfen muß'.

[24] Cf. Peter Lunenfeld, 'Digitale Fotografie. Das dubitative Bild,' in: Herta Wolf, ed., *Paradigma Fotografie. Fotokritik am Ende des fotografischen Zeitalters*, Suhrkamp: Frankfurt am Main, 2002, pp. 158-172 (here: pp. 166f).

[25] Thus Wolfgang Hagen, 'Die Entropie der Fotografie. Skizzen zu einer Genealogie der digital-elektronischen Bildaufzeichnung,' in: Herta Wolf, ed., *Paradigma Fotografie*, pp. 195-235, esp. pp. 234f.

[26] The remark is Barthes's, *Camera Lucida*, p. 87. Cf. Hagen, 'Die Entropie der Fotografie,' pp. 232f.

[27] This is already visible in the television-report in *Titel, Thesen, Temperamente*, and, following from this, a number of reports on the debate, the book and the TV report. See Sven Felix Kellerhoff: 'Moralisch nicht einzuordnen,' *Die Welt*, 16 October 2003; Ulrich Raulff, 'Vom Bombenhammer erschlagen,' *Süddeutsche Zeitung*, 18 October 2003; Andreas Platthaus, 'Bilderstreit um Tote,' *Frankfurter Allgemeine Zeitung*, 24 October 2003; Julius H. Schoeps: 'Holocaust und Bombenkrieg sind nicht vergleichbar,' interview, *Die Welt*, 24 October 2003; Wolfgang Benz, 'Man gibt die Opfer dem Voyeurismus preis,' interview, *Die Welt*, 27 October 2003; Joachim Günther, 'Finis Germaniae,' *Neue Zürcher Zeitung*, 3 November 2003; Georg Dietz, 'Der Bauch-Historiker,' *DER SPIEGEL*, 8 December 2003.

[28] After the publication of *Der Brand* and before the publication of *Brandstätten*, Jörg Friedrich said in an interview: 'Aus den Bildern des Luftkrieges könnte ich durchaus eine ähnliche Ausstellung machen wie die von Jan Philipp Reemtsma [über die Verbrechen der deutschen Wehrmacht] – mit den gleichen verbrannten Kindern, mit den gleichen Leichenfeldern.' See 'Deutsche Städte im Inferno,' *Focus*, 25 November 2002. However this illustrates that the mere facticity (that piles of corpses are piles of corpses) is not Friedrich's concern.

[29] For reviews, photographs were predominantly taken from this chapter. See Kellerhoff, Raulff, Dietz (all footnote 26). See also Reinhard Brockmann, 'Friedrich

zeigt alle Brandstätten-Bilder,' *Westfalen-Blatt*, 13 November 2003 and Christian Esch, 'Die Schrecken des Verlegens,' *Berliner Zeitung*, 17 October 2003. Esch describes the curious behaviour of Friedrich's publisher Propyläen, to distance themselves from their author (in an editorial notice to *Brandstätten*) but to market him nevertheless.

[30] From 1941 concentration camp inmates and POW's were used by the Organisation Todt to clear rubble and rescue operations all over Germany.

[31] See for example Schoeps, 'Holocaust und Bombenkrieg sind nicht vergleichbar'.

[32] Raulff, 'Vom Bombenhammer erschlagen'.

[33] Friedrich, *Der Brand*, pp. 496, 498, 503.

[34] Ibid., here the chapter 'Stein,' pp. 515-39.

[35] Friedrich, *Brandstätten. Der Anblick des Krieges*, Propyläen: Munich, 2003, p, 239: 'Ich habe nach Bildern gesucht, die erzählen, was Worterzählungen übersteigt.'

[36] Hans Erich Nossack, *Der Untergang. Hamburg 1943* [1948]. Photographs by Erich Andres. Ernst Kabel Verlag: Hamburg, 1981, p. 21. Further references as (U, page number).

[37] Ibid., p. 143. The quote is from the afterword by Erich Lüth, with reference to Siegfried Lenz's encomium for Nossack.

[38] Ibid., p. 7, again on pp. 27, 108, 28; see also p. 132: 'unvorstellbar'.

[39] Ibid., p. 68. Cf. p. 72: 'In Gegenden, die ich zu kennen glaubte, habe ich mich völlig verirrt.'

[40] Ibid., p. 59 and p. 98.

[41] Gert Ledig, *Die Vergeltung, Roman* [1956]. With an afterword by Volker Hage. Suhrkamp: Frankfurt am Main, 1999. Further references as (V, page number).

[42] Ibid., pp. 130f, 186-188.

[43] Ibid., pp. 186-88, esp. p. 188.

[44] Wolfgang Iser, *Der Akt des Lesens. Theorie ästhetischer Wirkung* [1976], Fink: Munich, 1984, esp. pp. 219-256.

[45] Roland Barthes uses this term for the reconstructive work of the structuralist. See Barthes, 'Die strukturalistische Tätigkeit,' translated by Eva Moldenhauer, in: *Kursbuch* Nr. 5, (1966), pp. 190-196.

[46] Alexander Kluge, *Der Luftangriff auf Halberstadt am 8. April 1945* [1977], in: <u>Chronik der Gefühle</u>, vol. II, *Lebensläufe*, Suhrkamp: Frankfurt am Main, 2000, p. 42. Further references as (LH, page number).

Annette Seidel Arpacı

Lost in Translations? The Discourse of 'German Suffering' and W. G. Sebald's *Luftkrieg und Literatur*

W.G. Sebald's *Luftkrieg und Literatur* has been credited, both nationally and internationally, with re-opening the discourse on memory of the Allied bombings, an allegedly 'silenced' and taboo subject. The chapter examines Sebald's concept of trauma and use of Holocaust tropes in *Luftkrieg und Literatur*, together with the international reception of his theses, arguing that the alleged 'taboo' constitutes an act of forgetting of the commemoration and assessment of the effects of the war in the 1950s.

In the wake of the publication of Jörg Friedrich's bestselling *Der Brand*,[1] another book on the aerial bombing of Germany received once more increased attention: W. G. Sebald's *Luftkrieg und Literatur*, which was published in German three years earlier in 1999.[2] My basic premise here is that Sebald's work contributes in this context significantly to a discourse concerned with establishing competitive and exculpating notions of 'German suffering' and 'German victimhood' in relation to National Socialism and the Second World War.[3]

To begin with, I would like to point to the problematic connotation of the terminology: '*German* suffering' necessarily implies that a whole population had suffered *as* Germans and that 'Germans' were targeted as such and not as the society which brought about National Socialism and war. Thus an appropriation of Holocaust discourse and of the de facto suffering of Jews *as a group* emerges almost inevitably. Furthermore, the term excludes German Jews and other minorities and individuals victimised by the Nazis – not to say, by Germans. The term in the context of the discourse implicitly likens the political agenda of National Socialism and the Allies. 'German (wartime) suffering' is thus a loaded term with far-reaching implications as it is aimed at describing the living situation and wartime experience of those Germans – the majority – that were at least co-responsible for the Nazi crimes, in short it turns a society of perpetrators and bystanders into a society of at least 'also-victims'. Hence the difference between the common-place recognition that war necessarily produces human suffering and the specificity of the German self-imagination as victimised group is obscured entirely.

When in January 2005 delegates of the neo-Nazi party NDP in Saxony's parliament used the term 'Bombenholocaust' to refer to the Allied air raids[4] they thus merely condensed within this term a sentiment already publicly expressed in far more respectable form in recent years. It is the claim to an 'equal status of victimhood' for Germans; this claim is expressed in discussions of 'German suffering' and the use of terminology and images tied to the Holocaust. Most notable in recent years for appropriating terms of Holocaust discourse to 'German suffering' was Friedrich's bestselling *Der Brand*.[5] The project of constructing a 'German victimhood' is intertwined with the assertion that until very recently there had been a silence about Germans as victims of war and expulsion and that this silence was a form of repression and resulted from trauma and/or taboo.

It is therefore no coincidence that I refer so prominently to Friedrich's *Der Brand*. However, while his book is generally viewed in scholarly circles as at the very least highly controversial, Sebald's theses on German (literary) memory and the Allied air raids were received much less critically, or, as we will see later on, are questioned from a very different angle. Moreover, on the back cover of *Der Brand* we find praise from W. G. Sebald: 'Einzig der Militärhistoriker Jörg Friedrich hat sich genauer mit der Evolution und den Konsequenzen der Zerstörungsstrategie der Alliierten befasst.'[6]

However, instead of focussing on Friedrich's *Der Brand* with its notorious appropriations, I direct my attention here to W. G. Sebald's *Luftkrieg und Literatur*. I discuss this work in conjunction with the problematic translation and format of its English version *On the Natural History of Destruction* and in relation to its reception in Germany and beyond. I argue that not only Friedrich's but already Sebald's use of language contributed to the ingredient imagery for the creation of a term like 'Bombenholocaust.' However, I do not want to charge Sebald with any explicitly revisionist political agenda with respect to the debates on National Socialism, the Holocaust and memory but rather discuss his choice of language and argument by reading him in the context of writings by critics and in the context of the wider reception of his theses.

Sebald's focus – as the title of his book suggests – was to be what he analyses as a nearly complete silence in German literature about the

Allied air raids and their apparent effects on German society. In the course of the essay on the air raids it becomes clear that Sebald attributes this alleged silence to all levels of social interaction. He charges post-war German writers for the failure of not having addressed the alleged psychological devastation as a result of the bombings and seems to suggest that the silence of these writers contributed to or perpetuated the silence prevalent in German society as a whole. That the claims of a general silence in society about the air war, just as about 'German wartime suffering' in general, cannot be upheld has been shown for instance in publications that resulted from research into intergenerational transmission of memory as well as into Catholic and Protestant responses to the Holocaust and National Socialism.[7] Having said that, much work still needs to be done on the 'private' but also the 'public' discourse of 'German wartime suffering,' not least in the fields of war memorials, debates in political parties and organisations, in film, to name but a few. Here, however, I will concentrate on Sebald's language resulting in an implicit appropriation of Holocaust discourse to the Allied air raids, the politics of translation into English and on the reception and scholarly readings of *Luftkrieg und Literatur*.

Both the German edition and the English translation contain in their respective first chapters Sebald's series of lectures at the University of Zurich in 1997, during which he introduced his theories on the air war and German literature and, in addition, an essay on the writer Alfred Andersch. However, an interesting editorial decision has been made for the publication in English: two more essays have posthumously been added to the English edition of the book. We learn in a translator's note at the beginning of the book that

> this is the foreword as written for the German edition of the book published by Hanser in 1999. The English edition, it will be seen, also includes essays on Jean Améry and Peter Weiss which were not part of the original German publication. I have no doubt that if he had lived to see the final text of the full translation – he had already approved the whole of the earlier part – W. G. Sebald would have revised or added to the foreword in order to include mention of these two authors.[8]

We have to consider here the politics of translating and publishing, and the role these politics play for cultural translations, which leads to a number of questions. Why did the publishers of the English edition so substantially alter the book, and why were the essays on Améry and Weiss not included in the original German edition? It is no longer possible to verify the reasons for the sole appearance of the essays in the English edition. Is it conceivable that precisely Weiss and Améry – with their vigorous anti-Fascism and in particular the latter's insisting on his right to 'Ressentiments' – were considered as not suitable for the German mainstream audience?[9] This option seems plausible in particular in the context of a work which aims to scandalise the alleged silence about 'German suffering,' and which includes already one very critical article on Alfred Andersch that, as Mark McCulloh puts it, 'illustrates the lengths to which some Germans were willing to go in order to deny their own participation in the aggression that – in the final analysis – brought on the destruction of Germany's cities.'[10] It is also likely that Sebald himself may have never considered the essays on Améry and Weiss for the original German publication of the book.

The inclusion of the essays in the English edition thus strongly points to a division into an internal/'inner Nation' discourse and an international discourse. The addition of the two essays could thus constitute an attempt to 'soften' or to 'balance' this 'inner Nation' discourse for an 'outside.' In the case of Sebald's book, the publishers of the English edition seem to have taken this 'balancing' approach to avoid publishing a book possibly considered 'too German' for an English language readership if it were to focus mainly on 'German suffering', the Allied and, in particular, the British air raids. Other ways of 'softening' for an English language readership lie in the language translation as such. According to translator Anthea Bell, Sebald had 'approved the whole of the earlier part', and, since he died before he could have revised his foreword to include Améry and Weiss, he had obviously seen neither their inclusion nor how these texts were translated and presented. Astonishingly enough, neither the issue of translation nor, as we will come to see, Sebald's problematic use of language in the original German is questioned by critics.

On the very first page of his *Luftkrieg und Literatur: Züricher Vorlesungen* Sebald writes in the German original that the air war against Nazi-Germany was an 'in der Geschichte bis dahin einzigartige Vernichtungsaktion,' (LL, 11) which Bell translated for the English edition as a 'destruction, on a scale without historical precedent'.[11] Sebald, having approved of the translation, must have been aware that it does not quite carry the connotation of the German original. Why, then, did Sebald choose this phrasing in German to begin with? For, as Sebald would have known, the term 'Vernichtung' – in particular as a noun – can hardly be used in German language at this point in time without connoting first and foremost the murder of the Jews in Europe, generally the murder of people whose lives were considered 'unwert' as well as the *Vernichtungskrieg* of the *Wehrmacht*. The term 'Vernichtung' has a disturbingly close proximity to what Victor Klemperer has called the 'Language of the Third Reich'[12] and may not be a term that we want to use for the murder of human beings. Nonetheless, the term acquired this connotation on a broad basis at least since the 1980s in the wake of the increasing public discourse on National Socialism and the Holocaust. 'Vernichtung' then was translated for the English edition as 'destruction' rather than as 'annihilation', or, as 'extermination.' The word 'destruction' resonates much more with the meaning of 'Zerstörung' (for instance, of buildings) than with 'Vernichtung.' I do think, therefore, that Sebald – an author very attuned to the subtleties of language – chose his terminology here as precisely as Friedrich did at similar points. Furthermore, Sebald doubles his linguistic effort on appropriation with the addition of the term 'Aktion' to 'Vernichtung.'

Considering the connotation of the term 'Aktion' which was also used by the Nazis for raids to round up Jews for deportation to the camps, as well as that of 'Vernichtung', this use of language results in shifting a part of German guilt and responsibility onto the Allies via the shifting of terms from one discursive context into another. Sebald's choice of language thereby implicitly compares the bombing of German cities to the Shoah and the German war in the East. Thus 'everyone' can be viewed as victim and perpetrator; 'everyone' is caught up in 'the natural history of destruction.' Stuart Taberner notes 'that the devastation of German cities could be seen as natural disaster, that is, as an event that was unprovoked and undeserved' emerged much more in the title of the English edition of the book.[13] Moreover, Sebald, by describing the Allied air war as 'in der Geschichte bis dahin einzigartig' inevitably overwrites the German bombing of other countries and thus the utter destruction of cities like Warsaw – and due to this prominent introductory statement to *Luftkrieg und Literatur,* Sebald even overwrites his own references to Coventry and other places destroyed by German air raids.

However, the translation does follow the German original at another critical point, when Sebald speaks of 'die erstaunliche

Fähigkeit der Selbstanästhetisierung eines aus dem Vernichtungskrieg anscheinend ohne nennenswerten psychischen Schaden hervorgegangenen Gemeinwesens' (LL, 19).[14] Sebald's term 'war of annihilation' is ambiguously connoted here and can be read as referring to the air war against Germany, and once more he applies terminology that has been used for the war of the *Wehrmacht*, in particular, in Eastern Europe. Moreover, Sebald appropriates the term precisely at the moment in time (in 1997) when the role of the *Wehrmacht*, and with it the term 'Vernichtungskrieg', had been the subject of heated debates in Germany in the wake of the exhibition *Verbrechen der Wehrmacht 1941-1945*.[15] Sebald's *Luftkrieg und Literatur* begins with the following sentence:

> Es ist schwer, sich heute auch nur eine halbwegs zureichende Vorstellung zu machen von dem Ausmaß der während der letzten Jahre des zweiten Weltkriegs erfolgten Verheerung der deutschen Städte, und schwerer noch, nachzudenken über das mit dieser Verheerung verbundene Grauen. (LL, 11)

That an author who had also written *The Emigrants* should focus on 'German suffering' and their experience of 'horrors' during the Second World War may seem surprising and remarkable at first impression. It is not so, however, if we consider that Sebald seems to be concerned with a very generalised notion of 'breaking silence(s)' and in particular with the universalisation of 'trauma,' which, finally, in *The Emigrants* and *Austerlitz* leaves only traumatised human beings, who are able to connect through their experience. We are left on an individualised psychological plane that does not – despite being embedded in historical developments – refer back to subjective decisions and responsibilities. In *Luftkrieg und Literatur* the 'Vernichtungskrieg' and 'Verheerung' *are* entities encountered by human beings in a traumatising course of history. Dominick LaCapra's cautioning is therefore transferable to the debate about the air war and its scholarly readings in light of the construction of 'silence' and 'taboo':

> The apparent discursive superiority of the liberal left even threatened to conceal the fact [...] that the Historians' Debate allowed for the entry into a broader public arena of reactive if not reactionary feelings, thoughts, and attitudes that earlier had been kept private or confined to small circles. [...] 'After the wall' these sentiments could be circulated more freely and with fewer inhibitions, and they might have currency in politics.[16]

Considering both Sebald's book as well as its reception, we have to ask whether any public debate and mourning for the 'German' victims of a war that Germany brought on itself will inevitably lead to a calculation of suffering and thus to further attempts at relativising Nazi Germany's crimes. Sebald argued against such relativism, and yet seemed surprised by some of the letters he received after a number of his lectures on 'air war and literature' had been published. Apparently, he did not see the link between the content of his lectures and some of the written replies afterwards. Thus Sebald noted,

> Bleibt mir zum Schluß noch ein Brief zu kommentieren, der mich, über die Redaktion der *Neuen Zürcher Zeitung*, Mitte Juni vergangenen Jahres aus Darmstadt erreichte als bislang letzte Zuschrift zum Thema Luftkrieg und den ich mehrmals durchlesen mußte, weil ich zuerst meinen Augen nicht traute, enthält er doch die These, die Alliierten hätten mit dem Luftkrieg das Ziel verfolgt, die Deutschen durch die Zerstörung ihrer Stadt von ihrem Erbe und Herkommen abzuschneiden und so die dann in der Nachkriegszeit tatsächlich erfolgte Kulturinvasion und allgemeine Amerikanisierung vorzubereiten. Diese bewußte Strategie, so heißt es in dem Brief aus Darmstadt weiter, sei ersonnen worden von den im Ausland lebenden Juden. (LL, 104-105)

Sebald's astonishment seems odd, even when considering the anti-Semitism of the letter, but in particular because he himself attests many of the letters he received 'einen leicht paranoiden Zug' (LL, 89). The common tropes of 'cultural invasion' and 'Americanisation', interlinked with the anti-Semitic fantasies of plans for a complete destruction of Germany, are equally common and expressed, for instance, in various schemes ascribed to Henry Morgenthau.[17] After diagnosing the writers of letters to him with paranoia, Sebald notes

> von einem gewaltigen und gewissermaßen subterranen Echo auf den Zusammenbruch des Reiches und die Zerstörung seiner Städte kann bei dem, was mir übersandt wurde, nicht die Rede sein. Vielmehr handelt es sich in der Regel um eher muntere Reminiszenzen, gekennzeichnet von jenen (ungewollt) eine bestimmte gesellschaftliche Ausrichtung und innere Verfassung zum Ausdruck bringenden Wendungen, die mich, wo immer ich ihnen begegne, mit dem größten Unbehagen erfüllen. (LL, 89)

Thereafter, Sebald lists – not without cynicism – a whole range of such 'Wendungen', and comes to the conclusion that it is difficult

> die Art der Deformation zu definieren, die in solchen Retrospektiven fortwirkt, doch hat sie sicher etwas mit der besonderen Ausprägung zu tun, die das kleinbürgerliche Familienleben in Deutschland fand. Die von Alexander und Margarete Mitscherlich in ihrer Schrift *Die Unfähigkeit zu trauern* präsentierten Krankengeschichten lassen zumindest erahnen, daß es einen Zusammenhang gab zwischen der unter dem Hitler-Faschismus sich vollziehenden deutschen Katastrophe und der Regulierung intimer Gefühle in der deutschen Familie. (LL, 89-90)

The universalised notion of trauma underlying Sebald's reading of these letters – as further examples of 'Krankengeschichten' – combined with an understanding of history as catastrophic beyond specificity leads to more ambiguous formulations such as the all-encapsulating 'German catastrophe'. From his vantage point as 'insider – outsider' who has concerned himself with a literary narrativisation of the traumatic experience of individuals victimised by the Nazis – or, the Germans? – Sebald extends this approach to history as such. Thus we may have to rethink Sebald's astonishment about letters such as the above in view of excerpts like the following:

> und niemand, auch die mit der Bewahrung des kollektiven Gedächtnisses der Nation betrauten Schriftsteller nicht, durfte uns später, gerade weil wir unsere Mitschuld erahnten, so schmachvolle Bilder in Erinnerung rufen wie jenes vom Dresdner Altmarkt zum Beispiel, auf dem im Februar 1945 6865 Leichen auf Scheiterhaufen verbrannt wurden von einem SS-Kommando [sic] mit Erfahrung in Treblinka. Jede Beschäftigung mit den wahren Schreckensszenen des Untergangs hat bis heute etwas Illegitimes, beinahe Voyeuristisches, dem auch diese Notizen nicht ganz entgehen konnten. (LL, 103-104)

In *Luftkrieg und Literatur*, the '600,000 Zivilpersonen in Deutschland' and the inhabitants of Cologne or Dresden, 'fell victim to the air raids' of 'the Royal Air Force,' which – unlike the 'civilians in Germany' – is clearly nameable and hence can be determined as responsible (LL, 11). Moreover, the terms 'civilians in Germany' and 'inhabitants of Cologne' in Sebald's reading have to necessarily exclude the Jewish civilians, as most Jews had been deported and murdered before Germany's cities were massively bombed. In the above piece on Dresden it seems at first utterly unclear what the purpose of including the 'SS-Kommando' but even more so their 'experience in Treblinka' in the scene may be. It does neither render the suffering of those experiencing the bombing 'worse' nor does this information increase the number of dead people. The reason Sebald included this information can be found in the term 'Mitschuld.' This shows that he was very aware about ongoing debates about the 'air war' and 'German suffering,' that these debates – and hence his emphasising of 'Mitschuld' – were in Dresden as in other cities much more steeped in 'Selbst-Mitleid' and resentment of the Allies rather than the acceptance of 'Mitschuld' or even less, 'Schuld.' Thus Sebald's 'SS-Kommando' from Treblinka figures in this scene, on the one hand, as reminder of the German crimes, confronting the 'civilians of Germany' with their own responsibility, but, on the other hand, it can be read in the sense that 'the Nazis' did not differentiate between dead Jews and dead Germans. Thereby 'Germans' are turned into potential victims of 'the Nazis,' drawing on a juxtaposition of

'Germans' and 'Nazis' which we will encounter again in Welzer et al's *Opa war kein Nazi.*

To further discuss the place of *Luftkrieg und Literatur,* we might want to return to Fuchs's *Die Schmerzensspuren der Geschichte.* Fuchs also discusses the lines on the first page of the 'Zurich Lectures,' which I have already referred to in view of its translation into English. It reads in full:

> Die in der Geschichte bis dahin einzigartige Vernichtungsaktion ist in die Annalen der sich neu konstituierenden Nation nur in Form vager Verallgemeinerungen eingegangen, scheint kaum eine Schmerzensspur hinterlassen zu haben im kollektiven Bewußtsein, ist aus der retrospektiven Selbsterfahrung der Betroffenen weitgehend ausgeschlossen geblieben, hat in den sich entwickelnden Diskussionen um die innere Verfassung unseres Landes nie eine nennenswerte Rolle gespielt, ist nie, wie Alexander Kluge später konstatierte, zu einer öffentlich lesbaren Chiffre geworden – ein durchaus provokanter Sachverhalt, wenn man bedenkt, wie viele Menschen dieser Kampagne Tag für Tag, Monat für Monat, Jahr für Jahr ausgesetzt waren und wie lange sie, bis weit in die Nachkriegszeit hinein, konfrontiert geblieben sind mit ihren realen, jedes positive Lebensgefühl (wie man hätte meinen müssen) erstickenden Folgen. (LL 11-12)

This long sentence seems to be a key to the project of the book. When Sebald wrote of the air raids as an 'until then singular act of annihilation in history' he must have been absolutely aware that he was using a phrase that attempted to describe and situate in history the specificity of the Holocaust. However, as we will come to see, there are more problems with this excerpt.

Fuchs quotes this piece – yet only up to 'zu einer öffentlich lesbaren Chiffre geworden' after which she puts a full stop – in the beginning of her subchapter 'Heimat als Ruine und Ruine als Heimat: *Luftkrieg und Literatur.*[18] Similar to my own reading she regards this very piece as revealing the 'charakteristische Tonlage' for the whole following essay, and she notes thereafter:

> Auf diese Verdrängungsthese, die Sebald an dieser Stelle noch losgelöst von der parallelen Verdrängung des Holocaust formuliert, folgt im zweiten Teil die kritische Durchsicht der wenigen literarischen Beispiele, die sich Sebalds Lesart zufolge in der Nachkriegszeit überhaupt auf den Bombenkrieg und seine katastrophalen Folgen eingelassen haben.[19]

Fuchs does not take issue with Sebald's appropriative use of language and affirms the thesis about an apparent 'Verdrängung,' of both the Holocaust and the 'Vernichtungsaktion' that allegedly had been the Allied air war. Yet Fuchs notes that in her work she will not concern herself with either correction or consolidation of Sebald's thesis but rather with the 'obsessive Tonalität von Sebalds Essay, die in der

auffällig repetitiven Qualität der Argumentationslinie durchscheint'.[20]
Fuchs attributes Sebald's apparent obsessive voice in *Luftkrieg und
Literatur*, which she rightly calls a 'symptomatisches Narrativ',[21] to a
melancholic synthesis of 'Heimatkritik' and nostalgia.[22] However, in
the next chapter of Fuchs's book, titled 'Die Leere der Gegenwart:
Sebalds Gedächtnistopografie', her critical reading of Sebald as a
nostalgic author becomes clearer with respect to the present. She
notes, '1989 und danach scheint in Sebalds Gedächtnistopografie
kaum vorzukommen'.[23] The reason for Fuchs's critique of Sebald's
'memory topography' is that he does not seem to notice the major
changes in German *Vergangenheitsbewältigung*:

> In Sebalds mentaler Deutschland-Topografie sind die *wesentlichen* Zäsuren
> [emphasis mine] der deutschen Gedächtniskultur nicht verzeichnet: Seine
> Arbeiten nehmen keine Notiz von Richard von Weizsäckers berühmter Rede vom
> 8. Mai 1985. [...] Damit wurde die problematische alte Vorstellung der
> Vergangenheitsbewältigung   zu   Gunsten   des   Konzepts   der
> Vergangenheitsverantwortung abgelöst. Diese Zäsur wird von Sebald genauso
> ignoriert wie die Bedeutung der Wehrmachtsdebatte, der Goldhagen-Diskussion
> in der breiten Öffentlichkeit oder die Diskussion um das Holocaust-Denkmal in
> Berlin Ende der 90er Jahre.[24]

Fuchs's critique of Sebald is essentially linked to his refusal to
acknowledge the 'wesentlichen Zäsuren' in Germany. It is thus
interesting to ask whether the events and debates mentioned by Fuchs
actually *are* (all) the 'relevant' ones, from whose perspective they
would be read like this and how this reading itself constructs a
'relevant' discourse. It is therefore a question of how these above
debates are analysed: do they contribute to a conscious concern with
remembering and working through, or are they perpetuating a
melancholic 'forgetfulness'? Fuchs in fact seems to locate a problem
in Sebald's work in his acknowledging of the Shoah as a rupture that
defined the 20th century:

> Sebalds Deutschland erstarrt gleichsam in den fünfziger Jahren, ein Befund, der
> nur unzureichend mit der Auswanderung des Autors nach Großbritannien Anfang
> der siebziger Jahre erklärt wird. Seine Indifferenz gegenüber den jüngsten
> geschichtlichen Bewegungen gründet vielmehr in dem Verständnis von 1945 als
> Zäsur von einer geradezu manichäischen Kraft: Angesichts der Ungeheuerlichkeit
> des Holocaust erscheinen alle geschichtlichen Entwicklungen danach als bloße
> Fußnoten in der Geschichte der menschlichen Selbstzerstörung.[25]

I would agree that there is indeed an obsessive vocality to *Luftkrieg
und Literatur* but would argue that it can be read contrary to Fuchs's
argument. The construction of Sebald's long introductory sentence
deserves again attention in this respect: Sebald builds a narrative,

which arches from the 'singular act of annihilation' to the effects that the alleged trauma has up to the present day. The initial traumatising experience is emphasised by the repetitious pattern 'day by day, month by month, year by year', suggesting a seemingly endless and agonising suffering. Reading the sentence leaves one breathless for more than one reason, and with the impression that precisely this *breathlessness* is a key point. Sebald concludes that the Allied air raids have had 'reale' and '*erstickende* Folgen [emphasis mine]', effects which *suffocated* 'jedes positive Lebensgefühl' (LL, 12). Does this structuring breathlessness and its linguistic linking reveal a desire for Germans to be recognised equally as victims, like their victims who suffocated in the gas chambers? In this sense, it would not differ significantly from Friedrich's use of the term 'crematoria' to describe cellars in air raided cities,[26] yet Sebald is highly praised both by scholars inside and outside of Germany for pointing to an alleged gap in scholarship and wider discourse. However, while Friedrich is precisely concerned with claiming a competitive status of 'victimhood' for Germans, Sebald universalises 'suffering', not, as Fuchs seems to argue, because of his neglecting German debates but rather in spite of them. In a review of Sebald's *Luftkrieg und Literatur* the German literary scholar Carole Anne Constabile-Heming even goes as far as to say: 'I find unfathomable the extent to which the sufferings of German civilians during World War Two have been ignored.'[27] She wonders about 'the greater issue at hand, namely, that historians, political scientists and literary scholars *have been one-sided in our approach* [my emphasis] to *Vergangenheitsbewältigung*'. However, taking Fuchs's assessment into account according to which Sebald remained stuck in the 1950s and over-determined by the Shoah, it leaves us wondering whether Sebald in fact read the Allied air raids and 'German suffering' through the lens of someone intensely affected by the events of the Holocaust – without considering for once the 'inner-German' discourse in the present and the problematic effects his thoughts on the bombing of German cities would have in this respect.

In Ernestine Schlant's comprehensive and critical analysis of West German literature and the Holocaust, it is precisely W. G. Sebald, whom she regards as a kind of exemplary writer, who breaks and shifts the 'language of silence' which is to be found in various forms in post-Holocaust German literature. In her chapter 'Post-Unification'

Schlant discusses works by Bernhard Schlink, Peter Schneider and W. G. Sebald. Schlant writes about Sebald's *The Emigrants*:

> Sebald's text is steeped in images of the Holocaust and a language of mourning and melancholy so pervasive that it applies even when the texts speak of other events and times. In this mourning, Sebald restitutes individuality to the victims he portrays and in doing so introduces a new kind of silence – the silence of the victims.[28]

Schlant's words here would also be suitable for Sebald's novel *Austerlitz*, and yet it was this latter work which for me raised even more doubts as to whether Schlant's categorisation of 'German writers' is not a rather difficult one. To what extent can Sebald be called a 'German writer' in the sense of which Schlant speaks: one who expresses a general public discourse (and what about 'non-German-German' writers in Germany)? Sebald writes *Luftkrieg und Literatur*, as I have pointed out above, as an 'outsider' – not only do critics receive his work in this way but he himself seems to have considered his lectures not as part of a German discourse of 'wartime suffering'.

In *Austerlitz,* the narrator seems to give us important insights into some of the reasons why he had left Germany and did not return, while recalling a visit to the fortress of Breendonk in Belgium:

> Was ich aber im Gegensatz zu dieser in Breendonk ebenso wie in all den anderen Haupt- und Nebenlagern Tag für Tag und jahrelang fortgesetzten Schindereien durchaus mir vorstellen konnte, als ich schließlich die Festung selber betrat und gleich rechterhand durch die Glasscheibe einer Tür hineinschaute in das sogenannte Kasino der SS-Leute, auf die Tische und Bänke, den dicken Bullerofen und die in gotischen Buchstaben sauber gemalten Sinnsprüche an der Wand, das waren die Familienväter und die guten Söhne aus Vilsbiburg und aus Fuhlsbüttel, aus dem Schwarzwald und aus dem Münsterland, wie sie hier nach getanem Dienst beim Kartenspiel beieinander saßen oder Briefe schrieben an ihre Lieben daheim, denn unter ihnen hatte ich ja gelebt bis in mein zwanzigstes Jahr.[29]

Through his narrator, Sebald makes it very clear that he can easily imagine the people who considered murder as 'a normal day's work', and Sebald's closing sentence, in particular his emphasising phrase 'after all' seems to be full of indignation. So we could indeed be tempted to ask if Sebald's position is that of an 'insider' or an 'outsider', siding with a dominant majority or rather opting for the outside to the extent of being literally outside, in self-chosen exile in Britain. And yet, *Luftkrieg und Literatur* and its role in the 'Luftkrieg-Debatte' in Germany emphasises the fact that emigration – considering the above quote from *Austerlitz* – does not mean giving up a dominant/inside perspective of a native country. Taberner therefore rightly observes with respect to Sebald's critics,

> Thus there appears to exist, amongst scholars in the United States and Great Britain in particular, a consensus that the conventions of reception which shape their sceptical approach to German texts dealing with Nazism do not apply here. Sebald's literary output is thus framed as being in some way 'removed' from the social and political debates within which contemporary German literature is typically contextualised and interrogated.[30]

Taberner points here to the reception of Sebald in the US and the UK which, I would argue, turns highly problematic in the case of scholarly readings of *Luftkrieg und Literatur*. Here a point has been reached in the debate when it is maintained that the hegemonic memory in German society on 'German victimhood' had not even existed. Thereby – in a move to right the wrong of this 'one-sided approach' (Constabile-Heming) – the already and always dominant memory paradoxically emerges as finally 'coming/being out' but now unquestioned *as such* and even viewed as 'progressive' discourse. It is asserted that German society now begins to remember that which was forgotten. Actually, it is precisely happening in reverse: the discourse expresses a forgetting about remembering, a forgetting that a memory about the Allied air raids, the 'Vertreibung' and other effects of Nazism had always existed. And it expresses a forgetting about the fact that this memory was preserved, (re-) shaped and transferred throughout society, publicly and – not least – within family narratives. An interesting new aspect in this discourse of victimisation is the stress on trauma

However, the forgetting about a remembering can be linked to what the Mitscherlichs had analysed as enormous psychological energy needed for the deployment of a set of defence mechanisms, foremost the 'derealisation' (Entwirklichung) of the past.[31] The Mitscherlichs were very aware that a derealisation meant not German society's collective *re-narrating* of the Nazi period but rather a *denial* of National Socialism altogether. This explains why many immediate post-war observers 'from outside' and Jewish survivors stated their shock about the consistent refusal to acknowledge guilt and responsibility.[32] Moreover, this collectively internalised version of the Nazi past links, for instance, with the most recent studies finding that still today 'Germans' and 'Nazis' are perceived as entirely different groups, such as in Welzer et al.

In their study entitled *Opa war kein Nazi*, Welzer, Moller and Tschuggnall take as their point of departure the distinction/mutual interlinkage between what they refer to as 'Lexikon' and 'Album'. 'Lexikon' stands for the knowledge about history, as learned, for instance, at school, and it represents the critical, 'worked through' and distanced relationship to National Socialism. 'Album', however, denotes another, an emotionally more important system of reference for the interpretation of the past: family and relations, letters, photographs and personal documents.

Thus, as Welzer et al state, the 'Album' of the 'Third Reich' is 'en-imaged/pictured' (bebildert) with war, heroism, suffering, victimhood, hardship, fascination and fantasies of greatness, and not, like the 'Lexikon', with crime, exclusion and annihilation.[33] With reference to Raul Hilberg's formulation that in Germany the Holocaust was family history, the authors note that thus the 'Lexikon' and the 'Album' stand side by side on the living room shelf, their contradictory contents having to be brought in line with each other. However, according to Welzer et al, this is solved in most cases by assigning parents and grandparents a role that exempts them from everything which is listed in the 'Lexikon'.[34] The research by Welzer et al suggests the predominant presence of stories about the Germans' own suffering, bombings, war and imprisonment by the victorious forces within family memory. What is more, they show convincingly that these topics are not communicated in the families as *knowledge* but as *certainty*.

Most instructive is Welzer et al's thesis that *knowledge* (Wissen), thus a part of the 'Lexikon' that is mediated through schools, memorial sites and film, is entirely different from the *certainty* (Gewissheit), which one has as a member of a community of memory (Erinnerungsgemeinschaft) about a shared past. According to Welzer et al, this is not least due to family memory being made up from the continuity of its 'presentialising' (Vergegenwärtigung).[35] Against the background of their categories of analysis, it is therefore not surprising that Welzer et al find that 'Wissen' and 'Gewissheit' can easily co-exist in complete detachment. This results in self-perceptions as 'victim' as well as – at the very same time – in what the authors call 'cumulative heroisation'.[36] The scandal around the term 'Bombenholocaust' used by the neo-Nazi party NPD could thus consist in their transgression of the boundaries of the 'Album,' that is, in the attempt of merging 'Gewissheit' and 'Wissen' in a parliamentary setting which is ultimately accessible/audible in a wider (international) context. The problem of transferring terminology from Holocaust discourse lies in the competing nature of the claims using this language. Thus the claims to '*German* victimhood' will inevitably be received in tandem with a minimising of the Shoah, and hence bring us to the unproductive debate about the singularity of the Nazi crimes. LaCapra rightly notes, 'if it is not redefined to refer to the transgression of an outer limit, the concept of uniqueness easily becomes an emblem in a grim competition for first place in victimhood'.[37] One could add that this competition is even more difficult to understand and even more grim in the case of Germans trying to claim a (first?) place in victimhood vis-a-vis victims who were murdered in their very name.

As becomes apparent through a critical look at W. G. Sebald's *Luftkrieg und Literatur*, the gap between the discourse on German responsibility and remembrance of the victims of the Nazi crimes and the desire for recognition of '*German* wartime suffering' leads us back to the question whether *Luftkrieg und Literatur* is not precisely an attempt to bring 'Lexikon' and 'Album' in line with each other. Sebald, not content with the two detached volumes on the shelf, seems to leap across the gap and merge these two by insisting on the content of the 'Lexikon', and, in spite of his sceptical view on family memory and its anaesthetic function, letting the 'Album' take over and fill in its blanks through the language of the 'Lexikon'. At the time of the 60th anniversary of the liberation of the camps and Germany's capitulation, the Allied bombing of German cities has almost sidelined the commemoration of the victims of the Holocaust. Thus the headlines about 'German suffering' in German newspapers and magazines overtook the facts about the reasons for the Second World War. With that even more linguistic inhibitions fell, and it became opportune to speak about 'German suffering' in a language that appropriated the horrors of the camps. Sebald has contributed to that discursive development, yet we will never know whether he would approve of – or even be interested in – the directions the debates are taking within Germany and beyond.

Notes

[1] Jörg Friedrich, *Der Brand: Deutschland im Bombenkrieg 1940-1945*, Propyläen: Munich, 2002.

[2] W. G. Sebald, *Luftkrieg und Literatur*, Fischer: Frankfurt am Main, 2001. Further references in the text as (LL, page number). The English translation, *On the Natural History of Destruction* was published in 2003, Hamish Hamilton, Penguin: London. Anne Fuchs speaks of the 'von Sebald losgetretene Diskussion um den Bombenkrieg und seine Folgen' and I would follow her in so far as I would suggest it was indeed Sebald's *Luftkrieg und Literatur* which addressed for the first time the supposed 'silence' about 'German wartime suffering' and the air raids within a 'respectable' setting and turned this into the concern of an author that could hardly be suspected of right-wing ideological leanings. See Anne Fuchs, *Die Schmerzensspuren der Geschichte: Zur Poetik der Erinnerung in W. G. Sebalds Prosa*, Böhlau: Köln, 2004, p. 154.

[3] The recent debate about 'German suffering' in relation to National Socialism is not at all a new one as is often alleged in literary and scholarly writing since the late 1990s. For example Jörg Arnold states in a review of Friedrich's *Der Brand* that a certain strand in the current debate 'feeds off a discourse that emerged during the final years of the war and is grounded in local memory.' Jörg Arnold, 'On Friedrich's, *Der Brand:* A Narrative of Loss,' review on H-Net German/History (3 Nov. 2003), www.h-net.org/reviews.

[4] See *Stern* magazine (21.1.2005), www.stern.de/politik/Deutschland/535592.html.

[5] For a critique of *Der Brand* – albeit omitting the highly gendered aspects in some of the images and terms Friedrich uses to construct 'German victimhood' – see Hannes Heer, *Vom Verschwinden der Täter: Der Vernichtungskrieg fand statt, aber keiner war dabei*, Aufbau Verlag: Berlin, 2005. Heer has discussed Friedrich's language extensively and come to the conclusion that the author indeed suggests a Holocaust perpetrated on Germans, see p. 296.

[6] Sebald's praise, though, refers not to *Der Brand* which was published three years after *Luftkrieg und Literatur*, but to Friedrich's 1995 work *Das Gesetz des Krieges*, Sebald, p. 76.

[7] See Harald Welzer, Sabine Moller and Karoline Tschuggnall, *'Opa war kein Nazi': Nationalsozialismus und Holocaust im Familiengedächtnis*, Fischer: Frankfurt am Main, 2002, Suzanne Brown-Fleming, *The Holocaust and Catholic Conscience: Cardinal Aloisius Muench and the Guilt Question in Germany*, University of Notre Dame Press: Notre Dame/Indiana, 2006, as well as Matthew D. Hockenos, *A Church Divided: German Protestants Confront the Nazi Past*, Indiana University Press: Bloomington, 2004. These works make clear that not only has there been no 'silence' about 'German suffering' but that, on the contrary, Germans imagined themselves as being persecuted by the Allies. Jörg Friedrich himself shows, probably

unintentionally, that the claims of a 'silence about the air war' cannot be upheld: the bibliography of *Der Brand* is full of titles such as *Würzburg im Feuerofen, Eine Stadt im Feuerregen, Alliierter Bombenterror, Köln >39-45<, Der Leidensweg einer Stadt* and *Die gemordete Stadt*. It is noteworthy that most of the titles are closely tied to a Christian biblical interpretation; this is most obvious with respect to the 'Leidensweg', literally the Via Dolorosa, the passion of Jesus Christ. Hence we are confronted with Christian martyr imagery. The 'Feuerofen' resonates with the fiery furnace of Nebuchadnezzar (Daniel 3.12); the 'Feuerregen' reminds one of Sodom and Gomorrha. These books were published throughout the post-war decades, some of them dating back to 1946 and to the early 1950s. As this is evidence contrary to the alleged 'silence,' Friedrich writes in his editorial: 'Über den Bombenkrieg ist viel geschrieben worden, seit langem aber nichts über seine *Leideform*', Friedrich, p. 543. I would argue that the titles of the books in Friedrich's bibliography themselves already sufficiently express a most empathic writing about this 'Leideform.' This 'Leideform' is given voice in graphic detail by Friedrich, who chooses a narrative format without footnotes for his almost 600 page book. In addition to the literal meaning, Friedrich apparently draws on the grammatical meaning of the term: the passive construction in a sentence ('passive voice'), which is even more interesting with respect to constructing 'passive subjects' and their suffering.

[8] W. G. Sebald, *On the Natural History of Destruction*, p. vii. However, in the English hardback edition we can find no acknowledgement of the source for these two essays on Améry and Weiss. Thus the English reader was left with the question about the time of Sebald's writing of these texts. Only in the later English paperback edition do we learn that these essays had previously been published in German: 'Against the Irreversible: On Jean Améry,' was originally published as 'Mit den Augen des Nachtvogels. Über Jean Améry,' in *Études Germaniques* 43 (1998), 3, pp. 313-327 and 'The Remorse of the Heart: On Memory and Cruelty in the Work of Peter Weiss' appeared first as 'Die Zerknirschung des Herzens. Über Erinnerung und Grausamkeit im Werk von Peter Weiss,' in *Orbis Litterarum* 41 (1986), 3, pp. 265-278. See Sebald, *On the Natural History of Destruction*, Penguin Books: London, 2004.

[9] See Jean Améry, 'Ressentiments,' in: Améry, *Jenseits von Schuld und Sühne*, Klett-Cotta: Stuttgart, 1977, pp. 102-29.

[10] Mark McCulloh, *Understanding W. G. Sebald*, University of South Carolina Press: Columbia, 2003, p. 177.

[11] Sebald, *On the Natural History of Destruction*, pp. 3-4.

[12] See Victor Klemperer, *'LTI – Lingua Tertii Imperii: Notizbuch eines Philologen*, Reclam: Leipzig, 1975.

[13] Stuart Taberner, 'German Nostalgia? Remembering German-Jewish Life in W. G. Sebald's *Die Ausgewanderten* and *Austerlitz*,' in *The Germanic Review*, vol. 79, no. 3 (Summer 2004), pp. 181-202 (here: p. 182).

[14] The translation reads: 'the extraordinary faculty for self-anaesthesia shown by a community that seemed to have emerged from a war of annihilation without any signs of psychological impairment.' Sebald, *On the Natural History of Destruction*, p. 11.

[15] For a comprehensive discussion of the debates on the exhibition and for a critique of its inner politics and the subsequent changes of its conception, see Hannes Heer, *Vom Verschwinden der Täter*. Heer, who was one of the historians who initiated the project, also points to another political-linguistic link: The news-magazine of the governing Bavarian Christian Social party CSU attacked the exhibition as a 'moralischen Vernichtungsfeldzug gegen das deutsche Volk', Heer, p. 19.

[16] Dominick LaCapra, *History and Memory after Auschwitz*, Cornell University Press: Ithaca and London, 1998, p. 71.

[17] Saul Friedlander, for instance, notes that in 1985 the editor-in-chief of *Der Spiegel*, Rudolf Augstein, devoted an important part of an article 'to Roosevelt's Jewish secretary of the treasury, Henry Morgenthau. [Augstein] describes Morgenthau's plans to subjugate a defeated Germany and decides that Hitler missed in him a good follower.' Moreover, Friedlander states, Augstein informed his readers that 'Theodore Nathan Kaufman, the president of the American Peace society, advocated the general sterilization of the German population in order to bring about its disappearance.' Saul Friedlander, *Memory, History, and the Extermination of the Jews of Europe*, Indiana University Press: Bloomington and Indianapolis, 1993, p. 13.

[18] Fuchs, p. 152.

[19] Ibid.

[20] Ibid., p. 154.

[21] Ibid., p. 156.

[22] Ibid., p. 157.

[23] Ibid., p. 166.

[24] Ibid., p. 167.

[25] Ibid.

[26] Friedrich, p. 195.

[27] Carole Anne Constabile-Heming, 'On Sebald's *Air War and Literature*,' review on H-Net German/History (3 Nov. 2003), www.h-net.org/reviews.

[28] Ernestine Schlant, *The Language of Silence: West German Literature and the Holocaust*, Routledge: New York and London, 1999, p. 234.

[29] Sebald, *Austerlitz*, Fischer: Frankfurt am Main, 2003 [2001], pp. 37-38. In the translation, the 'Münsterland,' located between Dortmund and Osnabrück and thus in North-West Germany, turns into the 'Bavarian Alps,' which make up the Southern border, presumably for reasons of more easily recognisable geographical location for the English language readers. This is nonetheless worthy of note for a British edition, since the 'Münsterland' came after 1945 under British administration while Bavaria was in the US-American sector. See Sebald, *Austerlitz*, Penguin: London, 2002, p. 29.

[30] Taberner, 'German Nostalgia?,' p. 181.

[31] See Alexander and Margarete Mitscherlich, *Die Unfähigkeit zu trauern*, Piper: Munich, 1977 [first 1967], p. 47f.

[32] See, for instance, Eva Kolinsky, *After the Holocaust: Jewish Survivors in Germany after 1945*, Pimlico: London, 2004, pp. 224-225. Hans Frankenthal, *Verweigerte Rückkehr: Erfahrungen nach dem Judenmord*, Fischer: Frankfurt am Main, 1999. Available in English translation as *The Unwelcome One: Returning Home from Auschwitz*, Northwestern University Press: Evanston, 2002.

[33] Welzer, Moller and Tschuggnall, p. 10.

[34] Ibid., pp. 9-10.

[35] Ibid., p. 210.

[36] Ibid., p. 209. 'Cumulative heroisation' means in this context that with every new generation the role of great-/grand/parent(s) is increasingly glorified, and, as Welzer et al show, this occurs to the extent of complete revisions of even a known role as perpetrators into a role of supporters of Jews.

[37] LaCapra, *History and Memory after Auschwitz*, p. 57.

Odile Jansen

Wahrheit und Erinnerung. Die Spuren des Jahres 1945 in Texten von Christa Wolf

This chapter explores the meaning of the return of the memories of aerial bombing, flight and expulsion, mass rapes and war captivity. With the return of these memories, the year 1945 enters centre stage again, the year of the end of the war and the year of liberation of the concentration camps. The public exposure of perpetration in 1945 caused a crisis in perception of the past and of identity that was already fended off by the Germans immediately after the war by reference to their own suffering. In the texts of Christa Wolf (born 1929) who experienced the end of the war fleeing from the Red Army, the traces of the year of 1945 are visible as a conflict between personal and historical truth.

'Die Chiffre "1945" ist ins deutsche Erinnerungskollektiv zurückgekehrt' schrieb der Historiker Nicolas Berg 2003 in einem Feuilletonartikel für *DIE ZEIT*.[1] Mit der Rückkehr der kollektiven Erinnerungen an 'Luftkrieg', 'Flucht und Vertreibung', Massen-Vergewaltigungen und Kriegsgefangenschaft in die öffentliche Debatte, tritt in der Tat das Jahr 1945 in den Vordergrund, ein Jahr das in vielerlei Hinsicht eine Zäsur bildet.[2] Historisch, denn Deutschlands Niederlage bedeutete das Ende des Deutschen Reichs; biographisch, da die Ereignisse von 1945 für Millionen zu einer Entwurzelung ihrer Existenz führte, von der Flucht vor der Roten Armee im Januar und Februar, dem Erlebnis des Kriegsendes, bis zu der Zwangsmigration von Deutschen aus den ehemaligen Reichsgebieten und von deutschsprachigen aus Ost- und Mitteleuropa als Folge der Potsdamer Konferenz von Juli-August 1945.

1945 – Krise in Wahrnehmung, Erzählen und Erinnern

Was bedeutet diese Rückkehr der Erinnerungen an 1945? Sie stellt zweifellos die Spur eines Traumas dar, aber welchen Traumas? 1945 symbolisiert schließlich auch eine andere Zäsur, die des Jahres der Befreiung der Lager. Mit dem Vormarsch der alliierten Truppen im Frühling '45 in Deutschland und Österreich wurden nach und nach die Nazi-Verbrechen vor den Augen der Welt enthüllt.[3] Die totale Entwertung aller menschlichen Werte in den Lagern offenbarte einen Zivilisationsbruch, der das integrative Vermögen der Erzählung außer Kraft stellte. Im Anblick dieser Orte versagte die Sprache, wovon zahllose Berichte alliierter Befreier und Kriegskorrespondenten Zeugnis ablegen. So schrieb *Time*-Reporter Percy Knauth nach seinem Besuch in Buchenwald, kurz nach der Befreiung des Lagers im April 1945: 'Buchenwald is beyond all comprehension. You just can't understand it, even when you've seen it.'[4]

Diese Krise der Wahrnehmung, des Erzählens und Erinnerns, wie sie in der Literatur zu 1945 beschrieben ist,[5] bezieht sich nicht nur auf die Perspektive der alliierten Seite. Die Konfrontation der Zivilbevölkerung mit den Nazi-Verbrechen im Frühling '45 durch Poster oder durch Führungen durch die Lager im Rahmen der 're-education', führte zu einem Schock, belegt u.a. in den Arbeiten Aleida Assmanns und Dagmar Barnouws. Der deutsch-jüdische Architekt Julius Posener, der vor dem Krieg nach Palästina ausgewandert war und als Officer der British Intelligence Service nach Deutschland zurückkehrte, bemerkte in seinem Bericht über das Kriegsende und das Nachkriegsdeutschland:

> Die Deutschen – ich meine das Volk im großen und ganzen, nicht die aktiven Mitglieder der Partei – erlebten damals zwei Erschütterungen: die der Niederlage und die der kollektiven Schuld. Es muß wohl zugestanden werden, dass man in Deutschland von den Greueln nichts oder nur wenig wußte, die nun nach den Funden in Belsen in jeder Stadt und jedem Dorf in Wort und Bild den Leuten vor Augen geführt wurden. Die Frage, wieviel man wußte, bleibt trotzdem etwas dunkel.[6]

Die landesweit übliche Beteuerung nach der Konfrontierung mit dem Grauen der Lager: 'Wir haben es nicht gewußt!', verriet das schlechte Gewissen, auf Grund einer passiven Mitverantwortung für die Verfolgung, von der nicht alles, aber immerhin genügend gewusst wurde.[7]

Die Rückkehr zu den Erinnerungen an 1945 bedeutet deswegen nicht nur eine Rückkehr zu der deutschen Leidensgeschichte, sondern auch eine Rückkehr zu dem Moment einer traumatischen Erkenntnis deutscher Täterschaft, die nachträglich die Vergangenheit und das Selbstbild grundlegend in Frage stellte.[8] Diese Erkenntnis und ihre Abwehr bilden zugleich den Anfang der konfliktreichen Geschichte der 'Vergangenheitsbewältigung'. Ein Bedürfnis, sich von der historischen Erfahrung des Holocaust abzugrenzen und eine unbehelligte Identität für sich in Anspruch nehmen zu können, tauchte schon gleich nach dem Kriegsende auf. Die Frage der Schuld und Mitverantwortung wurde 1945 und in den nachfolgenden Jahren häufig abgewehrt, unter Verweis auf die eigenen, immerhin reellen

Leidenserfahrungen, deren Ursachen aber nicht hinterfragt wurden. Ein Beispiel dieser Strategie, die den Verlust der nationalen Identität bekämpft,[9] bietet der Briefwechsel zwischen dem österreichischen Schriftsteller jüdischer Herkunft Hermann Broch und dem jungen deutschen Emigrant Volkmar von Zühlsdorff. '"Flohbisse" nannte ein Amerikaner die Sünden der Deutschen im Vergleich zu der totalen planmäßigen Verwüstung', schreibt von Zühlsdorff in Sommer 1945 an Broch, und fragt ihn einige Monate später, ob die Juden in Amerika nicht eine Hilfsaktion anregen sollten:

> für die hungernden und verhungernden deutschen Kinder [...] – erstens um der Kinder willen, und zweitens um klarzumachen, dass Morgenthau nicht für 'die Juden' spricht?[10]

Diese Haltung der Aufrechnung und Apologetik, wobei ein Vergleich zwischen dem Leiden der deutschen Zivilbevölkerung unter vor allem dem Luftkrieg und dem Leiden der Opfer des Holocaust offen zutage tritt – die 'Öfen von Auschwitz sind die Glutherde von Hamburg und Dresden [...]',[11] schreibt zum Beispiel von Zühlsdorff – ist ein frühes Zeichen eines sich-nicht-auseinandersetzen-(könnens) mit der Vergangenheit. Als symptomatische Begleiterscheinungen dieser gesellschaftlichen Wunde gestalten sich neben dem Opferdiskurs das häufig beschriebene, plötzliche Verschwinden der Nazi-Ideologie nach dem Krieg und ein bemerkenswertes Schweigen darüber, was in Deutschland und im übrigen Europa geschehen war.[12]

Trauma und Repräsentation

1945 als 'Wahrheitskrise' führt zu der Frage, inwiefern es möglich ist, die Vergangenheit als real gelebte Wirklichkeit zu kennen und darzustellen. Die Vergangenheit bildet schließlich keine Entität an sich, sie entsteht nur in und durch ihre Repräsentation. Erst der Vorgang von narrativer Ergänzung, Deutung und kausaler Klärung transformiert Erlebnisse in Erfahrungen. Traumata zerstören diesen Prozess der Symbolisierung und Sinngebung. Das Trauma als interpretatives Vakuum zieht nie endende Deutungsversuche nach sich, wie Freud in seiner Theorie der Nachträglichkeit darstellte.[13] Das Trauma macht sich als Trauma gerade kennbar durch diesen Prozess der nachträglichen Übersetzung und Transformierung eines nicht-erfahrenen Ereignisses. Was stellt also die referentielle Ebene der Erinnerungen an traumatische Erlebnisse dar? Diese Frage nach der Authentizität der Erinnerung, die seit dem Anfang der Traumaforschung eine zentrale Rolle spielt, kann auch formuliert

werden als eine Frage nach der 'Wahrheit'. Bezieht die Erinnerung
sich auf die Vergangenheit oder gibt sie eher eine – chiffrierte –
Vorstellung der Vergangenheit?

Diese Problematik möcht ich am Beispiel verschiedener Texte der
DDR-Autorin Christa Wolf darstellen, in deren Arbeit die Spuren des
Jahres 1945 als individuelles Trauma und kollektive Krise
eingeschrieben sind. Für die Autorin, geboren 1929 in der ehemaligen
ost-brandenburgischen Provinzstadt Landsberg a.d. Warthe, das
heutige polnische Gorzów Wielkopolski, bildet '1945' eine
Primärerfahrung. Ende Januar '45 flüchtete sie mit ihrer Familie vor
der Roten Armee westwärts und erlebte während dieser Flucht das
Kriegsende. In ihren schriftstellerischen Arbeiten nimmt 1945 als
Thema oder Motiv eine Rolle ein seit den ersten unveröffentlichten
Manuskripten, den so genannten Hanna-Geschichten aus den Jahren
1955-56 über das Leben des Flüchtlingsmädchens Hanna zwischen
Februar 1945 und September 1946. Zu dieser Erzählung schreibt die
Dichterin:

> Kern der Handlung ist der Weg der zu Beginn sechzehnjährigen Hanna durch das
> völlige innere Chaos, über die verschiedensten Irrwege, bis an die Schwelle eines
> neuen Lebens.[14]

Gegen den Hintergrund des Erlebnisses der Flucht und der
historischen Traumata des Holocaust und des 'Dritten Reichs'
gestalten diese Prosatexte sich als autobiographische Sinnkonstrukte
nach einer Erfahrung von massivem Sinnverlust

Wahrheit und Erinnerung

Den Kernkonflikt von 1945, die Entfremdung von der eigenen
Vergangenheit nach den Erkenntnissen des Holocaust und der
Verunsicherung der Identität als Teil eines nationalen Kollektivs, hat
Christa Wolfs um zwei Jahre älterer Generationsgenosse Martin
Walser in seinem autobiographischen Roman *Ein springender
Brunnen* (1998) über seine Jugend während des Nationalsozialismus
so dargestellt:

> Solange etwas ist, ist es nicht das, was es gewesen sein wird. Wenn etwas vorbei
> ist, ist man nicht mehr der, dem es passierte. Allerdings ist man dem näher als
> anderen. Obwohl es die Vergangenheit, als sie Gegenwart war, nicht gegeben hat,
> drängt sie sich jetzt auf, als habe es sie so gegeben, wie sie sich jetzt aufdrängt.[15]

Am Ende dieses Romans finden wir einen in dieser Hinsicht
bedeutungsvollen Hinweis auf die Erschütterung des Alter Egos des

Autors, Johann, als er 1945 von der Verfolgung der jüdischen Mutter seines Dorfgenossen Wolfgang erfährt:

> Er hatte gespürt, dass Wolfgang, was er ihm erzählt hatte, erzählt hatte, weil Johann das wissen müsse. Vielleicht meinte Wolfgang, dass Johann ein Vorwurf zu machen sei, weil er all das nicht gewußt, nicht gemerkt hatte. Johann wehrte sich gegen diesen vermuteten Vorwurf. [...] Er wollte von sich nichts verlangen lassen. [...] Niemand sollte ihm eine Empfindung abverlangen, die er nicht selber hatte.[16]

Die Symptome des Traumas von 1945, die Empfindungen von Schuld und Scham, werden in diesen Textstellen vor allem sichtbar im Verlust der Identität, als Vorstellung eines einheitlichen, affirmativen Narrativs zu der eigenen Vergangenheit. Die Konstruktion einer Lebensgeschichte zielt aber auf eine Wahrheit, die weniger Korrespondenz mit der Realität zu haben braucht, als man meinen könnte. Der Versuch, die Vergangenheit darzustellen, wie sie 'wirklich' gewesen ist, als wäre es eine archäologische Fundstelle, die man nur auszugraben hätte, verkennt den Konstruktionscharakter narrativer Darstellungen der Vergangenheit und den Faktor 'narrativer Wahrheit'.[17] Die Überzeugungskraft von Geschichten beruht nicht nur auf ihrer Faktizität, sondern auch auf ihrer ästhetischen Qualität. Formale Merkmale wie ein passendes Erzählschema und Konsistenz liefern einen nicht unwichtigen Beitrag zu dem Maß, in dem eine Geschichte als 'wahr' empfunden wird. Gerade das nachträgliche Wissen, über welches Walser schreibt, zerstört die Empfindung der eigenen Vergangenheit und Identität als lebensgeschichtlicher Einheit.

Die Vermittlung der historischen Erfahrung von Krieg und Nationalsozialismus, die Christa Wolf bereits früh als das Ziel ihrer schriftstellerischen Arbeit erwähnt hat, zieht diese Darstellungsproblematik der 'historischen Wahrheit' wie selbstverständlich nach sich, thematisiert sie auch als unauflösbaren Dauerkonflikt. Der Versuch, als 'Chronikschreiber' die Zeitgeschichte als Erfahrungsgeschichte darzustellen, führt zwangsläufig zu einem Konflikt zwischen dem subjektiven Empfinden, Opfer des Krieges zu sein, und der deutschen Täterschaft. Walter Benjamin postulierte in seinem Essay 'Der Erzähler' (1936) das Ende der Erzählung als Erfahrungsmedium nach dem Ersten Weltkrieg, dem ersten kollektiven Schockerlebnis der westlichen Welt.[18] In den 'Erfahrungstexten' Christa Wolfs, wo die Grenze zwischen Literatur und Egodokument völlig verwischt ist, können wir ein mimetisches Paradoxon beobachten, nämlich den Versuch, die unterschiedlichen traumatischen Ereignisse, die zusammen das Erlebnis des 'Kriegsendes' formen, darzustellen. Dieser Versuch führt zu einem Rückzug auf das Bildliche, vielfach Szenen von Tod, Gewalt und Verlust, in denen zum Ausdruck kommt, wie der Extremcharakter der Ereignisse von 1945 den Blick auf die Wirklichkeit geändert hat.

'Wandlung'

Das Wesen des Traumas von 1945 als ein radikaler Bruch in der Wahrnehmung wird wohl kaum so klar gezeigt wie in 'Gedächtnis und Gedenken' (1972). Die Kluft zwischen den Lebenswelten von Verfolgten und Nichtverfolgten, sowie die 'Blindheit' der Nicht-Verfolgten für den Terror des nationalsozialistischen Regimes, werden anschaulich in einer zitierten Szene aus *Der siebente Brunnen,* einem Roman von Fred Wander, Schriftsteller und Überlebender von Auschwitz und Buchenwald. An dieser Stelle beschreibt Wander, wie auf einem kleinen Bahnhof vor Buchenwald bei Fliegeralarm ein Zug mit toten und lebenden Gefängenen hält. Frauen und Kinder, die nach dem Alarm aus einem Luftschutzbunker herauskommen, gehen an diesem Zug vorbei:

> Mit unheimlicher Affektlosigkeit wird berichtet, wie das Unheimliche, das Unglaubliche geschieht: dass die Frauen, die ganz dicht vorübergehen, den Zug nicht *sehen* und nicht die 'merkwürdigen Gestalten, die aus den Waggontüren kollerten.' Dann aber, doch: Eine junge Frau fällt in Ohnmacht. 'Sie hatte gesehen. Nur eine hatte gesehen.' Am Rande der Straße lagen, wie Eisenbahnschwellen gestapelt, in langer Reihe, zwei Meter hoch, Leichen. Dies 'nur eine hatte gesehen' geht einem nach. Ist diese mutwillige Blindheit wirklich schon erklärt? Ist sie erklärbar? [19]

In dieser Erkenntniszene, die eine starke Ähnlichkeit mit den 'Erkenntnisszenen' nach der Befreiung der Lager aufweist, als die alliierten Truppen der örtlichen Bevölkerung im Rahmen der 're-education' die Verbrechen zeigten und Bilder verbreiteten, wird der Schleier vor dem Bewusstsein weggerissen und die Häftlinge als Menschen erkannt. Die grauenhafte Wirklichkeit der Lagerwelt, die sich in dieser Szene plötzlich den unbeteiligten Zuschauern offenbart, lässt die angebliche Normalität des Kriegsalltags verbleichen. Ähnliche emblematische Szenen, die als Wiederholung einer traumatischen Erkenntnis von Schuld erscheinen, kommen in den Texten Christa Wolfs vor, wo die getrennten Welten von Verfolgten und Nicht-Verfolgten während der Flucht aufeinander stoßen. In der autobiographischen Kurzgeschichte 'Blickwechsel' (1970) bilden die befreiten KZ-Häftlinge, denen der Flüchtlingstreck unterwegs begegnet, ein Menetekel für den bisher nicht wahrgenommenen Unrechtscharakter des Nationalsozialismus:

> Dann sahen wir die Kzler. Wie ein Gespenst hatte uns das Gerücht, dass sie hinter uns hergetrieben würden, die Oranienburger, im Nacken gesessen. […] Sie sahen anders aus als alle Menschen, die ich bisher gesehen hatte, und dass wir unwillkürlich vor ihnen zurückwichen, wunderte mich nicht. Aber es verriet uns doch auch, dieses Zurückweichen, es zeigte an, trotz allem, was wir einander und was wir uns selber beteuerten: Wir wußten Bescheid. Wir alle, wir Unglücklichen, die man von ihrem Hab und Gut vertrieben hatte, von ihren Bauernhöfen und aus ihren Gutshäusern, aus ihren Kaufmannsläden und muffigen Schlafzimmern und aufpolierten Wohnstuben mit dem Führerbild an der Wand – wir wußten: Diese da, die man zu Tieren erklärt hatte, und die jetzt langsam auf uns zukamen, um sich zu rächen – wir hatten sie fallenlassen. […] Und mit Entsetzen fühlte ich: Das ist gerecht, und wußte für den Bruchteil einer Sekunde, dass wir schuldig waren. Ich vergaß es wieder. [20]

Diese kathartischen Erkenntnisszenen bilden den Auftakt zu dem, was in den Prosaarbeiten Christa Wolfs als 'Wandlung' beschrieben wird, ein Prozess geistiger Erneuerung des Subjekts in intensiver Auseinandersetzung mit der Vergangenheit. In diesem Begriff ist das Jahr 1945 als Krise der (Selbst-)Wahrnehmung reflektiert, wie sie in den Erkenntnisszenen anschaulich wird, die Passagen in Martin Walsers *Ein springender Brunnen* nicht unähnlich sind. Mit der Verwendung des Begriffs 'Wandlung' zeigt Christa Wolf sich dem frühen DDR-Schulddiskurs und seinem typischen literarischen Exponat, dem so genannten Wandlungsroman, verpflichtet. Der Wandlungsroman, ein Produkt der ostdeutschen Literaturpolitik der fünfziger Jahre, hob die Schuldfrage des Individuums hervor, und schuf auf diese Weise die Prämisse für die Entwicklung eines individuellen Täterbewusstseins. Dadurch forderte dieser Romantypus, der sich an das klassische Genre des Bildungsromans anlehnt, eine Entwicklung, die sich konträr zu der in der DDR vorherrschenden Dimitrovdoktrin ausnahm, welche den Faschismus als Folge des Klassenkampfes erklärte. Der Wandlungsroman, der sich an der Generation orientierte, die den Krieg als Jugendliche oder junge Erwachsene erlebt hatten, stellte die Transformation, von vor allem ehemaligen Hitlersoldaten in schuldbewusste Muster-Antifaschisten, sprich engagierte DDR-Bürger, dar. [21]

Die Formel der Wandlung leitet sich vermutlich aus dem Aufsatz 'Schicksalswende', [22] den der ungarische Literaturwissenschaftler und Marxist Georg Lukács nach der Befreiung des Vernichtungslagers Lublin (Majdanek) durch die Rote Armee im Juli 1944 schrieb. Die

Nachrichten über diese 'Todesfabrik' erschütterten die deutschen Kommunisten im Exil, für die Majdanek ein bleibendes Symbol der Lager blieb. Mehrere Aufrufe an die deutsche Bevölkerung folgten,[23] in der Hoffnung, dass die 'Stunde der Peripetie', wie Lukács schrieb, gekommen war.

1945 – Wendepunkt und Lebenskrise

Die Erinnerung Christa Wolfs an 1945 als historischen Wendepunkt und Lebenskrise wird dabei gekennzeichnet durch eine extreme Ambivalenz, wie die autobiographische Geschichte 'Zu einem Datum' (1971) zeigt. In dieser Kurzgeschichte, verfasst aus Anlass des 25. Jahrestags der Vereinigung von SPD und KPD zur SED am 21. April 1946, beschreibt die Autorin ihre ideologische Wandlung von ehemaliger BDMlerin zum Marxismus. Dieser Schritt, symbolisch dargestellt durch die Lektüre der ersten marxistischen Schrift, wird nach einer Periode der ideologischen Enttäuschung getan, in einer von Erfahrungen des Hungers, der materiellen Not und dem Verlust der Heimat geprägten Nachkriegszeit. Die Konstruktion dieses lebensgeschichtlichen Abschnitts entspricht ganz der klassischen Wandlungsgeschichte mit ihrem biblischen Muster des skeptischen Ungläubigen, der zur Umkehr findet.

'Zu einem Datum' beginnt mit der Beschreibung des einzigen ihr bekannten Kommunisten durch das erzählende Ich und endet mit einer Reflexion über den Bauernaufstand unter Führung von Thomas Müntzer im Jahre 1525, der im selben Thüringer Ort blutig endete, wo die Flüchtlinge ansässig geworden sind. Mit dieser symbolischen Schlussszene schreibt die Ich-Erzählerin sich ein in die geschichtliche Tradition des anderen Deutschland, das Deutschland der Aufklärung und der Reformbewegungen. Die Geschichte stellt kurzum ein Bekenntnis zur DDR und ihrer sozialistischen Tradition da. Die Ambivalenz, die diesen Prozess des ideologischen Objektwechsels begleitet, der ebenso hochtrabenden wie naiven Schlussszene zum Trotz, ist gekennzeichnet durch die Phrase 'Entwirklichung der Wirklichkeit'. 'Tempora mutantur, die Zeiten ändern sich [...] und wir ändern uns in ihnen', läßt der Lateinlehrer in der Notschule, die die Ich-Erzählerin morgens besucht, übersetzen.[24] Die 'nagelneue Zeit' steht aber nicht im Zeichen einer kathartischen Wandlung, sondern der Entfremdung und des Selbstverlustes: 'Wenn ich etwas erfahren hatte, so dies: Wie einstmals Wirkliches allmählich unwirklich wird [...].'[25]

Unwirklich ist die ehemalige Begeisterung für den BDM geworden, wie auch das Kriegsende. Der Verlust des Haltes in der nationalsozialistischen Ideologie und die Erfahrung des Zusammenbruchs der Gesellschaft, ihrer Normen und Werte führt in 'Zu einem Datum' zu einer Derealisierung der Vergangenheit.

Die Derealisierung, die in dieser Geschichte dargestellt wird, spiegelt das merkwürdige, spukhafte Verschwinden des Nationalsozialismus nach 1945. Die augenscheinlich nach dem Krieg mit dem Übertritt zum Marxismus kaltgestellte Vergangenheit kehrt dennoch zurück, wie in dem Debut *Moskauer Novelle* aus dem Jahre 1961 zu sehen ist, dessen Hauptperson, eine junge deutsche Ärztin mit einem Hintergrund als Flüchtling und BDM-Mädel, so sehr an ihren Schuldgefühlen über den Krieg leidet, dass sie anstatt der Russen, die sie besucht, selbst als das traumatisierte Opfer erscheint. In diesen und anderen Versuchen Christa Wolfs, zwei Geschichten gleichzeitig zu erzählen, einerseits die Geschichte der Verwicklung in den Nationalsozialismus und andererseits die Geschichte eines Verlustes der Heimat und einer ungebrochenen Identität, tut sich eine konflikthafte Selbstbestimmung über die Bilder auf, die die Vergangenheit hervorruft. Dies lässt sich an der autobiographischen Kurzgeschichte 'Blickwechsel', die eine Vorstudie zu dem ebenfalls autobiographischen Roman *Kindheitsmuster* (1976) bildet, ablesen.[26]

'Blickwechsel' thematisiert das Kriegsende und seine unterschiedlichen Lesarten. Wie die Chiffre '45 ist der 8. Mai 1945, der Tag der deutschen Kapitulation, mit Ambivalenz umgeben. Das Kriegsende bedeutete zwar das Ende von Nationalsozialismus, Terror und Kriegsgewalt, wurde aber von einer Mehrheit der Bevölkerung nicht als Befreiung empfunden. Die Empfindung, eine Niederlage erlitten zu haben, der Ideologieverlust, die Erfahrungen von Flucht, Zwangsmigration, Kriegsgefangenschaft, Gewalt gegen Frauen, die Toten, die zu betrauern waren und die materielle Notlage nach dem Krieg im Allgemeinen, verleihen den Erinnerungen an das Kriegsende ihre eigentümliche Ambivalenz. Der Streit um die Bedeutung, die dem 8. Mai '45 beigemessen werden sollte, der in der Bundesrepublik lange andauerte, war in der DDR, wo der 8. Mai '45 als 'Tag der Befreiung' bewertet wurde, abwesend, damit fehlte aber auch ein offener Dialog über die Vergangenheit.[27]

In 'Blickwechsel' wird diese offizielle DDR-Lesart des Kriegsendes als 'Befreiung' konterkariert mit einer Darstellung der

Flucht vor der sowjetischen Armee im Januar 1945, dem Erlebnis des Kriegsendes als persönlicher Katastrophe und Hinweisen auf andere DDR-Tabuthemen wie die Vergewaltigungen durch die sowjetische Besatzungsmacht. Die implizite Kritik an der DDR-Vergangenheitspolitik in dieser Geschichte ist eingebunden in einen Prozess des kritischen Erinnerns.

Die veränderte Perspektive auf die Vergangenheit, die die 'Befreiung' als einen Prozess des Erinnerns darstellt, bildet das Hauptthema dieser Erzählung, wie der Titel bereits andeutet. Das Paradoxon des Endes des Krieges als Befreiung vom Nationalsozialismus und Anfang eines persönlichen Verlusts wird in 'Blickwechsel' an Hand von Erinnerungsbildern repräsentiert, die bekannte Topoi aus der kollektiven Erinnerung an 1945 repräsentieren: Bilder der Flucht im Januar '45; Bilder vom Tieffliegerbeschuss, von der Konfrontation mit befreiten KZ-Häftlingen und der ersten Begegnung mit den alliierten Truppen. In der Interpretation dieser einschneidenden Erlebnisse in der eigenen Lebensgeschichte zeigt sich ein Bemühen um eine historisierende Distanzierung.

Wie sehr aber diese Erfahrung emotional unverarbeitet geblieben ist, zeigt das Erzählmuster, in das der Krieg plötzlich einbricht als ein schockartiges Erlebnis in eine idyllische Situation. Das Trauma manifestiert sich in der Darstellung der Flucht, die zu allen späteren Kenntnissen konträr ist. Die Funktion der 'Deckerinnerung', die die Erinnerung an die Flucht in der Nachkriegsgeschichte häufig bekommen hat, d.h. eine Erinnerung, die das Verhalten vor '45 verdeckt, kommt hier zwar nicht zum Vorschein, es stellt sich aber dennoch eine Identifizierung mit der Opferschaft her. Die Divergenz von emotionalem Empfinden und nachträglicher Kognition spricht aus der Beschreibung des Krieges als eine Katastrophe, an die das erzählende Ich sich hilflos ausgeliefert fühlt. Gesprochen wird von Selbstentfremdung, einer Betäubung der Affekte, Spaltung der Persönlichkeit, kurzum von Selbstverlust als Folge des Einbrechens des Unerwartbaren, das dargestellt wird in der bildhaften Schlüsselszene, als die Ich-Erzählerin beschreibt, wie sie an einem 'kalten Januarmorgen in aller Hast auf einem Lastwagen' ihre Stadt verließ, und etwas in ihr sagte: 'Das siehst du niemals wieder.'[28] Diese Vertreibung aus dem Kindheitsparadies, eine Szene die als Chiffre des Verlusts zahllosen Texten Christa Wolfs eingeschrieben ist, wirkt wie abgeschnitten vom Rest der Erzählung als ein 'dissoziertes Wissen'. Das Bild des Heimatsverlusts weist hin auf die Erfahrung eines 'psychischen Tods', gewinnt aber in 'Blickwechsel' wie in anderen Erzählungen und Texten über das Kriegsende die zusätzliche Bedeutung eines Verlusts der Identität. Im Erinnerungsbild des Abschieds der Heimatstadt verdichten sich die Trauer-, Schuld- und Schamgefühle, die so kennzeichnend sind für die biographische Zäsur 1945.

Die Darstellung von 1945 als biographische Zäsur, in der sich persönliche Verlusterfahrungen der Heimatstadt, der Kindheit, und einer positiven – nationalen – Identität verschränken, wiederholt sich in *Kindheitsmuster* (1976). Dieser autobiographische Roman über eine Jugend im 'Dritten Reich', der allgemein als ein Höhepunkt in der DDR-Literatur zum Thema Faschismus und Vergangenheitsbewältigung betrachtet wird, gestaltet sich vor allem als die Geschichte eines Identitätsverlusts. Dieser Verlust ist schon in der Form erkennbar, nämlich einer Reise zürück an die Orte der Kindheit in der ehemaligen deutschen, heute polnischen, Heimatstadt L., einer Komposition, mit der faktisch eine umgekehrte Fluchtbewegung beschrieben wird. Die Rekonstruktion der Erinnerungen an diese Reise wird unterbrochen durch zahllose Rückblenden aus der Kindheit, dem Krieg und der Nachkriegszeit und mit Szenen aus der (DDR-)Gegenwart. Dem Versuch der Identitätsfindung zum Trotz, stellt *Kindheitsmuster*, vor allem durch die fragmentierte Erzählweise und die dreifache Aufteilung der Erzählinstanz unter Vermeidung der ersten Person Singular, das Unvermögen dar, die verschiedenen Erlebnisse und Zeitschichten in einer Erzählung zu integrieren. Die Geschichte der Leidenserfahrung als Flüchtlinge kann nicht erzählt werden ohne die Geschichte der – eigenen – Verwicklung in den Nationalsozialismus, was gleichzeitig eine Entfremdung dieser Leidenserfahrung bedeutet. In *Kindheitsmuster* gestaltet dieser Konflikt sich u.a. in der Szene, wo die Erinnerung an den Kriegsanfang die Lust an der Beschreibung des Kriegsendes zerstört:

> Heute vor fünfunddreißig Jahren hat mit der Eroberung von Polenstädtchen durch deutsche Soldaten ein großer Krieg begonnen. Mit einem Mal ist dir das Interesse dafür abhanden gekommen, zu beschreiben, wie einige Leute – Deutsche – das Ende dieses Krieges erlebt haben.[29]

Die Darstellung der Flucht als zeitgeschichtliches Ereignis und subjektive Erfahrung, kann anscheinend nur in der Form einer 'verschnittenen' Wahrheit gelingen:

Das Gewissen des Schreibers hat sich, so sieht es aus, nur um die Wahrheit zu bekümmern, 'die reine Wahrheit und nichts als die Wahrheit'. Da aber die Mitteilung zum Wesen der Wahrheit gehört, produziert er, oft zweifelnd, eine vielfach gebundene Wahrheit: an sich selbst gebunden, den Mitteilenden, und den immer begrenzten Freiheitsraum, den er sich abgezwungen hat [...]. Nicht 'rein' – mehrfach getrübt ist die Wahrheit. [...] Die 'Flucht' zum Beispiel – wenig beschrieben. Warum? Weil die jungen Männer, die über ihre Erlebnisse später Bücher schrieben, Soldaten waren? Oder weil dem Gegenstand etwas Heikles anhängt? Allein das Wort...Es verschwand später. Aus Flüchtlingen wurden Umsiedler [...].[30]

Dieses Flüchtling-sein wird als dominante Nachkriegsidentität beschrieben: 'Nelly und ihre Verwandten näherten sich fluchtartig Schwerin (nannten sich noch Jahre nach dem Krieg "Flüchtlinge") und glaubten zu wissen, wovor sie flohen.'[31] Die Identifizierung der Erzählerin mit Opferschaft, geht aber zusammen mit einem Schuldkomplex über ihre Mitgliedschaft im BDM. Schuld und Trauma ergänzen sich kurzum wechselseitig in diesem Roman.

Die Widersprüche in den Erzählungen Christa Wolfs zum Kriegsende, die Fragmentierung der Geschichte und der Identität zeigen die Unmöglichkeit einer Darstellung der Zeitgeschichte als Erfahrungsgeschichte. Das 'Wirkliche' des Traumas, das unbekannte Wissen des Subjekts und der Gesellschaft, das sich der Symbolisierung entzieht, kommt in diesen Aporien des Erzählens zum Vorschein. Gerade in und durch dieses paradoxe Erzählen zeigt sich aber auch die Abhängigkeit von der Erzählung als einziges Medium zur Erkundung der Vergangenheit. Rückkehrend zu der Frage, die ich am Anfang stellte, ob es eine 'authentische Erinnerung' gibt, lautet die Antwort, dass die 'Wahrheit' der Erinnerung vor allem eine narrative Wahrheit ist, wie gerade die Texte Christa Wolfs durch ihren Verlust der Fiktion einer einheitlichen Erzählung über Vergangenheit und Identität enthüllen.

Anmerkungen

[1] Nicolas Berg, 'Eine deutsche Sehnsucht,' *DIE ZEIT*, 6 November 2003, S. 38.

[2] Vgl. Jürgen Kocka, '1945: Neubeginn oder Restauration?,' in: Carola Stern und Heinrich August Winkler, hg., *Wendepunkte deutscher Geschichte. 1848-1990*, Neubearbeitete und erweiterte Ausgabe, Fischer: Frankfurt am Main, 1994, S. 159-192; Klaus Naumann, *Der Krieg als Text. Das Jahr 1945 im kulturellen Gedächtnis der Presse*, Hamburger Edition: Hamburg, 1998.

[3] Das erste Lager, das befreit wurde, war das Vernichtungslager Majdanek. Majdanek wurde bereits Juli 1944 durch die Rote Armee befreit, dennoch wurden die Bilder der 1945 befreiten Lager in Deutschland und Österreich zum universalen Symbol des Holocausts. Vgl. Barbie Zelizer, *Remembering to Forget. Holocaust Memory through the Camera's Eye*, The University of Chicago Press: Chicago/London, 1998. Für die Befreiung der Lager in Deutschland und Österreich siehe auch: Robert H. Abzug, *Inside the Vicious Heart. Americans and the Liberation of Nazi Concentration Camps*, Oxford University Press: New York/Oxford, 1985; Jon Bridgman, *The End of the Holocaust. The Liberation of the Camps*, B.T. Batsford: London, 1990. Das Wort 'Enthüllung' bezieht sich übrigens besonders auf die visuelle Repräsentierung durch Bilder und Filme. In der alliierten Presse und in der Öffentlichkeit waren bereits vor und während des Krieges Berichte über die (Vernichtungs-)Lager erschienen, wie z.B. das Pamphlet des jüdisch-britischen Verlegers Victor Gollancz, *"Let My People Go". Some Practical Proposals for Dealing with Hitler's Massacre of the Jews and an Appeal to the British Public*, Victor Gollancz: Covent Garden, 1943.

[4] Percy Knauth, *Time: The weekly newsmagazine* (Air Express Edition), 30 April 1945, S. 28.

[5] Aleida Assmann & Ute Frevert, *Geschichtsvergessenheit – Geschichtsversessenheit. Vom Umgang mit deutschen Vergangenheiten nach 1945*, DVA: Stuttgart, 1999; Dagmar Barnouw, *Germany 1945: Views of War and Violence*, Indiana University Press: Bloomington/Indianapolis, 1996; Cornelia Brink, *Ikonen der Vernichtung. Öffentlicher Gebrauch von Fotografien aus nationalsozialistischen Konzentrationslagern nach 1945*, Akademie Verlag: Berlin, 1998; Shoshana Felman & Dori Laub, *Testimony. Crises of Witnessing in Literature, Psychoanalysis, and History*. Routledge: New York/London, 1992; Zelizer, *Remembering to Forget*.

[6] Julius Posener, *In Deutschland. 1945 bis 1946*, Siedler Verlag: Berlin, 2001, S. 24. Original: 'Julius,' *In Deutschland 1945-1946*, Edition Dr. Peter Freund: Jerusalem, 1947.

[7] Hans Mommsen, 'Was haben die Deutschen vom Völkermord an den Juden gewußt?,' in: *Der Judenpogrom 1938. Von der 'Reichskristallnacht' zum Völkermord*, Walter H. Pehle, hg., Fischer: Frankfurt am Main, 1988, S. 176-200; Volker Ullrich, '"Wir haben nichts gewusst". Ein deutsches Trauma,' *1999: Zeitschrift für Sozialgeschichte des 20. und 21. Jahrhundert*, 6.4 (1991), 11-46. Peter Longerich, *'Davon haben wir nichts gewusst!' Die Deutschen und die Judenverfolgung 1933-45*, Siedler: München, 2006.

[8] Vgl. die Ambivalenz Ernst Jüngers, der die Frage der Verantwortung externalisiert: 'Diese Mordhöhlen werden auf fernste Zeiten im Gedächtnis der Menschen haften, sie sind die eigentlichen Mahnmale dieses Krieges wie früher Douaumont und Langemarck. Doch jene konnte neben dem Leide auch Stolz umweben; hier bleiben nur Trauer und Demut, denn die Schändung war derart, dass sie das ganze menschliche Geschlecht berührte, und keiner sich der Mitschuld entziehen kann.'

Ernst Jünger, 'Der Friede,' [1945], <u>Sämtliche Werke. Essays I. Betrachtungen zur Zeit</u> (Zweite Abteilung. Essays) Band 7. Klett-Cotta: Stuttgart, 1980. S. 194-236 (hier: S. 202-203).

[9] Vgl. die Bemerkung des Historikers Dan Diner: 'Auch die Deutschen haben also eine Leidensgeschichte zu erzählen – die Bombenopfer, die verschleppten Wehrmachtsangehörigen, die vergewaltigten Frauen zum Ende des Krieges. Doch diese Geschichte vermag nicht angemessen erzählt zu werden – so jedenfalls wird geklagt. Denn mit dem ständigen Hinweis auf 'Auschwitz' werde den Deutschen ein "Recht auf Öffentlichkeit" verwehrt, ihrem eigenen Leid Gehör zu verschaffen. Es drängt sich der Eindruck auf, als warte diese als unterdrückt empfundene Geschichte darauf, endlich ihre Erzähler zu finden. Bis das *nationale* Narrativ auch als nationales erzählt werden kann, müht sich der energetische Mahlstrom ersatzweise am Diskurs vom Holocaust ab.' Dan Diner, 'Schulddiskurse und andere Narrative,' in: *Gedächtniszeiten. Über jüdische und andere Geschichten*, C.H.Beck: München, 2003, S. 180-200 (hier: S. 200).

[10] Hermann Broch, *Briefe über Deutschland 1945-1949: Die Korrespondenz mit Volkmar von Zühlsdorff*, Suhrkamp: Frankfurt am Main, 1986, S. 23 und S. 45.

[11] Broch, *Briefe über Deutschland*, S. 110.

[12] Vgl. die Äußerungen Elliot Cohens, weiland Redakteur des jüdisch-amerikanischen Magazins *Commentary*: 'Es herrscht hier ein Schweigen, das Schweigen eines Grabes. Besonders beredt und unheilvoll ist dies Schweigen in einem bestimmten Bereich: wo bleiben die Worte der Nächstenliebe, der Seelenpein und der Selbstprüfung, der Diagnose und der Therapie, der Wiederherstellung und der Weisheit, welche manche von uns angesichts dieser ungeheuerlichen geschichtlichen Tragödie von den führenden Männern der Kirche und des Glaubens in Deutschland erwartet hatten, von den Gelehrten, den Historikern, den Dichtern und Schriftstellern? Wie wenig wurde gesagt – fast nichts. […] Ich halte es für fruchtlos, die Frage der Kollektivschuld zu erörtern; soviel aber sei hier gesagt: selbst wenn man zugesteht, dass die Deutschen in ihrer Gesamtheit für das Verbrechen der Vergangenheit nicht verantwortlich zu machen sind – sollten sie nun nicht bald den Mund auftun, sollten sie nicht Maßnahmen ergreifen, die der Welt zeigen, dass sie sich des begangenen Unrechts bewußt sind – Schritte zur Besserung, zur Selbsterkenntnis und zur erzieherischen Aufklärung des gesamten Volkes über dieses Übel und seine Bedeutung, so werden tatsächlich alle Deutschen, ob sie nun schuldig oder unschuldig am Verbrechen der Vergangenheit sind, als belastet gelten.' Elliot Cohen, 'Deutsche und Juden. Eine Rede in Berlin,' *Der Monat* 3 (1951), S. 375-379 (hier: S. 376).

[13] Vgl. J. Laplanches und J.-B. Pontalis' Umschreibung von Freuds Konzeption der Nachträglichkeit: 'Nicht das Erlebte allgemein wird nachträglich umgearbeitet, sondern selektiv das, was in dem Augenblick, in dem es erlebt worden ist, nicht vollständig in einen Bedeutungszusammenhang integriert werden konnte. Das Vorbild für ein solches Erleben ist das traumatisierende Ereignis.' J. Laplanche und J.-B.

Pontalis, *Das Vokabular der Psychoanalyse*, übers. Emma Moersch, Suhrkamp: Frankfurt am Main, 1996, S. 314.

[14] *Christa Wolf. Erzählungen 1960-1980*, Sonja Hilzinger, Luchterhand Literaturverlag: München, 1999. Vgl. Sonja Hilzingers Bemerkungen zu der Entstehung, Veröffentlichung und Rezeption der *Moskauer Novelle* in diesem Band, S. 554-560 (hier: S. 555-556).

[15] Martin Walser, *Ein springender Brunnen*, Suhrkamp: Frankfurt am Main, 1998, S. 9.

[16] Ebd., S. 401.

[17] Donald Spence, *Narrative Truth and Historical Truth. Meaning and Interpretation in Psychoanalysis*, W.W. Norton & Company: New York/London, 1982.

[18] Siehe Walter Benjamin, 'Der Erzähler. Betrachtung zum Werk Nikolai Lesskows,' in: Benjamin, Gesammelte Schriften, hg. V. Rolf Tiedemann und Hermann Schweppenhäuser, Bd. II.2, Suhrkamp: Frankfurt am Main, 1977, S. 438-465.

[19] Christa Wolf, 'Gedächtnis und Gedenken,' in: *Die Dimension des Autors. Essays und Aufsätze, Reden und Gespräche 1959-1985. Bd. 1*, Luchterhand Literaturverlag: Frankfurt am Main, 1990, S. 133-144 (hier: S. 143-144).

[20] Christa Wolf, 'Blickwechsel,' in: *Gesammelte Erzählungen*, Luchterhand Literaturverlag: Frankfurt am Main, 1988, S. 5-19 (hier: S. 16).

[21] Vgl. Christel Berger, *Gewissensfrage Antifaschismus. Traditionen der DDR-Literatur, Analysen, Interpretationen, Interviews*, Dietz Verlag: Berlin, 1990; Heinrich Küntzel, 'Von *Abschied* bis *Atemnot*. Über die Poetik des Romans, insbesondere des Bildungs- und Entwicklungsromans, in der DDR,' in: Jos Hoogeveen und Gerd Labroisse hg., *DDR-Romane und Literaturgesellschaft*, Rodopi: Amsterdam, 1981, S. 1-32; Martin Straub, '"Die Abenteuer des Werner Holt" oder die Sehnsucht nach dem gefährlichen Leben,' in: Annette Leo und Peter Reif-Spirek, hg., *Helden, Täter und Verräter: Studien zum DDR-Antifaschismus*, Metropol: Berlin, 1999, S. 211-231; Frank Trommler, 'Von Stalin zu Hölderlin.' Über den Entwicklungsroman in der DDR,' in: Reinhold Grimm und Jost Hermand, hg., *Basis: Jahrbuch für Deutsche Gegenwartsliteratur II*, Athenäum Verlag: Frankfurt am Main, 1971, S. 141-190.

[22] Georg Lukács, 'Schicksalswende,' in: *Marxismus und Stalinismus. Politische Aufsätze*, Ursula Schwerin et al., hg., Rowohlt: Reinbek 1970, S. 50-68.

[23] Vgl. u.a. die Erklärung des Lateinamerikanischen Komitees der 'Freien Deutschen', 'Zu Hitlers Todesfabriken,' in: *Freies Deutschland,* 11 (1944), 10; Alexander Abusch, 'Hitlers Todesfabriken und die Verantwortung der Deutschen,' in: *Freies Deutschland*, 12 (1944), S. 13-15; sowie Thomas Mann, *Deutsche Hörer!* 55

Radiosendungen nach Deutschland von Thomas Mann. 2. Ausgabe, Bermann-Fischer Verlag: Stockholm, 1945.

[24] Christa Wolf, 'Zu einem Datum,' in: *Erzählungen 1960-1980*, S. 129-36 (hier: S. 133).

[25] Ebd., S. 135.

[26] Christa Wolf, *Kindheitsmuster*, 1976. Luchterhand: Darmstadt /Neuwied, 1987.

[27] Peter Hurrelwinkel, *Der 8. Mai 1945 – Befreiung durch Erinnerung. Ein Gedenktag und seine Bedeutung für das politisch-kulturelle Selbstverständnis in Deutschland*, Dietz Verlag: Bonn, 2005.

[28] Wolf, 'Blickwechsel,' S. 10.

[29] Wolf, *Kindheitsmuster*, S. 266.

[30] Ebd., S. 296-297.

[31] Ebd.

Helmut Schmitz

Historicism, Sentimentality and the Problem of Empathy: Uwe Timm's *Am Beispiel meines Bruders* in the Context of Recent Representations of German Suffering

Beginning with a critique of the representation of the student movement as the originators of an 'empathy-taboo', this chapter tries to set up a theoretical framework for thinking about representations of suffering Germans from a perspective of empathy. Highlighting the problems inherent in a number of fictional and non-fictional representations of German suffering, the chapter closes with a discussion of Uwe Timm's memoir *Am Beispiel meines Bruders*.

> 'In my opinion it is high time that we illustrate our history ourselves'
> Bernd Eichinger, writer and producer of *Downfall*
> (2004)[1]

I. The Student Movement as Origin of an Empathy-Taboo

The recent controversies about representations of German suffering and these very representations in fictional and non-fictional media have one common vanishing point: the student movement. The students of 1968, and a psycho-pathologically motivated explanation of their hostility, or at least indifference, to their parents' wartime suffering serve as the central point of legitimation for current engagements with German war experiences from the perspective of empathy.

As I have argued elsewhere, the re-legitimation of empathy with the German war experience is the implicit and sometimes explicit concern of a number of controversial interventions into the German memory discourse, from the 'historians' controversy' to the Walser-Bubis debate.[2] The notion of breaking with a taboo is central in recent attempts to construct a German experience of suffering from the perspective of empathy. This was already visible from the mis-reception of both W.G. Sebald's Zurich lectures *Luftkrieg und Literatur* (1999) and of Grass's novella *Im Krebsgang* (2002) in the German press. In both instances the reviews alleged that the authors had broken a long-standing 'taboo' on engagement with German suffering.[3] The origin of this taboo was quickly located: it was the student generation of 1968 which had collectively refused to empathise with their parents' wartime suffering and instead had come to regard them exclusively as perpetrators. The student movement is thus seen as the origin of a binary discourse of memory which bars the Germans from empathising with their own suffering and locates all empathy with the victims of Nazism. Peter Schneider argues: 'Radikaler als die kritischen Geister der Grass-Generation haben die 68er alle Geschichten über Deutsche, die nicht ins Bild der "Täter-Generation" passten, aus ihrem Geschichtsbild ausgeblendet'.[4] According to Schneider, the sweeping postulation of a 'perpetrator generation' by the student movement had silenced the issue of the legacy of National Socialism as a matter of inner-familial traumatisation:

> Es hat unter den Aktivisten jener Jahre selbstverständlich viele Söhne und Töchter von Überlebenden und Zeugen der alliierten Flächenbombardements und der Vertriebenen gegeben. Ich kann mich nicht erinnern, dass einer oder eine von ihnen je vom Schicksal der Eltern gesprochen hätte.[5]

The argument of the student movement's self-expulsion from family genealogy is so frequently repeated both in fictional and non-fictional engagements with the issue of German suffering that it assumes the status of an explanatory paradigm. It is central to Günter Franzen's condemnatory review of Uwe Timm's *Am Beispiel meines Bruders* which I will briefly analyse as it exemplifies the pitfalls of this line of argument.

According to Günter Franzen, the inability or unwillingness of the German left to empathise with German wartime suffering is the consequence of a 'strikte Zweiteilung der Welt in [...] Täter und Opfer, Freund und Feind' as a result of the emotional pressure the second generation experienced in the face of the moral complexities of historical reality.[6] Franzen criticises the morally unambiguous position of 'hindsight' in the 68 generation's approach to the legacy of National Socialism. The 'narcissistic gain' of this approach, says Franzen, depends on a facile identification with the victims of National Socialism and results in an 'Enthaltsamkeitsgebot in der Frage des nationalen Gedenkens':

> Der narzißtische Gewinn [...] besteht also zweifellos darin, die individuellen, aus der familiären Vergangenheit herrührenden Abhängigkeits- und Ohnmachtsgefühle einzufrieren und sich über die durchgehende Identifikation mit den Opfern des Nationalsozialismus der eigenen Humanität zu versichern.[7]

In this argument, the Mitscherlichs' theses from their seminal 1967 study *The Inability to Mourn* take on the status of an explanatory model with which to assess the student movement's relation to their parents. According to the Mitscherlichs, the German collective had withdrawn their affective energies from their affiliation with National Socialism thus avoiding dealing with the loss of Hitler.[8] The result of this, they allege, was a 'derealisation' of the collective past both with respect to the role during National Socialism and the fate of the Nazi victims and with respect to their own losses:

> Ein weiterer Grund für die mangelnde Einfühlung in das Schicksal der Opfer der Naziverbrechen ist die erwähnte Derealisierung dieses ganzen Zeitabschnittes. [...] Und obgleich sie ein ehrendes Angedenken finden, bleiben auch die Toten der Schlachtfelder und unserer gegen Ende des Krieges in Schutt und Asche versinkenden Städte hinter diesem Schleier des Unwirklichen zurück.[9]

The student movement, in return, is said to have repeated this withdrawal of libidinous energy with respect to their parents' wartime experience out of a feeling of shame. This line of argument is central to Peter Schneider, Bernhard Schlink's *Der Vorleser* (1995), Ulla Hahn's *Unscharfe Bilder* (2003), Stephan Wackwitz's *Ein unsichtbares Land* (2003) and Gerd Koenen's memoir *Das rote Jahrzehnt* (2001).[10] The result of this, Franzen implies, is that the student generation, rather than realising its own implication in the legacy of National Socialism, casts itself in the light of belated Nazi victims.[11]

My contention is not that the representation of the student movement as refusing to acknowledge the previous generation's suffering is incorrect but that it serves in the current debates to legitimise representations of German suffering from a position of empathy that is not without problems. The reductive interpretation of the student movement's position towards National Socialism as a transposition of inner-familial dynamics onto the political sphere forgets that the political stage of 1968 is haunted by the spectre of National Socialism *on all fronts*, student movement, state institutions and mass media. The castigation of the student movement thus forgets the extremely charged political scenery of 1968, in order to postulate the lifting of the 'taboo on empathy'. The implicit argument in the accusation of the student movement as originators of this empathy taboo is that it is now possible to suspend the binary discourse and represent the Germans both as perpetrators as well as acknowledge their suffering.

However, there are several problems with this. First and foremost, Franzen's and Schneider's argument that the student movement evaded the realisation of their own 'Verstrickung' into the guilt of the parents by identifying with the victims implies that empathy with their parents' suffering would have led to a realisation of their own entanglement in the legacy of Nazism. The issue of transgenerational transmission of both trauma and Nazi legacies has attracted increasing scholarly attention over the last decades, both from within Psychoanalysis and Cultural Studies.[12] The mobilisation of this argument for a contemporary *representation* of suffering Germans replaces the issue of insight into possible continuities of inner-familial Nazi legacies with the re-creation of the historical immediacy of the traumatic experience of war. This is visible from Franzen's denunciation of the student movement's safe and facile position of *a posteriori* judgement and ethical non-ambiguity, a position that he ultimately regards as inauthentic and inappropriate to the historical reality. This juxtaposition of experiential perspective of immediate authenticity in the generation of war participants and inauthentic *a posteriori* knowledge is central to Dieter Wellershoff's wartime memoir *Der Ernstfall* (1995) and Ulla Hahn's novel *Unscharfe Bilder*, both narrative attempts to re-create the 'authentic' historical experience of soldiers at the Eastern Front. Both texts try to replace an *a posteriori* perspective of judgement with a 'therapeutical' attitude of listening, in order to facilitate the understanding of the period: 'Doch um [...] Antworten zu erhalten, muss man erst einmal Vertrauen schaffen, wie beim Beginn einer Gesprächstherapie.'[13] In Hahn's novel the same argument is deployed to make the second generation aware of their potential for implication in the same structures that engulfed their parents: 'Ihr habt ein Recht, zu fragen, aber nicht immer Recht auf eine Antwort.'[14] Included in this perspective is the demand that the post-war generation suspend their moralising attitude in an appreciation and even appropriation of the perspective of 'immediacy' that acknowledges their position of ignorance and moral incompetence. As Franzen's argument makes clear, however, what is at stake in the representation of German suffering from a position of empathy is the creation of a national collective of commemoration where the children who died in the air raids are configured as 'imaginäre Geschwister'.[15]

II. Empathy and Representation of Historical Trauma

The current form of belated empathy seems to finally enact the Mitscherlichs' 1967 demand for Germans to re-empathise with themselves. However, there is an important difference. The Mitscherlichs had called on the Germans to re-empathise with themselves for the purpose of mourning their Nazi-selves. Empathy, in the Mitscherlichs' use, is bound up with critical self-knowledge and insight.[16] After forty years and the representation of German wartime experience in literature, film, historiography and mass media, however, we are no longer on the level of personal and inter-subjective empathy and mourning but on the level of public representation and collective memory. Over the following pages I want to address a number of theoretical approaches to the problem of empathetic representations of historical trauma, before discussing Uwe Timm's memoir *Am Beispiel meines Bruders*.

In *Writing History, Writing Trauma*, Dominick LaCapra insists on the categorical distinction between victims of traumatic events and 'others not directly experiencing them', specifically the historian as 'secondary witness'.[17] To mark the precarious position of the 'secondary witness', he introduces the distinction between 'empathetic unsettlement' and 'extreme' or 'unchecked identification' with the victim.[18] Empathetic unsettlement recognises the difference of one's own position to that of the victim. It 'resists full identification with, and appropriation of, the experience of the other'. In contrast, unchecked identification merges one's subject position with that of the victim, resulting in 'making oneself a surrogate victim'.[19] LaCapra warns against the dangers of unchecked identification with historically specific victim positions as it may give rise to the transvaluation of trauma 'into a test of the self or the group and an entry into the extraordinary'. Moreover, for specific groups, extremely traumatic events may become narratives of 'founding traumas – [...] the valorised or intensely cathected basis of identity for an individual group rather than events that pose the problematic question of identity'.[20]

For my purpose, I want to distinguish between sentimental, historicist and critical empathy in the representation of German suffering. Furthermore, it is important to separate the enaction of empathy (e.g. by the historiographer/writer), the production of empathy in the reader/viewer (e.g. by narrative/filmic means) and the staging of empathy (e.g. by a character in a novel). Following LaCapra, I describe as sentimental empathy forms of identification that gloss over the distinction between the viewer/writer and the suffering represented, abstracting from the person's historically particular position. I understand historicist empathy to be an objectifying historisation that purports to represent historical suffering 'as it really was', isolating the trauma and pain from its historico-political context and setting it in an 'absolute' past, cutting the ties to the present. Historicist empathy, as we shall see, may slip over into sentimental empathy as the apparent 'authenticity' of the representation of trauma frequently eschews the ideological complexity of the historical situation. As critical empathy I regard a form of representation that engages with that complexity of the simultaneity of suffering and Nazi community.

III. Sentimental and Historicist Empathy

Both the transvaluation of traumatic events as a 'test for [...] a group and an entry into the extraordinary' and the creation of a foundational myth are at stake to varying degrees in a number of representations of German suffering, particularly in Jörg Friedrich's *Der Brand* and Roland Suso Richter's television film *Dresden*, broadcast on the second German TV channel ZDF on 5 and 6 March 2006. Friedrich's *Der Brand* has been criticised for enlisting terminology usually associated with the Holocaust with regard to his 'thick' description of the effects of the Allied bombing campaign on German cities and civilians.[21] Since Friedrich explicitly states that there exists no analogy 'zwischen Judenvernichtung und Bombenvernichtung', the purpose of the repeated use of Holocaust terminology is not directly a relativising comparison between Jewish and German suffering. The primary function of Friedrich's rhetoric is to de-stabilise the assumed predominant perspective on the bombing war as a morally legitimated form of retaliation against the genocide committed by Nazi Germany: 'Den Zusammenhang von Genozid und Sühnebombardement stellt die Moral des Betrachters her, doch er ist keiner, der je existierte.'[22] The Holocaust serves as a model prototype of traumatic excess against which the excess of the German traumatisation needs to be valorised; its discursive model is the relationship between horror, trauma and the trope of ineffability in Holocaust discourse.[23]

The configuration of German suffering and victim status is thus validated with recourse to *topoi* from Holocaust discourse.[24] In Ulla Hahn's *Unscharfe Bilder* the topos of ineffability and unimaginability of the soldiers' experiences at the Eastern Front likewise assumes central significance for the daughter's validation of the father's status as a victim. This is also true for Friedrich's representation of the horrors of the bombings which, in their intensity, remain inaccessible to experience as the suffering consciousness reacts with a 'Panzerung des Empfindens'.[25] Empathy with suffering Germans is thus frequently constructed through a paradox, relying on representations of atrocities in both word and image while the ineffability of experience is constantly underlined. The atrocities thus have the rhetorical function of being simultaneously unimaginable *and* graphically represented, legitimising the collective status of victim precisely because of their relation to the Holocaust with respect to traumatic intensity. Friedrich's 600-page volume repeatedly recounts the gruesome destruction of German cities and the horrific deaths of their inhabitants; repetition and a fascination with excessive figures and horrific detail are one of the hallmarks of its style. This is yet another (and probably voyeuristic) aspect of the current engagement with German suffering that begs the question what insight, beyond the mere acknowledgement of the infernal realities of war, is produced by the obsessive concern with Germans as objects of atrocities rather than as their cause.[26] This question may be tentatively answered with recourse to Martin Walser's praise for Friedrich's book. Walser, who in 1998 had admitted to 'looking away' from visual representations of the Holocaust, something he referred to as the 'Dauerrepräsentation unserer Schande',[27] enthusiastically endorsed *Der Brand* since its 'homeric' epic narrative was 'jenseits der sonst üblichen Einteilung in Gut und Böse'.[28] As Friedrich's book portrays the British Bomber Command as aggressor in a war of annihilation aimed at German civilisation, heritage and tradition, Walser's comment about Friedrich's transcendence of moral binaries refers more to the Germans themselves than to the two sides of the war. Thus it may be assumed that the representation of atrocities is more palatable when it is possible to re-inscribe them into a context of national suffering. Moreover, Friedrich's representation of the Allied bombing as a gigantic destruction of history and loss of connection to a living past transfigures this loss into a 'Zivilisationsbruch' analogous to the

Holocaust.[29] In conjunction with the lament for the destroyed cities as a 'nichtangeeignete Geschichte', *Der Brand* is ultimately a mythography of the historically 'rootless' present, a foundation myth with destruction as origin.[30]

Daniel Fulda has argued that Friedrich's much criticised lack of contextualisation of the bombing war is due to his refusal to employ a '*master narrative*' or 'Zentralperspektive', opting instead for a multi-perspectival approach that is in accordance with the current trend of the dissolution of homogenising historical narratives in a globalised world.[31] However, Friedrich's perspectivism is by no means a 'Verzicht auf eine Hierarchisierung der gebotenen Perspektiven' as Fulda makes out.[32] Friedrich's portrayal of the destruction visited upon German cities and their population is, implicitly and explicitly, ethically cathected; while Friedrich reproduces the perspective of the Bomber squads, empathy does not extend to the Allied perspective. Rather than de-stabilise its readers' moral identification, *Der Brand* keeps it tightly focused on the horrors of the firestorms, arriving at a central perspective of the bombing war in its (collective) 'Leideform'.[33] Furthermore, as Heinz-Peter Preußer argues in this volume, the bombing victim becomes a 'universal prototype' for Friedrich which finally overwhelms the narrative stance into a complete identification where the narrative stance turns into the suffering 'Ich': 'Das Erforderliche vollbringe ich wie außerhalb meiner selbst.'[34] The rhetoric of *Der Brand* is defined by what LaCapra has described as 'acting out' where 'the past is performatively regenerated or relived as if it were fully present rather than represented in memory and inscription'.[35]

LaCapra insists on the structural framing and marking of empathetic unsettlement, denying the historian the identification with any of the positions of victim, perpetrator and bystander, instead demanding that s/he investigate them. Unchecked identification harbours the danger of 'dubious identity politics', of 'simply repeating and further legitimating or acting out the subject positions with which one begins without subjecting them to critical testing'.[36]

The idea that representations of historically traumatic events and victimisation should lead to a checking of identity positions is also articulated by Gillian Rose, here with respect to fictional and visual representations. In 'Beginnings of the day. Fascism and Representation', Rose reflects on the problem of empathy and insight, from a position that takes into account both the structures by which (visual) media make us empathise with representations and the fact that by now the Nazi era is predominantly represented in mass media. With reference to Spielberg's *Schindler's List*, Rose claims that the film's 'anxiety that our sentimentality be left intact' results in a binary representation of demonic Nazis and transfigured victims.[37] Rose's argument is essentially that the film's representation of pure, innocent victims manipulates the audience's empathy into a strict divide between absolute good and evil. This, she argues, is ultimately sentimental as it stabilises our own subject position by its self-gratifying voyeuristic nature. Thus it does not cause a 'crisis in identification' that may be the beginning of knowledge.[38] Rose's critique of empathy is primarily aimed at the production of empathy for audience gratification and sentimentality. Her argument, similarly to LaCapra's, is that uncritical identification leaves our subject positions intact and affirms our sense of identity, as our 'sympathies can be so promiscuously enlisted.'[39] An uncritical representation of Germans as victims is thus frequently in danger of reproducing collective notions of identity based on ethnically dubious concepts. This is all the more important, as the focus on individual experience in fictionalised accounts is in danger of being implicitly or explicitly extrapolated onto a collective level, as Stuart Taberner has pointed out.[40]

This is illustrated by the TV-movie *Dresden* which shares a number of similarities with *Der Brand*. While the movie painstakingly tries to avoid any simplistic reversal of moral positions and attempts to represent *all* perspectives from a point of empathy – German, British and Jewish – it ultimately relies on a distinction between 'ordinary' Germans and 'evil' Nazis that is redolent of the 1950s. The language of the Third Reich is virtually cleansed from the dialogue of all but the uniformed Nazi characters. This is facilitated by the narrow focus of the first two hours of the film on the love story between Anna, a nurse working in her father's hospital, and Robert, a British bomber pilot who hides in the hospital cellar after his plane is shot down. The final 40 minutes of high-production-value destruction, horror, suffering and mayhem caused by the bombing is thus visited upon a series of individuals, witnessed mainly through the eyes of the two main characters. This creates a sense of visual immediacy that de-contextualises the suffering, reducing it to a pure spectacle of horror.

The film ends by cutting from a photograph of the destroyed Frauenkirche to the consecration of the re-constructed church on 30 Oct 2005, the year of the 60th anniversary of the bombing. The extracts from the speeches at this festive event evoke a message of peace and pacifism and an ultimately Christian narrative of redemption. While the camera pans the faces of the mass of citizens standing outside the church, a voiceover by the main character inscribes this celebration into a narrative of survival, successful reconstruction and post-war effort of 'not looking back': 'jeder, der überlebt hat, hatte die Verpflichtung etwas Neues zu schaffen.' While the end credits roll over the image of the restored cupola of the church, the voice of the mayor is heard reading out the message 'peace be with you' in English, French, Hebrew and Russian. The bombing of Dresden thus ends up as a foundation myth; the film squeezes a meaningful narrative of collective effort and overcoming out of the historical event, not unlike *Schindler's List* itself. Moreover, *Dresden*'s ultimate anti-war message relies on a de-Nazification of the people's community for a universalised image of suffering.

Despite the sentimental and melodramatic nature of its plot, *Dresden* is animated by a historicist agenda. The frequent insertion of historical footage seeks to suggest that the framework of what we are watching is historically accurate. A historicist perspective is by definition based upon empathy with that which is represented and withholds its own representational agenda from consideration. The danger is thus that it favours a naïve approach to representations that exculpates the recipient from any responsibility towards that which is represented and the issue of representation as a whole. The further the historical phenomenon of National Socialism recedes in time, the more difficult it becomes for contemporary audiences to understand its normative ethical universe that is so categorically different from our globalised consciousness. This facilitates a historicist approach to National Socialism that presents the period as 'completed' and reduces it to a spectacle of entertainment for the delectation of its audiences, with no ideological implications for the present.[41] Furthermore it is in danger of reproducing the 1950s division of Germans into innocent victims and evil Nazis. Stefan Berger has criticised Friedrich for drawing a 'sharp line between the majority of innocent German civilians and the minority of nasty German Nazis'.[42] This applies equally to *Dresden*, Ulla Hahn's *Unscharfe Bilder* and, as

Paul Cooke points out in this volume, to the 2004 blockbuster *Der Untergang*. Not only does the film's producer claim that the film is 'authentischer als alle vorherigen',[43] its historicist agenda has been largely successful with respect to reception, both in 'high' and 'low' terms. The film's historical accuracy was generally praised at the 2004 German Historians' Conference. Its popular reception seems to run along two interdependent lines: the first is an expression of joy that finally a German blockbuster could be made on that topic, that it has 'come home' so to speak.[44] The second is the conviction that what we are watching is actually historical reality itself.[45]

In the debates around representations of German suffering, the issue of historisation represents the other side of the coin of traumatic immediacy; at stake are narratives that reproduce the perspective of 'how it really was' without being clouded by hindsight.[46] The historicist agenda of Günter Franzen's demand for a suspension of the *a posteriori* perspective is also articulated by Dieter Wellershoff's *Der Ernstfall* and Ulla Hahn's *Unscharfe Bilder*. Franzen, Wellershoff and Hahn deploy their critique of *a posteriori* judgement with the argument that it prevents insight into one's own ethical fallibility and positions us in a secure moral certainty. Here, we are requested to empathise with the plight of Germans by imagining how we would have behaved in the same situation.[47]

This 'uninhibited' historicist perspective, however, is problematic because it is always 'pre-politicised'. It does not exist independently of an always already polarised field of public discourse of German politics of memory. Furthermore, as Welzer, Moller and Tschuggnall have pointed out in their study *Opa war kein Nazi*, even individual memories of suffering are influenced by models of thought and perception pre-formed in public discourse and media images.[48] The demand for abstraction from political and ethical categories by allocating them a position of 'hindsight' implies that these categories had been unavailable at the time in question. There might be some truth in this. In his recent book *Täter. Wie aus ganz normalen Menschen Massenmörder werden*, Harald Welzer argues that National Socialism very quickly and successively created a normative ethical framework in which Nazi victims and particularly Jews were perceived to be outside the *Volksgemeinschaft* and thus not only are eliminated from perception as being part of a common humanity but also come to constitute a problem that needs to be solved: 'Im

Ergebnis treten sich Täter und Opfer als Angehörige zweier vollständig verschiedener Menschengruppen gegenüber'.[49] The Mitscherlichs had argued in 1967 that Hitler had effectively turned German conscience 'upside down' by installing himself as the only institution to which the individual bore any responsibility and that the Allies' entry into Germany effectively represented the re-establishment of a pre-war moral conscience.[50] If Welzer and the Mitscherlichs are correct, National Socialism was able to establish a 'normative model' in which the persecution of designated others was not considered or even perceivable as unethical.[51] However, the normative ethical universe of Nazi Germany, the sedimentation of racial and supremacist thought in the average mind, as evident for example from the letters of German soldiers, is absent from most memoirs and representations that otherwise attempt to recreate a perspective of immediacy. Thus a perspective of experience is accepted as 'authentic' that is, more often than not, cleansed from the Nazi-perspective on the world and by definition amalgamated with the contemporary ethical universe. Consequently, the current perspective of historicist empathy is largely determined by the desire for a German perspective freed from issues of ideology and perpetration. This means that in literary and visual representations suffering Germans are frequently constructed on an axis of sameness to our contemporary experience that is out of touch with recent historical and socio-psychological research.[52]

The call for a historically more differentiated view of Germans under National Socialism beyond the perpetrator/victim divide frequently coincides with an attempt to legitimise a sentimentally empathetic approach to Germans as innocent victims. Furthermore, the representation of German wartime experience from a perspective of immediate traumatic intensity does little to facilitate insight into the ethical complexities of the Nazi period as the representation of traumatic events and traumatic excess tends to de-contextualise the historical and political aspects of the suffering persona. This emerges from Ulla Hahn's *Unscharfe Bilder* whose title illustrates its narrative purpose. Hahn prefaces her novel with a quote from Wittgenstein that suggests that an out-of-focus image of a person is more human than a focused one: 'Ist eine unscharfe Fotografie überhaupt ein Bild eines Menschen? Ja, kann man ein unscharfes Bild immer mit Vorteil durch ein scharfes ersetzen? Ist das unscharfe nicht oft gerade das, was wir brauchen?' However, the development of a more complex image beyond simple perpetrator/victim dichotomy and a humane, forgiving image of the wartime generation are two different matters. The former demands a more focused gaze whereas the latter is ultimately in the interest of closing family ranks.[53] In the course of Hahn's novel, for example, the daughter ultimately ends up sharing in the father's trauma, relinquishing her post-war perspective: 'Sie hatte geglaubt zu wissen, Vergangenes zu wissen. Nun wurde aus dem Vergangenen, dem Vorbeisein ein Mit-Dabeisein.' (UB, 121) The result of the simultaneous realisation of her own moral incompetence and empathy with respect to the father's situation in the war is a validation of the collective status of his entire generation as victim. This acceptance is expressed in an explicit image of genealogical linking through inheritance, signifying reconciliation with the wartime generation:

> Wenn wir die Erben der Verstrickung unserer Väter und Mütter in die Nazijahre sein wollen, wenn wir ehrlich Verantwortung für diese Geschichte mit übernehmen wollen, dann müssen wir auch die Erben der Leiden, der Verletzungen werden, all der zerstörten Lebenspläne der Deutschen dieser Jahre (UB, 145)

The representation of German wartime suffering and traumatisation is thus troubled by two complementary issues, that of the valorisation of trauma (i.e. immediacy) and that of historisation (i.e. distance), both of which take recourse to an argument about the purported 'authenticity' of experience and can be frequently encountered in the various recent literary, filmic and historiographical representations of suffering Germans. The danger of such an uncritically empathetic approach is an amalgamation with a sentimental desire for a 'clean' or 'uninhibited' image of German suffering which can be approached with a gesture of compassion and mourning. What is at stake is thus frequently not a question of empathy in the Mitscherlichs' sense but an act of 'mercy' extended towards the German experience:

> Uwe Timm [...] könnte sich seines Bruders erbarmen. Er könnte den Kopf des seiner Uniform, seiner Gewaltinsignien und seiner pubertären Großmäuligkeit beraubten, auf seine kreatürlichen Abmessungen geschrumpften Jungen in seinen Schoß betten und ihm das Sterben erleichtern.[54]

This is based on a complex act of attempted identification that ultimately validates the experiential perspective of the suffering Germans by the recognition of the impossibility of imagining their plight, their existential and ethical situation. Franzen's invocation of Christian categories thus entails essentially a relativisation of the

ethical and political dimensions of National Socialism.[55] Rather than
constituting an act of stereoscopic vision – acknowledging the
simultaneity of perpetration and suffering – it is frequently
characterised by what Welzer, Moller and Tschuggnall have described
with respect to memory of National Socialism in German families as
'Wechselrahmung': the image of the perpetrator is exchanged for that
of the victim.[56] The price for this is more often than not a repression of
the mediation of the particular fate with what Dieter Wellershoff has
referred to as 'Unheilszusammenhang'.[57] The result is that the
political persona disappears behind the individual fate.

   With this in mind I would like to look at Uwe Timm's *Am Beispiel
meines Bruders* which is in many ways an engagement with the
problem of representing German suffering and, while reassessing the
student generation's relationship with the war participants, self-
consciously avoids the pitfalls that characterise Hahn's text and other
narratives.

IV. The impossibility to mourn – Critical Empathy in Uwe Timm's *Am Beispiel meines Bruders*

Am Beispiel meines Bruders is Uwe Timm's attempt to shed light on
the private and political person of his elder brother Karl-Heinz who
died on the Eastern Front in 1943 as a member of a SS death's head
division at the age of 19. The first thing that is necessary to note is that
mourning in the strict Freudian sense is an option that is not open to
Timm: he has almost no memories of the brother who is 16 years
older than him.[58] Instead, the presence of the dead brother makes itself
felt in his absence that casts a melancholic shadow over him and the
family, a motif that is also central to Hans-Ulrich Treichel's *Der
Verlorene*:

> Anwesend und doch abwesend hat er mich durch meine Kindheit begleitet, in der
> Trauer der Mutter, den Zweifeln des Vaters, den Andeutungen zwischen den
> Eltern. Von ihm wurde erzählt […]. Auch wenn nicht von ihm die Rede war, war
> er doch gegenwärtig, gegenwärtiger als andere Tote, durch Erzählungen, Fotos
> und in den Vergleichen des Vaters, die mich, den Nachkömmling, einbezogen.[59]

Timm explicitly connects his first memory of selfhood with his
brother, who is also his godfather and is held up as a 'Vorbild' (AB,
18) to him throughout his childhood. His narrative is a belated
attempt, after the death of all other family members, to approach the
dead brother with all the questions that have remained unanswered
because they have not been asked out of consideration for his mother

and sister. The process of writing is deliberately connected with the desire to establish identity and continuity: 'Sich ihnen [brother and father, HS] schreibend anzunähern, ist der Versuch, das bloß Behaltene in Erinnerung aufzulösen, sich neu zu finden.' (AB, 18)

Timm's brother leaves behind a sparse diary of his time as a soldier, filled with short, impersonal entries, and cryptic remarks ('*Viel Beute!*', AB, 15) which neither provide any access to his individual experiential perspective, nor any clues as to his status or feelings as perpetrator and give rise to frequent unanswerable questions:

> Kein Traum ist in dem Tagebuch erwähnt, kein Geheimnis. [...] War er schon einmal mit einer Frau zusammengewesen? (AB, 28) Wie sah der Bruder sich selbst? Welche Empfindungen hatte er? Erkannte er etwas wie Täterschaft, Schuldigwerden, Unrecht? (AB, 88)

Timm's narrative thus circles around this double absence of his brother, as family member and as potentially involved in the atrocities of Hitler's war of annihilation in the East, for example in the re-capturing of Charkov in which his brother's unit participated in 1943. It is a sensitive, probing enterprise that through an act of careful reading attempts to extract from the brother's sparse remnants as much of a spectre of a personality as possible. The narrative is fragmented into short pieces and Timm frequently recurs to the same memory or piece of evidence from a different perspective. His reflections on his brother's diary extracts are contrasted with historical documents that shed light on the ideological nature of the war in the East. Timm's ruminations about his brother are furthermore embedded into a subtle memoir of the post-war family atmosphere that resulted from the lost war, including a psychological portrait of his father, a World War One veteran and free corps fighter with close affinities to the 'Organisation Consul' and *Luftwaffe* officer in World War Two.[60] What emerges is not so much a clearer image of his brother than an impression of the historical and family context in which the brother and Timm himself grew up.

I would like focus on two moments of Timm's family memoir that highlight Timm's procedure. The first is one of his brother's letters in which he describes the bombing of Germans as 'nicht human' due to its targeting of civilians – explicitly women and children: 'Das ist doch kein Krieg, das ist ja Mord an Frauen und Kinder (sic)' (AB, 24). Seventy pages later, Timm returns to this letter, contrasting it with a simple factual statement from his brother's diary on the removal and destruction of Russian household ovens for the building of roads for the German army. In contrast to letters from other soldiers which either mention with 'größter Selbstverständlichkeit' (AB, 91) the killing of civilians, Jews and Russians, or document outrage or pity with the suffering people, his brother's diary entry is characterised by the complete absence of any emotion and perspective. Timm reads the simultaneity of his brother's conception of bombing of German civilians as 'nicht human' and his emotional distance to Russian civilians as evidence of a split in perspective that is part of the normal German soldier's ideological make-up:

> Es ist schwer verständlich und nicht nachvollziehbar, wie Teilnahme und Mitgefühl im Angesicht des Leids ausgeblendet wurden, wie es zu dieser Trennung von human zu Hause und human hier, in Russland, kommt. (AB, 90)

Timm's *a posteriori* judgement may be characterised by a lack of empathy ('nicht nachvollziehbar'), based on compassion with the brother's potential victims that seems to fit Franzen's model of easy identification of perpetrator and victim. However, Timm's careful narration enables him to both enquire into his brother's human dimensions and insert his role (and that of his family) into the context of the Nazi enterprise as a whole. Timm describes his brother as a gentle, sickly and patient child who grows up into a world of masculinity and military values embodied by his father. This portrait suggests that the world of Nazi values ultimately swallowed him up. As a result of Timm's narrative technique the micro-perspective of the family is continuously put in context with the macro-perspective of (Nazi) politics; the penetration of the family with Nazi and military values remains visible throughout Timm's narrative. The 'Unheilszusammenhang' (Wellershoff) lights up in the fragmented nature of Timm's exploration: his own personal memory of an air raid shelter, and an extract of his brother's letter voicing his incredulity at the destruction of Hamburg is followed by the sober, factual statement: 'Juden war das Betreten des Luftschutzraums verboten' (AB, 38) The effect of Timm's montage technique is that the suffering Germans become recognisable as the Nazi *Volksgemeinschaft*. This is to say, Timm captures the simultaneity and interdependence of traumatic suffering and political reality that is frequently eschewed in representations of German suffering.

The second example is Timm's memory of the 1950s which are of a time when '[d]ie Vätergeneration, die Tätergeneration' (AB, 99) was coping either by complete silence or by constantly talking about the war. This talk takes the form of 'anecdotes' which have the function to manage the experience of horror and make it disappear in *Gemütlichkeit*:

> Das Eigentümliche war, wie der Schock, der Schreck, das Entsetzen durch das wiederholte Erzählen langsam in seinen Sprachformeln verblasste. (AB, 39)
> Die Frauen und Alten erzählten von den Bombennächten in der *Heimat*. Das Fürchterliche wurde damit in Details aufgelöst, wurde verständlich gemacht, domestiziert. Es löste sich meist beim gemütlichen Zusammensein in Anekdoten auf, und nur selten, urplötzlich, brach das Entsetzen hervor. (AB, 99)

Like Sebald who remarks on the 'stereotypen Wendungen [...] der Augenzeugenberichte', Timm chronicles the transformation of traumatic horror into formulaic language.[61] The other function he ascribes to the repeated war-stories is coping with the damage to the sense of self-worth as a result of military defeat. Timm connects the talk of the war in post-war families with the psychological damage to the masculine sense of self and the re-establishment of a fragile parental authority: 'Eine Generation war politisch, militärisch, mentalitätsmäßig entmachtet worden, und sie reagierte beleidigt, mit Trotz, Verstocktheit.' The 'Herrschaftsanspruch' (AB, 71) survives at home in the education of their children under the ideals of obedience and in the men's frequent re-visitation of the battlefields from the perspective of military strategy, 'abendfüllende Themen für diese Generation' (AB, 75). This evening talk at home is set in context with the representation of war and soldiers in the 1950s in newspapers, militarist brochures, dime novellas in the tone of the 'SS Totenkopfdivision' and the popular memoirs of Nazi generals like General Field Marshal von Manstein's *Verlorene Siege*. Timm's incorporation of italicised typical vocabulary of the 'war experience' in the East like *Gefrierfleischorden, Hitlersäge, Heimatschuss* reminds the reader of how much the soldier's jargon still accompanied his 1950s childhood, reflecting 'gleichermaßen Verrohung und Verdrängung in der Sprache' (AB, 96).[62] Timm's memoir is thus a reminder of the continuities, both mentally and discursively, between war and post-war mentalities:

> Es ist aus heutiger Sicht kaum nachvollziehbar, dass nach dem Krieg und mit dem Wissen um die systematische Tötung – die *Ausrottung* – der Juden öffentlich eine breite, ernsthafte Diskussion darüber geführt werden konnte, wie man den Krieg doch noch hätte gewinnen können. (AB, 95)

Timm reads the penetration of language by military and Nazi jargon, the 'Sprachverstümmelungen', as correlative to the visible physical mutilations around him, 'die Hinkenden, an Krücken Gehenden, die mit einer Sicherheitsnadel hochgesteckten leeren Jackenärmel, die umgeschlagenen Hosenbeine, die quietschenden Prothesen' (AB, 98). Thus he shows how the self-exculpatory narratives of the perpetrator-generation, of '*Davon haben wir nichts gewusst*' of '*Die anständige Luftwaffe*. […] *Die anständige Wehrmacht*' (AB, 98), serve to not only hold at bay any engagement with guilt but also to master the war generation's own suffering:

> Sprache wurde nicht nur von den Tätern öffentlich missbraucht, sondern auch von jenen, die von sich selbst sagten, *wir sind noch einmal davongekommen*. Sie erschlichen sich so eine Opferrolle.[63] (AB, 103)

The focus on the construction of the post-war family atmosphere out of the defeated spirit of National Socialism, however, does not preclude compassion with the father's suffering. Timm mentions a single incident when the father's memories of the experienced horrors break through the barriers of self-pity and grandiloquence that define his post-war persona. However, this suffering remains essentially uncommunicated and thus does not lead to a breach of the increasing distance between father and son:

> Wie er da stand und weinte, war etwas von dem Grauen und der Erinnerung gegenwärtig, abgrundtief, verzweifelt, kein Selbstmitleid, ein unsägliches Leid, und auf meine Fragen schüttelte er nur immer wieder den Kopf. (AB, 99)

Hans-Joachim Schröder has pointed out, how little the real experience of the soldiers in the Nazi war has become part of collective consciousness and tradition.[64] Schröder argues, though, that the soldiers' deep-seated traumatisation is a product of *both* suffering and committed atrocities:

> Die Mauer kollektiver Verdrängung bekommt jedoch allmählich immer tiefere Risse, und damit wird zugleich deutlich, mit welcher umfassenden Gründlichkeit unter den Deutschen eine schuldbeladene Vergangenheit verharmlost und verdrängt worden ist.[65]

Schröder refers to the German war of extermination in the East as a 'zweite Völkermord' that has not been sufficiently addressed.[66] Timm's memoir makes visible the correlation between silence, guilt and victim rhetoric, keeping mindful of the origin of the rift between the war generation and their children as well as of the uncanny context of suffering and perpetration. While he acknowledges both his father's distress and his continuous silence, Timm frames them with the 'alltäglichen Geschichten, die nach dem Krieg erzählt wurden', stories of victory and atrocities, like the story by one of his father's employees about shooting Russian POWs out of a whim.

Timm's narrative illustrates the context of continuities between National Socialism, the war and the immediate post-war period. This is achieved by continuous juxtaposition of his brother's diary and Timm's family memories with historical documents, army orders of the day, historical research like Christopher Browning's *Ordinary Men*, and survivors' memoirs like Primo Levi's *The Drowned and the Saved* which are inserted to counterpoint any exclusive focus on the brother or father as pure victim. The image that emerges is not only one of the interdependence of the perspective of German suffering with that of the Nazi victims. Timm's memoir also stresses that the fate of the individual soldier cannot be torn from the 'context of disaster' as a whole without losing sight of the political context.[67]

Rather than being determined by a position of condemnation or judgement, Timm's memoir is essentially characterised by a sense of emotional distance. The honesty with which this distance is acknowledged, historicized and reflectively negotiated turns it into a history lesson. What makes Timm's narrative so useful is that it is an attempt to approach the 'perpetrator generation' with understanding and empathy that does not repress his own *a posteriori* perspective but sheds light on the historical context in which memory, empathy and suffering are to be situated. The father's political persona does not disappear behind the recognition of the legitimacy of his suffering, neither is it appropriated by Timm as it remains essentially alien due to its distance and lack of communication. Throughout his narrative, Timm thematises the act of memory and the 'Gefahr, glättend zu erzählen' (AB, 36). His narrative reflects on itself as a self-conscious public act of creating meaning through narration. As an *a posteriori* explanation it documents the essential unavailability of a 'naïve' perspective together with the necessity to narrate.

Far from being the merciless tribunal that Franzen makes it out to be, Timm's narrative thus manages to combine a compassionate approach to the brother (or rather to his leftovers and memories) with a critical reflection on his own origins in the restrictive post-war society, the stifling family atmosphere of the 1950s and the 'normal violence' in school, at home and in the streets (AB, 145). The post-war family and its internalised structures of authority, combined with the humiliation of defeat, is remembered as the origin of the rebellion of his generation. Timm's evaluation of 1945 as 'Befreiung von den nach Leder riechenden Soldaten, den genagelten Stiefeln, dem Jawoll, dem Zackigen, diesem stampfenden Gleichschritt der genagelten Knobelbecher' (AB, 65) is a decidedly (leftist) post-war perspective. Timm historicises the student movement's rejection of their parents' world, by tracing his own growing alienation from his father in the course of the 1950s as the pre-history of 1968. His experience remains recognisable as the experience of a particular historical moment which is one of the strengths of the narrative. This, however, does not preclude the recognition and acknowledgement of the suffering of his father's generation when it becomes visible. As is visible from contemporary fictional and filmic re-creations of the Nazi period, they frequently forego critical narrative in favour of narrative immediacy. They belong increasingly to a nationalising imaginary that attempts to figure National Socialism without its extermination politics. Timm's *Am Beispiel meines Bruders* illustrates that the complete picture includes both Germans and Nazi victims, with their irreconcilably different perspectives.

Notes

[1] Joachim Fest and Bernd Eichinger, *Der Untergang. Das Filmbuch*, Michael Töteberg, ed., Rowohlt: Reinbek, 2004, p. 458.

[2] See my 'The Birth of the Collective from the Spirit of Empathy: From the Historians' Debate to German Suffering,' in: Bill Niven, ed., *Germans as Victims: Remembering the Past in Contemporary Germany*, MacMillan: Basingstoke, 2006, pp. 93-108.

[3] See Annette Seidel-Arpaçi's contribution in this volume. On the German reception of Sebald, see Stefan Braese, 'Bombenkrieg und literarische Gegenwart,' *Mittelweg 36*, (1, 2002), 2-24. On Grass's *Im Krebsgang* see the relevant chapter in my *On Their Own Terms. The Legacy of National Socialism in Post-1990 German Fiction*, University of Birmingham Press: Birmingham, 2004, pp. 263-286.

[4] See Peter Schneider, 'Deutsche als Opfer. Über ein Tabu der Nachkriegsgeneration,' in: Lothar Kettenacker, ed., *Ein Volk von Opfern? Die neue Debatte um den Bombenkrieg 1940-45*, Rowohlt: Berlin, 2003, pp. 158-165 (here: pp. 162-163).

[5] Ibid.

[6] Günter Franzen, 'Links, wo kein Herz ist', *DER SPIEGEL*, 44, 2003, pp. 216-218 (here: p. 218).

[7] Ibid. p. 216 and p. 218.

[8] See Alexander and Margarete Mitscherlich, *Die Unfähigkeit zu trauern. Grundlagen kollektiven Verhaltens*, Piper: Munich 1977 [first 1967], pp. 15-90, esp. pp. 29-39.

[9] Ibid., p. 46.

[10] On Schlink see my 'Malen nach Zahlen? Bernhard Schlink's *Der Vorleser* und die Unfähigkeit zu trauern,' *German Life and Letters*, 3 (2002), 296-311. On Wackwitz see my 'Annäherung an die Generation der Großväter: Stephan Wackwitz' *Ein unsichtbares Land* und Thomas Medicus' *In den Augen meines Großvaters*,' *BIOS*, January 2007. On Hahn see my 'Reconciliation between the Generations: The Image of the Ordinary German Soldier in Dieter Wellershoff's *Der Ernstfall* and Ulla Hahn's *Unscharfe Bilder*,' in: Stuart Taberner and Paul Cooke, eds., *German Culture, Politics and Literature into the Twenty-First Century. Beyond Normalization*, Rochester: Camden House, 2006, pp. 151-166.

[11] Koenen and Wackwitz also see the 1968 students in the grip of a narcissistic injury which causes them to withdraw all affective energies from their parents and displace them onto the ethically untainted Jewish father figures of the Frankfurt School. See Koenen, *Das rote Jahrzehnt*, Kiepenheuer & Witsch, Cologne, 2001, p. 96 and Stephan Wackwitz, *Ein unsichtbares Land*, Fischer: Frankfurt am Main, pp. 257-258.

[12] See for example the articles in Jörn Rüsen and Jürgen Straub, eds., *Die dunkle Spur der Vergangenheit. Psychoanalytische Zugänge zum Geschichtsbewußtsein*, Suhrkamp: Frankfurt am Main, 1998, esp. the articles by Brigitte Rauschenbach, pp. 242-255, Werner Bohleber, pp. 256-274 and Michael B. Buchholz, pp. 330-353. See also Sigrid Weigel, 'Telescopage im Unbewussten. Zum Verhältnis von Trauma, Geschichtsbegriff und Literatur,' in: Elisabeth Bronfen, Birgit R. Erdle, Sigrid Weigel, eds. *Trauma. Zwischen Psychoanalyse & kulturellem Deutungsmuster*. Böhlau: Cologne, Weimar, Vienna, 1999, pp. 51-76.

[13] Dieter Wellershoff, *Der Ernstfall, Innenansichten des Krieges*, Kiepenheuer & Witsch: Cologne, 1995, p. 272.

[14] Ulla Hahn, *Unscharfe Bilder*, DVA: Munich, 2003, p, 66. Further references as (UB, page number).

[15] Franzen, p. 218.

[16] A. and M. Mitscherlich, p. 88.

[17] Dominick LaCapra, *Writing History, Writing Trauma*, Johns Hopkins University Press: Baltimore and London, 2001, pp. ix and 78.

[18] Ibid., pp. 40, 47 and 78-9.

[19] Ibid., p. 78 and p. 79.

[20] Ibid., p. 23, also p. 81.

[21] Jörg Friedrich, *Der Brand. Deutschland im Bombenkrieg 1940-1945*, Propyläen: Munich, 2002, quoted from the paperback edition, Berlin: List, 2004. Friedrich frequently describes the Allied campaign as 'Vernichtung' (pp. 164, 194, 195), the cellar in the firestorm 'arbeitete wie ein Krematorium' (p. 194), the victims 'wurden [...] vergast' (p. 378). For a list of critical responses to Friedrich see Heinz-Peter Preußer's chapter in this volume, p. 159, footnote 26.

[22] Friedrich, p. 342.

[23] Aleida Assmann asks whether in Friedrich the Holocaust is used as a 'Traumaparadigma [...] das auch anderen traumatischen Erfahrungen zur Artikulation verhelfen soll.' Aleida Assmann, *Der lange Schatten der Vergangenheit. Erinnerungskultur und Geschichtspolitik*, C.H.Beck: Munich, 2006, p. 188.

[24] See for example Primo Levi's repeated dreams of his inability to make himself understood to people outside the camp. Levi, *If this is a man/The Truce*, Abacus: London, 1987, p. 66 and also, more generally: 'Perhaps one cannot, what is more, one must not understand what happened. [...] If understanding is impossible, knowing is imperative.' Afterword, pp. 395-396.

[25] Friedrich, p. 503.

[26] In this context it may be worth pointing out Primo Levi's deliberate refrain from focusing on the atrocities and horrors of his experience at Auschwitz, since, he claimed, they stand in the way of knowledge. See Levi's preface to *If this is a man*, p. 15.

[27] See Martin Walser, 'Die Banalität des Guten. Erfahrungen beim Verfassen einer Sonntagsrede,' *Frankfurter Allgemeine Zeitung*, 12 October 1998, p. 15.

[28] Martin Walser, 'Bombenkrieg als Epos,' in: Lothar Kettenacker, ed., *Ein Volk von Opfern? Die neue Debatte um den Bombenkrieg*, Berlin: Rowohlt, 2003, pp. 127-130 (here: p. 130).

[29] Friedrich, p. 169. Friedrich speaks of the 'Krieg gegen das Wurzelreich der Vergangenheit', p. 190.

[30] This foundation myth can also be found in Hanns-Josef Ortheil's parent novels *Hecke* and *Abschied von den Kriegsteilnehmern* and in Günter Grass's novella *Im Krebsgang*. On Grass see Stuart Taberner, '"Normalisation" and The New Consensus on the Nazi Past: Günter Grass's *Im Krebsgang* and the Problem of German Wartime Suffering,' *Oxford German Studies*, 31 (2002), 161-186. On Ortheil see the relevant chapter in my *On Their Own Terms*, pp. 27-54.

[31] Daniel Fulda, 'Abschied von der Zentralperspektive. Der nicht nur literarische Geschichtsdiskurs im Nachwende-Deutschland als Dispositiv für Jörg Friedrichs *Der Brand'*, in: Wilfried Wilms and William Rasch, eds., *Bombs Away! Representing the Air War over Europe and Japan*, Rodopi: Amsterdam, 2006, pp. 45-64 (here: p. 50).

[32] Ibid., p. 63.

[33] Friedrich, p. 542.

[34] Friedrich, p. 502. See Heinz-Peter Preußer's chapter in this volume, p. 150.

[35] LaCapra, p. 70

[36] LaCapra, pp. 198-199 and p. 41.

[37] Gillan Rose, 'Beginnings of the day: Fascism and Representation,' in: Rose, *Mourning becomes the Law*, Cambridge, CUP, 1996, pp. 41-62 (here: p. 48).

[38] Ibid., p. 53.

[39] Ibid., p. 48.

[40] See Stuart Taberner, 'Representations of German Wartime Suffering in Recent Fiction,' in: Bill Niven, ed., *Germans as Victims*, pp. 164-180 (here: p. 173). Samuel Salzborn criticises the 'narrative Kollektivierung individueller Schicksale' as a central rhetorical praxis in the non-fictional representation of expellees. See Samuel Salzborn, 'Opfer, Tabu, Kollektivschuld,' in: Michael Klundt, Samuel Salzborn, Marc Schwietring, Gerd Wiegel, *Erinnern Verdrängen Vergessen. Geschichtspolitische Wege im 21. Jahrhundert*, Netzwerk für politische Bildung, Kultur und Kommunikation e.V.: Gießen, 2003, pp. 17-41 (here: p. 21).

[41] See LaCapra's critique of an objectified representation of history: 'Concentrating on objectified and abstracted (or "split off") past contexts also confines understanding to a purely interpretive or contemplative role that blocks sustained consideration of the problem of the implication of the interpreter both in the object of interpretation and in contemporary discussions of it.' LaCapra, *Representing the Holocaust. History, Theory, Trauma*, Cornell University Press: Ithaca and London, 1994, p. 71.

[42] Stefan Berger, 'On Taboos, Traumas and Other Myths: Why the Debate about German Victims of the Second World War is not a Historians' Controversy,' in: Bill Niven, ed, *Germans as Victims*, pp. 210-224 (here: p. 220).

[43] Bernd Eichinger, *Der Untergang. Das Filmbuch*, p. 458. See Paul Cooke's chapter in this volume, pp. 257-258.

[44] A sentiment voiced by the film's producer, Bernd Eichinger, himself, p. 458. Eichinger's statement implies that hitherto this history has been illustrated by (non-specified) 'others'.

[45] See the SPIEGEL's report on the reception of Der Untergang at the 'Deutsche Historikertag', http://www.historikertag.uni-kiel.de/pressemit/SPIEGEL160904.htm and the film discussion internet board filmszene.de http://www.filmszene.de/kino/u/untergang.html.

[46] These arguments were central to the debate about historisation and 'Alltagsgeschichte' of National Socialism between Martin Broszat and Saul Fiedlander in the 1980s. The debate is reprinted in Peter Baldwin, ed., Reworking the Past: Hitler, the Holocaust and the historian's debate, Beacon Press: Boston/Mass., 1990, pp. 103-134.

[47] LaCapra dismisses empathy with the perpetrator for the discovery of the reader's/spectator's own fascist self as a form of ahistorical blurring, p. 202.

[48] See Harald Welzer, Sabine Moller, Karoline Tschuggnall, 'Opa war kein Nazi'. Nationalsozialismus und Holocaust im Familiengedächtnis, Fischer: Frankfurt am Main, 2002, esp. ch.5. pp. 105ff. Samuel Salzborn refers to a study by Hiddo M. Jolles which notes this phenomenon as early as 1965, p. 36.

[49] Harald Welzer, Täter. Wie aus ganz normalen Menschen Massenmörder werden, Fischer: Frankfurt am Main, 2005, esp. pp. 49-75 (here: p. 64).

[50] A. and M. Mitscherlich, pp. 29ff and pp. 32 and 34.

[51] 'Die Deutschen fühlten sich zur Zeit des Nationalsozialismus einem normativen Modell verpflichtet, das die Erniedrigung und Verfolgung anderer Menschen nicht verurteilte, sondern forderte, und das im letzten Drittel des "Dritten Reiches" auch vorsah, dass es notwendig und gut sei, zu töten.' Welzer, Täter, p. 69. In contrast, Peter Longerich's 'Davon haben wir nichts gewusst!', Munich: Siedler, 2006, which documents in detail the public nature of the persecution and elimination of Jews from Germany, comes to the conclusion that the Nazi machinery's anti-Semitic propaganda was counterproductive and the 'Anstrengungen zur Ausrichtung der Bevölkerung auf die "Endlösung"' were unsuccessful and produced widespread rejection. Longerich argues that, due to the manipulated public sphere and the difficulty of independent opinion formation, it makes little sense to speak of a homogenous 'Volksmeinung', p. 313.

[52] See for example Götz Aly's controversial study Hitler's Volksstaat, Fischer: Frankfurt, 2005, which argues that National Socialism was able to achieve mass acceptance by bolstering its ideology of a homogenous Volk through the distribution of goods from expropriated Jews and the mass distribution of wealth acquired from the occupied countries during the war.

[53] See also Harald Welzer, 'Schön unscharf. Über die Konjunktur der Familien- und Generationenromane,' *Mittelweg 36*, 1 (2004), 53-64.

[54] Franzen, p. 218.

[55] See Salzborn, p. 21.

[56] Welzer, Moller, Tschuggnall, pp. 81ff.

[57] Dieter Wellershoff, 'Das Kainsmal des Krieges', encomium for Hannes Heer on receiving the *Carl von Ossietzky-Medaille* as representative of the exhibition *Vernichtungskrieg. Verbrechen der Wehrmacht 1941-1944* of the Hamburg Institute for Social Research (7 Dec 1997), in: Wellershoff, *Das Kainsmal des Krieges*, Verlag Landpresse: Weilerswist, 1998, pp. 13-34 (here: p. 13).

[58] Mourning for Freud is connected to a conscious working through of the memories of the lost object: 'Each single one of the memories and expectations in which the libido is bound to the object is brought up and hypercathected, and detachment of the libido is accomplished in respect of it.' Freud, 'Mourning and Melancholia', *Standard Edition*, vol. XIV, The Hogarth Press: London, 1957, pp. 241-258 (here: p. 245).

[59] Uwe Timm, *Am Beispiel meines Bruders*, Kiepenheuer & Witsch: Cologne, 2003, p. 8. All further references as (AB, page number). On Treichel's *Der Verlorene* see Stuart Taberner, 'Hans-Ulrich Treichel's *Der Verlorene* and the Problem of German Wartime Suffering,' *Modern Language Review*, 1 (2002), 123-134. I only became aware of Anne Fuchs's article 'The Tinderbox of Memory: Generation and Masculinity in *Väterliteratur* by Christoph Meckel, Uwe Timm, Ulla Hahn and Dagmar Leupold' after the completion of this chapter. In: Anne Fuchs, Mary Cosgrove and Georg Grote, eds. *German Memory Contests. The Quest for Identity in Literature, Film, and Discourse since 1990*, Camden House: Rochester, 2006, pp. 41-66.

[60] The 'Organisation Consul' was a clandestine right-wing conspiracy formed after the prohibition of the notorious *Brigade Erhard* following the failed *Kapp-Putsch* in 1922. It was responsible for the murder of Walther Rathenau (1922), foreign minister of the Weimar Republic, and connected to the murder of Matthias Erzberger (1921), who had signed the 1918 armistice. See the homepage of the Walther Rathenau Gesellschaft, www.walther-rathenau.de/wrg.htm.

[61] Sebald, *Luftkrieg und Literatur*, Fischer: Frankfurt am Main, 2001 [first Carl Hanser Verlag: Munich, 1999], p. 32. See also p. 86 where Sebald remarks on the 'Neigung zum Vorgeprägten, zur Wiederholung des Immergleichen' in eye-witness accounts.

[62] *Gefrierfleischorden* was the bitterly ironic soldier's term for the 'Medal Winter Battle in the East' 1941/42, introduced by Hitler in spring 1942. *Hitlersäge* was the

soldier's jargon for the MG42 machine gun and a *Heimatschuss* was an injury sufficient for transfer to a hospital in Germany.

[63] A reference to Thornton Wilder's play *The Skin of Our Teeth* (1943) which was extremely popular in post-war Germany in its translation *Wir sind noch einmal davongekommen*. The extent to which this expression expressed – and still expresses – the feeling of Germans having survived can be seen from the frequency with which it is used both in commemorations of the 60th anniversary of the end of the war and in contemporary witness memories. See for example Wolf Jobst Siedler's book *Wir waren noch einmal davongekommen*, Munich, 2005. Theo Sommer, editor-at-large of *DIE ZEIT*, refers to Wilder in his commemorative speech 'Vor sechzig Jahren: Kriegsende und Neubeginn', held in the city hall of Osnabrück, www.osnabrueck.de/Vortrag_zum_Kriegsende.pdf. The phrase also appears in Peter Bachér, 'Ein Tag mit zwei Gesichtern', *Welt am Sonntag*, 8 May, 2005, without reference.

[64] See Hans-Joachim Schröder *Erzählgeschichten und Geschichtserzählungen im Interview. Der zweite Weltkrieg aus der Sicht der ehemaligen Mannschaftssoldaten.* Niemeyer: Tübingen, 1992, p. 135.

[65] See Schröder, 'Erfahrungen deutscher Mannschaftssoldaten während der ersten Phase des Rußlandkrieges,' in: Bernd Wegner, ed., *Zwei Wege nach Moskau. Vom Hitler-Stalin-Pakt zum Unternehmen 'Barbarossa'*, Piper: Munich, 1991, 309-325 (here: p. 318).

[66] Ibid., p. 321.

[67] Schröder stresses 'wie sehr Armeebefehlshaber und die "einfachen Soldaten" an einem Strang zogen'. Schröder, 'Erfahrungen deutscher Mannschaftssoldaten', p. 219.

Stuart Taberner

Literary Representations in Contemporary German Fiction of the Expulsions of Germans from the East in 1945

This chapter examines contemporary literary representations of the expulsions of ethnic Germans from East Prussia, Poland and Czechslovakia at the end of the Second World War. It argues that depictions of the actual events are relatively uncommon and that the majority of texts are concerned with how 'private memories' of the hardships endured by 'ordinary' Germans were passed down within families in the post-war period. Finally, it is argued that a number of texts also reflect on the purposes and possibilities of literature itself in relation to a theme which continues to provoke powerful emotions and intense political debate.

In Dagmar Leupold's autobiographical novel *Nach den Kriegen. Roman eines Lebens* (2004), the narrator hastens to Germany from the United States to sit at her father's hospital bed as he is about to pass away. The daughter has long been the writer that the father aspired to be and the story she recounts here of his life is in effect the story that he never succeeded in committing to paper, with the repeatedly thematised difference that *her* version is disrupted by epistemological anxiety with regard to the 'truth-value' of the accounts of wartime experience which had circulated around her family when she was a child and by her persistent inability to understand or, more specifically, empathise with her father's mindset. In particular, she returns time and again to his wartime diaries and is repelled by their sentimentality and tendency to aestheticise combat in metaphysical terms, and by his self-presentation, reminiscent of Gottfried Benn and Ernst Jünger, as a uniquely sensitive spirit unconcerned with the 'banal' reality of Nazism. Above all, she is outraged by his self-stylisation as a victim, first in Poland and later, following his expulsion, in West Germany: 'Eine Kontinuität der Kränkungen: als Deutscher in Polen, als Flüchtling in Deutschland.'[1]

Leupold's novel, as may be surmised from the brief digest above, is intensely personal, and yet it is also exemplary of the wealth of narratives which began to appear from the early 1990s concerned with the experiences of 'ordinary Germans' during the Nazi period. The fact that the text was most likely written some years after the father's

death in 1986 points to a changed social and political context and to a
different mood with regard to the depiction of the choices, collusion
and circumstances of individual Germans not directly or
disproportionately involved in Nazi crimes. Thus, in contrast with the
typically condemnatory tone of the *Vaterromane* of the 1970s and
1980s, *Nach den Kriegen* presents a complex individual who, in the
1960s, 1970s and even beyond, unthinkingly supported the *Bund der
Vertriebenen*'s revisionist complaints and yet was also just as
impulsively critical of Kurt Georg Kiesinger, so much so in fact that
he became pathetically enamoured of Beate Klarsfeld, talking
excitedly of the 'Unerschrockenheit der *jungen Frau* und ihre
Attraktivität' (NK, 97, italics in original) when she slapped the
Chancellor in protest at his links to the Nazi period. In Leupold's
novel, we glimpse a man who, in the post-war era, was
'aufgeschlossen, liberal' with 'Sympathien für die 68er', but whose
instinctively nostalgic sensibility and adopted political stance
remained uncannily irreconcilable: 'sentimentales Festhalten am
Vergangenen und pragmatisches Ablehnen des politisch
Unvernünftigen' (NK, 218).

This more differentiated presentation of the wartime generation, an
early precursor of which was Hanns-Josef Ortheil's *Abschied von den
Kriegsteilnehmern* (1992), in which a son is haunted by his inability to
connect with his father's experiences on the Eastern Front,[2] relates to
a sense, after 1990, that the post-war period had come to a close:
division, the most visible consequence of the lost conflict, had been
overcome and the lessons of Germany's disastrous expansionism
seemingly learnt, and, perhaps more mesmerising for younger
Germans, the wartime generation would soon be passing away. The
main focus of interest in the Nazi past, whether in literature,
historiography or public debate, thus shifted from a more or less
'political' insistence on the structures of fascism to a less judgmental
attention to the everyday experience of individual, 'ordinary'
Germans. This development was encouraged by events such as the
publication in German of Christopher R. Browning's *Ordinary Men:
Reserve Police Battalion 101 and The Final Solution in Poland* in
1993 and the exhibition *Vernichtungskrieg: Verbrechen der
Wehrmacht 1941-1944*.[3] More broadly, a line may be drawn from the
attempts made by conservative historians such as Ernst Nolte, Michael
Stürmer and particularly Andreas Hillgruber in the course of the

Historikerstreit of the mid-1980s to 'historicise' the Nazi past to a less obviously 'political' 'ongoing process of broadening understanding'[4] in the 1990s, as described by Bill Niven, vis-à-vis the multifaceted reality faced by different groups during the Hitler period. By the late 1990s, this 'broadening understanding' had come to encompass the controversial theme of 'German wartime suffering', specifically the firebombing of German cities, the mass rapes of German women and girls by the advancing Red army, and the arbitrary killings and brutal expulsions of ethnic Germans from Eastern Europe.

However, a closer examination of literary representations of the Nazi past in the post-unification period reveals that, for the most part, the primary focus is less on the actual events than on the manner in which they have been remembered, discussed and depicted in the decades since the end of the Second World War. For example, Bernhard Schlink's *Der Vorleser* (1995) engages with the legacy of the student protesters of 1968 and their perhaps overzealous condemnation of their parents; Martin Walser's *Ein springender Brunnen* (1998) similarly criticises 'politically-correct' interpretations of the past,[5] whereas Marcel Beyer's *Spione* (2000), Tanja Dückers's *Himmelskörper* (2003), Stephan Wackwitz's *Ein unsichtbares Land* (2003), and Thomas Medicus's *In den Augen meines Großvaters* (2004) all deal with the transmission of wartime experiences across three generations. Even a novel such as Marcel Beyer's *Flughunde* (1995), portraying the entanglement of its protagonist Karnau in Nazi crimes, is, as Niven argues in a discussion of post-1990 depictions of Nazi perpetrators, one of a number of similar texts which 'are more focused on the problems and processes of addressing that period than [...] on this past itself'.[6] The result, as Anne Fuchs and Mary Cosgrove have argued, is a more or less self-reflexive engagement with a multiplicity of 'memory contests' centred on the Nazi past.[7]

This attention to the dialogue (more often disconnection) between generations is especially evident in texts featuring stories of 'wartime suffering'. Photographs, diaries, fragments of older relatives' conversations remembered from childhood or discussions with a wartime generation about to pass away thus motivate the interrogation of family history in novels such as Leupold's *Nach den Kriegen*, Hans-Ulrich Treichel's *Der Verlorene* (1998), Günter Grass's *Im Krebsgang* (2002), Ulla Hahn's *Unscharfe Bilder* (2003) or Uwe Timm's *Am Beispiel meines Bruders* (2003),[8] or in texts by younger writers such as Dückers's *Himmelskörper* (2003) or those collected in the volume edited by Dückers and Verena Carl, *stadt land krieg. Autoren der Gegenwart erzählen von der deutschen Vergangenheit* (2004). Common to the majority of contemporary literary ruminations on the transmission between generations of wartime stories, to a greater or lesser degree in each, moreover, are three key topoi: 1) an engagement with contemporaneous debates on the supposed near-absence since the 1950s of literary depictions of 'German wartime suffering'; 2) a broader reflection on the way in which the Nazi period has been remembered at key moments in the post-war period, in East and West Germany; 3) a more metaphysical anxiety with regard to the traumatic disruption of family histories and legacies.

The first of these topoi is more often than not simply a matter of responding to the contention that a taboo had previously existed on speaking of the devastation caused by Allied bombing, or of the mass rapes, arbitrary executions or expulsions. In Timm's *Am Beispiel meines Bruders*, for example, the narrator notes in relation to the Royal Airforce's firebombing of Hamburg in July 1943: 'Noch Jahre nach dem Krieg, mich durch meine Kindheit begleitend, wurden diese Erlebnisse immer und immer wieder erzählt'.[9] The narrator of Leopold's *Nach den Kriegen* similarly recalls how the talk amongst her relatives was always of 'Angriffen, Lazaretten, Schußwunden und Schlesien' (KN, 44). These and other similar texts, in fact, contribute to the debate sparked by W. G. Sebald's assertion in his 1997 Zurich lectures (published in 1999 as *Luftkrieg und Literatur*) that there had been no adequate literary depiction of the destruction of Germany's cities and add weight to the counter-claim that in family settings at least, there had always been talk of the horrors inflicted upon mothers and fathers, aunts and uncles, and grandparents. In effect, recent fictional portrayals of the post-war era echo the findings of the oral history project undertaken by Harald Welzer, Sabine Moller and Karoline Tschuggnall, *'Opa war kein Nazi'. Nationalsozialismus und Holocaust im Familiengedächtnis* (2002). Moreover, as Aleida Assmann argues, 'family narratives' frequently seeped, until the 1980s, into the public-political realm and were often instrumentalised by the *Bund der Vertriebenen* and others hoping to keep alive German claims for restitution or even to relativise German crimes.[10]

More interesting, and perhaps less expected, is the way in which recent literary depictions of 'German wartime suffering' feed into the current interest in historicising the pre-1990 Federal Republic and the ex-GDR. Many of the texts in question, then, ruminate on family life and the public-political sphere in the 1950s, 1960s and beyond and reveal the fractures running through the foundations of the post-war order in both East and West Germany. And what they suggest is that Sebald, whilst mistaken in his claim that the air raids, for example, are absent from German fiction – Volker Hage proved the converse in *Zeugen der Zerstörung. Die Literaten und der Luftkrieg* (2003) – may have been correct in his assertion that German society after the war was irrevocably marked by its origins in the death, destruction and devastation inflicted upon its precursor. (Sebald speaks only of West Germany but we may extend his arguments to include the former GDR). This insight represents a dramatic shift in the way in which post-war Germany is to be seen. In the place of a storyline focused on ideological divides – the two states, Cold War rivalry, generational conflict, dissent and the state in the ex-GDR, the fall of the Wall, and so on – an alternative narrative emerges with trauma at its core. A more complex narrative comes into view in which different generations are not so much similarly insistent, and thus implacably opposed, on diametrically different readings of the past – German innocence versus German perpetration – as differently traumatised, but uncomfortably conjoined, by the same instinctive recoil from the destruction of home, heritage and history.

In what follows, I examine recent literary representations of the expulsions of ethnic Germans from the East in 1945 and immediately after the end of the war. The arguments I make here, however, may also be applied to texts having to do with other aspects of 'German wartime suffering', ranging, for example, from Dieter Forte's *Der Junge mit den blutigen Schuhen* (1995), a reflection on the supposed 'concreting-over' of the physical traces and horrific memories of the Allied bombing campaign,[11] to Timm's *Am Beispiel meines Bruders,* a very different book exploring the impact of the death of his older brother, an *SS* soldier, and the way in which this became part of a post-war narrative of 'victimisation' within the family. Although my primary concern is with the manner in which contemporary novels reflect on familial and public-political discourses on 'German wartime suffering' at various points in the history of the pre-1990 FRG and the GDR, I am also crucially interested in how authors have recognised that this is a subject which, because it is simultaneously intensely

'human' and yet also of such great political import, allows them to
reflect on the purposes and possibilities of literary fiction itself.

The Transmission of Trauma
In Arnold Stadler's novel *Sehnsucht* (2001) the narrator recalls a
former schoolteacher of his, Schultze, a 'Heimatvertriebener' who
took his pupils to the north German coast and bid them to 'alles
aufsagen, was vorbei und verloren war, vor allem die Inseln'.[12]
Schultze, he insists, 'war wohl kein Revisionist, er hatte nur vielleicht
ab und zu mal Heimweh, was er verschwieg'. In the wake of the
liberalisation of social and sexual mores and the advent of an
unforgivingly self-critical avowal of German crimes after 1968,
'Heimweh' for that which was irretrievably lost at the end of the war
had come to be commonly regarded as 'peinlicher als Küssen unter
freiem Himmel' (S, 287).

Stadler's oeuvre formulates a critique of the contemporary Federal
Republic and of its erasure of all ties to its (non-Nazi) history and
traditions for the sake of a politically-correct insistence on contrition,
rationality and its credentials as a modern (and model) Western
constitutional democracy. In *Ich war einmal* (1989), expellees from
East Prussia and Italian guest workers inhabit the ugly new
settlements now ubiquitous in the Swabian hinterland: the Federal
Republic is a functional (although increasingly permanent) abode for
those whose roots are elsewhere, not a true home. And in the author's
Büchner-prize-winning *Ein hinreißender Schrotthändler* (1999),[13] a
brilliant satire on the state of the nation after the elections of 1998, it
is only the narrator's recollection of an expellee who lived in his
village in the south-west German provincial hinterland of
Kreenheinstetten, Irmelda Swichtenberg, that offers 'ein letzter
Beweis, daß es Heimat gibt'.[14] In a country in which any positive
perspective on the past is blocked by political correctness and all
remaining vestiges of an authentically 'German' heritage are being
eradicated by the willing surrender to international brand names and
'universal' liberal values, it is only in the pain of those who were
forcibly expelled half a century ago that the loss of *Heimat* so eagerly
embraced by today's generations of global consumers can be
glimpsed.

Stadler's work typically depicts the trauma of dispossession and
displacement in Heideggerian terms, that is, with a distinctly

metaphysical edge, but it nevertheless also locates it within the particular historical context of (West) Germany post-'68 and more specifically in relation to the present-day Berlin Republic. To this extent, it delivers a critique of a mode of coming-to-terms with the past which, in insisting on the broad social and political significance of issues of perpetration and complicity, designates 'felt experience' as invalid – Stadler's literary fiction, like that of his mentor Martin Walser, is a defence of individual subjectivity and memory[15] in the face of what Walser has termed the 'Tugendterror der political correctness'.[16] Yet, in addition to a general criticism of the FRG's commemorative culture, the emphasis throughout Stadler's work is more explicitly on the disrupted transmission of traumatic memories of a 'German loss' from generation to generation, and between individuals. More pointedly, this disruption is seen as traumatic in itself. At the end of *Ein hinreißender Schrotthändler*, the narrator declares that he only ever wanted to tell his wife – a native of the northern German city of Hamburg and a member of the Republic's impeccably 'rationalist', politically-correct liberal-left elite – of a childhood fall, a moment of physical pain and metaphysical dislocation: 'wie weh es tat, wie einst, als ich vom Dreirad gefallen war' (HS, 235). We may take this superficially banal comment on the state of his marriage as a far-reaching metaphor for his melancholic mindfulness of the incommunicability of an 'authentic' past, of *Heimat*, of the sudden loss of orientation and certainty, and perhaps even of a fall from grace, within a society which privileges an entirely opposed form of memory.

Stadler's insinuation of a 'secondary trauma' generated by the disrupted transmission of an original trauma, that is, of the pain endured even by those who never directly experienced the original hurt, may be reminiscent of recent theories of 'postmemory', as formulated by Marianne Hirsch,[17] for example. In this case, however, the 'postmemory' of the expulsions of ethnic Germans from the East (or, indeed, other forms of anguish undergone by 'ordinary' Germans at the end of the war) implies a form of suffering inflicted upon the descendents of the perpetrators – a form of 'German victimhood', then. This sense of victimisation may be present even – or perhaps precisely – at those moments when the author insists that the Holocaust – a German crime, after all – has destroyed all hope that *Heimat* might be reconstituted in the modern age. 'Ja, dieses

Jahrhundert [...] bot ein Leben in der Nachbarschaft von Verbrennungsöfen', he begins in an essay of 1999, then to continue: 'Wo soll da noch Heimat sein?'.[18] The generalising formulation of 'dieses Jahrhundert' detracts from a *German* responsibility for the death camps and implies a broader social and historical dislocation – modernity perhaps; likewise, the question 'Wo soll da noch Heimat sein?' may suggest a melancholic resignation related to an existential torment apparently visited upon all humankind in the contemporary period. As in the work of W. G. Sebald, expulsion, exile and eradication occasionally feature as the defining impulses of modernity. Unlike Sebald, however, Stadler does not always distinguish between the instigators and principal agents of the horrors of the 'terrible twentieth century' (Jonathan Glover's epithet in his *Humanity: A Moral History of the 20th Century* [2000]) and those who were its primary victims.[19]

Hans-Ulrich Treichel's *Der Verlorene* (1998) is both more directly concerned with the expulsions from the East and less indulgent of the self-pitying inability of the wartime generation to place 'German suffering' in relation to German perpetration and of the melancholic internalisation on the part of a subsequent generation of the problematic legacy of loss they have inherited from their parents. Broadly speaking, *Der Verlorene* depicts the gulf between the narrator Arnold and his parents in the 1950s as Arnold, on the one hand, struggled to understand why his existence appeared so marginal within the family and his mother and father, on the other hand, laboured unsuccessfully to come to terms with the 'loss' of their older son in early 1945 during one of the treks from East Prussia. More specifically, as I have argued elsewhere, the novel undermines both the wartime generation's exclusive focus on its own suffering and scandalous negligence of German perpetration and the often morally motivated indifference to their parents' wartime experience displayed by the children who would later come to constitute the generation of '68.[20] Yet, when read in the context of the wave of texts focused on the passing down of wartime stories between the generations which have appeared since the novel's publication in 1998, it becomes clear that *Der Verlorene* is also centrally concerned with the 'secondary trauma' experienced as a result of the breakdown of communicated memory within the family *per se*. Arnold's manifest irrelevance to stories which preceded his birth, his exclusion from his parents' whispered conversations, and their unexplained secrecy and unpredictable emotions all underscore his sense of inhabiting a 'non-place'. His parents' loss is real, and thus, to an extent, capable of being mourned, however inadequately, but his is intangible and hence all the more destabilising. At the end of the novel, his mother 'fails' to recognise 'Findelkind 2307' as her own child – this grown boy is not the baby she lost and for whom she has grieved – whereas the narrator remains haunted by the prospect that this boy, or any other, that is, this past or another manifestation of a past that is not his, might return at any time and re-establish the prior claim of a memory of *Heimat* in which, by definition, he simply does not feature.

In his contribution to Lothar Kettenacker's collection *Ein Volk von Opfern? Die neue Debatte um den Bombenkrieg 1940-45*, Peter Schneider asks in relation to his own generation, the generation of '68, and to those still younger: 'Benehmen wir, die Kinder und Enkel, uns nicht zuweilen immer noch wie Traumatiker?'.[21] Treichel's *Der Verlorene* provides a potent impression of this 'secondary trauma' but any possible impulse towards a self-serving melancholia or self-stylisation as victim is undercut by satire: the second-born son is 'ein zu dick geratener pubertierender Knabe',[22] bloated by his over-indulgence in a material and gastronomic plenty unthinkable only a decade or so previously and incapable of rising above his egotistical fretfulness that he might have to share his room with his 'lost' older brother if he should ever be 'found'. The existential melancholia endured by Stadler's protagonists as they contemplate the incommunicability of pain within the family, and between individuals, in a society from which all allusions to a shared experience of trauma have been expunged for the sake of political correctness appears in Treichel's text as a rather more prosaic self-pity, and even self-obsession, on all sides.

Treichel's work more generally offers an insight into the 'homelessness' experienced by the post-war generation as a consequence both of their material and psychological disconnection from the past and their fraught relationship to parents whose life-stories are so alienating, even repellent. Two volumes of essays, *Von Leib und Seele* (1992) and the ironically-titled *Heimatkunde oder alles ist heiter und edel* (1996) thus detail with laconic dexterity his parents' flight from the Russians at the end of the war, the story of the older brother 'lost' on the trek (later reworked in *Der Verlorene*), and the utter emptiness of the author's own West German childhood in his 'ostwestfälischen Heimat'.[23] The sense that the adopted home inhabited by the post-war generation can never be anything more than a shadow of the *Heimat* sorely remembered by dispossesed parents also haunts the protagonists of Treichel's *Tristanakkord* (2000) and *Der Irdische Amor* (2002). The narrator of *Tristanakkord* who, similar to Treichel himself, thus has an ex-soldier father with a prosthetic arm – an autobiographical reference, certainly, but here no doubt also a metaphorical allusion to an irreplaceable loss and an inadequate substitute – is cut off from his own childhood memories by the river Ems, 'der Strom des Vergessens',[24] and yet, on the other side of the river, as a German abroad, lacks the kind of worldly self-confidence which, paradoxically, can only come from knowing where home is. In *Der Irdische Amor*, similarly, the protagonist, a student of art history, travels to Italy in the footsteps of Herder, Winckelmann and Goethe, but is plagued by flashbacks to his childhood as the son of refugee parents who had fled the Russian advance.[25]

Depicting Expellees in the GDR

Christoph Hein's *Landnahme* (2004) certainly responds to the post-unification fascination with the ex-GDR and ties its depiction of the former communist state in the 1950s and 1960s to the present-day interest in 'German wartime suffering'. Yet its aim is less a postmodern reflection on the 'authenticity' or otherwise of contemporary cultural memory than the making good of an omission: East Germany's historical refusal to recognise the difficulties endured by the substantial number of expellees amongst its population in integrating into a society for which the brutal evictions (and mass rapes) inflicted by the (now allied) Red Army simply did not feature in the official record of the war and its aftermath.[26] Hein's choice of the fate of a former expellee in the GDR as a theme, therefore, reflects this East German writer's desire to add to the historicisation, and timely examination, of the GDR's ideals and reality.

Hein's *Die Landnahme* tells of Bernhard Haber, the son of a refugee from what became Polish territory after 1945, his struggle for acceptance in a community hostile to 'outsiders', and how this antagonism deforms him. It reveals, for example, how Herr Voigt, the mathematics teacher at the local school, humiliated the newly arrived pupil in front of his future classmates and insisted that he use the

Polish name Wrocław for the city of Breslau from which he was so recently expelled;[27] we also learn that the carpentry business established by Haber's father was burnt down and that Haber's efforts to get the police to investigate what was clearly an act of arson were peremptorily rebuffed, leading the boy to turn against his neighbours. In the course of the rest of the novel, a series of different narrators piece together the story of Haber's life once he has left the town. His first girlfriend tells of how he fell under the influence of a young political activist, Sylvie, and became part of the troop sent round to 'encourage' farmers to take part in the collectivisation programme. Peter Koller relates the same story and Haber's response when he asked him why he participated in this brutality: 'Rache ist süß, Koller' (L, 239); Koller also reveals that he and Haber were involved in smuggling people across the border to West Germany. Next, Katharina Hollenbach claims to have seduced him before he married her sister, and, finally, Sigurd Kiterow, a businessman, divulges that he slept with Haber's wife, and reports that it was likely that Haber's father was murdered by locals. Common to all of these stories is the hint of an underlying resentment of the variously named *Vertriebene*, *Umsiedler* or *Polacken*, a resentment which persisted even after Haber became a pillar of the community in the years after the fall of the wall in 1989.

Hein's novel is concerned above all with the narrow-mindedness of the townspeople. Yet, more generally, its presentation of the problems encountered by expellees in integrating into East German society offers a useful contrast with novels which depict *West* Germany in the same period. Thus, whereas *Der Verlorene* suggests that, broadly speaking, expellees in West Germany were able to achieve economic success and a degree of social status relatively quickly, even as they continued to hanker for their lost *Heimat* – the father's purchase of ever more expensive cars is heavily satirised – *Landnahme* implies that it was far more difficult for refugees in East Germany to re-establish themselves. The hostility expressed by the locals in *Landnahme*, then, is subtly sanctioned by the state insofar as the authorities consistently side with the indigenous population against the *Vertriebene* and create a climate in which it is understood by all that the expellees are an uncomfortable, and undesired, reminder of the brutality of the (now allied) Red Army. This stands in stark contrast with the status of expellees in West Germany as presented in *Der*

Verlorene: in Hein's novel, the town's police conspires in the exclusion of Haber and his father; in Treichel's text, the narrator's widowed mother is wooed by a local officer. In the Federal Republic, of course, the experiences of the expellees were useful precisely *because* they cast the communist Eastern bloc in a bad light. In *Landnahme*, consequently, the alienation experienced by the children of expellees is expressed primarily in relation to a *regime* which does not recognise the suffering endured by their parents: Haber alternates between rebelling against the GDR and cynically participating in its worst excesses in order to take revenge against the individuals who degraded his father. In *Der Verlorene*, on the other hand, the alienation of the post-war generation is expressed first and foremost in relation to the *family*, that is, to parents, aunts and uncles, and grandparents, who appear not as victims of the West German state but as beneficiaries of its deliberate neglect of their connivance in Nazism and collaborators in its repression of the past.

A significant consequence of these different emphases may be the relative 'universality' of texts set in East Germany compared with those set in West Germany. Literary works which reflect on the transmission of a collective memory of the expulsions in the Federal Republic thus appear for the most part as a continuation, albeit in a more differentiated fashion, of the rather inwardlooking 'familial dialogue' begun in the 1970s in the West German *Vaterroman*, with a very strong insistence on the specific historical circumstances of the Nazi era and the causal precedence of German crimes over 'German suffering'. More generally, writers concerned with depicting West Germany may feel that the spectre of historical revisionism, ever present in the Federal Republic in the 1950s and 1960s and intermittingly observable in the 1970s and 1980s, means that their literary fiction must necessarily be conceived of as an intervention in a particular set of debates. Novels focusing on the fate of expellees in the ex-GDR, in contrast, are less narrowly focused on the damaging dynamics resulting from incompatible narratives within the family, or on a broader discussion of coming-to-terms with the Nazi past, and more concerned with expulsion and displacement as an issue with a global dimension that resonates in the present day. Hein's *Landnahme*, then, generalises its critique of the manner in which the GDR population, subtly encouraged by the state, marginalised expellees seeking to build a new life in East Germany in the post-war period into a commentary on the way refugees from today's conflicts are similarly excluded in post-unification Germany. At the end of the novel, Haber's son forcibly ejects two Fijians, exiles from the crisis in that country in the year 2000 no doubt, from a carneval procession, 'ein deutsches Fest', but is berated by his father: 'Lass die Leute zufrieden, Paul. Es sind arme Flüchtlinge, ihnen geht es schlecht genug. Sie tun uns nichts, und sie nehmen uns nichts weg'. And if the connection were not already obvious, Haber subsequently adds emphatically: 'Dein Großvater war auch ein Vertriebener' (L, 352-3).

Hein's interest in addressing the historical injustice of the manner in which expellees in the GDR were treated by the state and the indigenous population and his related, more global concern with the welcome extended (or denied) to refugees in the present extends the scope, and significance, of his fictionalisation of a period in East German history and implies literature's ability to generalise universal messages from the specific events it depicts. What may be omitted, of course, is the focus on the possible complicity of expellees in the rise of National Socialism. Here, Hein's *Landnahme* may be compared with Reinhard Jirgl's *Die Unvollendeten* (2003), which begins (unusually) with a depiction of the rape, murder and expulsion of Germans by Czech soldiers and civilians in the course of the *wilde Vertreibungen* of 1945 and early 1946 but then turns to the fate of Hanna and Maria and their mother Johanna in the GDR. Jirgl's novel, then, tells of the discrimination endured by expellees in East Germany and of the continuing resonance of their dispossession – '*Heimat* ist ferner als der Tod'.[28] Yet there are also hints that participation in Nazi crimes was often unwilling – Anna's lover relates how he was indoctrinated, conscripted and implicated in the murder of Jewish internees (72-76) – and a suggestion that the standard insistence that Germans were perpetrators before they were victims is not always tenable: it turns out that Hanna is half-Jewish (the result of Johanna's brief affair with a Dutch businessman). Jirgl's intention is most likely to generate sympathy for the 'ordinary' German victims of expulsion and to relate this to the plight of refugees in more recent times (in Bosnia or Kosovo, for example), as adumbrated by the novel's allusions to 'FLÜCHTLINGSKONTINGENTE' (DU, 6) or its universalising statements: 'Denn wo Flüchtlinge sind, sind immer auch Die Lager....' (DU, 6); 'Die Angst der *Flüchtlinge*, man würde sie hier=drinnen zusammenpferchen und die Scheune in Brand

setzten….. – diese Ur-Angst aller Deportierten' (DU, 29). For all the
modernist self-reflexivity implied by its unique orthography, however,
it may be that *Die Unvollendeten* – with the best of intentions –
dissolves the historical specificity of what led to Germans being
expelled within an undifferentiated victimhood: 'Die Lager' (with the
capitalised 'Die' adding emphasis), for instance, conventionally
evokes the concentration camps and its use here may thus parallel
German refugees interned in 1945 (and present-day refugees) with the
Jewish, Sinti and Roma, homosexual and 'political' inmates of the
Nazi sites of mass killings.

'German Wartime Suffering' and German Literature at the End of the 1990s

Jirgl's empathetic depiction of his three Sudeten German characters
certainly runs the risk, as indicated above, of detracting from the fact
that the expulsion of Germans from the East was preceded by brutal
German expansionism. Yet it would be wrong to conclude that this
East German author's undoubted sympathy with 'ordinary' people
caught up in global conflicts predisposes him to the brand of historism
promoted in West Germany in the mid-1980s by historians such as
Michael Stürmer and Andreas Hillgruber and by conservative forces
more generally in the 1990s. Stürmer and Hillgruber, and even more
so the neo-conservative writers of the early post-unification period,
were thus concerned to undermine the essentially 'political' insistence
within the Federal Republic's culture of 'coming-to-terms with the
past' on Germans' historical responsibility for the Holocaust by means
of a plea for greater understanding of the 'impossible' circumstances
faced by individuals. Jirgl, on the other hand, encourages empathy
with 'ordinary' Germans *not* in order to shortcircuit a critical
perspective on the past but precisely in order to confront a historical
injustice. The difference, of course, is that Jirgl's focus is on the
GDR's failure to treat its citizens equitably and, indeed, its
unacknowledged continuities with Nazism. To this extent, *Die
Unvollendeten* continues the project the author has pursued in a range
of novels published in the 1990s, including his trilogy *Genealogie des
Tötens*, written in the GDR between 1985 and 1990 but first available
in print only in 2002.

In focusing on three women who were transparently innocent of
complicity in Nazism, the author sidesteps the thorny issue of whether

empathy would be appropriate in respect of other individuals who, although mistreated by the Red Army or its allies in 1945 and later victimised by the East German regime, had also been supporters of the Nazi system or even directly involved in its atrocities. Of more immediate interest here, however, is Jirgl's insinuation that literature has a social and political role to play: both in 'coming-to-terms' with the GDR and, as already noted, in its apparent intervention in contemporary debates in post-unification Germany on the integration of refugees from the wars in the ex-Yugoslavia. Most obviously, this ascription of a political purpose to fiction distinguishes Jirgl's empathetic approach to his characters' experiences from the (only) purportedly *a*political emphasis on individual life-stories favoured by critics and authors such as Karl Heinz Bohrer, Ulrich Greiner, Frank Schirrmacher and Martin Walser, who have rightly been seen as counterparts in the cultural sphere to historians Stürmer and Hillgruber,[29] that is, as proponents of a mode of representation which would promote 'understanding' of 'real' people's embeddedness in their time rather than retrospective moralising.

More specifically, however, Jirgl's *Die Unvollendeten* explicitly aligns itself against the 'new German pop literature' of the late 1990s. In a somewhat unexpected excursus, then, the narrator rails against the contemporary trend of 'lifestyle writing': 'zeitgeistparfümiert, kaum 1 Satz ohne zerkwätschte Amerikawortbrocken, das Joop-Doitsch internett —. Globalistisches Empfinden —', and in particular against the marketing of the 'Bubi & Frollein Wunder' (DU, 194), that is, of ostentatious male dandies – Alexander von Schönburg, Benjamin von Stuckrad-Barre or Christian Kracht, for example – and fragile young women, e.g. Judith Hermann, Karen Duve or Julia Franck.[30] The brutal expulsion of tens of thousands from their homes, in 1945 but also in the present is a more important topic for fiction than the currently fashionable fascination with a globalised consumer culture. And empathetic insight into individuals' interactions with complex social and historical realities, it is further suggested, is the *raison d'être* of any literature worthy of the name.

In fact, it might be argued more generally that many of the novels published from the late 1990s onwards concerned with the expulsion of ethnic Germans from the East, and with 'German wartime suffering' as a whole, are as much a response to the dismissal of socially-engaged writing, by conservatives initially but also, by the end of the 1990s, more broadly, and to the popularity of 'lifestyle writing', typically modelled on Anglo-American fiction, as they are a response to the resurgence of interest in the events themselves. To this extent, such texts participate in contemporary discussions of *aesthetic* matters: the challenge to the socially-engaged fiction associated with writers such as Günter Grass or, in East Germany, Christa Wolf, or with '68ers' such as Uwe Timm, F C Delius and Peter Schneider; the 'commodification' of literature, and the acceleration of globalisation and the 'threat' to 'German' culture. In the final section of this article, I consider the most noteworthy fictional work representing 'German wartime suffering' to appear in the period from the late 1990s, Grass's *Im Krebsgang* (2002), and examine it as an intervention in a debate about literature, politics, present-day society and German identity which goes beyond its narrow focus on the sinking of the *Wilhelm Gustloff*, a former *Kraft durch Freude* cruise liner packed with over 7,000 refugees and a small number of military personnel, by a Soviet submarine in January 1945.

Günter Grass's *Im Krebsgang*

The impression communicated in Jirgl's *Die Unvollendeten* of a younger generation of writers interested only in lifestyle and indifferent to more 'universal' concerns, is, of course, not entirely accurate. Tanja Dückers's *Himmelskörper* (2003), notably, thus deals precisely with the subject of 'intergenerational trauma' related to the expulsion of the narrator's grandparents from East Prussia in 1945; Olaf Müller's *Schlesisches Wetter* (2003), likewise, narrates his family's expulsion from Poland. Both texts point to a wish on the part of the grandchildren and great-grandchilden to relate 'learnt' history to the 'real' individuals, about to fade away, with direct experience of the war. In *Himmelskörper*, then, the narrator sets out to reconstruct the story of a generation which had 'selbst in brennenden Häusern gesessen, auf Viehwagen geflohen' or had been 'als Sechzehnjährige in den Krieg, als Kleinkinder in den Bombenkeller geschickt'.[31] For Freia, the aim is not to excuse her grandparents, Party members given preferential treatment during their flight from the East, but to bring the past to life and establish a coherent familial and national narrative. A similar interest in what Dückers, in her introduction to a collection of short stories edited with Verena Carl, *stadt land krieg. Autoren der Gegenwart erzählen von der deutschen Vergangenheit* (2004), terms the 'intergenerationelle Weitergabe von Themen' may also be detected in texts by other younger writers, including, for example, Katrin Dorn's 'Memory' or Leander Scholz's 'SS' (in *stadt land krieg*), or even in novels in which the Nazi past is mentioned only in passing such as Jenny Erpenbeck's *Geschichte vom alten Kind*, Julia Franck's *Liebediener* or Elke Naters's *Lügen* (all 1999). More generally, the 'Versuch einer Tradierungsgeschichte darzustellen' and the 'emphatische Suche [...] nach den historischen Rollen und Weltsichten [der] Großeltern', noted by Harald Welzer in relation to Dückers's *Himmelskörper* and, by implication, the work of other younger authors,[32] most likely contribute to the much-discussed 'normalisation' of post-unification Germany's relationship to the National Socialist past, that is, in the evolution of a less determinedly 'political' perspective on the era and a more tolerant curiosity with regard to the 'lived' experience of the wartime generation.[33]

I have written elsewhere of how Grass's *Im Krebsgang* reflects on the 'normalisation' debate of the late 1990s and new millennium.[34] In brief, then, the novella responds to the widespread conviction, frequently repeated in the extensive media coverage which followed the text's publication in March 2002, that a culture of 'coming-to-terms' with the past focussed on German perpetration had rendered discussion of what 'ordinary' Germans had endured taboo and that only by following a similarly intensive engagement with its *own* 'suffering' might the country become truly 'normal'. 'Eigentlich, sagt er, wäre es Aufgabe seiner Generation gewesen, dem Elend der ostpreußischen Flüchtlinge Ausdruck zu geben', notes the *Arbeitgeber* Günter Grass, the fictional projection of the author, before continuing with a partial justification: 'die eigene Schuld [war] übermächtig und bekennende Reue in all den Jahren vordringlich'.[35] In order to make good a 'Versäumnis' described as 'bodenlos' (IK, 99), the *Arbeitgeber* enjoins his narrator, Paul Pokriefke, to tell the story of his mother, Tulla, also a character in *Katz und Maus* (1961), *Hundejahre* (1963) and *Die Rättin* (1986), of her flight from the Red Army in January 1945, the sinking of the *Gustloff*, and his birth on the *Löwe*, a boat sent to the rescue. Paul, indeed, tells this story, albeit with a sense of enduring frustration at his mother's attempts to style herself as an 'absolute' victim, along with the tale of his own failure as a journalist, husband and father and in competition with Tulla's interjections and an account of how Konrad, his son, unduly influenced by Tulla,

founded an internet site dedicated to 'German suffering'. Konrad's
story, in fact, comes to dominate: he shoots dead Wolfgang Stremplin,
an internet adversary who, in a pointlessly philo-Semitic gesture,
styles himself as David Frankfurter, the Jew who murdered the Nazi
Party representative in Switzerland for whom the ship *Gustloff* was
named. In sum, the text suggests that the story of 'German wartime
suffering' *does* need to be transmitted from one generation to the next
for the sake of social cohesion. The way in which the novella's
different 'voices' are paralleled and thereby relativise one another,
however, as Kathrin Schödel argues, inhibits any 'narrative
normalisation' of this story and, indeed, undermines any attempt to
'normalise' the Nazi past more generally.[36]

Grass's novella is self-evidently concerned with intergenerational
trauma in the post-war German family: Tulla's obsession with her
own loss which squeezes out any possible recognition of, or empathy
with, the victims of the German crimes which, temporally and
casually, preceded her expulsion, predicts her son's angry rejection of
any connection to *this* past and his own obsessive insistence that
German perpetration can only be undermined by allusions to German
suffering. This, in turn, provokes a revisionist backlash on the part of
Konrad. The seeming impossibility of shaping a shared narrative of
the past which allows for empathy with individuals but also
acknowledges the relationship between German victimhood and
German guilt means that German families do not function as they
should. Thus Paul's refusal to accept his mother's story regarding the
coincidence of his birth with the moment the *Gustloff* disappeared
beneath the waves may symbolise the breakdown in dialogue between
the wartime generation for whom post-war Germany drew its first
painful breaths amidst the death and destruction raining down from
Allied bombers high above or Soviet artillery and their children, the
generation of '68 for whom the very notion of a transmitted *German*
narrative was, by definition, suspect. Bereft of a father as a result of
the war (the war *is* the unwanted and unloved father of his
generation), moreover, and instinctively ill at ease with the 'narrative
authority' expected of the parent within the family, Paul fails as a
father to his own son. This is a failure which in no small part
contributes to Konrad's susceptibility to dangerous political extremes.

In *Im Krebsgang*, Grass integrates 'German wartime suffering' into
a larger narrative of the period in which the emphasis on German

perpetration is still paramount: Konrad's and Tulla's allusions to the 'unprovoked' injustices inflicted on Germans are constantly undermined as inflammatory hyperbole reminiscent, all too often, of Nazi propaganda. As such, it reiterates the author's anxiety in the early 1990s that a reawakened interest in formerly German territories further to the East in the newly expanded, post-unification Federal Republic might lead to revisionism or even revanchism: *Unkenrufe* (1992) tells of German expellees from Poland returning to stake out burial plots in their old *Heimat*, insensitive to the fears of the present-day inhabitants.[37] More broadly, however, but as yet relatively unexplored, *Im Krebsgang* also, and significantly, intervenes in current debates on the purpose of literature and in particular on the possibility of a *German* literature in today's globalised world.

The question in *Im Krebsgang* is not whether socially-engaged writing automatically precludes empathy and identification with 'real' people but whether empathy necessarily precludes critical reflection. Ruminating on how best to depict the final moments of passengers trapped on the *Gustloff*, therefore, Paul begins by insisting that he will not

> das Grauenvolle in ausgepinselte Bilder [zu] zwingen, sosehr mich jetzt mein Arbeitgeber drängt, Einzelschicksale zu reihen, mit episch ausladender Gelassenheit und angestrengtem Einfühlungsvermögen den großen Bogen zu schlagen und so, mit Horrorwörtern, dem Ausmaß der Katastrophe gerecht [zu] werden. (IK, 136)

There will be no epic narration or forced empathy, he says. Yet individual fates are so compelling that he cannot help but relate them. His self-admonition, 'aber ich darf keine weiteren Storys erzählen', sounds increasingly unconvincing as he tells of lifeboats so packed that they capsized, of wounded soldiers left to die, women trapped inside the promenade deck, Dr Richter who delivered Tulla's baby, and the 'allseits beliebten Bordfriseur' (IK, 138-9). Yet elsewhere in Paul's narrative, empathy with 'his' characters is integrated into the broader historical setting and a factual detailing of German culpability for the disaster: Nazi accounts of Soviet atrocities, designed to encourage Germans to fight to the end, provoked the perilous flight of civilians; casualties on the *Gustloff* were much greater as a result of lack of life boats, and the German High Command had transformed the ship into a legitimate target by recklessly boarding submarine crew and members of the Navy Auxiliary Troop. Empathy, a literary device, is thus relativised by another entirely conventional literary

technique – juxtaposition – generating a *critical* understanding of how
the lives of 'real' people relate to the larger context.

Grass's *Im Krebsgang* responds simultaneously to different, but
interlinked contexts: the 'primary' debate on 'German wartime
suffering'; the related debate on the supposed incompatibility of
socially-engaged writing with an empathetic, properly 'literary'
engagement with a *German* past, and, more broadly, the debate on the
social utility of literature *per se* in the internet age – the narrator's
deliberate, digressive and ultimately more differentiated 'thick
description' of individual fates and the historical framework, 'etwa
nach der Art der Krebse' (IK, 8), contrasts with Konrad's
inflammatory internet broadsides.[38] Just as important, however, *Im
Krebsgang* also addresses the desire implicit in both the re-emergence
of interest in 'German stories' and the turn against socially-engaged
writing as an 'abnormal', that is, a 'non-organic', even 'non-native',
post-war deviation, for a *national* narrative tradition. Grass, then,
reminds his readership of the sustained German-language tradition of
socially-engaged – often socially-critical – literary texts via the
subtitle *Eine Novelle*, gesturing towards the work of nineteenth-
century writers such as Keller, Kleist or Storm,[39] turn-of-the-century
and early twentieth-century authors such as Stefan Zweig,
Hauptmann, Hofmannsthal, Werfel, Schnitzler, Heym and Thomas
Mann,[40] and many others subsequently right through to Grass himself
(*Katz und Maus*, for example), Timm, Delius and Schneider, to name
but a few. In short, the author of *Im Krebsgang* is continuing here his
project begun in the 1980s (itself deriving from Herder, of course) to
promote the notion of a *Kulturnation*.[41] Telling 'German stories',
whether in order to embed a collective memory of the experiences of
previous generations or to secure local identity in an age of internet
'non-places' and the globalised consumer culture, need not – indeed
must not – Grass implies, be left to revisionists, Neo-Nazis or other
'Rechtsgestrickten' (IK, 99), but can be accommodated within a
healthy – because self-critical – literary tradition.

Conclusion

The *Arbeitgeber*, a.k.a. Günter Grass, in *Im Krebsgang* is clearly a
figure who might all too easily inspire an entirely epigonal imitation
in his successors. Indeed, Paul, a chronicler of the past already
profoundly unsure of his capabilities both as a story-teller and as a

credible voice on social and political affairs, suffers a second form of trauma related to the passing down of narratives: the 'anxiety of influence' appears evident in the narrator's comment: 'Er sagt, mein Bericht habe das Zeug zur Novelle. Eine literarische Einschätzung, die mich nicht kümmern kann. Ich berichte nur.' (IK, 123) The *mea culpa* delivered by the *Arbeitgeber*, the admission that his generation had 'failed' to render the past in its full complexity, may thus be intended to encourage subsequent generations of writers (and subsequent generations of Germans) to have the courage to deal with the Nazi past in a manner appropriate to their own time. Grass's novella certainly offers a defence of a self-critical approach to both the past and the present but it also recognises the need for a literature which intervenes in current affairs to be responsive to previous omissions and the challenges of the future.

Contemporary German novels concerned with the expulsions from the East, and indeed with 'German wartime suffering' as a whole, engage not only (and often not even primarily) with the events themselves but also participate in a series of related discussions: how to present the history of the post-war period in the ex-GDR and FRG and particularly the history of successive modes of speaking of the past within the family; how to portray the experiences of 'real' people as part of a larger historical context and whether it is possible to achieve a balance between empathy and analysis, and the extent to which a socially-engaged literature can tell authentically 'German' stories and offer a German readership the opportunity of identifying with a national tradition rooted in a discursive engagement with social reality rather than disturbing revisionist mythologies. For the most part at least, recent literary representations of 'German wartime suffering' may thus imply not the end of critical engagement with the Nazi past, as has sometimes been argued, but rather a renewed interest in German fiction in the relationship between writing, politics, history and society. Indeed, literature may be able to explore this relationship in a more subtle and sophisticated fashion than currently more 'fashionable' forms of public remembrance such as monuments and memorials, television films (e.g. the 2006 ZDF production *Dresden*), sensationalising or sentimentalising historical exhibitions, or commemorative days.

Notes

[1] Dagmar Leupold, *Nach den Kriegen. Roman eines Lebens*, C.H. Beck: Munich, 2004, p. 167. Hereafter *NK*.

[2] See Helmut Schmitz, *Der Landvermesser auf der Suche nach der poetischen Heimat. Hanns-Josef Ortheils Romanzyklus*, Verlag Hans-Dieter Heinz: Stuttgart, 1997.

[3] See Bill Niven, *Facing the Nazi Past*, Routledge: London, 2002, pp. 143-74.

[4] Bill Niven, *Facing the Nazi Past,* 5.

[5] See Kathrin Schödel, 'Normalising Cultural Memory? The "Walser-Bubis-Debate" and Martin Walser's Novel *Ein springender Brunnen*,' in: Stuart Taberner and Frank Finlay, eds., *Recasting German Identity*, Camden House: Rochester, 2002, pp. 69-87.

[6] Bill Niven, 'Representations of the Nazi Past [1]: Perpetrators,' in: Stuart Taberner, ed., *Contemporary German Fiction: Writing in the Berlin Republic*, Cambridge University Press: Cambridge, forthcoming 2007.

[7] See Anne Fuchs and Mary Cosgrove, eds., *Memory Contests*, special number of *German Life and Letters*, 59:2 (2006). See also Anne Fuchs, Mary Cosgrove and Georg Grote, eds., *German Memory Contests: The Quest for Identity in Literature, Film and Discourse since 1990*, Camden House: Rochester, 2006.

[8] See Helmut Schmitz, 'Representations of the Nazi Past [2]: "German Wartime Suffering",' in: Stuart Taberner, ed., *Contemporary German Fiction.*

[9] Uwe Timm, *Am Beispiel meines Bruders*, Kiepenheuer & Witsch: Cologne, 2003, p. 39.

[10] Aleida Assmann, 'On the (In)compatibility of Guilt and Suffering in German Memory,' *German Life and Letters*, 59:2 (2006), 187-200.

[11] See my 'Representations of German Wartime Suffering in Recent Fiction,' in: Bill Niven, ed., *Germans as Victims: Remembering the Nazi Past in Contemporary Germany*, MacMillan: Basingstoke, 2006, pp. 164-80.

[12] Arnold Stadler, *Sehnsucht*, Dumont: Cologne, 2002, p. 290. Hereafter S.

[13] See my '"Nichts läßt man uns, nicht einmal den Schmerz, und eines Tages wird alles vergessen sein". The Novels of Arnold Stadler from *Ich war einmal* to *Ein hinreißender Schrotthändler*,' *Neophilologus*, 87 (2003), 119-132.

[14] Arnold Stadler, *Ein hinreißender Schrotthändler*, Dumont: Cologne, 1999, p. 136. Hereafter HS.

[15] See my 'A Matter of Perspective?: Martin Walser's Fiction in the 1990s,' in: Martin Kane, ed., *East and West German Responses to Unification*, Peter Lang: Bern, 2002, pp. 149-165.

[16] Martin Walser, 'Über freie und unfreie Rede,' in: Martin Walser, *Deutsche Sorgen*, Suhrkamp: Frankfurt am Main, 1997, pp. 468-475 (here: pp. 473-474).

[17] See, for example, Marianne Hirsch, 'Past Lives: Postmemories in Exile,' in: Susan Rubin Suleiman, ed., *Exile and Creativity: Signposts, Travelers, Outsiders, Backward Glances*, Duke University Press: Durham and London, 1998, pp. 418-446.

[18] Martin Walser, 'Erbarmen mit dem Seziermesser,' *Badische Zeitung*, 248, 26 October 1999, p. 15.

[19] See my 'German Nostalgia? Remembering German-Jewish Life in W. G. Sebald's *Die Ausgewanderten* and *Austerlitz*,' *The Germanic Review*, 79:3 (2004), 181-202.

[20] See my 'Hans-Ulrich Treichel's *Der Verlorene* and The Problem of German Wartime Suffering,' *The Modern Language Review*, 97 (2002), 123-134.

[21] Peter Schneider, 'Deutsche als Opfer? Über ein Tabu der Nachkriegsgeneration,' in: Lothar Kettenacker, ed., *Ein Volk von Opfern? Die neue Debatte um den Bombenkrieg 1940-45*, Rowohlt: Berlin, 2003, pp. 158-65 (here: p. 159).

[22] Hans-Ulrich Treichel, *Der Verlorene*, Suhrkamp: Frankfurt am Main, 1999, p. 139.

[23] See my 'sehnsüchtig traurig und unerlöst': Memory's Longing to Forget. Or Why *Tristanakkord* is not Simply a Reprise of Martin Walser,' in: David Basker, ed., *Hans-Ulrich Treichel*, University of Wales Press: Cardiff, 2004, pp. 79-93.

[24] Hans-Ulrich Treichel, *Tristanakkord*, Suhrkamp: Frankfurt am Main, 2000, p. 17.

[25] See Rhys Williams, '"Caravaggio in Preußen": Hans-Ulrich Treichel's *Der irdische Amor*,' in: David Basker, ed., *Hans-Ulrich Treichel*, pp. 94-110.

[26] The mass rapes of German women by Soviet soldiers already featured in Christoph Hein's 1989 short story 'Die Vergewaltigung' (1989).

[27] Christoph Hein, *Landnahme*, Suhrkamp: Frankfurt am Main, 2004, pp. 18-19. Hereafter L.

[28] Reinhard Jirgl, *Die Unvollendeten*, Carl Hanser Verlag: Munich, 2003, p. 155. Hereafter DU.

[29] See Stephen Brockmann, 'The Politics of German Literature', *Monatshefte*, 84:1 (1992), 46-58.

[30] See my *German Literature of the 1990s and Beyond*, Camden House: Rochester, 2005.

[31] Tanja Dückers, *Himmelskörper*, Aufbau Verlag: Berlin, 2003, p. 94.

[32] Harald Welzer, 'Schön unscharf. Über die Konjunktur der Familien- und Generationenromane,' *Mittelweg* 36:1 (2004), 53-61 (here: p. 63).

[33] See Stuart Taberner and Paul Cooke, eds., *German Culture, Politics and Literature into the Twenty-First Century: Beyond Normalization*, Camden House: Rochester, 2006.

[34] See my '"Normalization" and the New Consensus on the Nazi Past: Günter Grass's *Im Krebsgang* and the "Problem" of German Wartime Suffering,' *Oxford German Studies*, 31 (2002), 161-186.

[35] Günter Grass, *Im Krebsgang*, Steidl: Göttingen, 2002, p. 99. Hereafter IK.

[36] See Kathrin Schödel, '"Narrative Normalization" and Günter Grass's *Im Krebsgang*,' in: Stuart Taberner and Paul Cooke, eds., *German Culture, Politics and Literature into the Twenty-First Century*, pp. 195-208.

[37] See Julian Preece, *The Life and Work of Günter Grass*, Palgrave: New York, 2001, pp. 180-187.

[38] See Kristin Veel, 'Virtual Memory in Günter Grass's *Im Krebsgang*,' *German Life and Letters*, 57:2 (2004), 206-218.

[39] See Roger Paulin, *The Brief Compass. The Nineteenth Century German Novelle*, Oxford University Press: Oxford, 1985.

[40] See David Turner, *Mental Processes and Narrative Possibilities in the German Novelle 1890-1940*, Edwin Mellen Press: Lewiston, New York, 2005.

[41] See Michael Braun, 'Günter Grass' Rückkehr zu Herders "Kulturnation" im Kontrast zu Martin Walser und Günter de Bruyn: Essays und Reden zur Einheit,' in: Volker Wehdeking, ed., *Mentalitätswandel in der deutschen Literatur zur Einheit (1990-2000)*, Erich Schmidt Verlag: Berlin, 2000, pp. 97-110.

Paul Cooke

Der Untergang (2004): Victims, Perpetrators and the Continuing Fascination of Fascism

This chapter examines the controversy surrounding Hirschbiegel and Eichinger's 2004 film about the last days of Hitler. It suggests that the image of the war and the National Socialist regime it presents is highly reminiscent of films from the immediate post-war period, a time when the representation of the Germans as 'victims' was commonplace. At the same time the film tries to accommodate the agenda of the New German Cinema, which looked to hold the nation accountable for its complicity with Hitler. Finally, I suggest that a key intention behind the film would seem not to be to engage with debates about whether Germans were 'victims' or 'perpetrators', but to present an image of the past that can capitalise the 'authenticity' offered by its German-speaking cast.

Introduction

In recent years German cinema has provoked a level of international interest it has rarely achieved in the post-war period. For example, if one takes the Oscars as a measure of international success, since unification German films have been nominated six times in the category of 'Best Foreign Language Film'. This compares with nine nominations for German films in the previous forty years.[1] Initially, the current success of German films abroad seemed to coincide with a shift in the interests of filmmakers. Key figures in the New German Cinema of the 1960s and 1970s – the last time that German film had made an impact on the international cinematic scene – including Rainer Werner Fassbinder, Alexander Kluge and Wim Wenders, had attempted to provoke German society with their challenging works, intent upon forcing the older generation to face up to the legacy of National Socialism. For those filmmakers responsible for this new interest in German cinema, at first it appeared that the National Socialist period was losing its relevance, with films such as Tom Tykwer's hugely successful *Lola rennt* (1998) owing more to MTV and computer game culture than any specifically German historical legacy.[2] However, a brief glance at the list of Oscar nominations, from Michael Verhoeven's *Das Schreckliche Mädchen* (1990) to Caroline Link's winning entry *Nirgendwo in Afrika* (2001) as well as the most recent nomination, Marc Rothemund's *Sophie Scholl – Die letzten Tage* (2005), makes it clear that an examination of the Nazi period remains the best way for a German film to gain international recognition.[3] Yet although such films continue Germany's cinematic engagement with the legacy of National Socialism, the manner of this engagement has clearly shifted, both in terms of aesthetics and political point of view. As Eric Rentschler puts it, while the likes of Wenders and Fassbinder produced avant-garde film texts that 'interrogated images of the past in the hope of refining memories and catalysing changes', many recent mainstream films can best be described as a form of 'cinema of consensus' that lacks 'oppositional energies and critical voices', intent solely on achieving box-office success.[4]

As the present volume shows, this move towards a 'cinema of consensus' coincides with a time when we are witnessing a general cultural shift in the way Germany is exploring National Socialism and the legacy of the War. This has allowed for a, frequently highly controversial, engagement with the question of German wartime suffering, and the extent to which Germans might be seen as victims of, rather than accepting responsibility for, the events of history. As I shall discuss in this article, this has been particularly evident in recent German cinema, not least in the 2004 film *Der Untergang*, directed by Oliver Hirschbiegel, co-written and produced by Bernd Eichinger – the head of Constantin Film, Germany's biggest film company. In terms of box office, *Der Untergang* is to date the most successful of the new wave of internationally acclaimed films, grossing $92 million worldwide on its initial release and nominated for an Oscar in 2005.[5] Based on Joachim Fest's book of the same name, as well as on the memoirs of Traudl Junge, Hitler's private secretary (made into a documentary film in 2002),[6] *Der Untergang* gives a detailed account of the last days of Adolf Hitler, played by Bruno Ganz, a veteran of the New German Cinema. The film is told predominantly from the point of view of Junge (Alexandra Maria Lara), showing the spectator her experience of life in the *Führerbunker* as Berlin suffers the onslaught of, and finally capitulates to, the Red Army. Presenting the spectator with many of the stock images of Hitler's final days, we see the growing hysteria of his inner circle as their leader refuses to accept the reality of the situation the nation is facing until his final suicide, which is then followed by a wave of deaths, perhaps the most disturbing (and well known) being those of Goebbels's children, who are murdered by a mother that cannot imagine a world without

National Socialism. Throughout the film, life in the bunker is interspersed with stories from above ground, where we are shown the terrible effects of the war on the ordinary population of the city. Here we look at the world through the eyes of the SS-Doctor Ernst-Günter Schenck (Christian Berkel), who battles his way through the Russian bombardment in order to help look after the injured, and the boy soldier Peter Kranz (Donevan Gunia), who is seen fighting the Soviets in the streets and being decorated by Hitler during the leader's well documented final public appearance (a further stock image from the story), before grasping the futility of his actions and returning to his father who is desperate to protect him.

In Germany the film provoked a huge debate, largely due to its presentation of Hitler's 'human side', that is as a man who, along with willingly sacrificing civilians in a war that had no hope of success, could also be kind to his secretary and who loved his dog. Of course, representing Hitler in film is not new. From Chaplin's *The Great Dictator* (1940) onwards cinema has been fascinated with the image of the Nazi leader. Indeed, the 1970s in Germany saw what became known as a *Hitlerwelle*, with numerous films and books appearing that dealt with aspects of his life. The most notable film to come out of this wave is probably Hans-Jürgen Syberberg's seven hour epic *Hitler – ein Film aus Deutschland* (1978), also produced by Eichinger. However, in stark contrast to Syberberg, who attempts to distance his spectator from the cinematic text through the use of avant-garde aesthetics, *Der Untergang* offers an intimate portrayal of the dictator in the style of a Hollywood war movie, much more akin to the presentation of the same story in George Schaefer's *The Bunker* (1981), starring Anthony Hopkins as Hitler. As such, the film was considered by its supporters, not least Eichinger and Hirschbiegel, to signal a 'Tabubruch' and cultural 'Neuland' for German-language cinema.[7] For, as Christine Haase notes, it had long been considered that a realist mode for the representation of the horrors of National Socialism was simply inappropriate for a German film.[8] Those who defended it, therefore, such as Eckhard Fuhr writing in *Die Welt*, considered the film an important 'Zeichen der Emanzipation', suggesting that 'Die Deutschen haben ihre Geschichte, aber sie haben sie nicht mehr am Hals'. This distance from the past was allowing filmmakers, for the first time, 'Hitler in die Augen zu schauen', and should be seen a part of the necessary broader 'Versöhnung mit der

Tätergeneration' currently taking place in Germany.[9] The film seemed to be a product of German 'normalisation' in action, evidence of a new and very welcome relationship to history at work in the Berlin Republic.[10] As such, for its supporters the film marked a timely step beyond the agenda of the New German Cinema, and in particular the need of the earlier generation to hold their parents to account for their complicity with National Socialism. While there is a continued acceptance of the fact that this was a generation of 'Täter' which must continue to accept its guilt, it was now possible to offer an image of wartime experience that could highlight how the Germans also suffered as their leader took the nation towards its destruction.

For critics of the film, however, most notably the New German Cinema director Wim Wenders, any attempt to move on from the agenda of his generation in *Der Untergang* was nothing short of a trivialisation of the crimes of National Socialism. After seeing the film he experienced, he claims, 'ein tiefes Erschrecken über etwas, was ich nur "Verharmlosung" nennen kann'.[11] The UK's *Daily Mail* was similarly troubled by the film, going much further than the filmmaker in its criticism, asking: 'Is Germany finally forgiving Hitler?' In a discussion so preposterous that, whatever one's own view might be, one cannot help wondering if the reviewer ever actually saw the film, Allan Hall suggests that *Der Untergang* presents Hitler as 'a softly spoken dreamer' and, even more outrageously, that

> his misery and descent into madness, as his vision of the 1,000-year Reich finally disintegrates, are sympathetically portrayed. Indeed, the moment he and his new wife, Eva Braun, commit suicide together, on April 30, 1945, as the Russians close in on his Berlin bunker, may even bring a tear to the eye of German cinema-goers.

The film, Hall claims, allows the German spectator to indulge their purportedly natural inclination towards National Socialism, which he goes on to suggest is still very evident amongst the population. Here, he cites an apparent recent growth in German neo-Nazi websites. Moreover, Hall criticises what he sees as the film's indulgence of Germany's new tendency to 'wallow in a victim role' which is ostensibly based on a wish to avoid culpability for the past.[12]

In this article I explore how the film's representation of Hitler and the end of the Third Reich does indeed explicitly engage with the question of German wartime suffering and the extent to which this can be seen as part of a 'Verharmlosung' of the National Socialist period. However, far from breaking a taboo, I argue that the film marks a return to an earlier period of German filmmaking, against which the artists of the New German Cinema were largely rebelling. At the same time, the film engages with, or at least tries to accommodate, the agenda of the New German Cinema. As such, I suggest that the film attempts to be all things to all spectators, in order that it can achieve its ultimate aim of presenting a mainstream war story which can profit from the added authenticity with which its German-speaking cast provides it and which can, in turn, feed the international media market's continued voyeuristic fascination with the workings of Hitler's regime.

The German Nation as Hitler's Victim
As mentioned above, there have been other filmic representations of Hitler and indeed, to suggest that by offering a 'realistic' image of Hitler *Der Untergang* signals a 'Tabubruch' for German-language cinema is also incorrect. In 1955, the Austrian actor Albin Skoda played Hitler in G.W. Pabst's *Der Letzte Akt*, a film which uses a realist mode to trace the final days of the Nazi regime, offering the spectator a similar diet of the well-known moments in the story. In the German-speaking world this film, like *Der Untergang*, sparked an intense media debate. It was also very successful abroad, being sold to 52 countries worldwide. However, as Michael Töteberg notes, and as can be seen in the reception of *Der Untergang,* 'in Deutschland verschwand der Film nach kurzer Zeit aus den Kinos, und selbst umfangreiche Filmgeschichten wissen nichts von ihm'.[13]

Indeed, it is not only in regard to the international impact of the film or its use of cinematic realism to represent the *Führer* that Hirschbiegel's film invokes an earlier period in German filmmaking. *Der Untergang* recalls many of the aspects of German cinema of the immediate post-war period. This was a time when, as Robert G. Moeller notes, 'a past of German suffering was ubiquitous' across German culture, with the discussion of topics such as the Allied bombing campaign, the treatment of German POWs, the plight of the expellees and the relationship of the indigenous population to the occupying powers commonplace, the specific emphasis being, to a degree at least, contingent on the ideological system articulating them.[14] Here we might mention, for example, the *Trümmerfilme*, the first films made in post-war Germany, such as Wolfgang Staudte's *Die Mörder sind unter uns* (1946) or Gerhard Lamprecht's *Irgendwo in Berlin* (1946), both produced with the support of the newly-formed DEFA (Deutsche Film-AG) in the Soviet zone, as well as a number of high-profile West German war films of the 1950s, including *Der Letzte Akt* or Bernhard Wicki's Oscar-nominated *Die Brücke* (1959). Throughout these films the spectator is presented with an image of the recent past that tends to confirm the status of ordinary Germans as victims twice over, of the Hitler dictatorship on the one hand and of the Allied campaign on the other. Generally, an unambiguous view of Germany's relationship to National Socialism is constructed that allows the clear identification of the criminals of the previous regime, the 'Mörder' of Staudte's film, in order that the masses might be exonerated. At the same time, such films tend to have a strong pacifist message. In Pabst's film, for example, the story of Hitler's demise is juxtaposed with that of a disillusioned *Wehrmacht* officer who is shot as he tries to stop the *Führer* from flooding an S-Bahn tunnel filled with Berliners hiding from the onslaught of the Red Army. As the man lies dying, he uses his last breath to implore the young boy solider Richard (Gerd Zöhling) – Pabst's version of the Peter Kranz character in *Der Untergang* (whom we similarly see being decorated by Hitler) – to reject his blind obedience to the Nazi war machine: 'Seid wachsam!', the boy is told, 'Sagt nie wieder Jawohl!' In some respects, however, it is *Irgendwo in Berlin* that most closely recalls the sentiment of the Kranz narrative in *Der Untergang*. The central relationship of Lamprecht's film is that of a returning POW (Harry Hindemith), to his young son Gustav (Charles Brauer). The father, who through his experience of war has become a confirmed pacifist, has a fraught relationship with the boy. Gustav, like all the children in the city, has almost become feral, spending his days playing war games with friends amongst the bomb craters of the city. During one such game we see Gustav's best friend Willi (Hans Trinkaus) fall as he climbs up the outside wall of a ruined building. This accident, which leads to the child's death, reminds us of the extent to which the population continues to suffer the legacy of the allied bombing campaign. Through this tragic accident the children are, at least, shaken out of their violent ways, and as the story ends we see father and son reunited, the boy collecting his friends together to help his father clear away the rubble from the man's workshop so that he can reopen his business and thus begin to rebuild his life.

Der Untergang reflects the sensibility of these earlier films in a number of ways. Most importantly, the film presents an image of the Third Reich in which it is reasonably easy to divide the population into good and bad Germans. This is made explicit in a sequence where we see Schenck and his comrade attempt to prevent a group of military policemen from murdering deserters, the two groups finding themselves for a moment in a standoff, their weapons aimed at each other in a dramatic performance of this moral divide. As already mentioned, Schenck is a member of the SS. The actual historical figure Ernst-Günter Schenck was found guilty after the war of carrying out experiments on concentration camp prisoners.[15] In the film, however, he is presented as a wholly sympathetic character, who, as Jan Weyand suggests, functions less as a member of a Nazi organisation than as a metaphor for the German people as a whole, with whom the spectator is encouraged to identify positively. In turn:

> Der Konstruktion der 'Guten' korrespondiert die der 'Bösen', Hitler und Goebbels, die gegen die 'Guten' profiliert werden. Das Muster ist immer das Gleiche: Postives Identifikationsobjekt oder Nebenfigur bittet für das 'Volk', Hitler oder Goebbels reagieren mit einer Hasstirade auf die Deutschen.[16]

Throughout the film a binary opposition is created, with the ordinary, 'normal' Germans constructed as the victims of the insane violence of a Nazi leadership intent upon their destruction. 'Wo das Volk als namenlose Masse auftaucht, werden Opfer, Verletzte und Tote in allen Variationen, Frauen und Alte gezeigt. Der Zuschauer bekommt bebildert, was Hitler meint, wenn er von "Ausrottung" spricht'.[17] Indeed, even many of those who are convinced followers of National Socialism are seen not as perpetrators complicit with a barbaric regime but rather as having been duped by it and consequently are also portrayed to a lesser or greater extent as its victims. At one end of this spectrum we find Albert Speer, torn between his personal loyalty to the *Führer* and his conscience as he refuses to follow Hitler's 'scorched earth' policy, thereby helping to save the German nation. As such, he is portrayed as being fundamentally moral, having simply been led astray by Hilter's charisma.[18] At the other we find Magda Goebbels, who is presented not as part of the Nazi elite but as a woman caught up by an incomprehensible hysteria. Driven by her obsession with Hitler, she would rather murder her children than see them live in a post-Nazi state.

Above ground, the boy soldier Peter Kranz strongly recalls the children of Lamprecht's film as well as other examples of post-war pacifist cinema. To a degree the film might, in fact, be seen as a much delayed prequel to *Irgendwo in Berlin*. Kranz is intent upon defending his *Führer* to the bitter end, risking his life in an increasingly futile battle. His father, having returned injured from the front, tries to take his son home, predicting his death and the deaths of his young comrades if they continue to fight, only to be branded a coward by the boy as he runs away. Eventually, however, Kranz comes to understand the senseless destruction of war as his friends lie dead in the streets of Berlin and he is reconciled with his father. At the end of the film, he, like the children in *Irgendwo in Berlin*, becomes a symbol for the future of the nation, when we see Kranz join Hitler's secretary, taking her by the hand and protecting her as she walks, quaking with fear, through the ranks of celebrating Soviet soldiers, a clear allusion to the mass rape of German women at the hands of the Red Army. The child symbolically helps the woman to negotiate her way through the trauma of the war into the world of post-war Germany. And, in the final sequence of the main body of the film this is confirmed as we see Junge and Kranz cycle off together in the sunshine having survived the downfall of the Nazi regime, suggesting the new dawn that was to come for the nation.

Addressing the agenda of the New German Cinema?
In presenting an image of ordinary Germans as victims of National Socialism who suffered the trauma of the war, *Der Untergang* returns us to the immediate post-war period of German filmmaking. At the same time, in the final shot of Junge and Kranz riding off together the spectator is provided with a quintessential image of the type of contemporary cinematic 'consensus' attacked by Rentschler. However, there are moments when the film seems explicitly to reject this charge. In this regard the film also incorporates the position of earlier more radical filmmakers, such as Fassbinder, and their need for Germans to accept their culpability for National Socialism alongside its representation of ordinary Germans as victims. After the final shot of Junge and Kranze we are presented with a series of captions that summarise the effects of the war and which remind us that '6 Millionen Juden waren in *deutschen* Konzentrationslagern ermordet worden'.[19] Thus the film places German wartime suffering in the

context of German perpetration, reminding the spectator of the Holocaust and the responsibility of the nation as a whole for allowing 6 million Jews to be murdered in '*deutschen* Konzentrationslagern'.

The film is also framed by two clips from the 2002 documentary about Junge, where we see the woman accept that she has been tainted by her past: 'Ich habe das Gefühl, daß ich diesem Kind, diesem kindischen jungen Ding bös sein muß oder daß ich ihm nicht verzeihen kann, daß es die, die Schrecken ... dieses Monster nicht rechtzeitig erkannt hat'. Although she insists that she was 'keine begeisterte Nationalsozialistin', and, as we have already clearly seen in the main body of the film, that she was very young and naïve when she came to work for Hitler, she also declares that these facts are no defence for her complicity with the regime.[20] She claims that one day, as she walked past the memorial for Sophie Scholl, who was executed for her work with the resistance group *Weiße Rose*, she noticed that they were both the same age and that Scholl was killed the year that Junge took the job as Hitler's secretary: 'Und in dem Moment habe ich eigentlich gespürt, daß das keine Entschuldigung ist, daß man jung ist, sondern daß man auch hätte vielleicht Dinge erfahren können.'[21] Consequently, the final image of the film is of an individual accepting her responsibility for the past and with it the culpability of her generation. As such, *Der Untergang* would seem finally to offer an engagement with National Socialism that acknowledges the complicity of the nation in the crimes of the past, reminding the spectator that it is not only the elite that must carry the burden of guilt. In so doing, the film acknowledges the agenda of much of the New German Cinema, ostensibly offering a more complex image of history than the one depicted in the main body of the film.

Fascinating Fascism

For critics of the film, however, such as Wenders, the acknowledgement of this more critical agenda at best only ever pays lip service to the need to acknowledge the question of German guilt for the past, since there is no *reflection* on this issue in the body of the film. Indeed, he suggests that the film even neutralises its own potential to challenge the spectator from within its realist mode:

> Hitler bittet seinen Adjutanten Wünsche, er möge Benzin besorgen, 'damit die Russen meine Leiche nicht zur Schau stellen können'. 'Ein schrecklicher Befehl, aber ich will ihn ausführen', entgegnet der Untergebene. Und was tut der Film? Er führt Hitlers Befehl tatsächlich aus! Alles sieht man in *Der Untergang*, nur

Hitlers Tod nicht! Der Mann gibt sich (und seiner Eva) hinter verschlossener Tür das Gift und die Kugel. So wie Hitler sich abwendet, wenn seine Schäferhündin Blondie stirbt, so wendet sich der Film ab, wenn der Führer stirbt.[22]

For Wenders the film worryingly obeys Hitler's own last wish, preventing his death from becoming a public spectacle, thereby giving it a dignity it does not deserve and missing the opportunity of using the film's realism to challenge the spectator by representing something that truly would have been a 'Tabubruch'. Furthermore, although the film is framed by Junge's *mea culpa*, this does not change the fact that she, like Schenck and Kranz above ground, provides a point of identification for the spectator with events in the bunker, her naïve gaze allowing the spectator access to this world while also maintaining a degree of distance from it that means there is never any need for moral engagement.

However, according to its producer, the aim of the film is actually to be deliberately non-reflective. As Eichinger put it in an interview with NDR:

Es gibt keine Moral. Es ist ganz wesentliche Aufgabe des Drehbuchs und der Unternehmung gewesen, dass wir überhaupt in keiner Weise moralisieren, denn das wäre ja wiederum eine Interpretation dessen, was wir tun. Was wir versuchen, ist – soweit wir das irgend können – die Fakten darzustellen, die Geschichte zu erzählen. Und nicht die Geschichte zu interpretieren.[23]

Here we begin to see a major impulse behind the film. While *Der Untergang* might present a humanised version of Hitler there is never any attempt to challenge the spectator to reflect upon the past, to explore the motivation for the leader's drive to destroy the nation, or indeed to examine the fact that much of this same nation was willing to follow him to its destruction.

Instead the film indulges what Susan Sontag identified in her seminal 1975 essay 'Fascinating Fascism', namely the enduring popular obsession with the minutiae of the Third Reich. As she notes, 'Nazism fascinates in a way other iconography staked out by the pop sensibility (from Mao Tse-tung to Marilyn Monroe) does not'.[24] A cursory glance at the programming schedule of the British television Channel 5, or the internationally broadcast History Channel (often referred to colloquially as the 'Hitler Channel'), shows the continuing international public appeal of documentaries and fiction films about all aspects of National Socialism and in particular the life of the Nazi leader, both real and imagined. Along with the *The Bunker* from 1981, mentioned above, in recent years this fascination has, for example, produced Menno Meyjes's *Max* (2000), which tells the imaginary story of Hitler's early life as an art student, as well Ken Stott's performance as the dictator in the story of his relationship with his niece in *Uncle Adolf* (Nicholas Renton, 2005).

Der Untergang, however, appears to have trumped all other attempts to portray Hitler by virtue of its attention to detail and, in particular, the degree of authenticity it is afforded by virtue of its German credentials. Clearly Eichinger was aware of the potential of this film from the outset. His Constantine Film company has made its name backing films that will sell internationally, from *Das Boot* (Wolfgang Petersen, 1981) to *Resident Evil* (Paul W.S. Anderson, 2002). As Thomas Elsaesser points out, Eichinger 'more than anyone else, takes credit for being the strategist and driving force of the Germans' apparently savvy, but in any event unapologetic commercial turn in movie-making'.[25] It is within this context that *Der Untergang* was made, the investment of €13.5 million signalling that Eichinger always had an eye on an international market, since this is a sum of money that could never be amortised domestically. Eichinger was also careful to make the most of what Sabine Hake has identified as the growing 'star-based physiognomy of the Third Reich' in German cinema, casting a number of actors that have made a name for themselves in this new wave of films that represent aspects of the National Socialist past. Interestingly, the 'star text' of many of these figures seems further to undermine any clear moral response to the events portrayed in the minds of the audience, running counter to binary division of the population into 'good' and 'bad' Germans within the diegesis. Hake mentions figures such as Ulrich Matthes who plays Goebbels in *Der Untergang*, but whose performance overtly recalls his portrayal of a Catholic priest on leave from Dachau in Volker Schlöndorff's *Der Neunte Tag* (2004), thereby 'blurring the boundaries between individual films', to present 'a performative reenactment of history through the identificatory structure of the star system', which again allows the spectator to evade an individual moral engagement with the specific events presented.[26]

Although there was some criticism of the film abroad, its reception was overwhelmingly positive. Specifically, it is continually claimed that the film offered audiences something that they had not seen before, namely an *authentic* image of Hitler's last days. The historian Ian Kershaw, for example, suggests: 'Of all the screen depictions of the *Führer*, even by famous actors such as Alec

Guinness or Anthony Hopkins, this is the only one which to me is compelling. Part of this is the voice. Ganz has Hitler's voice to near perfection. It is chillingly authentic.'[27] Ganz does indeed give a very convincing portrayal of the man in the last stages of his life. Along with his perfect mimicry of the man's speech, one might also mention his constantly shaking arm, signalling the first signs of Parkinson's Disease. The authenticity of the performance is then further compounded by what Haase describes as the film's explicit 'fetishisation of realism and authenticity' which constantly parades the filmmakers' attention to detail. We are given lingering shots of the everyday items with which people at the time lived, from the omnipresent military insignia of the Third Reich to the toy soldiers with which children played. We are even given a close up of Hitler's dinner as he eats one of his last meals in the bunker, the image of a half-eaten plate of mashed potato and spinach highlighting the fact that Eichinger and Hirschbiegel know that the man was a vegetarian.

Crucially, however, while the film is filled with details about life in the Third Reich, these details never help us understand the period. As A.O. Scott observes, the represention of this world is 'fascinating without being especially illuminating', holding the spectator's attention 'without delivering any dramatic or emotional satisfaction in the end'.[28] While the debate surrounding the film is interesting in its own right, it would seem to have little to do with the impulse behind this project. If anything it simply provides further proof that in the movies there is no such thing as bad publicity, showing that, from a business point of view Eichinger was very justified in organising such a major financial investment in the project. Internationally, *Der Untergang* without doubt hit a nerve, providing a perspective on the war and the Nazi regime that many felt they had not previously seen, offering them what one reviewer saw as 'one of the best war movies ever made', a claim that became a tagline of the film's international publicity campaign.[29] The film eschews the types of aesthetic devices used by the filmmakers of the New German Cinema that attempted to force the spectator to reflect upon their relationship with the National Socialist past. Instead, *Der Untergang* provides us with another example of Germany's shift towards the cinematic mainstream, its narrative, filmed in the style of a Hollywood war epic, allowing the audience to identify with, yet distance themselves from, the world we see through the eyes of the naïve Traudl Junge. At the same time, it highlights the fact that Germany's past remains a highly marketable 'unique selling point' for the nation's filmmakers. Nonetheless, for some at least, it is still problematic that, while the film instrumentalises its Germanness, it deliberately ignores the obvious moral implications of making a German film about this most controversial moment in German history.

Notes

[1] See http://www.oscar.com/nominees/bestforeignlanguagefilmnominee4.html (accessed 6 March 2006).

[2] For further discussion see Owen Evans, 'Tom Tykwer's *Run Lola Run*: Postmodern, posthuman or "post-theory"?' *Studies in European Cinema*, 1 (2004), 105-115.

[3] For further discussion of this point see my 'Abnormal Consensus in Contemporary German Cinema,' in: Stuart Taberner and Paul Cooke, eds., *German Culture, Politics and Literature into the Twenty-First Century: Beyond Normalization*, Camden House: Rochester, 2006, pp. 223-237.

[4] Eric Rentschler, 'From New German Cinema to the Post-Wall Cinema of Consensus,' in: Mette Hjort and Scott Mackenzie, eds., *Cinema and Nation*, Routledge: London, 2000, pp. 260-277 (here: pp. 263-4).

[5] Figures taken from Box Office Mojo, http://www.boxofficemojo.com/movies/?id=downfall.htm (accessed 5 March 2006).

[6] André Heller and Othmar Schmiderer, *Im toten Winkel — Hitlers Sekretärin*, (2002). See also Traudl Junge with Melissa Müller, *Bis zur letzten Stunde. Hitlers Sekretärin erzählt ihr Leben*, Berlin: Ullstein, 2003.

[7] See The Editor, 'Ein Film über die letzten Tage im Berlin des "Führers",' *Berliner Morgenpost*, 25 August 2004; Jan Schulz-Ojala, 'Der Übersterbensgroße – von Monstern und Menschen: Bernd Eichinger und sein Team stellen in Berlin ihren Hitler-Film *Der Untergang* vor,' *Tagesspiegel*, 23 August 2004.

[8] Christine Haase, 'Ready for his Close-up? On the Success and Failure of Representing Hitler in *Der Untergang*,' *Studies in European Cinema*, 3 (2006), forthcoming.

[9] Eckhard Fuhr, 'Auf Augenhöhe,' *Die Welt*, 25 November 2004.

[10] For further discussion of normalisation debates see Taberner and Cooke, *German Culture, Politics and Literature into the Twenty-First Century: Beyond Normalization.*

[11] Wim Wenders, 'Tja, dann wollen wir mal,' *Die Zeit*, 21 October 2004.

[12] Allan Hall, 'Is Germany finally forgiving Hitler?,' *The Daily Mail*, 25 October 2004.

[13] Michael Töteberg, 'Hitler – eine Filmkarriere: Der letzte Akt und andere Filme über das Ende des Führers,' in: Michael Töteberg, ed., *Der Untergang: das Filmbuch*, Rowohlt: Reinbek, 2005, pp. 405-425 (here: p. 417).

[14] Robert G. Moeller, 'Remembering the War in a Nation of Victims: West German Pasts in the 1950s,' in: Hanna Schissler, ed., *The Miracle Years: a Cultural History of West Germany 1949-1968*, Princeton University Press: Princeton, 2001, pp. 83-109 (here: p. 85). For a discussion of the relationship between politics and constructions of German victimhood see Graham Jackman, 'Introduction,' *German Life and Letters*, 57 (2004), 343-356.

[15] Alexander Ruoff, 'Die Renaissance des Historismus in der Populärkultur: über den Kinofilm Der Untergang,' in: Willi Bischof, ed., *Film Ri:ss. Studien über den Film Untergang*, Unrast: Münster, 2005, pp. 69-78 (here: p. 70).

[16] Jan Weyand, 'So war es! Zur Konstruktion eines nationalen Opfermythos im Spielfilm Der Untergang,' in: Bischof, *Film Ri:ss*, pp. 39-68 (here: p. 46).

[17] Weyand, p. 48.

[18] This is a position offered by Speer himself in his autobiography, *Inside the Third Reich* (1969). In recent years, however, this has been problematised by the work of Gitta Sereny, *Albert Speer: His Battle with Truth*, Knopf: New York, 1995.

[19] Bernd Eichinger, 'Der Untergang,' in: Töteberg, pp. 236-401 (here: p. 399). My emphasis.

[20] Eichinger, p. 236.

[21] Eichinger, p. 401.

[22] Wenders.

[23] 'Hitlers letzte Tage als Kinofilm,' http://www.ard.de/kultur/film-kino/-/id=8328/nid=8328/did=188420/zclncd/, 16 September 2004.

[24] Susan Sontag, 'Fascinating Fascism' in: Brandon Taylor and Wilfried van der Will, eds, *The Nazification of Art: Art, design, music, architecture and film in the Third Reich*, Winchester Press: Winchester, 1990, pp. 204 -219 (here: p. 216).

[25] Thomas Elsaesser, 'Introduction: German Cinema in the 1990s,' in: Thomas Elsaesser and Michael Wedel, *The BFI Companion to German Cinema*, BFI: London, 1999, pp. 3-16 (here: p. 4).

[26] Sabine Hake, 'Leaving the Bunker: On *Downfall* and the Historicization of the Nazi Past', unpublished manuscript generously provided by the author.

[27] Ian Kershaw, 'The Human Hitler,' *The Guardian*, 17 September 2004.

[28] Quoted in Haase.

[29] Eric Hansen, 'Downfall,' *Hollywood Reporter*, http://www.hollywoodreporter.com/ thr/reviews/review_display.jsp?vnu_content_id=1000630570 (accessed 6 March 2006).

Index of Contributors

Paul Cooke is Professor of German Cultural Studies at the University of Leeds. He is the author of *Speaking the Taboo: A Study of the Work of Wolfgang Hilbig* (2000), *The Pocket Essential to German Expressionist Film* (2002) and *Representing East Germany: From Colonization to Nostalgia* (2005). He is currently part of an AHRC-funded project investigating the cultural and political representation of 'German Wartime suffering' since 1945 and is working on a monograph for Manchester University Press on Contemporary German Film.

Hans-Joachim Hahn is Research Assistant at the Simon-Dubnow-Institute for Jewish History at the University of Leipzig after heading the Zentrum für Begegnung, Austausch und Forschung at the Gerhart-Hauptmann-Haus in Jagniątków (Agnetendorf), Poland, 2003-05. His research focuses on German memory culture and the history of anti-Semitism. His doctoral thesis *Repräsentationen des Holocaust. Zur westdeutschen Erinnerungskultur seit 1979* was published with Universitätsverlag Carl Winter in 2005.

Odile Jansen is a PhD student at the Dept of Literature at the University of Amsterdam and Tilburg, currently finishing her thesis on the traumatic heritage of 1945 and its traces in autobiographical writings. Her research focuses on cultural memory and *Vergangenheitsbewältigung*. She has published 'Doppelte Erinnerung: Täter- und Opferidentitäten in Christa Wolfs Rekonstruktion des Traumas der Flucht', *German Life and Letters* (4/2004) and 'Trauma Revisited: The Holocaust Memorial in Berlin' in: Gregory Ashworth and Rudi Hartmann, eds., *Horror and Human Tragedy Revisited: The Management of Sites of Atrocities for Tourism* (2005)

Gilad Margalit is Senior Lecturer in Modern German History in the History Department at the University of Haifa, Israel. His research interests focus on various aspects of German post-war processes of *Vergangenheitsbewältigung*. His recent publications include *Germany and its Gypsies. A Post-Auschwitz Ordeal* (2002) and *Guilt, Suffering and Memory. On German Commemoration of the German Victims of the Second World War* (in Hebrew, 2007).

Bill Niven is Professor of Contemporary German History at the Nottingham Trent University. He is the author of *Facing the Nazi Past* (2001) and *The Buchenwald Child* (2007), and editor of *Germans as Victims* (2006). Currently, he is preparing two edited volumes on memorialisation of the Second World War, and in the long term he plans a monograph on memory of the Holocaust in East and West Germany.

Heinz-Peter Preußer is Professor of German and Media Studies at the Institut für kulturwissenschaftliche Deutschlandstudien (IfkuD) at the University of Bremen. His main research is in the field of 20th century literary history and theory. He is the author of two monographs *Mythos als Sinnkonstruktion. Die Antikenprojekte von Christa Wolf, Heiner Müller, Stefan Schütz und Volker Braun* (2000) and *Letzte Welten. Deutschsprachige Gegenwartsliteratur diesseits und jenseits der Apokalypse* (2003), and editor of *Krieg in den Medien* (2005), *Weiblichkeit als politisches Programm? Sexualität, Macht und Mythos* (with Bettina Gruber, 2005), *Kulturphilosophen als Leser. Porträts literarischer Lektüren* (with Matthias Wilde, 2006) and *Mythos Terrorismus. Vom Deutschen Herbst zum 11. September* (with Matteo Galli, 2006).

Samuel Salzborn is a Diplom-Sozialwissenschaftler with a PhD in Political Sciences, currently working at the Institute for Political Sciences at the University of Gießen. His research focuses on political theory, political psychology, Zeitgeschichte and European minority politics. He has published the monographs *Grenzenlose Heimat. Geschichte, Gegenwart und Zukunft der Vertriebenenverbände* (2000) and *Ethnisierung der Politik. Theorie und Geschichte des Volksgruppenrechts in Europa* (2005).

Annette Seidel Arpacı works as Research Fellow for the AHRC-funded project 'Discourses of "German Wartime Suffering"' at the Dept of German at the University of Leeds. She received a PhD in 2005 at the Centre for Jewish Studies at Leeds for her thesis on Holocaust Memory, Migration and 'Otherness' in Renationalised Germany. She has co-authored a comparative study on *Racisms in Feminist Psychosocial Networks* (1999), and has published articles on representations of Jewishness and Blackness, Holocaust remembrance, migration and pedagogy, on Maxim Biller's and Esther Dischereit's writing, and on Hito Steyerl's films.

Helmut Schmitz is Associate Professor of German at the University of Warwick. His research focuses on the representation of National Socialism in German literature. He has edited *Entgegenkommen. Dialogues with Barbara Köhler* (with Georgina Paul, 2000) and *German Culture and the Uncomfortable Past* (2001) and is the author of *On Their Own Terms. The Legacy of National Socialism in Post-1990 German Fiction* (2004).

Gregor Streim is Assistant Professor at the Institute for German and Dutch Philology at the Freie Universität Berlin. He is the author of the monographs *Das 'Leben' in der Kunst. Untersuchungen zur Ästhetik des frühen Hofmannsthal* (1996) and *Berliner und Wiener Moderne. Vermittlungen und Abgrenzungen in Literatur, Theater, Publizistik* (with Peter Sprengel, 1998) and is co-editor of *Reflexe und Reflexionen von Modernität 1933-1945* (with Erhard Schütz, 2002). He has published a number of articles on the literary 'coming to terms' with the Third Reich and the Second World War.

Stuart Taberner is Professor of Contemporary German Literature, Culture and Society at the University of Leeds. He has published widely on German fiction since 1945 and has particular interests in the post-unification period. His major recent publications are *Recasting German Identity* (2005) and *Contemporary German Fiction. Writing in the Berlin Republic* (edited, 2007).

Helen Wolfenden is a PhD student at University College London. Her thesis examines West German war films of the 1950s, and contends that changes in the narrative representation of war are linked to changes in popular and political attitudes regarding the Nazi past that occurred in West Germany during this decade.

Printed in the United Kingdom
by Lightning Source UK Ltd.
135220UK00001B/133-153/P